PROBLEMS OF SEA POWER AS WE APPROACH THE TWENTY-FIRST CENTURY

A Conference Sponsored by the
American Enterprise Institute for Public Policy Research

D0916046

PROBLEMS OF SEA POWER AS WE APPROACH THE TWENTY-FIRST CENTURY

Edited by James L. George

American Enterprise Institute for Public Policy Research
Washington, D.C.

Library of Congress Cataloging in Publication Data
Main entry under title:

Problems of sea power as we approach the twenty-first
    century.

(AEI symposia ; 78F)
Papers at a conference held Oct. 6 and 7, 1977, in
Washington, and sponsored by the American Enterprise
Institute.
    1. Sea power—Congresses. 2. United States. Navy—
Congresses. 3. Twenty-first century—Forecasts—
Congresses. I. George, James L. II. American Enter-
prise Institute for Public Policy Research. III. Series:
American Enterprise Institute for Public Policy Research.
AEI symposia ; 78F.
V25.P76   359'.03'0905   78-18422

ISBN 0-8447-2133-6
ISBN 0-8447-2132-8 pbk.

Printed in the United States of America

2 1 5 3 7 0

PARTICIPANTS

Congressman Charles E. Bennett
Chairman, House Seapower Subcommittee

Alva M. Bowen, Jr.
Analyst in National Defense, Congressional Research Service

Vice Admiral William Crowe, *USN*
Deputy Chief of Naval Operations for Plans, Policy and Operations

James Hessman
Editor, Sea Power Magazine

Senator Daniel K. Inouye
Chairman, Senate Merchant Marine Subcommittee

Herschel Kanter
Brookings Institution

David Kassing
President, Center for Naval Analyses

Robert Kilmarx
Georgetown Center for Strategic and International Studies

Rear Admiral Robert E. Kirksey, *USN*
Carrier Programs Division

Rear Admiral Gene La Rocque, *USN (ret.)*
President, Center for Defense Information

Reuven Leopold
Naval Ship Engineering Center

William S. Lind
Office of Senator Gary Hart

Michael MccGwire
Dalhousie University

James M. McConnell
Center for Naval Analyses

CONTENTS

INTRODUCTION

James L. George

At the close of World War II, the United States had 5,718 ships in the active fleet, including 98 aircraft carriers, 23 battleships, 72 cruisers, and over 700 destroyers and destroyer escorts. While the Soviet Union still had a rather large submarine force, its effective major surface combatant force was insignificant except for some former American and British ships on loan. Also of importance is that in this period Great Britain still had a very large fleet.

Perhaps more important than the numbers is the fact that at the end of World War II the U.S. Navy finished with a distinguished record of victories that can compare proudly with those scored by ancient Greece at Salamis, the Europeans at Lepanto, or Great Britain in its naval heyday. On the other hand, the record of the Soviet navy could at best be called dismal. At the beginning of World War II, the Soviet Union had the largest submarine fleet in the world, outnumbering the German fleet by approximately three to one; yet it accomplished virtually nothing in the war. One of the few bright spots on the Soviet navy record was performed by the young Soviet Rear Admiral Gorshkov, who displayed courage and imagination in supporting the army in the Black Sea area. Although smaller than the American navy in World War II, the British fleet and those of some of its Commonwealth allies such as Canada and Australia carried on the great British sea power tradition. During World War II, Canada actually had the third largest Western navy. In short, at the end of World War II and the beginning of what would be called the cold war, the United States and its Western allies had not only a preponderance of strength in naval force numbers but also an absolute preponderance in the equally important perception of sea power.

A lot has changed since those days. While striving for a 600 ship navy (which is actually lower than the pre–World War II level) the U.S. Navy has slipped to around 460 ships and most analysts wonder if there will even be a 500 ship navy in the next twenty-odd years towards the twenty-first century. On the other hand, since World War II, the Soviet navy has slowly grown and now has a greater number of ships than the American navy has. An additional point often overlooked by American planners is that the fleets of some of our major allies are also shrinking. The United Kingdom has only one attack aircraft carrier and that is slated for retirement in a year or two. The British gave up their fleet "east of Suez" long ago and now make only an occasional deployment beyond their home waters.

While these numbers are interesting, especially when compared with the immediate post–World War II levels, the change in perceptions is also interesting. Not only has the Soviet navy become quantitatively superior to the American fleet, it also has changed its quality and types of ships. The latest and undoubtedly most intriguing is the appearance of the new Soviet "aircraft carrier," the Kiev class, which in size is equal to the old American Essex-class carriers. Equally interesting in the world of perception and images is the publication of two books by Admiral Gorshkov, *Red Star Rising At Sea*[1] and *Sea Power and the State*. A survey of the literature shows nothing written in modern times to compare to these two books—perhaps nothing since Mahan's works. Although these books cannot be compared to Mahan in content or thought, the very fact that a Soviet naval writer—rather than a Westerner— would write a comprehensive sea power book says something about the changing times. In short, since World War II, American sea power has shrunk from absolute predominance to a "slim margin of superiority." In the world of perception and images, it might even be said that the West is actually on the defensive, or at least that the issue is "confused."

Missions

No issue generates more confusion and debate than that of naval missions. There are three parts to this debate, but there probably should be four. The first debate centers on the question: What are the missions of the navy? In the era of ICBMs, laser beams, and neutron bombs, some would question whether we even need a navy. The second and undoubtedly most intriguing debate centers on the mission of the Soviet navy. Has the Soviet navy gone beyond its traditional role of only defending the coastline and supporting the army? The third debate centers on the role and missions of the U.S. Navy. This debate has obvious effects on deployment and less obvious ones on ship design. The fourth debate would be the role and mission of our allies. Unfortunately this debate is rather subdued, despite the contribution than can still be made by Britain and our other Western allies.

---

[1] This is actually a series of articles written by Admiral Gorshkov for a Soviet navy journal that was published by the United States Naval Institute.

From the American viewpoint, the most interesting and important debate concerns the role and mission of the Soviet Union as we approach the twenty-first century. The Soviet navy has had, like most navies, internal debates on its role. Since the revolution, there have been sporadic Soviet plans to build a blue water fleet, complete with battleships and aircraft carriers, but for a number of reasons—economic limitations, World War II, the death of Stalin—generally the role and mission of the Soviet navy has been defensive in nature. This was the conclusion of the first definitive book on Soviet naval strategy,[2] and, at the time, few would have disputed it. The only other role seriously suggested was that of interdiction of the Western sea lines of communication (SLOC) by the large Soviet submarine force, but then the anti-SLOC mission is essentially defensive.

The debate on the role and mission of the Soviet navy opened in 1967 with two significant events. The first was the confirmed appearance of the small Moskva-class antisubmarine cruiser, a helicopter carrier which gave hints of a change in ship design and mission. The second significant event was the 1967 Arab-Israeli War. The Soviet navy had made only occasional forays into the Mediterranean and other far-flung areas, but the Soviet navy has been continuously deployed in them since that time. No careful commentator has yet suggested that the Soviet navy now has an offensive or a blue water fleet, but most now talk about forward deployments that border on that role. The two Okean exercises in 1970 and 1975, which demonstrated the Soviet Union's effective command, control, and communications (C^3) capability with worldwide fleets, have added to the debate on Soviet roles and missions. Although the Soviet navy might not yet be in a position to control the sea, it might have reached the level of the German fleet in World War I, when it challenged the British fleet.[3] And, of course, if present trends continue, the challenging roles could be reversed by the twenty-first century.

On the surface, there would seem to be no problem with the roles and missions of the U.S. Navy. Most authorities would cite Title 10 of the U.S. Code, which says, in part:

> The Navy shall be organized, trained, and equipped primarily for prompt and sustained combat incident to operations at sea. It is responsible for the preparation of naval forces necessary for the effective prosecution of war except as otherwise as-

---

2 Robert Waring Herrick, *Soviet Naval Strategy* (Annapolis: United States Naval Institute, 1968).

3 Alva M. Bowen, Jr. "The Anglo-German and Soviet-American Naval Rivalries—Some Comparisons," in Paul Murphy, ed., *Naval Power in Soviet Policy* (forthcoming).

signed and is generally responsible for naval reconnaissance, antisubmarine warfare, and protection of shipping.

Since this language can be interpreted rather broadly, most navy witnesses cite the missions of the navy as "sea control" and "power projection." While these are traditional terms, indeed the sea control mission can easily be traced to Mahan, there is the feeling in some quarters that these terms are not definitive enough for the roles and missions of the 1970s, let alone the twenty-first century. In other words, at the same time that there is debate on the roles and missions of the Soviet navy, there is growing debate within the United States on the roles and missions of the American navy.

The problem regarding missions may again be that of perception. Some analysts are putting forth a "mirror image" explanation of the motives behind the Soviet forward deployment decisions and especially behind the decision to build an aircraft carrier in the 1970s, after years of deprecating their role in the age of missiles and nuclear weapons. According to this mirror image theory, the Soviet Union is building a large blue water fleet only to reflect the size, role, and missions of the U.S. Navy. On the other hand, this mirror image explanation should provoke a certain sense of irony, since many of the same analysts are arguing about the roles and missions of the U.S. Navy. Also, in the past ten years, the size of the American fleet has shrunk by over 50 percent, while that of the Soviets has slowly grown. In short, while the debate over the roles and missions of the two superpowers is important and fascinating, it might also be the classic example of the "chicken and egg" dilemma of any arms race. Therefore, to help resolve and understand the missions debate, it becomes necessary to look first at the potential areas of conflict.

Areas of Conflict

Anyone who makes predictions about potential conflicts takes a risk. Who in the 1950s would have predicted a ten-year war in Vietnam, and who would have predicted that a small country like Cuba would be involved in African wars? Certain things can be said, however, about the events during the next twenty-odd years that are predictable. The question is: Will these events involve the use of sea power?

The Mediterranean Sea is the region of most concern because it has the greatest immediate potential to involve the two superpowers, despite their best intentions to resolve the conflicts there. Since the 1967 Middle East war, both the United States and the Soviet Union have maintained approximately sixty ships in the Mediterranean Sea. During the 1973 Arab-Israeli War, according to Admiral Zumwalt, there was a "political" confrontation that reminded him of the 1962 Cuban missile crisis, though, unfortunately, the roles were reversed.[4] For the first time since World War II, the U.S. fleet found itself in a very uncomfortable position. This is why this is the area of most immediate concern, and until the Arab-Israeli conflict is resolved, this will always be a potential source of superpower struggle on the seas. In fact, even if this conflict is resolved, the rivalry among the Arab nations and the continuing importance of Middle East oil will make this an important sea for U.S.–Soviet rivalry.

There are other predictions that can be made concerning the Mediterranean area. For example, Tito *will* die and the Yugoslavian relations with the Soviet Union are bound to change in some manner. Soviet use of Yugoslavian bases at the same time the United States seems to be losing bases in the Eastern Mediterranean will have an effect on Sixth Fleet operation. The Turkish-Greek situation will undoubtedly fester well into the twenty-first century with the possibility that the Soviet Union will intervene on one side or the other. Finally, even the threat of Eurocommunism in Italy and France could have devastating effects on the operation of the Sixth Fleet. These are problems that will continue for many years. There are other situations that might occur. What will be the future of Spain, Gibraltar, and some of the volatile countries of North Africa? Of all the areas of the world, the Mediterranean Sea definitely seems to have the greatest potential for conflicts that would involve sea power.

While the Mediterranean region might have the greatest potential for conflict, perhaps the most important area is the North Sea/Baltic region—an area usually ignored by American analysts. The reason for its importance is simple—two of the four Soviet fleets must transit this area to reach the open sea. The area is patrolled by Norway, Denmark, West Germany, and England—all NATO allies—but the U.S. Navy takes only an occasional cruise there. Since this is the most important transit area for the Soviet navy, perhaps this American priority will have to change in the next twenty years. There are few conflicts in this area, though Iceland threatened to pull out of NATO because of its so-called Cod War with the United Kingdom. Without the use of Iceland, NATO control of the so-called G-I-UK gap (Greenland, Iceland, and United Kingdom) would be in jeopardy, allowing easier access for Soviet submarines to the Middle and South Atlantic.

---

[4] Admiral Elmo R. Zumwalt, *On Watch* (New York: Quadrangle, 1976), pp. 444-445.

In some respects, the Indian Ocean is a new area in American naval thinking. This was a region long patrolled by Great Britain and France, with only a small Middle East force of two destroyers and a flag ship maintained by the United States. It has become a new area of concern because of the recent forays of the Soviet fleet and, of course, the importance of the Middle East oil, and it is an area of immense potential conflict. Southern Africa can be expected to continue to broil for many years, together with other parts of the continent, such as the Horn of Africa. Southern Africa and the Horn of Africa provide the only recent incidents of a non-African country, Cuba, intervening in what could be called projection ashore.

Despite the great sea battles of World War II and the recent war in Vietnam, the Western Pacific has become an unknown area. Little is written about this region or the Philippines, Indonesia, Thailand, Korea, Japan, or Taiwan, even though they are all islands or peninsulas and susceptible to a sea power strategy. Perhaps this lack of interest reflects uncertainty about American actions after Vietnam and about the potential Sino-Soviet conflict. Resolution of this conflict would certainly allow both of these powers to concentrate more time on other areas.

Pro-Western forces in Indonesia were able to stage a successful attack on communist sympathizers in the early 1960s, but the same might not be true in the early 1990s. Many of the tense situations in Indonesia, the Philippines, and other countries might eventually erupt, and the insular positions and the presence of the dominant Seventh Fleet that has insulated them from hostile sea power projections ashore may no longer be effective in twenty years.

Finally, there is the Caribbean, the only area of actual open confrontation of the two superpowers on the high seas. Some analysts feel that it was the 1962 Cuban missile crisis that caused the Soviet Union to build a blue water navy, though others contend the decision was made prior to 1962. Regardless, the missile crisis surely was an impetus for Soviet naval planners. While there have been some Soviet deployments in this area since the 1962 crisis, they have not been an area of major concern to American naval planners. However, the remoteness of the Caribbean from the Soviet Union and the inclination to consider it an "American lake" could make it a good indicator for future conflict. The possibility that other countries in the region might follow the Cuban example cannot be ruled out, and this would certainly focus more attention on this sea.

In sum, the forward areas, or the flanks, depending upon one's viewpoint, offer some interesting perspectives. The Mediterranean Sea is the area of most immediate potential conflict, while the North Sea/Baltic Sea

6

area may be the most important. The Indian Ocean area is becoming a new area to watch, while the Western Pacific has become somewhat unknown. Finally, the Caribbean might be most useful as an indicator of future sea power conflicts. The important point is, *if* the Soviet Union wants to take advantage of situations that will surely erupt in the flanks, they must eventually go to sea.

Sea-Based Air Power

The subject of most interest to naval planners is ships, especially aircraft carriers and the future of sea-based air power. The aircraft carrier has been the capital ship of the fleets since the 1930s. Any doubt about that among battleship enthusiasts was erased at Pearl Harbor. As soon as World War II ended, however, the war over aircraft carriers began. The argument was made then, as now, that in the age of long-range and supersonic airplanes, and later missiles and fast attack nuclear submarines, the aircraft carrier is too vulnerable *and* too expensive. The cost of a new nuclear powered aircraft carrier is now over $2 billion. Added to this old debate are two new questions: (1) Can land-based air actually be used for sea control, at least in an area such as the Greenland, Iceland, and United Kingdom gap? (2) Will V/STOL[5] make virtually every destroyer-size ship an aircraft carrier?

It is interesting that one of the most radical ship designs that can be predicted as we approach the twenty-first century will be in the most important of the capital ships of the line. Although there might be one more large nuclear powered carrier,[6] according to the chief of naval operations, the eight large attack carriers slated to be retired around the turn of the century will be replaced by V/STOL carriers.[7] If this happens, land-based aircraft might be forced to take over some of the responsibilities of sea control.

The debate over carriers is a significant one, which is not fully appreciated. The debate is not just over land-based versus sea-based air, or V/STOL versus CTOL[8] planes, but over the whole future of Western sea power. According to all navy witnesses, our "slim margin of superiority" over the Soviet navy exists only because of our large attack carriers, and if these capital ships are not replaced, the result would seem to be self-evident.

---

[5] V/STOL stands for "vertical and/or short takeoff and landing."

[6] For a discussion on the present and proposed different aircraft carrier types, see James L. George, "Maintaining A Western Carrier Capability," *United States Naval Institute Proceedings,* October 1977, pp. 30-41.

[7] Admiral James L. Holloway III, USN, "The Transition to V/STOL," *United States Naval Institute Proceedings,* September 1977, pp. 9-13.

[8] CTOL stands for "conventional takeoff and landing."

Balance of the Fleet

The carrier debate, important as it is, is only part of the whole fleet puzzle that must be pieced together for the twenty-first century. What will be the balance of the whole fleet? Will there be radical ship designs? Can the fleet be protected? Just what will be the size of the fleet?

There have probably never been so many ship designs with potentially significant changes for the fleet. Many new designs are operational or in an experimental mode—hydrofoil, air cushion, surface effect, SWATH—and the final evaluation of them will probably not be completed for several years. Since it takes a minimum of five years to build any ship, however, can the planner ignore any new designs that might make the present ones obsolete? Can even the mission planners ignore these new designs? If some of these new concepts do prove feasible, there could be a full resurgence of the debate between the "young school" and "old school"[9] on the type of ships the fleets of the future will contain. There are, in fact, nascent criticisms now from younger analysts who, by supporting smaller ships, are rejuvenating the old debate.

Although it might be fun to speculate about sixty-knot ships, concerns over the propulsion systems of conventionally hulled ships may be more realistic. The shortage of oil reserves may be even more acute in the next ten or twenty years. Logic would suggest nuclear ships, but their cost may become prohibitive. There will be a need for more nuclear ships, but there will also be a continuous need for more efficient fossil fuel ships. New ideas should emerge. Just as we have combined gas turbine-diesel systems, we might have combined nuclear-fossil fuel engine designs in the future.

But can any fleet, even a fleet with the most sophisticated defenses, be protected in this world of long-range missiles and orbiting spy satellites? It is easy to conjure a worst possible case in which a fleet, especially a fleet in a closed sea, can be destroyed in minutes. On the other hand, extreme cases seldom occur, and the question of protection of the fleet is still open. One of the problems with this debate is that most of it must be conducted in secret. Critics are free to suggest scenarios, but defenders may not elaborate on the sophistication of new computerized systems, such as the Aegis, which will join the fleet in the 1980s.

Finally, there must always be a return to the numbers game. Just what will be the size of the fleet around the turn of the century? Officially, the navy is striving for 600 ships, but that figure could not be

---

[9] In brief, the old school (Mahan) calls for a traditional, balanced high-seas fleet complete with large capital ships, while the "young school" (Aube) calls for smaller ships.

reached before the 1990s and it can be reached then only if shipbuilding is increased. Perhaps a more important question is, Does the United States really need a 600 ship navy? To answer that requires an analysis of the missions of the navy which brings the debate full circle.

In considering these important questions as we approach the twenty-first century, we should remember that the navy does not operate in a vacuum. The navy is only a part, albeit an important part, of the sea power equation. Perhaps of equal importance are the uses of the sea, which require analyses of the merchant marine, fisheries, ocean-ography, offshore mining, and the like in relation to sea power. Here also, there has been a drastic change since World War II. The Soviet merchant marine, fishing, and oceanographic fleets, virtually nonexistent at the close of World War II, have now surpassed the United States in quantity and, in many cases, in quality. If there is any truth to the axioms about the relationship between the navy and the merchant fleet, even more naval problems can be anticipated in the future.

After World War II and the advent of the atomic bomb, the late 1940s and the 1950s were the era of air power concerns. Who can forget the famous (or infamous) bomber and missile gaps? In the 1960s and early 1970s, with Vietnam, the spotlight was on the army, as counterinsurgency and guerrilla warfare became the major concerns.

Will the 1980s and 1990s be the era of sea power, and will there be a "navy gap"? There is good reason to predict the former and to be concerned about the latter. Turmoil can be expected in many Third World nations, and there will be other problems in overseas areas. Moreover, the West will need raw materials that are no longer available in their own countries and must be transported over the sea lines of communication. All of this adds up to a greater need for sea power in the future. Although no one is predicting a "naval gap," the Soviet Union is building a fleet capable of forward deployments. It is now numerically superior to the U.S. fleet, whose slim margin of superiority is due to the large attack aircraft carriers which are not to be replaced. It is obviously not too early to start looking at some of the problems of sea power as we approach the twenty-first century.

PART ONE

CHANGING NAVAL MISSIONS

The two papers in this part set the historical background of the U.S. and the Soviet navies. In the first, Vice Admiral Crowe, deputy chief of naval operations for plans, policy, and operations, gives us a cogent look at the past, present, and future roles and missions of U.S. naval forces. The United States entered the international arena as a maritime nation after the Spanish-American War, in which, according to Admiral Crowe, American forces demonstrated the efficacy of Mahan's concept of command of the sea. The United States quickly gained a position of preeminence on the high seas, and after World War II, it was left with a legacy of responsibilities and challenges that persist to this day. As the navies of our Western allies—especially Great Britain—decreased in size and scope, the U.S. Navy took over their former role of protecting remote sea lines of communication. At the same time, the Soviet navy was growing at an unprecedented rate. In the period 1964–1976, it outbuilt the American navy by 1,323 to 302 in all types of ships.

According to Admiral Crowe, the U.S. Navy has two basic missions: sea control and power projection. Sea control is the primary mission, since it is a prerequisite for the success of other naval operations. Power projection encompasses a broad spectrum of actions, from launching strategic nuclear weapons to conducting surgical air strikes and amphibious landings.

Regarding the future, Admiral Crowe states that uncertainties about the outcome of the U.S.–U.S.S.R. relationship will continue to be of global concern. Economic factors—especially increasing U.S. reliance on overseas resources—will accentuate the importance of sea power. New ship designs and sophisticated weapons systems will enhance the need for skilled manpower. But no matter how accurate our predictions, the admiral notes, unforeseen developments, involving even our NATO or

Asian allies, could disrupt our long-range plans. Nevertheless, sea control will remain the principal mission of the U.S. Navy because it affords maximum flexibility in the management of unexpected events.

In the second presentation, James McConnell of the Center for Naval Analyses, points out that the history of Soviet, indeed of Russian, sea power is marked by "discontinuities," displaying "spasmodic off-again, on-again patterns." Since World War II, priorities assigned to Soviet naval missions—for example, strategic strike capability, sea control, strategic defense, and interdiction of sea lines of communication—have varied from "important" to "most important" to "main" or "secondary." No wonder the debate over the role and missions of the Soviet navy is so intriguing.

James McConnell notes that one of the "novelties" of the post-Stalinist period is the resumption of Third World naval diplomacy. He predicts that traditional interior power projection will not be a future Soviet mission. Instead, the U.S.S.R. will maintain a credible offshore presence in order to inhibit any U.S attempt to reverse successes gained by Soviet client states.

Because of past discontinuities, it is hard to predict the future role or missions of the Soviet navy. As McConnell points out, with a change in current trends, we may see a decline in the resources allocated to the Soviet navy. If present trends continue, however, the size of the Soviet navy will decrease by approximately 10 percent in actual number of ships, but it will increase in tonnage by 30 percent. In short, we can expect larger, more sophisticated ships, like the Kiev. *In fact, if the Soviets build ships of this class at a normal rate, they could have thirteen by the year 2000. Thirteen, of course, is the number of aircraft carriers now in the U.S. fleet.*

Western Strategy and Naval Missions Approaching the Twenty-First Century

William Crowe

This paper briefly examines the strategic concepts and international circumstances that catapulted the navy onto the world stage, the challenges posed by the growth of Soviet sea power, the current maritime balance, and the nature of naval missions through the remainder of this century. Volumes have been written about naval warfare, the international environment, the pressures on Western navies to expand or contract over the last seventy-five years, and the enormous impact of science and technology on the development of naval weapons systems. This paper, therefore, addresses only the basic and rather broad elements that have shaped current U.S. naval policy and are likely to have important impacts in the next twenty-five years.

The Past

In considering the future, it is appropriate first to examine the past. An appreciation of history can help us understand where we are and where we are going. What principles of naval warfare were gleaned from experience? How did two world wars and two industrial revolutions affect the roles, size, and structure of our navy? What pressures now argue for a maritime posture second to none?

Approach to Sea Power

The history of Western civilization, particularly the British experience, is bound up with the use of naval forces—to transport armies, to fend off invasion, to safeguard lines of communication to overseas trading posts. Certainly, England's fortunes in the American Revolution were tied directly to its ability to control the seas. Thus, it was only natural for our founding fathers to view the oceans as avenues for economic development and as barriers for defense. As early as 1793, Thomas Jefferson addressed this matter in a letter to the House of Representatives:

As a branch of industry our navigation is valuable, but as a resource of defense . . . our navigations will admit neither neglect nor forebearance. The position and circumstances of the United States leave them nothing to fear on the land board, and nothing to desire beyond their present rights. But on their seaboard they are open to injury, and they have there too a commerce which must be protected.[1]

The U.S. Navy was founded on October 13, 1775. For the next eighty years or so, the United States remained safe from invasion and occupied itself primarily with the consolidation and development of its vast western land masses. In the early 1860s its energies were concentrated on the Civil War. During this conflict the North mounted a shipping blockade against the Confederacy, which greatly contributed to the South's defeat. Nevertheless, the large land battles of the Civil War eclipsed the contribution of sea power. In the 1880s American naval policy was limited to local defense, the protection of ocean-borne commerce from raiders, and the opening of new trade frontiers with such countries as China and Japan. By the end of the nineteenth century, however, the United States was beginning to look to sea.

Mahan's concept of gaining command of the sea by destroying enemy formations with a superior battle fleet was confirmed by the U.S. Navy in the Spanish-American War. As a result of that victory, the United States entered the twentieth century with mounting world influence, confidence in naval power, and national security interests that extended deep into the Pacific as well as more traditional waters such as the Atlantic and Caribbean. This emerging naval role and posture called for increased attention to maritime policy.

Experience of Two World Wars

As World War I broke upon the European continent, the German fleet and submarine warfare presented a direct challenge to international commerce and freedom of the seas—and with telling effect. Countering this threat required unprecedented resources, technical innovations, and tactical adjustments. The superb effort by the British and American navies to ensure the security of the transatlantic lines of communication enabled us to project decisive military power on and over the seas, to resupply U.S. and allied forces, and in time, to collectively win the land battle in Europe. This performance elevated the United States onto the

[1] T. Jefferson, "Report on the Privileges and Restrictions on the Commerce of the United States in Foreign Countries," *The Writings of Thomas Jefferson*, Paul Leicester Ford, ed. (New York: G. P. Putnam Sons, 1899), vol. 6, pp. 470-484.

world stage as one of the world's great naval powers—along with Great Britain, Japan, France, and Italy. In the period between World War I and World War II, technological and tactical advances combined not only to improve the effectiveness of our traditional warships but also to develop entirely new weapons systems for improved submarines and sea-based aircraft. The U.S. Navy played an important part in this revolution, particularly in developing the carrier task group.

During World War II the ability of U.S. and British forces to resupply Europe across the North Atlantic again proved decisive. By destroying the Japanese fleet and merchant marine, carrier-based air power and submarines performed a key role in ending the war in the Western Pacific. Utilizing amphibious warfare concepts and equipment developed by the navy and the marines between 1920 and 1938, American forces carried out an island-hopping campaign that drove the Japanese back into their home waters. The use of carrier-based aircraft provided naval forces with an unprecedented capability for projecting power over great distances and far inland. In the closing days of the war, the startling introduction of nuclear weapons introduced an entirely new variable into the strategic equation and profoundly altered our thinking about military strategy. It also posed a host of difficult questions for naval thinkers.

Postwar Legacy and Challenges

Immediately following World War II, the U.S. Navy found itself unchallenged on the seas but without justification for the large number of ships that had fought in the Atlantic, Mediterranean, and Pacific theaters. For roughly five years (1945–1950), the United States demobilized its naval forces and for a time, the new Department of Defense dissipated its energies over the bomber versus carrier controversy. During this period American scientists and engineers were working on such new developments as carrier-based jet aircraft, aircraft-borne nuclear weapons, and missile technology, and naval designers began thinking about nuclear-powered submarines and the complexities of antisubmarine warfare in a nuclear age.

The forward deployment of U.S. naval forces continued into the postwar years. Commencing in 1948, the United States gradually inherited the British role of buttressing peace and stability in the Mediterranean. A similar pattern developed in the Far East, where the Seventh Fleet remained in support of American shore-based units and national commitments. The practice of keeping peacetime naval forces forward deployed in both Europe and the Western Pacific has persisted to this day.

15

In 1950 the Unted States found itself embroiled in Korea and its first "limited" war. The U.S. Navy, along with army and air force units, was quickly commited to defending South Korea. The navy's effectiveness in interdicting troops and materiel moving down from North Korea testified to the utility of forward deployed forces. During this conflict, the United States relied heavily on its reserve of personnel and World War II ships. Given the limited character of the Korean War and the absence of a seaborne enemy, the fleet's principal role was power projection.

During and after the Korean conflict the threat of communist expansion dominated American foreign policy. To contain Soviet aggression our national strategy called for a U.S.-based strategic nuclear deterrent and a series of alliances and security pacts with allied nations. These arrangements called for unprecedented peacetime deployment of U.S. ground combat forces to Europe and Asia and the establishment of major air and naval bases overseas. The U.S. perceived the fundamental military threat to be land combat power projected by a seemingly monolithic communist bloc.

The forward-deployed fleets fitted nicely into U.S. contingency planning. With the postwar spread of communism in Europe and Asia, strategists placed heavy emphasis on the navy's role in maintaining stability. The overseas fleets could quickly apply power, using tactical air and amphibious forces in response to a wide spectrum of crises in a variety of locations. These were valuable assets in an unsettled and threatening world.

Through most of the 1950s, U.S. carrier forces helped enhance the credibility of our doctrine of massive retaliation. At the same time, the navy was moving rapidly toward a radically new concept of warfare—the fleet ballistic missile submarine—which in time would become a key element of the U.S. strategic deterrent.

In the postwar years, the economic well-being of the United States and its allies became increasingly dependent on sea lines of communication. Without a seaborne threat, however, this fact was not self-evident, and free passage on the world's oceans was, for all practical purposes, taken for granted. Predictably, a power-projection philosophy dominated U.S. naval thinking throughout this period, but change was in the offing. The first significant clue was the Cuban missile crisis of 1962. Once again, the critical importance of sea control was demonstrated—this time rather close to our own shores.

Many believe that the Cuban missile crisis accelerated the growth of the Soviet navy, which was already large. Whatever the cause, Soviet naval forces soon mushroomed in quantity and improved in quality. By the early 1970s the Soviet Union had matched U.S. expenditures for military research and development, and from roughly 1964 to 1976, the number of Soviet naval research institutes nearly doubled. More visibly, in the twelve-year period following the Cuban missile crisis, the Soviet Union built a total of 1,323 ships of all classes compared with 302 for the United States. Among the new Soviet ships were 120 major surface combatants, 83 amphibious units, and 53 auxiliaries. Moreover, Moscow entered the nuclear propulsion competition in earnest. By 1976 Admiral Gorshkov could boast 188 nuclear submarines, including 46 ballistic missile-carrying submersibles. New and sophisticated weapons systems began to appear with stunning frequency, of which the most important were several generations of surface-to-surface, air-to-surface, and submarine-to-surface cruise missiles. Routine deployment of Soviet naval forces far from the homeland and the presence of these ships in various oceans of the world soon became a major factor in U.S. and allied calculations of the maritime balance.

Unfortunately, other uncontrollable events of the 1960s and early 1970s, not directly related to sea control, were making their impact on the size and quality of the U.S. Navy. The operational demands and fiscal constraints imposed by the war in Vietnam effected a marked decline in the material readiness of our surface combatants. While naval aircraft continued to be replaced and improved during the Vietnam conflict, many ships suffered from age and neglect. For more than five years an in-depth assessment of these problems and the funds to replace worn-out or obsolete surface combatants and weapons systems were deferred because of the war.

In June 1968, the U.S. Navy had 976 active ships in commission, of which fifteen were attack carriers and eight, antisubmarine warfare carriers. Faced with high operating costs, uncertain reliability, and block obsolescence, the navy decided after careful deliberation to retire many of these ships and to invest any accrued savings in new construction. Because of high inflation and tightening appropriations, the outcome of this step was a fleet with less than half as many ships as in 1968.

The Present

Today, the U.S. Navy is still striving to modernize and expand the active fleet and to build in the combat characteristics required to further long-range national objectives. Resources, however, are not unlimited, and navy planners are constantly on the defensive. Many inside and outside of government argue that present force levels are sufficient for the next few years and vigorously resist any increase in capital investment. Budgetary factors such as the high cost of skilled manpower, maintenance, peacetime training and readiness, improvements in command and control capabilities, and basic research and development also inhibit new construction. Rising costs are, of course, not unique to the navy. Still, the United States can ill-afford to delay fleet modernization and expansion.

International Milieu. U.S. national security and international relations —political, economic, and military—rely heavily on free and unimpeded passage on the world's oceans. For several reasons this dependence impacts directly on U.S. strategy and demands a posture that will assure naval superiority.

First, our geopolitical situation compels us to remain a maritime nation. The United States is bound on the north and south by only two international frontiers, across which are friendly nations that pose no threat; to the east and west are thousands of miles of coastline. Two states—Alaska and Hawaii—and all U.S. territories are linked to the mainland by sea lines of communication. The petroleum presently being drawn from Alaska's North Slope punctuates our need for a strong maritime posture in the Eastern Pacific, and the Arctic Ocean may not long remain a defensive barrier with little relevance to national security.

Second, the United States is inextricably involved in an increasingly interdependent world economy. Prior to World War II, we relied heavily on domestic production of natural resources and served as a net exporter of many strategic materials. Since then, U.S. reliance on imports has increased to the point where we now consume one-third of the world's annual production of minerals and energy. In many cases, we have depleted our domestic reserves, and U.S. industrial production has become dependent on imported raw materials. For instance, we import over 40 percent of our petroleum, of which one-half comes from Africa and the Middle East. We purchase overseas nearly 100 percent of our cobalt, manganese, natural rubber, tin, chromite, and columbium–tantalum, and 90 percent of our antimony, nickel, and industrial diamonds. Moreover, our chemical industries rely heavily on petroleum products for the manufacture of synthetic materials. Despite the tremendous advance in air transport, 99 percent of the material exported and imported by the United States travels by surface ship. Thus, any extended disruption of our sea lines of communication would have an enormous impact on our domestic productivity and national security.

Third, our trading partners in Europe and Asia are even more dependent on free use of the seas. In their defense planning, these nations rely heavily on reinforcement and resupply from the United States. Japan, Korea, Australia, New Zealand, Israel, and the NATO countries, for example, continue to purchase American-made weapons systems. The customers assume that in a hostile environment, delivery of replacement units and spare parts can and will be assured by the United States.

Soviet Threat. At present, U.S. maritime strength and influence are directly challenged by the unprecedented growth of Soviet sea power, the scope of which cannot be explained simply by the organic needs of this major power. Rather, it seems to be motivated by both a Soviet perception of threat from the sea and an expansion of Soviet global interests and ambitions.

The Soviet territorial expanse dominates the Eurasian land mass, and the country has a large reserve of untapped natural resources and an expanding technological base. Its major allies—the Warsaw Pact countries—are contiguous to Soviet borders on the west; the only direct threat to Soviet security is along the Sino-Soviet border to the east. The NATO countries, with which the Soviet Union has an adversary relationship, occupy the same Eurasian land mass. Internal lines of communication facilitate reinforcement of the Warsaw Pact, deployment of Soviet military forces to the most probable areas of conflict, and transport of natural resources and industrial products. Such a situation would suggest a restrictive role for Soviet naval forces—coastal defense and flank support for land theaters of operation. Yet, in sheer number, the U.S.S.R. has constructed the world's largest navy—second only to the U.S. Navy in capability—and has deployed it worldwide. Clearly, the Soviet Union can no longer be thought of as an exclusively continental power. Rather, Moscow is using its maritime assets—military, commercial, and scientific—to spread Soviet influence and gain international acceptance.

In recent years the Soviet Union has expended enormous resources on antisubmarine warfare (ASW), including two new classes of aviation-capable ships, each of which reflects a radical change in the Soviet fleet. The Moskva class, with its heavy antisubmarine configuration and complement of helicopters, represents one of its early attempts to deal with the problem of countering nuclear submarines in distant waters. The much larger Kiev class has the capability of embarking vertical/short takeoff and landing (V/STOL) aircraft as well as helicopters. The Kiev is an impressive ASW platform with integral air defense and antisurface warfare capabilities. These ships greatly enhance the Soviet navy's overall ability to operate worldwide in time of peace or war. The Soviet navy has

19

also achieved significant improvements in land-based aircraft. In their naval configuration such planes as the Bear, Badger, and Backfire could present a severe threat to Western surface forces, especially when forward based and used in coordination with other elements of the Soviet navy. The Soviet air force has antishipping capabilities as well.

With their ability to operate the entire length of the North Atlantic as well as against other sea lines of communication, Soviet submarine forces pose a substantial threat to the United States and its maritime allies. In a protracted conflict, Soviet cruise-missile and torpedo-attack submarines can heavily reduce the necessary reinforcement and resupply of Western Europe and destroy much of the economic shipping upon which the United States and its allies depend. Moreover, the speed, endurance, and firepower of nuclear-powered submarines have rendered obsolete many traditional concepts of convoy protection, including some of the evasive tactics once pursued by convoy commanders, with or without the immediate support of antisubmarine forces.

Similar Soviet improvements in surface combatants have resulted in platforms capable of very effective performance in antisubmarine, anti-air, and antisurface-ship warfare. Since 1967, all new classes of principal surface combatants in the Soviet navy have been fitted with ASW equipment, including facilities to operate and maintain the Hormone A helicopter. In fact, the Soviet Union has designated every principal surface combatant in the past ten years as an ASW ship of one kind or another. The emphasis on ASW underscores Soviet concern with the qualitative advantages of U.S. and other Western SSNs. Moreover, Russian commanders have developed a sophisticated command network that not only permits centralized direction of the Soviet fleet but facilitates direct coordination among surface forces, submerged units, and land-based aircraft.

In addition to these and other naval developments, the Soviet Union has acquired the world's largest fishing, oceanographic, and scientific research fleets. It has the fifth largest merchant fleet and an expanding inventory of passenger liners. Quite obviously, Soviet dependence on the seas is not as great as that of the United States and its allies, but these developments illustrate the importance Soviet leaders attach to maritime affairs. The fact that all merchant and naval vessels remain under governmental control during peacetime also has important implications for the onset of hostilities in terms of intelligence gathering, mobilization capability, and coordination.

In recent years the Soviet Union has deployed its navy farther and farther from home ports and traditional operating areas. In 1970, it conducted its first worldwide naval exercise (Okean-70), which demonstrated a Soviet capability for coordinated air, surface, and submarine activity in both the Atlantic and the Pacific. Five years later Okean-75 gave the world a demonstration of even more sophisticated Soviet naval power and global coordination capabilities.

Increasingly, the Soviet Union has been emphasizing the utility of naval power in support of national defense and foreign policies. In the words of Fleet Admiral Gorshkov:

> The constantly growing capabilities of navies in carrying out strategic missions is elevating their role in warfare. The significance of oceanic theaters of military operations is also being elevated accordingly. As a result, an even further increase in the scale of naval warfare as one of the most important parts of warfare as a whole is foreordained.[2]

The U.S. Navy in National Military Strategy. As stipulated in Title 10 U.S. Code, the mission of the U.S. Navy is to be prepared to conduct prompt and sustained combat operations at sea in support of U.S. national interests. Within this mission, the navy is further tasked to perform specific and collateral functions in support of national military strategy:

> To organize, train and equip Navy . . . forces for the conduct of prompt and sustained combat operations at sea, including operations of sea-based aircraft and land-based naval air components—specifically, forces to seek out and destroy enemy naval forces and to suppress enemy sea commerce, to gain and maintain general naval supremacy, to control vital sea areas and to protect vital sea lines of communications, to establish and maintain local superiority (including air) in an area of naval operations; to seize and defend advanced naval bases, and to conduct such land and air operations as may be essential to the prosecution of a naval campaign.[3]

A distillation of this directive yields two primary functions with which the navy is currently charged: sea control and power projection. In addition, it assigns several collateral and subordinate functions to naval forces.

In essence, sea control is the navy's preeminent function, because it is a prerequisite for the successful conduct of other types of naval

---

[2] S. Gorshkov, "Certain Questions Concerning the Development of the Naval Art," *Morskoy Sbornik*, December 1974, pp. 24-25.

[3] Department of Defense, "Functions of the Department of Defense and Its Major Components," *DOD Directive 5100.1* (Washington, D.C.: Department of Defense, 1969), p. 9.

operations, including support of U.S. military forces deployed overseas. Effective sea control accomplishes several objectives: it enhances the survivability of the strategic submarine force by impeding enemy ASW operations; it protects commercial shipping vital to the economic well-being of the United States and its allies; it ensures the replenishment of combat consumables and equipment expended by U.S. and allied forces in time of war; and it provides secure operating areas from which to conduct air strikes or amphibious assaults against hostile shore areas.

Current doctrine seeks to achieve sea control by engaging and destroying air, surface, and subsurface forces threatening U.S. naval and merchant units or other friendly forces. The doctrine calls for the seizure or neutralization of threatening enemy bases and denial to enemy forces of access routes to open-ocean areas.

Power projection operations subsume a broad spectrum of offensive actions from strategic nuclear response by fleet ballistic missile submarines to surgical air strikes by carrier-based aircraft. Included in this continuum are the employment of amphibious assault forces and the bombardment of shore targets in support of land forces or other naval operations. Power projection operations can be essential to the achievement of sea control; for example, in the destruction of enemy naval bases and airfields to preclude replacement of hostile forces previously destroyed.

Thus sea control and power projection are closely related, and both functions depend in large measure on the same forces. Given an effective capability to perform these functions, the U.S. Navy can support national strategy in three ways: (1) by strategic nuclear deterrence which is a function of the essentially invulnerable ballistic missile submarine; (2) by components to be deployed overseas under a unified commander—capable of responding rapidly to national command authorities in regional contingencies and of supporting forward-positioned ground and air forces; (3) by units charged with the security of U.S. sea lines of communication—no mean feat.

U.S. Naval Developments

Given its assigned missions and the sharp decline in fleet strength since 1968, the U.S. Navy has had to rely heavily on technology and reconfiguration of its existing force structure to counter the mounting Soviet naval power. Its primary emphasis has been the threat posed by Soviet submarines, which continue to outnumber surface combatants (destroyers and frigates) in the U.S. fleet by a ratio of two-to-one. Thus, the U.S. Navy has moved toward the complementary use of various platforms in antisubmarine warfare and has sought to substantially improve the capabilities of each. Two new surface combatants—the FFG-7 Perry class and the DD-963 Spruance class—are being outfitted with the latest ASW equipment, including an improved version of the Light Airborne Multipurpose Sensor (LAMPS) helicopter. The submarine force has been given an expanded ASW role, with the new SSN-688 class nuclear-powered attack vessel in the forefront of this effort. Work continues on towed-array sonars, a new family of air-droppable sonobuoys, advanced ASW data-processing equipment, the MK-48 torpedo, and advanced mines for blocking key straits. In addition, research has commenced on a 3,000 ton surface effect ship combining the "dash" capability of helicopters with the "staying power" of a surface ship.

The decision to convert all Forrestal class carriers to a multipurpose power-projection and sea-control role was made in the early 1970s, based largely on the submarine cruise missile threat and the retirement of the Essex class ASW carriers. In essence, all of the technology gained from postwar carrier ASW operations was transferred intact to existing attack carriers and those under design or construction. This change in mission, coupled with the introduction of the S-3 and H-3 aircraft, gives these carriers an organic capability to counter submarine threats in distant areas, with or without the immediate support of land-based P-3 aircraft.

Concurrently, the U.S. Navy has been seeking to exploit both the offensive and defensive capabilities of precision-guided missiles. The NATO Sea Sparrow and the Vulcan Phalanx close-in weapon system provide surface ships with an effective, fast-reaction, close-in defense against low-flying, high-speed antiship missiles; Harpoon will provide surface, submarine, and air units with increased offensive power. Finally, engineering development has started on the Tomahawk cruise missile, a long-range precision-guided weapon suitable for installation in nuclear attack submarines and certain surface combatants. Overall, the navy is substantially increasing the missile-carrying and rapid-fire capabilities of all existing platforms.

Current Assessment. The U.S. Navy programs discussed above have been undertaken to counter multiple threats posed by the Soviet navy and to materially improve our general combat capabilities. The navy has placed maximum emphasis on the flexibility, complementarity, and effectiveness of existing platforms, particularly in sea-control missions. Our current assessment of relative capabilities, however, leads us to conclude that the naval balance between the United States and the Soviet Union will continue to deteriorate unless a sustained effort is made to increase not only the versatility but also the number of U.S. naval combatants.

Currently, the Soviet navy has almost a five-to-one advantage in number of ships, including major surface combatants, nuclear- and diesel-powered submarines, amphibious craft, minor surface combatants, mine countermeasures ships, and auxiliaries. Even without the auxiliaries, the numerical advantage is on the order of four-to-one. If we count only major surface combatants, submarines, and amphibious craft, the Soviet navy still has 50 percent more naval platforms than the U.S. Navy.

In displacement tonnage, the U.S. Navy has nearly a 30 percent advantage, mainly attributable to the thirteen aircraft carriers we carry in our force structure. It also has a two-to-one numerical superiority in operational aircraft over Soviet naval aircraft. Moreover, the carrier force—with its mixed complement of multipurpose aircraft, escorts, and support ships—provides the endurance and flexibility needed to respond to a wide spectrum of threats.

For the last seven or eight years, the Soviet navy's one-to-one ratio of ship acquisition to ship retirement has enabled it to remain relatively stable in number. For the past ten years the Soviet navy has concentrated heavily on nuclear-powered submarine programs, maintaining a numerical advantage over the United States in comparable units. This trend is especially significant to our allies, most of whom have no nuclear-powered submarines and no plans to develop them. On the other hand, U.S. attack and fleet ballistic missile submarines are qualitatively superior to their Soviet counterparts, particularly in sound propagation and sensor capabilities.

From 1968 to 1975, the U.S. Navy experienced a more than 50 percent decline in amphibious ships, while the Soviet navy's force level remained relatively constant, following a heavy buildup during the 1960s. Nevertheless, the U.S. amphibious assault capability remains superior to that of the Soviet Union, as it should to achieve U.S. sea-control objectives. With the introduction of the new Tarawa class ship, the United States will acquire a modern 20-knot amphibious force with significant troop-lift and vertical-envelopment capabilities.

The U.S.S.R. maintains a significant advantage in its access to geographically strategic areas—the sea of Japan, the Eastern Mediterranean, and the Norwegian Sea—because of the large number of guided missile fast-patrol boats in its inventory and the extended coverage provided by land-based aircraft. In these and other areas, the targeting problem tends to favor the Soviet navy because of the small number of U.S. platforms and widespread Soviet use of standoff missiles in its surface ships, submarines, and aircraft. Although the U.S. Navy maintains a numerical advantage in defensive systems, much of this advantage is based on our tactical air forces, including the F-14 aircraft with its multiple intercept capability.

In number of antisubmarine warfare platforms—surface ASW ships, attack submarines, land- and sea-based aircraft—the two navies have approached parity, but it is generally believed that the new weapons systems being introduced into the U.S. fleet are superior to those of the Soviet navy. Particularly significant is the advantage enjoyed by U.S. attack submarines as a result of quieting technology and geographic asymmetries. Also, the United States is maintaining an underway replenishment force that is considerably more versatile and capable than that of the Soviet navy.

U.S. naval weapons system components are generally believed superior to most Soviet systems because of our longer experience in electronics and avionic microminiaturization. We have improved the reliability and accuracy of our navigation equipment, guidance systems, and detection and surveillance sensors to the point where "blind" evasive maneuvering is well within the capability of weapons platform operators. The U.S. Navy also retains a significant advantage in combat-experienced personnel. The technical orientation of the average American recruit and our longstanding naval tradition tend to give U.S. Navy personnel a significant advantage over their Soviet counterparts. Such an advantage could be a critical factor in a showdown between the two navies.

Based on net assessments of all the aforementioned factors and other considerations, such as wargaming and international commitments, the U.S. chief of naval operations has testified before the Senate Armed Services Committee that:

> The United States Fleet has a slim margin of superiority over the Soviets in those scenarios involving the most vital U.S. national security interests. To maintain the future balance in favor of the United States, we must begin now to build the requisite number of ships if the U.S. Navy is not to surrender the capability to accomplish its mission and retain its current margin of superiority at sea.[4]

In the event of a war in Europe, the navy could control the North Atlantic sea lanes, but serious losses of Western shipping would probably

---

[4] James L. Holloway III, *Statement of Admiral James L. Holloway III, U.S. Navy, Chief of Naval Operations, before the Senate Armed Services Committee Concerning Maritime Posture on 3 February 1977* (Washington, D.C., February 1977), pp. 7-8.

occur in the early stages of hostilities depending on Soviet tactical priorities. Its ability to conduct operations in the Eastern Mediterranean, however, is questionable. The navy could also protect Pacific sea lines of communication to Alaska, Hawaii, and probably Guam, but would very likely find it difficult to extend this protection into the Western Pacific and Indian oceans because of insufficient combat and mobile logistic support forces.

The Future

The preceding examination of the "present" describes the starting point from which we look ahead to naval strategy and missions of the 1985–2000 time frame. Strategies are, by definition, evolutionary. In the real world, we cannot erase history and start afresh. Because of long lead times in translating concepts into fact, today's planner is always tied more or less to current forces, current base structures, current thought patterns, current weapons systems, and so on. Therefore, he must detect change early, hedge against the unforeseen, and react to new circumstances before his opponent. This is a major challenge, since none of us knows precisely what the future holds. Certainly our past record of predicting the strategic environment leaves a great deal to be desired.

Strategic Environment. As a first step in predicting the strategic environment, one must examine the geopolitical, economic, and technological factors likely to impact U.S. interests in general and the U.S. Navy's role in particular. Some of these factors show such evidence of continuity that they can be projected into the future with confidence. Others indicate probable change, instability, or high uncertainty. The goal is to discern developments that seriously threaten U.S. policy, offer new opportunities to further U.S. maritime interests, or significantly affect the naval balance.

Geopolitical factors. For the remainder of this century the predominant international political reality will be Soviet-American competition for global power and influence—a condition arising from fundamental differences in geographical location, history, political philosophy, resource availability, and socioeconomic outlook. During the period toward the twenty-first century, no nation other than the U.S.S.R. is likely to seriously challenge the United States, nor is any other nation or third-party combination apt to achieve "superpower" status.

We have every reason to believe that Moscow will continue to stress sea power. The Kremlin's tremendous investment in a fleet and success in expanding its influence into previously forbidding areas make it unlikely that Soviet leaders will reverse their current naval policy. This does not mean that the Soviet navy will necessarily increase in size, but we can expect to see consistent modernization and a constant search for new systems and tactics with which to outstrip the U.S. Navy.

Overall U.S. military strategy will remain defensive in nature. This implies a peacetime posture characterized by persistent monitoring of Soviet military developments and effective defenses against attack with little or no warning. The United States will attempt to meet the Soviet challenge in cooperation with other, like-minded nations. Barring a dramatic shift in international politics, the emphasis will remain on Western Europe and Japan. The strength and cohesion of this maritime alliance will depend on many factors, but in the military sphere the most important will be the U.S. capability to maintain an assured nuclear retaliatory response and to control essential sea lines of communication.

The United States and its allies will remain heavily dependent on Middle East petroleum for economic productivity and national security. Denial of this petroleum source would deplete Western reserves, slow down economic productivity, hamper defense industries, and possibly, threaten the outcome of any conflict with the Soviet Union. Such a crisis could occur as a result of political instabilities, renewed Arab-Israeli conflict, or Soviet intervention in the Persian Gulf. In addition, allied lines of communication in the Indian Ocean, South Atlantic, and the South and East China seas will remain highly vulnerable—for example, a super tanker departs the Persian Gulf every fifteen minutes bound for Japan, Europe, or the United States.

What are some of the uncertainties the United States may have to face? A major unknown in the global balance is the People's Republic of China. Will it continue to share strategic interests with the United States? How will its relations with the Soviet Union evolve? At present, Western European security is substantially enhanced by the number of Soviet ground and tactical air forces tied down in Asia. In turn, the Chinese benefit from U.S. naval power in the Western Pacific which is a counterpoise to the Soviet Pacific fleet. This relationship has no formal underpinnings, yet it has enormous implications for international peace and security and argues strongly for a U.S. naval presence in the Western Pacific. A dramatic shift in China's international situation could quickly throw our Asian policy into disarray. In this event, an effective U.S. naval presence in that part of the world becomes even more imperative.

As noted above, U.S. defense planning will continue to depend on allies, particularly NATO countries and Japan. No one can be certain, however, how these ties will evolve over time or under stress. Japan, for example, is not obligated by treaty to assist the United States or the NATO countries in a conflict with the Soviet Union. Its response to a crisis depends on many unpredictable factors. The growing strength of leftist elements in a number of European countries also clouds the future and might eventually threaten the cohesion of NATO itself. Reliance on petroleum makes Western Europe and Japan extremely sensitive to relations with the Arab states; the United States, on the other hand, continues to have a large stake in the survival of Israel. This situation alone could drive a sharp wedge between the United States and its allies. A shift from economic cooperation to sharp competition among Japan, the NATO nations, and the United States would also be decisive. While unwanted and unsettling, these possibilities strike at the heart of U.S. defense planning. It would be folly to ignore them in our strategic thinking.

Another uncertainty concerns the allied navies. Western sea power has been seriously diminished by the withdrawal of British forces "East of Suez" during the 1960s and the sharp decline in Royal navy combatants since then. No nation other than the United States could assume the British role. Similar trends may develop as other European allies become preoccupied with Soviet ground and air threats from the East or suffer increasing economic pressures. Given the national mood, any attempt to significantly expand Japanese naval forces would be met with alarm in that and other Pacific nations, including the People's Republic of China. In essence, an even greater share of the sea-control burden could fall on the United States.

Through most of the 1960s, U.S. defense planners focused almost entirely on the Soviet threat to transatlantic lines of communication. As the size of the U.S. fleet declined, more U.S. naval combatants were drawn into the Atlantic war-at-sea scenario. At present, we are faced not only with the foregoing problem, but also the problem of a Soviet Pacific fleet that includes some fifty surface combatants, about eighty submarines of various types, and nearly one hundred aircraft capable of delivering antiship missiles—all supported from an improved network of Soviet bases and repair facilities in the Far East. No one can predict exactly how the Soviet Union would employ these forces in a NATO conflict, but some possibilities include heavy pressure on Japan, interdiction of U.S. and allied shipping, disruption of petroleum shipments from the Persian Gulf, support of such Soviet client states as North Korea or Vietnam, or augmentation of Soviet units in the Atlantic. Whatever the case, the naval balance may be such that, in a hostile environment, U.S. interests in Europe, the Middle East, or Asia could best be protected by positive action to hold down or to neutralize the Soviet Pacific fleet.

In its approach to international security, the United States will continue to rely on a network of forward bases where politically feasible, tactically advantageous, and cost-effective to do so. However, during the last two decades, the number of relevant U.S. naval and air bases has declined from 150 to 30, and the trend will most likely continue for the remainder of this century. Also during this period, politicial requirements for redeploying ground troops from overseas areas may increase. The immediate example is the Second Division in South Korea, which is scheduled to be withdrawn by 1982. The utility of foreign bases will also be affected by constraints on U.S. military assistance programs for host governments, the multipolar political environment, conflicting assessments of national interests, and the reluctance of some countries to become involved in a superpower confrontation. Moreover, we could lose access to some of these bases rather suddenly during contingencies involving U.S. but not allied security interests. This clearly was the situation during the Arab-Israeli conflict of 1973, when much of NATO sought to divorce itself from the U.S. response.

Unknowns of a more limited nature center on countries that do not profess to be major powers or seek to become involved in Soviet-American competition but are still of interest to the United States. Some are in hostile and unstable environments and, left to fend for themselves, might invite intervention by the Soviet Union or one of its client states. Such dangers to international peace and security can often be deterred by the regular or periodic presence of U.S. naval forces. The political environment in the Eastern Mediterranean, the Persian Gulf, and East Africa, for example, could require special attention and a flexible U.S. military presence for the indefinite future.

Other international political factors capable of affecting U.S. naval forces in the 1985–2000 time frame are arms limitations talks and changes in the present sea regime. While arms control remains a valid and often selective approach to international peace and security, any agreements must take into account U.S. global interests, fundamental differences in the roles of the Soviet and U.S. navies (sea denial versus sea control, respectively), and the security of allies in Europe and Asia. It is difficult to conceive of an agreement that accommodates U.S. and Soviet interests equally. Nevertheless, attempts to reach such accords will undoubtedly continue, and the outcome could affect operational restraints. With respect to any sea regime proposal, our primary concern as a maritime nation should be to preserve the mobility and flexibility of U.S. as well as allied naval forces.

Economic factors. From a U.S. perspective, the dominant consideration in the 1985–2000 time frame will be our increasing dependence on and competition for imported resources. To pay for these imports, the U.S. will have to find new overseas markets for its agricultural and industrial products. Matters of vital economic concern will be the world's population growth, relations between developed and developing states, the cost and availability of petroleum and other natural resources, and the long-term impact of these pressures on economic stability.

With respect to critical raw materials, the gap between U.S. industrial demands and domestic production is projected to increase dramatically by the year 2000. For example, it is believed that over the next fifteen years U.S. demand for metallic elements will increase dramatically—aluminum, more than 600 percent; antimony, over 300 percent; nickel, over 200 percent; chromium, almost 300 percent; tin, 100 percent; manganese, just under 100 percent. Although these are estimates at best, they reflect the scope of the problem.

For all nations, economic development and productivity will remain central factors in governmental and industrial planning. How the plans are implemented will have a substantial impact on international peace and economic stability. A serious problem will be the distribution of gross world product (GWP). At present, the most developed nations account for 27 percent of the world's population and 79 percent of the GWP, while the poorest nations account for 73 percent of the world's population and 21 percent of the GWP.

Rapid population growth in the developing countries will exert unprecedented pressures on resources and governments. The world's population is increasing by 1.8 percent a year. By the year 2000, there will be a global population of 6.2 billion, four-fifths of it in the Third World. Simultaneously, the rising cost of raw materials (and, in some cases, mismanagement) will frustrate efforts by underdeveloped countries to meet both consumer demands and national development goals. These conditions will severely complicate the problems of the developed world.

The United States will play a leading role in trying to meet these global challenges through direct economic aid and revenue-sharing schemes administered by such international institutions as the United Nations and the World Bank. Nevertheless, the long-range strategic environment may well be fraught with increasing tensions, confrontations, and national conflicts. The United States will have to be prepared for such contingencies—to protect the lives and property of Americans overseas, to assure the safety of U.S. ships and aircraft engaged in international commerce, and to contain selected local or regional instabilities.

The availability of energy will be a major, if not the central, factor in the economic health and development of all nations. Since world

30

energy consumption is forecast to almost triple by 1990, the United States must pursue foreign and defense policies that preclude Soviet domination of vital oil-producing areas. A prime policy consideration will be the relative ease with which the Soviet Union can move ground and tactical air forces into the Middle East. In turn, an essential element of deterrence will be an American ability to evidence and project power in the Eastern Mediterranean and Indian Ocean areas. Naval forces are ideally suited to this task.

Economic trends also will have a significant impact on the U.S. defense potential. The costs of importing raw materials, of developing new sources of energy, and of sustaining economic productivity are bound to raise questions about outlays for defense both in the United States and among our industrial allies and trading partners. The rate of modernization or expansion of our armed forces may not be sufficient to meet existing or emerging threats. Western Europe, in particular, could become even more dependent on the U.S. naval forces, given the vast investment in research, development, and shipbuilding required to counter the sophistication of the Soviet navy.

All of these factors call for new approaches to collective and mutual security. Some of the searching has already started. The United States, for example, is encouraging standardization of allied military equipment in order to effect economies in research and development, to reduce the unit price of new weapons systems, to keep production lines open over a long run, and to enhance flexibility in combined operations. Through its military assistance programs, the United States is encouraging many of its allies to improve their ground and tactical air forces, while assuring them of our continued material and naval support. The need for a more far-reaching division of defense labor will be intensified over the next two decades, pointing up the importance of a U.S. commitment to maintain control over worldwide sea lines of communication. None of these initiatives can proceed in an orderly way, however, without a determined American effort to ensure political and economic stability in Western Europe, the Middle East, and Asia.

In summary, the long-term economic environment will present unprecedented challenges of resource distribution and management. The United States will seek to retain its present position of economic leadership, will rely increasingly on international commerce, and will acquire a much larger stake in world peace and stability. Under these circumstances, we will need a navy that can move about the world as necessary to maintain an equilibrium of military power that will inspire confidence in our allies and trading partners. The navy will also have to be able to control the sea lines of communication vital to the United States and its partners in trade. Certainly no nation other than the United States will be able to keep pace with Soviet naval developments, counter Soviet influence in underdeveloped regions, or preserve worldwide sea lines of communication.

Technological factors. Over the next three decades, technology will profoundly affect the characteristics of Soviet and American naval forces and the maritime balance in general. Yet it is an area of great uncertainty. In predicting the impact of basic science and applied technology on naval developments, it is virtually impossible to be specific or accurate. Many ideas and concepts too exist only in the minds of brilliant young men and women in graduate school or industrial laboratories. Still, some technological developments can be predicted with some confidence and discussed in terms of their impact on naval planning and operations.

It is reasonable to assume that the U.S. Minuteman or any other stationary weapons system will become increasingly vulnerable. If the Soviet Union continues to develop new generations of strategic missiles, improvements in accuracy are inevitable. In this sense, the U.S. sea-launched ballistic missile force will continue to be the least vulnerable component of the strategic Triad. However, we cannot ignore the heavy emphasis the Soviet Union is placing on antisubmarine warfare or the block obsolescence of the Poseidon submarines in the late 1980s and early 1990s. Thus, construction of the first of the new Trident class nuclear-powered ballistic missile submarine and an associated missile is an essential step toward retaining a credible deterrent and complicating the Soviet ASW problem. Related programs should focus on improving the accuracy of sea-launched ballistic missiles and investigating cruise missile configurations.

Also around 1990, the U.S. Navy will acquire a significantly improved ASW capability with a larger inventory of the Los Angeles class nuclear-attack submarine, a new generation of shipboard helicopter, and modified versions of the S-3 and P-3 series aircraft. Navy research and development efforts to surmount ASW problems will continue to be divided among surveillance systems, active and passive sonars, linear tactical towed arrays, advanced torpedoes, and mines. New ways of coordinating the use of various platforms will enhance the effectiveness of individual weapons systems.

The long-range requirement to project naval power ashore and our reliance on tactical aircraft for sea control missions have led the U.S. Navy to extend the service life of the Forrestal class carrier. Decisions are needed now, however, to resolve questions about replacement programs that must be initiated in the 1980s—How should the navy focus its research and development effort? What is required to ensure a successful marriage of carriers and potentially available aircraft? How can the cost of future production be kept within reasonable bounds? In terms of emerging technology, the most important factor will be the proven flexibility—but still uncertain tactical performance—of V/STOL aircraft. Thus, the future of sea-based tactical air power depends to a large extent on the investment we make now in V/STOL technology. This will be one of the most complex and important projects ever undertaken by the U.S. Navy.

Substantial improvements can be expected in the range and precision of radars—ship, shore, and aircraft. Laser beams that penetrate cloud cover may eventually be developed and used for target interrogation and acquisition. Less certain is improved technology for the detection and location of underwater platforms, but the high priority given to ASW implies continued efforts in this area.

Although this paper is a little more than a thumbnail sketch, it does suggest that seaborne forces will undergo some important changes as we approach the twenty-first century. Longer-range sensors, weapons systems, and helicopters will increase the effectiveness of individual ships. Smaller carriers and V/STOL aircraft may revolutionize the air picture. Single units will be capable of operating independent of task forces, and their range of missions will increase accordingly. At the same time more sophisticated command and control systems will weld these efforts into an integrated whole.

Other changes will undoubtedly occur in response to as yet unforeseen developments and pressures. Improvements in weapons technology may dictate different sizes or types of ships in order to complicate the targeting problem. Enhanced satellite sensors could mandate additional submarine functions. Soviet attack capabilities may dictate completely new ways of controlling, routing, and protecting merchant ships. The point of including such speculative issues is that we live in a scientific age that is constantly changing—often in unpredictable ways. The impact of scientific progress will surely continue to affect the future course of sea warfare.

In preparing for the twenty-first century, the U.S. Navy must do two things: (1) pursue a vigorous and varied research and development program, and (2) design sufficient flexibility and space into ships and aircraft to facilitate the retrofitting of new developments as they arise. It would be folly to do less.

Manpower Requirements. Skilled manpower is critical to the navy's ability to introduce new technology and rebuild its fleet. Yet, in an all-volunteer environment, manpower is one of the most uncertain factors in long-range planning. The ability to recruit and retain personnel is undoubtedly linked to economic conditions, but we are not as yet able to project the effects of this relationship. No one can predict the national employment rate or the cost of recruiting and retaining skilled personnel twenty years from now. A related question concerns military compensation and the defense budget—Will the rate of compensation increase faster than the rate of congressional appropriations, and if so, how will this affect funds designated for the procurement of new ships and aircraft? About 50 percent of the people needed to man ships, aircraft squadrons, and shore bases at the turn of the century will be born in the next few years. The education, self-discipline, and career orientation of these young people are important planning elements over which the navy will have little influence and virtually no control.

In addition to long-range uncertainties, the navy will be faced with the problem of manpower stability from year to year. It will be subject to continual pressures—to trim manpower costs; to change the present system of compensation; to defer retirement benefits; and the like. Some of these changes may be necessary and even desirable, but the way they are managed—especially in terms of funding and implementation—will profoundly affect naval recruitment and retention. Consider, for example, how difficult or even how unmanageable the situation would be if the navy were to enter the next century with inadequate recruits—in number or in skills—and too few petty officers to supervise the maintenance and operation of our highly complex weapons systems.

The nation must appreciate the importance of manpoyer and commit itself to resolving the uncertainties surrounding this factor long before the next century.

Management of the Unforeseen. The previous discussion focused largely on elements of national security that are exhaustively studied and widely accepted by government, private industry, professional scholars, and the media as fundamental to any consideration of long-term U.S. defense. It also indicated the extreme complexity, diversity, and uncertainty of the future strategic environment.

In seeking ways to economize and to make the planning process manageable, many budgeteers and analysts tend to oversimplify or to ignore uncertainty. Given the competition between the United States and the Soviet Union they are inclined to make some rigid assumptions—that our alliances with NATO and Japan will remain much as they are today; that Moscow's attention will be riveted to Central Europe; that a major European war will be of short duration; that the world's economy while troublesome will always be manageable and will not become a military problem. Policy makers often presume that the American people will not question the fundamental thrust of the U.S. defense posture, with its strong emphasis on Central Europe and Japan. Many also believe that if we could just get NATO and Japan to do more, the United States could spend less.

One can seriously question whether conventional wisdom of this sort will provide the United States with an appropriate defense posture. As the preceding discussion suggests, the remainder of this century is not likely to adhere to firm predictions or inflexible scenarios. U.S.–European relations, despite our best efforts, could undergo fundamental changes. Closer cooperation, increased defense expenditures, and a political shift to the center on the part of our NATO partners would all be welcome, of course. On the other hand, our ties with NATO may very well loosen over the next twenty-five years, particularly if European governments evolve toward a coalition of Communist and Socialist parties. Although such left-of-center governments would try to maintain their independence vis-à-vis the Warsaw Pact and probably welcome the presence of U.S. naval forces in the Eastern Atlantic and Mediterranean, they would most likely not permit us to station ground and air forces on their soil. Japan could also move toward more fragile ties with the United States—and with similar consequences.

Even if political and military relations with Japan and Western Europe do not change, the United States will very likely become increasingly reliant on other parts of the world for economic productivity. In recent years, Asia has overtaken Western Europe as our largest area of trade, and in future years the United States will acquire a much larger economic stake in the developing countries of the Southern Hemisphere. Consequently, we could find ourselves becoming more competitive with Japan and Western Europe—not only in industrial trade but in the search for guaranteed sources of energy and raw materials. The mushrooming world population will further exacerbate the situation. Such trends could lead to a demand for flexible and mobile forces that can promote stability and operate independent of allied support.

In an effort to intrepret the implication of such contingencies, policy planners often produce rather simplistic conclusions. For example, some argue that a weakening of security ties with Western Europe and Japan would allow the United States to reduce its forward deployments and thus, its expenditures on general-purpose forces. While it may be possible to reduce the number of ground- and land-based tactical air forces deployed to meet the threat in NATO's central region and northeast Asia, such a development would tend to magnify the Soviet maritime threat.

Moreover, without deployment of naval forces in forward areas, it would be a great deal more difficult to systematically keep track of Soviet naval deployments or to maintain an effective offshore defense posture. We failed to appreciate this fact in the 1930s, with disastrous results in the Pacific.

Similar miscalculations can result from dogmatic projections of Soviet behavior. For example, planners frequently portray the Soviet Union as preparing to fight an intense war of short duration on NATO's central front, giving little thought to other possibilities. They are convinced that a Soviet attack will occur where NATO is best prepared to counter it, and that both sides will be exhausted after the first round. Assumptions of this sort ignore the dangers of encirclement by coordinated attack against NATO's northern and southern flanks and forget that twice in this century victory in Europe depended on massive reinforcement and prolonged resupply from the United States.

Many proponents of this view attribute a purely defensive naval strategy to the Soviet Union. They tend to overlook a host of possible changes in the strategic environment that might prompt Moscow to shift its emphasis to the Middle East, Asia, or some other part of the world. Moreover, they ignore the impact of our naval posture on Soviet strategy —the fact that Soviet naval combatants remain relatively close to home because of perceived threats from our power projection forces. A withdrawal of U.S. naval forces from the Eastern Atlantic, the Mediterranean, or the Western Pacific could vastly change the military picture in these areas. It would increase Soviet flexibility to intervene in Third World conflicts and free more Soviet forces for interdiction of lines of communication essential to the United States. In effect, it would encourage the Soviet Union to adopt an offensive naval policy.

Similarly, preoccupation with the Soviet threat to Europe minimizes the significance of U.S. interests in Asia and the importance of China and Japan in the strategic equation. A strong U.S. naval presence is essential to the U.S.–Japanese alliance and, in the event of conflict, to ensuring Japan's sea lines of communication. The alternative would be to force Japan to reassess her position—particularly in the event of a U.S.–Soviet confrontation. On top of this is the uncertainty of mainland China's orientation. The most effective hedge in this situation is a visible and effective American fleet in the Western Pacific.

This discussion is not meant to suggest that the U.S. should abruptly change the basic premises of its strategy—NATO and our European connections are extremely important and will remain so into the foreseeable future. It is meant to suggest that tomorrow's world will be both uncertain and diverse, and that we must constantly hedge against a broad range of developments. Given the maritime character of our strategic environment, the best alternative to our inability to predict the future is a strong mobile navy with a wide range of wartime as well as peacetime capabilities.

From 1985 to the year 2000, sea control will be the navy's fundamental mission. Sea control will not only retain its historical usefulness but increase in importance. The ability to use the seas will permit us to preserve our vital links with industrial as well as Third World allies no matter what turns our economic and political relations take. Sea control will preserve the viability of our strategic deterrent—the cornerstone of any security policy. It will also widen U.S. choices for demonstrating interest, projecting limited force to maintain stability, and reacting to major and minor crises throughout large areas of the world. Naval forces offer a range of alternatives to today's overseas bases and shore-based logistics arrangements that could be extremely useful in tomorrow's world.

In essence, effective sea power can give the U.S. government the strategical and conventional flexibility needed to accommodate changes in the strategic milieu, if and when necessary. This should prove to be an invaluable asset as we move into the next century.

Conclusions

The evolution of the U.S. Navy has kept pace with the nation's increasing importance in world affairs. Today, the navy is supporting goals that are essential to national and international stability. Its strong fleet can be uniquely responsive to future changes in the world environment as well.

In planning for the future we must be cognizant of pitfalls, some of which can be illustrated by our experience in Vietnam. During the course of that conflict, we lost sight of the mounting strength of Soviet naval power and neglected to replace aging U.S. naval combatants in sufficient number or in the required time. As a result, the naval balance today is dangerously slim. The same sequence of events could happen again if we take too narrow a view in planning our future strategic requirements.

The precise number and mix of ships required over the next twenty years will derive from the total political process—that is, the continuing dialogue between the military community and the executive and legislative branches of government. No matter how farsighted or skillful the navy's leaders are in making the necessary security calculations and in advising their civilian masters, the U.S. political climate will, in the

37

final analysis, be the critical element in formulating security policy. The American people's sense of threat, the competing demand for resources, domestic priorities, and political reactions to these pressures will largely determine the health, character, and scope of our forces. It is not the purpose of this paper to predict the course of U.S. politics. But it is imperative for those knowledgeable in these matters to persistently strive to inform the American people of the mission and the potential of sea power, so that they can make wise rational choices among alternatives for structuring U.S. security forces.

Strategy and Missions of the Soviet Navy in the Year 2000

James M. McConnell

No one can speak with confidence of a situation a quarter century in the future; a great deal can happen over a quarter of a century. To the extent we do address the future, however, projections ought to be based on trends, or the lack of consistent trends, observed in the past and the present, which form a continuum with the future.

Accordingly, I will first deal briefly with some features of Russian naval development that have persisted over time, as well as some that have shown changes and fluctuations, especially those revealing regularities even in the process of change. Then I will deal at greater length with trends in our own period, since the 1950s, drawing on evidence from allocations, capabilities, operations, and especially stated intentions. In the final section, I will project strategy and missions for the year 2000, bearing in mind past and current trends and pointing out areas where history is a very uncertain guide. Attention will be paid to requirements and limitations imposed from the political side, as well as purely naval requirements, and to the state of the art and the technological potential for satisfying these requirements.

Continuity and Periodic Change in Russian Naval History

Since the time of Peter the Great there has been a large degree of continuity in Russian naval history, apparently due mainly to the formidable limitations set by geography. At the dawn of the eighteenth century Russia was blocked from the Baltic Sea by Sweden and from the Black Sea by Turkey; she had no merchant or fishing fleet. The Imperial Russian Navy was founded by Peter the Great in the late seventeenth century, not to protect maritime commerce, which is the usual pattern of national naval development, but to obtain it.[1] And even though this "urge to the

---

This paper represents the opinion of the author and not necessarily that of the Center for Naval Analyses, the Department of the Navy, or any other government agency.

[1] David Woodward, *The Russians at Sea* (New York, N.Y., 1966), pp. 13-14.

sea" bore fruit, the poor location of Russia's ports and naval bases relative to the main ocean routes of the world has handicapped her development as a naval as well as a maritime-commercial power.[2] As a consequence, for much of Russia's history, ambition has never risen above the objective of commanding the adjacent seas. Naval action was typically confined to coastal waters in direct support of land campaigns. Only rarely has the navy ventured out upon the world ocean, and then usually with the neutrality or benevolent support of the leading naval powers. Russia may long have been a great sea power as well as land power, as Soviet naval spokesmen repeatedly tell us, but surely the heavier accent has been on the latter, even though the difference in emphasis has recently been narrowing.

Within this framework of continuity with respect to objective limitations on naval ambition, there have been discontinuities in the interest displayed by the Russians in exploiting the potentialities actually open for naval development. Historically, Moscow's attention to its navy has shown a spasmodic off-again, on-again pattern. Several decades of intense activity in naval development have typically alternated with several decades of perfunctory activity, involving relatively slow growth or stagnation, sometimes even an absolute decline in capabilities. This fluctuating pattern of interest and apathy wrung from one Russian naval historian in 1905 the complaint that, for more than two centuries, "we have not shown ourselves capable of firmly deciding, not only what kind of fleet we need, but absolutely whether we need one at all."[3] The point was well taken, if exaggerated, and has been expressed by Westerners as well. According to Erickson, "the changing whims of Russia's leaders" since Peter's time have "made the development of the Navy a peculiarly 'stop and go' process marked by alternating periods of frenzy and inertia."[4] Similarly, Woodward has noted that "the waxing and waning of the Russian navy," first observed in the eighteenth century, "has repeated itself in Russion history down to the present day."[5]

Quantitatively the present post-Stalinist period has not been among those eras of the greatest rates of expansion—the reigns of Peter I, Catherine II, Nicholas I, Alexander III, or Stalin. Under Stalin, programs were initiated that led to an average annual increase of 8 to 9 percent in tonnage over the years 1926–1957. To be sure, the develop-

---

[2] Mairin Mitchell, *The Maritime History of Russia, 848–1948* (London, 1949), p. 340.

[3] Klado, *The Battle of the Sea of Japan* (London, 1906), p. 278.

[4] John Erickson, "Military Affairs," *Problems of Communism,* vol. 16 (Jan.-Feb. 1967), p. 63.

[5] Woodward, *Russians at Sea,* pp. 37, 42–44.

ment proceeded from a low base (only 139,000 tons in 1926),[6] but this source of percentage inflation was counterbalanced by the interruption of the expansion program throughout almost the whole of the 1940s, because of the war and the requirements of postwar recovery. Nor did the impetus behind naval development seem to be losing steam at the end of the period. The average annual increase in tonnage between 1950 and 1957 was higher than that for the whole 1926–1957 period.[7]

Since 1957, the rate of expansion has slowed appreciably. The crucial 1954 decision redefining the path of maritime development is said to have reduced the annual tonnage output of all types of warships by some 60 percent in favor of commercial construction.[8] In number of personnel and major combatants, the Soviet fleet today is actually down by roughly a quarter from that of two decades ago, although tonnage increased about 40 percent between 1957 and 1975, because of the larger size of submarines. Still, the average annual increase in tonnage over this period is only on the order of one-fifth to one-quarter of the 1926–1957 rate. Had expansion continued at the same rate after 1957 as before, the 1975 navy would have been more than triple its actual size. Moreover, about three-fourths of the tonnage increase actually registered is attributable, not to the traditional missions of fleet against fleet, but to a novel mission—strategic nuclear strikes directly against the shore. Were it not for this mission we would be speaking now of stagnation in Soviet naval development. The tonnage of major surface combatants (escorts and above) actually declined about 25 percent.

What is not only novel but also paradoxical about this period from a historical standpoint is that, in spite of the decline in personnel and combatant units and the much slower growth rate in tonnage, the Soviet navy has nevertheless managed to reduce appreciably the capabilities gap between itself and the leading navy of the world, now that of the United States; and it has also managed to break out of the straitjacket of geography onto the world ocean. It has done this by exploiting a technological trend that is relatively more favorable to them than to us in the naval sphere—what the Soviets call the revolution in military affairs, that is, nuclear warheads and nuclear power, missiles, and electronics. These innovations have tended to be great equalizers in some of the most important indexes of naval power. The fact that the U.S.

---

[6] S. G. Gorshkov, *Red Star Rising at Sea* (Annapolis: Naval Institute Press, 1974), p. 62.

[7] This and all subsequent tonnage figures are in terms of full-load displacement for surface ships and submerged displacement for submarines.

[8] Michael MccGwire, "The Soviet Navy in the Seventies," in *Soviet Naval Influence,* ed. Michael MccGwire and John McDonnell (New York, N.Y.: Praeger, 1977), p. 622.

Navy remains superior, having advanced qualitatively by the same technological means, is insufficient consolation when we consider that, for the first time, the Soviet navy can pose a direct threat to the continental United States; for the first time it can present a serious threat to the American surface fleet; and for the first time, through its navy, Russia has become a global power as well as a greater superpower, hence a formidable competitor in peacetime naval diplomacy. And while the costs of quality have come high—the investment value per ton of the 1975 combatant fleet seems to be more than three times that of the 1957 fleet[9]—the U.S.S.R. has succeeded in substantially reducing the U.S.–Soviet capabilities gap with a smaller national effort. In contrast to the trend during the Stalinist era, the real burden of the navy on the Soviet economy is almost certainly less today than in the mid-1950s, considering the faster pace of economic relative to naval expansion.

Current Trends In Naval Development and Missions

It has been reported that the U.S.S.R. not only has the standard five-year plans for naval development, which are tied in with the five-year plans for the national economy, [10] but also has ten-year and even twenty-year plans.[11] However, the objectives of these longer-range plans are not announced when adopted, and may never be announced. It was not until 1967 that Admiral Gorshkov revealed the goals of the Kremlin's 1954 decision that apparently replaced the Stalinist postwar long-range plan with a radically new one. The objective, he said, was to create an ocean-going fleet, capable of accomplishing tasks both in nuclear (world) war, and in conventional (local) wars, and also of protecting state interests at sea in peacetime.[12] There is no good reason to doubt that these were, in fact, the goals formulated in 1954;[13] such a formula-

[9] These and all subsequent investment values are based on the values per ton for the respective ship categories during various construction periods given in *World Armaments and Disarmament: SIPRI Yearbook 1975* (Stockholm: Stockholm International Peace Research Institute, 1975), p. 296.

[10] V. D. Sokolovskiy, ed., *Voennaya strategiya,* 3rd ed. (Moscow: Voenizdat, 1968), p. 378.

[11] Robert W. Herrick, *Soviet Naval Strategy* (Annapolis: Naval Institute Press, 1968), pp. 63-64; James A. Barry, "Soviet Naval Policy: The Institutional Setting," in *Soviet Naval Influence,* ed. MccGwire and McDonnell, p. 112.

[12] S. G. Gorshkov, "Development of the Soviet Naval Art," *Morskoy sbornik* (hereafter referred to as *MS*), no. 2 (1967), p. 20; Gorshkov, *Morskaya moshch' gosudarstva* (Moscow: Voenizdat, 1976), pp. 446-448.

[13] See Thomas W. Wolfe, "Soviet Naval Interaction with the United States and Its Influence on Soviet Naval Developments," *Soviet Naval Developments,* ed. Michael MccGwire (New York, N.Y.: Praeger, 1973), p. 253. For a different view, see MccGwire, "The Turning Points in Soviet Naval Policy," ibid., pp. 189-192.

tion at that time is consistent with (though not conclusively proved by) other data and considerations.[14] The plan was no doubt elaborated in greater detail than indicated by Gorshkov, but its indexes were probably not too specific or fixed; too much would depend on research and development payoffs, unforeseen initiatives and reactions of target countries, and other contingencies.

Regardless of original intentions, the result of two decades of development is a Soviet navy with features that contrast sharply with those of its predecessor.

- Essentially the navy was a local sea-going fleet in 1957; today all naval force-arms—subsurface, surface, and land-based and shipboard aviation—are overwhelmingly ocean-going, that is, designed to operate on or over the high seas in war.
- In 1957 the main arm of the navy was the surface ship, submarines making up only 25 to 30 percent of the investment value of the combatant fleet. In 1975 the submarine was the main arm, accounting for two-thirds of the investment value.
- The main allocation of resources within the navy is now to ballistic-missile submarines. Eighty percent of 1975 combatant tonnage, representing over 90 percent of combatant investment value, consists of ship classes introduced since 1957. The strategic-strike function alone accounts for over 40 percent of the investment value of these newer combatants.[15]
- Less has been invested in other functions. The open-ocean anti-ship and anti-submarine functions each account for something over 15 percent of investment value; coastal defense accounts for a little over 10 percent. None of the other functions, considered singly—interdiction of sea lines of communication, mine warfare, amphibious warfare—contribute as much as 5 percent.
- This distribution of investment, considered together with operations and stated intentions, may explain the navy's radically improved standing within the armed forces in some directions and its continued lag in others. When it comes to its role in "the combat system of the armed forces" (which relates only to the "armed

---

[14] I intend to discuss this more fully in the first chapter of a forthcoming book, tentatively entitled *Soviet Naval Diplomacy*, by N. B. Dismukes, J. M. McConnell et al., from the Center for Naval Analyses.

[15] Allocations to functions throughout this paper are based on Thorpe's Delphi-derived weights for the original missions of Soviet combatants, with the exception of the E-I submarine class which, after removal of its cruise missiles, is treated by analogy with the N class. See the unpublished paper by Claude Thorpe, *Mission Priorities of the Soviet Navy*, presented at the Soviet Naval Developments Conference held at the Carnegie Foundation, June 1977.

struggle" in war), the navy still ranks last; but when it comes to the system of national defense (which deals with the overall political and military struggle in war and peace), the navy stands second, after the strategic missile troops. This disparity in ranking may be attributable to the fact that the first two out of three of the navy's top missions are essentially politico-military, rather than purely military, in character.[16]

- The main assignment is strategic "operations against the shore" in "the national defense," which includes a sea-control mission for the protection of those submarine-launched ballistic missiles that apparently are to be withheld from the initial strikes, even in general nuclear war.
- The navy's second-ranking mission, referred to as "especially important," is "the protection of state interests abroad in peacetime, backed up by a local war doctrine should the political use of force fail in its aim.
- The navy's third-ranking mission—and the only one of the three that is essentially military in character—is that of strategic defense of the homeland against sea-based strike systems. It is designated "secondary."
- Thus, the contemporary Soviet navy seems to be the complex product of a particular technological trend and of political decisions flowing from a certain softening of the ideological confrontation in the post-Stalinist era, centering on the concepts of peaceful coexistence and the recognition of an intermediate Third World between the two blocs. These factors in combination have apparently had the effect of strengthening the political aspects of naval activity even in war, enhancing the importance of peacetime uses of the fleet, and to some extent shifting the axis of Soviet naval activity from the main Euro-American area of concern to the Third World periphery.

With the foregoing overall survey as a background, let us next consider individual missions in terms of their own particular trends and problems, as well as their interrelationship with other missions. The first category of tasks discussed will be that of general war, followed by that of peacetime and local war.

General-War Missions. With the exception of the traditional coastal defense mission of protecting the flanks of the Red Army in offense and

---

[16] See J. M. McConnell, "The Gorshkov Articles, the New Gorshkov Book and Their Relation to Policy," in *Soviet Naval Influence*, pp. 616-617.

defense, which is by no means neglected even today, the general-war category consists primarily of four basic naval tasks: (1) strategic strike, (2) sea control, (3) strategic defense, and (4) interdiction of sea lines of communication. Each of these four tasks is discussed below in its current relative order of importance.

Strategic strike. Moscow early evinced an appreciation for submarine strategic delivery systems; the Soviet navy had a "quick-fix" ballistic missile platform at sea as early as 1956, years before the appearance of the U.S. Polaris missile system.[17] However, for the first decade after the Kremlin's 1954 shift in policy, the emphasis was not on strategic strike. This mission accounted for only 15 to 20 percent of the investment value of combatants put into operation over the period 1960–1965. By contrast, over the next decade strategic strike accounted for almost half of combatant investment. At the beginning of 1966, on the eve of the deployment of the Soviet navy's *Yankee* class, strategic operations against the interior were, for the first time, declared first-priority, and this task has remained the main one ever since.[18]

It is important to know whether Soviet ballistic-missile submarines are part of the first strategic echelon intended for the initial strikes, or whether they are designated the second strategic echelon for military or political use in later stages of the war and in influencing the peace talks. The Soviets have always provided for operational and strategic reserves at all levels, and, given the submarine's inherent advantages in avoiding detection and targeting, it would have been only natural to think of it early in the reserve role. Based on Soviet statements, I have tentatively come to the conclusion that, in the early 1960s, when intercontinental ballistic missiles were first introduced, a division of labor was planned for land- and sea-based strategic launchers. Both the strategic missile troops and the navy's missile submarines would hit coastal targets. However, only the missile troops, supplemented by long-range aviation, would take part in the initial strikes against the interior.[19] A portion of the sea-launched missiles capable of these strikes would be withheld as a strategic reserve.[20]

---

[17] John E. Moore, *The Soviet Navy Today* (London, 1975), p. 72.

[18] McConnell, "The Gorshkov Articles," pp. 570-573.

[19] For example, compare the following three editions of the same work: V. D. Sokolovskiy, ed., *Soviet Military Strategy* (Englewood Cliffs, N.J.: 1963), pp. 307, 402, 404, 408, 422-423; *Voennaya strategiya,* 2nd ed. (Moscow: Voenizdat, 1963), pp. 369, 371-372, 380-381; ibid., 3rd ed. (Moscow: Voenizdat, 1968), p. 246.

[20] Again, compare Sokolovskiy, *Soviet Military Strategy,* pp. 304, 348, 420; 2nd ed., p. 396; 3rd ed., pp. 243, 308.

This decision was very shortly reversed; after 1962 the doctrine of withholding forces was scorned, perhaps on the grounds of the poor survivability of early submarine platforms, coupled with the urgent demand for initial-strike (first-echelon) forces. It was not until 1971, when strategic parity had been largely attained and submarine security was satisfied by the introduction or imminent introduction of the *Yankee* and *Delta* classes of missile submarines, that the earlier division of labor was restored. The strategic missile troops now have the most important first word in war, and the navy apparently the important last word.[21] Too, Soviet discussions turn so often on the blackmail potential of third-party fleets that one cannot help but wonder whether China is not a major factor in the Soviet doctrine of withholding forces.[22]

Sea control. A withholding strategy creates special problems for the U.S.S.R. that do not obtain for the United States. One problem derives from the old Russian enemy—geography. American submarines attain the security of the high seas almost immediately after leaving port. To reach their launching stations, however, Soviet *Yankee*-class submarines have to pass through choke-points under Western control (the Greenland-Iceland-United Kingdom gap). Then, there is the technological lag. Submarines of neither the *Yankee* class nor the *Delta* class (which, with its longer-range missiles, can launch from the relative safety of contiguous waters) are as quiet as their American counterparts; this makes them vulnerable to Western anti-submarine warfare, which in addition is relatively more advanced. It is not surprising, therefore, that from the very beginning of the nuclear era in the early 1960s, the Soviets have coupled a withholding strategy with the requirement to protect withheld submarines with surface ships, aircraft, and nuclear-powered torpedo-attack submarines, not only in their departure from base but also in their "deployment to the areas of combat operations," especially "in the areas of intense activity of enemy anti-submarine forces."[23]

After 1962, however, when the Kremlin evidently decided against the creation of second-echelon strategic reserves, criticism was voiced of "attempts to protect forces for the future, while rejecting their correct use in the present." It was only with the apparent return to withholding in 1971 that uniform praise was once again lavished on sea control.[24] According to Admiral Gorshkov, both world wars "have demonstrated

---

[21] McConnell, "The Gorshkov Articles," pp. 577-578, 585-592.

[22] Gorshkov, *Morskaya moshch' gosudarstva*, pp. 143, 146, 404.

[23] M. E. Stepanov, "Supporting the Development of Submarines During Wartime Operations," *MS*, no. 12 (1961), p. 39ff.; V. Prokof'ev, "The Main Strike Forces in the War at Sea," *Krasnaya zvezda*, 13 January 1962; I. Potapov, "Doctrine and the Navy," ibid., 26 September 1962.

[24] McConnell, "The Gorshkov Articles," pp. 596-604.

the erroneousness of the opinion that the submarine, by virtue of the secrecy of its movements after leaving base, can itself ensure its own invulnerability."[25] Sea control on behalf of missile submarines is not a secondary but, along with strategic strike, a "main goal,"[26] to be carried out (using surface ships, aviation, and general-purpose submarines)[27] as "the first and main task" from "the very beginning of the war."[28]

Of course, not all strategic forces are slated for the second-echelon reserve. Those on station before the war begins will presumably take part in the initial strikes, and if the war begins nonnuclear, they will evidently require protection. This may explain a recent report that Soviet torpedo-attack submarines are codeployed with patrolling missile submarines in the Atlantic.[29]

Strategic defense. In the late 1950s, even though strategic-defensive weapons systems were beginning to enter the inventory, the Soviet Union's main naval focus was still on the offshore mission, mainly in support of the land campaign.[30] After 1960, however, even though the navy had—and still has—the world's largest fleet of minor combatants for coastal protection, supplemented by an enlarged amphibious-marine force for theater use, this task was reduced to its current "secondary" level.[31]

For six years—and only six years, covering the period 1960 through 1965—the Soviet navy's main mission was said to be that of "combating the enemy fleet."[32] This task included, and still includes, as its most important component, "combating the strike forces of the enemy fleet" and "repelling their strikes from ocean axes,"[33] that is, what we (but not

25 Gorshkov, *Morskaya moshch' gosudarstva,* p. 319.

26 Ibid., pp. 352-354, 377.

27 D. P. Sokha, "Submarine Forces Past and Present," *MS,* no. 9 (1971), p. 28; G. Kostev, "The Battle under Water," *MS,* no. 3 (1973), p. 40; N. Vlasov, "The Past, Present and Future of Surface Ships," *MS,* no. 3 (1974), pp. 22, 27; N. V'yunenko, "On Certain Trends in the Development of Naval Tactics," *MS,* no. 10 (1975), p. 22.

28 Gorshkov, *Morskaya moshch' gosudarstva,* pp. 374, 380.

29 William Beecher, *Boston Globe,* 19 December 1975.

30 N. Malinovskiy, "The 40th Anniversary of the Soviet Armed Forces," *Krasnaya zvezda,* 23 February 1958; V. Kasatonov, "On Guard over Maritime Frontiers," *Pravda Ukrainy,* 27 July 1958; N. Vinogradov, "Fleet of the Great Soviet Power," *Sovetskiy flot,* 26 July 1959.

31 Sokolovskiy, *Soviet Military Strategy,* p. 423.

32 For example, V. Lizarskiy, "USSR Navy Day," *Sovetskiy patriot,* 31 July 1960; N. Kharlamov, "Under the Banner of the Soviets," *Trud,* 29 July 1962.

33 Sokolovskiy, *Soviet Military Strategy,* pp. 348, 420-422; Editorial, *MS,* no. 7 (1966), pp. 3-7, cited by MccGwire, "Soviet Strategic Weapons Policy, 1955-1970," in M. MccGwire, K. Booth, and J. McDonnell, *Soviet Naval Policy* (New York, N.Y.: Praeger, 1975), p. 486; Gorshkov, *Morskaya moshch' gosudarstva,* pp. 290-291, 360.

the Russians) refer to as strategic defense. Failure to grasp this and other examples of special Russian terminology is even today an unfortunate source of confusion.

In the first half of the period Moscow considered anticarrier warfare most important in the general task of combating strike forces.[34] By 1964, however, countering the carrier was deemed only "important" (not "most important," much less "main"),[35] even though carrier air still constituted, in the Soviet view, part of the "first strategic echelon" of nuclear strike forces. In 1966, in line with U.S. statements, the Soviets relegated the carrier to the "second strategic echelon"[36] and, beginning in the first half of the 1970s, the carrier's main mission in general war was said to be that of winning command of the sea (the Russian term for sea control), ahead of the reserve strategic-strike task.[37] This shift in perception of the carrier's mission priorities, plus the lack of references to anticarrier warfare as part of the mission of combating the enemy fleet, tempts me to infer that it may now be considered part of the Soviet sea-control mission, which is itself apparently no longer listed under the rubric of combating the enemy fleet.[38]

During the period 1963 through 1965, combating Polaris was the "main" or "first-priority task" of the Soviet navy.[39] Contrary to a widespread but unfounded impression, it has not been the primary task since then. In 1966 and 1967, though specifically denied to be a main task, countering Polaris was still considered to be "most important."[40] In 1968, however, it seems to have been downgraded to the "important" category,[41] and Gorshkov has recently referred to it as a secondary task.[42]

---

[34] S. G. Gorshkov, "True Sons of the Motherland," *Pravda,* 31 July 1960; Sokolovskiy, *Soviet Military Strategy,* pp. 420-422.

[35] V. Sokolovskiy and M. Cherednichenko, "Military Art at a New Stage," *Krasnaya zvezda,* 28 August 1964.

[36] N. M. Elagin and A. S. Ryzhov, "Gratitude from the Fleet for its Dictionary," *MS,* no. 2 (1967), p. 89.

[37] R. Tumkovskiy, "The Current and Future Status of Attack Carriers," *MS,* no. 7 (1974), p. 95.

[38] Gorshkov, *Morskaya moshch' gosudarstva,* pp. 354, 356; Yu Bystrov, "Winning Command of the Sea," *MS,* no. 3 (1977), p. 19.

[39] S. Shtemenko, "Scientific-Technical Progress and Its Influence on the Development of Military Affairs," *Kommunist Vooruzhennyth Sil,* no. 3 (1963), p. 29; P. P. Nevzorov, "The Use of Aviation in Combatting Submarines," *MS,* no. 9 (1964), p. 32; P. V. Nikolaev, "The Problem of Combatting Nuclear-Powered Submarine Missile Carriers," *MS,* no. 2 (1965), p. 23.

[40] N. V. Kharlamov, "Trends in the Development of Navies," *MS,* no. 1 (1966), pp. 32-36.

[41] Compare Sokolovskiy, *Voennaya strategiya,* 2nd ed., 1963, pp. 312-313, with 3rd ed., 1968, pp. 307-308.

[42] Gorshkov, *Morskaya moshch' gosudarstva,* p. 360.

We can probably attribute this downgrading of strategic defense to a failure of technology rather than to an acceptance of U.S. concepts of mutual assured destruction. Certainly Moscow is more realistic today in appraising its strategic-defense capabilities. From the fall of 1970 on, with the apparent revival of withholding but on a larger scale, coupled with the downgrading of strategic defense, both Soviet and U.S. missile submarines were proclaimed virtually invulnerable.[43] The strategic-defense objective today, according to Gorshkov, is "degrading to the maximum extent possible" enemy strikes on ground targets.[44] In line with current usage of the term *degradation,* this implies the Soviets feel they can knock out no more than 15 percent of Western sea-launched missiles.[45]

The overall distribution of general-purpose resources clearly ought to be in favor of sea control, since this is a main task, while combating Polaris is secondary. However, the allocation within individual force arms is not all that clear. One gains the impression from Soviet discussions that sea control has the clear edge in surface-ship missions, that both sea control and strategic defense are prominent in naval air but in uncertain proportions, and that combating Polaris seems to take priority only in the case of nuclear-powered torpedo-attack submarines.[46]

Interdiction of sea lines of communication. In the early 1960s the U.S.S.R. included interdiction in the overall mission of combating the enemy fleet, deeming it no less important than countering the carrier.[47] However, it is not generally appreciated that, even at this early date, the main method of interdiction was through ballistic-missile strikes—against communications terminals on shore (bases, ports), canals, straits, and shipbuilding and repair yards—rather than attacks on merchant shipping at sea, which received only a secondary accent.[48] It was

---

[43] G. A. Trofimenko, "Certain Aspects of U.S. Politico-Military Strategy," *SShA,* no. 10 (1970), p. 26.

[44] S. G. Gorshkov, "Navies in War and Peace," *MS,* no. 2 (1973), p. 21; Gorshkov, *Morskaya moshch' gosudarstva,* p. 360; S. Lobov, "Sea Power of the State and Its Defense Capabilities," *MS,* no. 4 (1976), p. 104.

[45] See O. Shul'man, "Formulating Combat Tasks," *MS,* no. 8 (1976), p. 19. Shul'man "assumes" that, in discussing combat objectives, annihilation *(unichtozhenie)* implies sinking or forcing the removal from the order of battle of 80-90 percent of enemy forces; smashing *(razgrom)* implies 70 percent; inflicting a defeat *(porazhenie),* 50 percent; substantial degradation *(sushchestvennoe oslablenie),* 30 percent; and simple degradation *(oslablenie),* 10-15 percent.

[46] Gorshkov, "Navies in War and Peace," p. 20; idem, *Morskaya moshch' gosudarstva,* pp. 307-308, 319, 327; Sokha, "Submarine Forces Past and Present," p. 28.

[47] Sokolovskiy, *Soviet Military Strategy,* p. 348.

[48] Ibid., pp. 420, 422-423.

felt that interdiction at sea could not be an urgent task in the initial period of the war, since general-purpose forces had to concentrate on nuclear-weapons carriers; only after resolution of the strategic struggle would attack submarines be redeployed on a large scale for disrupting communications in the "broken-back" phase of the war. From the mid-1960s interdiction was designated an important or secondary mission rather than a main or most important one. It was said that "ocean communications in the initial period . . . will not play any vital role, especially as the major ports and naval bases of the belligerents will most probably have been destroyed (put out of commission) by nuclear-missile strikes."[49]

In his recent book, Admiral Gorshkov seems to reduce the significance of interdiction at sea even further. He no longer includes the anticommunications assignment in the task of combating the enemy fleet. He considers it part of the overall mission of operations against the shore, a reclassification specifically attributed to the navy's "ability to fulfill strategic tasks of an offensive nature."[50] In other words, the change is apparently not the result of an arbitrary redefinition but of the even greater predominance of strategic strikes in interdiction. Speculation on the reason for this greater predominance might profitably focus on Moscow's recognition of a withholding strategy for both the United States and the U.S.S.R. Communications can now be disrupted, even in the later phase of a war, by a portion of withheld missiles, while the general-purpose forces formerly counted on for interdiction at sea in these later phases will no longer be available, because of the continuing requirement for sea control in support of Soviet missile submarines and for countering Western sea-based systems, also withheld.

This speculation is derived from the Soviet nuclear-war scenario. Unfortunately, it is the only scenario discussed by naval spokesmen, even though the general military literature in recent years seems to give more credence to a nonnuclear *phase* of inter-bloc war (though not, it would appear, to an inter-bloc war confined to the sea or a combined land-sea central war fought through to the end with conventional weapons). Speculation on the reasons for Russian silence on almost any subject is risky, but I am tempted to attribute it in this case to the possibility that mission priorities would not change substantially even in the context of an initial conventional phase. The Soviets may or may not intend

---

[49] S. I. Filonov, "Armed Conflict and Ocean Lines of Communication," *MS*, no. 3 (1965), pp. 39-41; Kharlamov, "Trends in the Development of Navies," pp. 35-36; Gorshkov, "Development of the Soviet Naval Art," p. 18; Sokolovskiy, *Voennaya strategiya*, 3rd ed., 1968, p. 308; K. A. Stalbo in *Istoriya voennomorskogo iskusstva*, ed. S. E. Zakharov (Moscow: Voenizdat, 1969), p. 540.

[50] Gorshkov, *Morskaya moshch' gosudarstva*, pp. 360-361.

to respect the inviolability of sea-based missiles in the conventional period; they could feel that the main task in the conventional period is to improve the U.S.S.R.'s military position should the war escalate. They also may or may not expect that we will avoid their strategic withholding areas, but they know they cannot count on it, and, if there is escalation, all restraints are surely removed. Submarines expended or deployed out of area on shipping lanes will not be available if the United States prosecutes strategic defense in the conventional phase or if there is an escalation to nuclear war. It seems likely that interdiction would receive a heavier allocation, but the basic forces would probably have to be assigned to, or held in reserve for, the more important sea-control and strategic-defense missions.

Peacetime Political and Local War Missions. One of the novelties of the post-Stalinist period is the resumption—after its lapse under Stalin—of Third World naval diplomacy, both cooperative and coercive. The nature of this discussion precludes a fully satisfactory treatment of this large, complex, and subtle problem, but I will briefly examine three of its principal aspects: (1) motivation, (2) capabilities, and (3) risk-taking propensities.

Motivation. The central precondition for contemporary Soviet naval diplomacy was Moscow's abandonment of the two-camp theory of the Stalinist era and the adoption of a more positive approach to Third World nationalism, the interests of which were thought to parallel those of the U.S.S.R. By 1955, with the single exception of coercive naval diplomacy, all the current instruments of Soviet Third World policy had already appeared: trade; cultural exchanges; political, economic, and arms aid; even cooperative naval diplomacy (official port visits). Moreover, the viability of some of these instruments would seem to depend on a forward naval presence. Trade and aid also meant the development of a merchant marine, which (along with the expanded fishing fleet) might require protection, especially in the case of sensitive arms shipments. Even more important, it might have appeared useless to generate an expensive stake in Third World regimes, only to see them toppled from within or without for the want of a forward-area military presence. A diplomacy of force based on this presence could protect and promote Soviet interests and create additional credit with grateful clients.

Capabilities. As Admiral Gorshkov testifies, a Third World diplomacy of force was already thought desirable in the mid-1950s, but it would take a full decade of development before sufficient capabilities could be accumulated to make this a part of operational doctrine. From the perspective of 1954, the U.S. attack carrier was the primary naval threat to the homeland in general war and the main strike force in local conflicts. By concentrating on anticarrier warfare (ACW), therefore, the Soviets were solving two problems in one developmental package. Initially the most urgent need was for ACW for strategic defense, but after 1965, when the carrier became a strategic reserve in the Soviet view, ACW in the local context may have been ranked as high as in the general-war context. Today the carrier's role in local war is mentioned ahead of its main sea-control mission in nuclear war.[51]

The vast bulk of Soviet ACW capabilities was introduced in the 1960s, especially in the first half, although their quality was vastly improved after 1965. The open-ocean antiship function accounted for about 30 percent of the tonnage and investment value of combatants introduced over the period 1960–1965, around 20 percent for the period 1965–1970, but only in the neighborhood of 10 percent during 1970–1975.

It is often argued that the Soviet navy is narrowly tailored to general nuclear war, that general-purpose forces on forward deployment are preoccupied with strategic defense of the homeland, and that there is no surplus available for a Third World diplomacy of force, especially in distant areas. It is true that the Soviet navy, like any other, was created for war[52] but, according to Gorshkov's testimony, it was not created for nuclear world wars alone but also for local wars; and on the basis of these dual war-fighting capabilities the navy has become an effective peacetime political instrument—deterrence and offensive pressure directly against the West on the one hand, the "protection of state interests" in the Third World on the other.

Further, the current strategic-defensive bias of Soviet forward deployments has been overemphasized. If strategic ASW against Polaris-Poseidon is crucial to peacetime forward deployment, we ought to find late-generation antisubmarine cruisers and large antisubmarine ships in the forward area—permanently, or at least during crises—when the danger of escalation is greater. We do find some *early generation* platforms formally designated as antisubmarine ships in the forward area— *Kresta* I, *Kashin, Kanin,* and modified *Kildin*—but these are apparently there as elements of anticarrier task groups, not for strategic ASW. What is typically missing in the permanent deployment are the later-generation

---

[51] Tumkovskiy, "Status of Attack Carriers," p. 95.

[52] J. M. McConnell, "Military-Political Tasks of the Soviet Navy in War and Peace," in *Soviet Oceans Development,* ed. John Hardt (Washington, D.C.: Government Printing Office, 1976), p. 200.

platforms—*Kiev, Moskva, Kara, Kresta* II, *Krivak*. These ships do periodically deploy and exercise in the forward area; however, the fact that there has been no augmentation during crises—indeed, a *Kara* in the Mediterranean went home at the first sign of trouble on the eve of the October War—suggests that the urgency of strategic ASW in the forward area immediately on the outbreak of war may have been exaggerated. It is necessary to remember that, in the apparent Soviet view, some portion of U.S. sea-based missiles are classified as strategic reserves, and that Russian strategic ASW forces, along with ballistic-missile submarines, are scheduled for sea-control support.[53] Taken together, all these observations imply that the anti-Poseidon task is not central to Soviet peacetime forward deployments and that the mission can stand deferral until a more favorable environment is created in nuclear war for its prosecution.

The core of the Soviet navy's permanent forward deployment is the ACW force. This contingent is augmented in crises; however, the Soviet concern is surely local rather than strategic. The carrier in general war is appraised as an immediate threat to the Soviet fleet (sea control) rather than to the homeland; and to the extent that it is regarded as a reserve strategic threat to the U.S.S.R., there is no reason why there should be a reaction to it but no reaction to the greater second-echelon threat posed by Polaris-Poseidon. However, even aside from these considerations, there is no contradiction between the general-war and local war missions of ACW task forces. As long as they are in the vicinity of their target, they are in a position to discharge either task. Nor does distance from the U.S.S.R. seem to be a significant factor in Soviet ACW capabilities. Moscow does not send large surface and submarine forces to nearby crisis areas and fewer forces to remote ones. If it chooses to respond at all in crises, it responds in a relatively uniform way, matching an ACW task group of a more or less standard surface and submarine composition with each U.S. carrier task group, regardless of the deployment distance—whether to the Indian Ocean,[54] the Atlantic off Angola,[55] or the Eastern Mediterranean.[56]

Aside from the periodic deployment of sea control and strategic ASW forces, then, the core of the Soviet navy's permanent and crisis-generated general-purpose forward deployment is made up of ACW

---

[53] Gorshkov, *Morskaya moshch' gosudarstva*, p. 354.

[54] J. M. McConnell and A. M. Kelly, "Superpower Naval Diplomacy in the Indo-Pakistani Crisis," in *Soviet Naval Developments*, ed. M. MccGwire, p. 444.

[55] MccGwire, "Soviet Navy in the Seventies," pp. 645, 652.

[56] Elmo R. Zumwalt, *On Watch* (New York, N.Y.: Quadrangle, 1976), pp. 437, 447; Jesse W. Lewis, *The Strategic Balance in the Mediterranean* (Washington, D.C.: American Enterprise Institute, 1976), p. 83.

forces (Mediterranean and elsewhere) useful for sea control in general war and countering the U.S. Navy in local conflicts, plus smaller, less specialized, and less formidable forces for local situations (Indian Ocean, Eastern Atlantic) where U.S. carriers are not permanently present.[57] So far, Moscow has not developed shipboard air and amphibious capabilities for long-range power projection; the *Kiev*-class flight-deck cruiser seems to be intended for sea control in general war rather than action against the land in the Third World.[58] However, the lack of these capabilities has not handicapped the U.S.S.R. in Third World intervention as much as one might think. Simultaneous with their creation of a navy for forward deployment, the Soviets were building up globally mobile military air transport and airborne forces. By the mid-1960s they probably had the capability for the simultaneous lift over long distances of one airborne division, today of two.[59] And where rapid reaction is not a requirement, they can draw on strategic reserves from other branches of the armed forces, as in the war of attrition in 1970. In this all-arms solution, the role of the Soviet navy is presumably to inhibit U.S. naval initiatives and reactions against the land and to secure the lifeline back to the U.S.S.R.

Risk-taking propensities. Success in military diplomacy hangs in the final analysis on a willingness to use force, and the Soviets have indicated they had a local war doctrine from the beginning of 1966.[60] In their definition, a local war is one limited in area, number of belligerents, means, and ends.[61] The definition does not bar the participation of one or both superpowers. While the risks of escalation to world nuclear war are high if the nuclear powers (plural) become involved,

---

[57] These are presumably designed to "establish a presence," protect sensitive lines of communication, and make demonstrations of force on occasions when Western great powers are not involved. However, except for the operationally insignificant time devoted to official visits, this does not involve high-quality forces and does not detract appreciably from the Soviet general-war posture.

[58] For emphasis on shipboard air with sea control, see B. L. Teplinskiy, "The World Ocean and U.S. Military Strategy," *SShA*, no. 10 (1972), pp. 21-22; V. Sysoev, "On the Maritime Blockade," *MS*, no. 12 (1976), p. 35.

[59] Graham B. Turbiville, "Soviet Airborne Troops," in MccGwire and McDonnell, *Soviet Naval Influence*, p. 284.

[60] J. M. McConnell, "Gorshkov's Doctrine of Coercive Naval Diplomacy in Both War and Peace," in *Admiral Gorshkov on "Navies in War and Peace,"* CRC 257, R. G. Weinland, M. K. MccGwire, and J. M. McConnell (Arlington, Va.: Center for Naval Analyses, 1974), pp. 102-103.

[61] V. Shelyag and T. Kondratkov, "Lenin's Analysis of the Essence of War and the Groundlessness of Criticism of It," *Kommunist Vooruzhennykh Sil,* no. 12 (1970), p. 16; Gorshkov, *Morskaya moshch' gosudarstva,* p. 381.

this is evidently judged less likely if vital interests are not at stake,[62] as is generally the case in the Third World. The Soviets, of course, would naturally prefer to avoid military solutions; a willingness to use force is only the grounding for its political use. The problem is to tailor the threat of force to Soviet local capabilities in situations where Moscow's strength of will is greater. From a no-risk policy before the mid-1960s, when its capabilities had not yet matured, the U.S.S.R. has gone over to what might be termed a policy of acceptable risk.

An examination of some twenty-five cases of Soviet coercive diplomacy since 1967 suggests that in the underdeveloped areas of Asia and Africa, where both superpowers can field credible forces and the interests at stake are evaluated as roughly equal, the key variable in relative superpower strength of will and politico-military impact turns on the question of which superpower, or the client of which superpower, is upholding the status quo strategically.[63] The Soviets know from experience that the United States is firm in upholding the status quo when its interests are at stake, but it can also conclude that Washington is reluctant to defend breaches of the status quo by its friends, even when maintaining the status quo involves injury to U.S. interests. Accordingly, Moscow can accept the risks of using force or the threat of force to secure transport even of arms and soldiers to friendly countries in peacetime; and it can demonstrate or actually intervene on behalf of recognized governments against domestic opposition and against foreign foes threatening the territorial integrity and viability of client states. It can also demonstrate on behalf of a client caught out in a breach of the international status quo, not in support of the breach itself but to confine the U.S. reaction to the breach to defensive ends.

On the other hand, with one exception, Moscow evidently considers it an unacceptable risk to violate the rights of others to the common sea, to threaten or employ force to help overthrow an established government from within, or to support a client in a strategic offensive against another state. The exception is when the United States itself is not committed to the status quo, because colonialism and racism are (or seem to be) involved, and therefore is unable to implement its own nonviolent alternative to the status quo, as was apparently the case in Guinea in 1970 and Angola in 1976. This Soviet approach to force

---

[62] For more on the change in Soviet attitude on risk-taking after the adoption of a local war doctrine, compare Sokolovskiy, *Voennaya strategiya*, 2nd ed., 1963, p. 242 and I. Zav'yalov et al., "Against Slander and Falsification," *Krasnaya zvezda*, 2 November 1963, with M. V. Zakharov, ed., *50 let Vooruzhennykh Sil SSSR* (Moscow: Voenizdat, 1968), p. 522.

[63] See McConnell and Kelly, "Superpower Naval Diplomacy in the Indo-Pakistani Crisis," pp. 449-451.

seems to be defensive—and it is, from the formal standpoint of the international order—but we have to remember that fanaticism and irresponsibility are also a part of the status quo,[64] and the mere fact of a superpower defensive commitment has often seemed enough to assure a client of the safety of offensive action, knowing that, if it failed, he would not lose everything.[65]

While the U.S.S.R. has become increasingly more committed to naval diplomacy, and the status of the mission has improved within the navy, there does not seem to have been any increase or decrease in risk-taking propensities over time. The actions taken have been various, but the variety seems to be a function, not of changes in the fundamentals of military policy, but of the different problems encountered in concrete situations, all still viewed as actionable or not actionable in light of the guidelines laid down in the original 1965 decision on local war and a diplomacy of force.

The Soviet Navy in the Year 2000

In extrapolating the role of the Soviet navy to the year 2000, one must consider two broad areas. The first involves the encouragement given to, and the constraints imposed upon, naval development by the Soviet system as a whole, especially as manifested in the ideological-political process. This bears largely, but not entirely, on the quantitative side of the problem—Moscow's willingness to allocate resources to the navy rather than to other competing claimants, as determined by the predominance of ideological or of pragmatic considerations and by the resulting level of aggressiveness of the system.

The second consideration centers on the requirement for missions imposed by the immanent logic of the military-naval system and the ability of the scientific-technical establishment to satisfy this requirement at a cost acceptable to the system as a whole. Although this area has a definite quantitative impact, in light of the projection problem as a whole its effect is treated here as primarily qualitative, bearing on missions, state of the art, and scientific-technological creativity.

The Ideological-Political Effect. In discussing the ideological-political effect I take two approaches to the question of the Soviet navy at the turn of the century: one based on a continuation of the current

---

[64] I am indebted to Abram N. Shulsky for this point.

[65] Edward N. Luttwak, *The Political Uses of Sea Power* (Baltimore, Md.: Johns Hopkins Press, 1974), pp. 35-37; Lawrence L. Whetten, *The Canal War* (Cambridge, Mass.: MIT Press, 1974), p. 9.

trend, and the other postulating a change in trend. Two methodological assumptions underlie both approaches—that the individual components of the Soviet system are interdependent and mutually compatible, and that anything posited about the future of this system has to be derived from its history. This does not mean that history repeats itself, only that there are long-term across-the-board trends and patterned regularities in historical change. The assumption is philosophically repugnant, since it limits the freedom of a human system and its individual components, but experience does seem to endow it with a certain utility for forecasting.

Continuation of the current trend. As mentioned earlier, the current trend in Soviet naval development originated in a 1954 policy decision. If this trend continues, the Soviet navy of the year 2000 will have perhaps 10 percent fewer major combatants than in 1975 but the tonnage of this component will be 50 percent larger; this projected increase in tonnage over twenty-five years should be compared with the 45–50 percent increase registered for the eighteen years between 1957 and 1975. At the turn of the century, the Soviet fleet will be appreciably more combat-effective and will represent a greater investment per ton. However, barring another revolution in military affairs, in neither aspect will the disparity between the 1975 and the year-2000 fleets be as great as between the 1957 and the 1975 fleets. This expectation is founded on trends in percentage increases in the investment value of the average major-combatant ton introducd during successive five-year periods compared with previous five-year periods since 1950: 25–30 percent for 1955–1960; 85–90 percent for 1960–1965; 80–85 percent for 1965–1970; but only 5 to 10 percent for 1970–1975.

The relatively modest increase projected in the size of the Soviet navy reflects a continuation of the lower level of aggressiveness manifested in the post-Stalinist period; it evidently makes a difference whether Moscow declares war to be inevitable or not. However, while continued adherence to peaceful coexistence will constrain the absolute level of naval expenditures in favor of alternative civilian uses, it will also tend to maintain—perhaps to enhance—the relative standing of the navy within the armed forces. Peaceful coexistence downgrades the armed struggle, not the economic, ideological, and political struggles; and the political includes the military-political. In a diplomacy of force the navy has unique advantages, both in peace and in war. In peace: deterrence and the application of pressure in the direct confrontation with the West; the protection of an expanding commerce on the high seas; and cooperative and coercive diplomacy in the meditated confrontation with the West in the Third World. In war: a strategic political as well as military reserve.

This projection implies continued political pressure within the U.S.S.R. for a sufficiently large sea-based deterrent, made secure by sea-control development. Whether it also implies the continued success of strategic arms limitation agreements depends in part on technological developments and disparities; nevertheless, it is tempting to assume that, if the will to agreement exists, a formula can be found to get around technical difficulties. Assuming a continuation of the current trend, the political atmosphere should be favorable, except for periodic short-term storms that put détente in jeopardy. Of course, the existence of large numbers of Chinese ballistic missiles by 2000 will complicate the problem of arms limitations.

However, the pressure from the Soviet political process for war-fighting missions, such as strategic defense against the long-range U.S. Trident missile, will presumably diminish, even though there will continue to be substantial political demands for such missions. Earlier we reasoned that the secondary rank Moscow currently assigns strategic defense stems primarily from the lack of a scientific-technological perspective, but Soviet accommodation to the failure of technology may have been helped by the Kremlin's increasing willingness to distinguish between deterrence and war-fighting. Until recently they have been reluctant to make this distinction—and still do not make it to the same degree, and with the same frankness, as Western spokesmen.[66]

Reversal of the current trend. If we are resigned to having the past determine our image of the future, then a reversal of the current trend is the more likely projection option, since periodic fluctuations are more faithful to Russian experience. Typically, several decades of relatively modest naval development have been succeeded by a roughly equal period of stormy expansion. However, no past trend in either direction has endured for the five decades posited in the previous projection. Others have noted this pendulum effect, but none seem to have noted its across-the-board character, the correlation between naval development and other indexes. At least since the end of the eighteenth century, relatively modest naval allocations have been associated with reform eras in Russian history, and intense development with periods of ideological-political and economic alienation.

We have to appreciate the wide swings displayed in this historic alternation of trends. Whereas there was only a 40 percent increase in combatant tonnage during the eighteen years after 1957, there was a

---

[66] McConnell, "The Gorshkov Articles," pp. 616-617.

ten- to eleven-fold increase over the thirty-one years preceding 1957. In 1928, the real burden of defense on the Soviet economy was around 2.5 percent;[67] by the early 1950s, if the burden was underestimated to the same extent as later, it must have been close to 30 percent; today it is 11–13 percent.[68] To be sure, one would not expect a retrogression to Stalinism, but it would not require the revival of slogans on the inevitability of war, only on the heightened danger of war, to effect a doubling, and perhaps even a tripling, of fleet tonnage by the year 2000. In the short term, shipbuilding facilities reallocated from military to commercial construction in the 1950s could be returned to military production; in the longer term Moscow could add new facilities as well. One could reasonably expect such a shift in emphasis since, historically, periods of rapid naval expansion have also been periods of economic isolation and declining (or declining rates of increase in) international trade;[69] and today international trade primarily governs merchant marine development.

A reversal of the current trend would have profound effects. Although the Soviet navy would improve its position in absolute terms, it would suffer relative to some other branches of the armed forces as a result of the displacement of interest from peace to war and from the political to the military use of force. Of course, military force would have a political impact—that political impact would even be enhanced—but it would be based on war-winning capabilities rather than on the capabilities for punitive retaliation implied by the less ambitious objec-

---

[67] A. Yugoff, *Economic Trends in Soviet Russia* (London, 1930), p. 246; Abram Bergson, *The Economics of Soviet Planning* (New Haven, Conn.: Yale, 1964), p. 309.

[68] A real burden of 15-18 percent for 1952 is given in Lincoln P. Bloomfield, Walter C. Clemens, and Franklyn Griffiths, *Khrushchev and the Arms Race* (Cambridge, Mass.: MIT Press, 1966), p. 110. This figure should probably be appraised in connection with the Central Intelligence Agency publication, *Estimated Soviet Defense Spending in Rubles, 1970–1975*, SR 76-1012H, May 1976, p. 16, which points out that the real burden in recent years is actually almost twice previous estimates.

[69] The long swings are clearly visible in Russian trade statistics, which are available from 1793. Eliminating years of war and blockade at the beginnings and ends of long swings, the average annual rates of increase in the value of foreign trade are, by period: 1793-97 to 1801-5, 5.8 percent; 1816-1820 to 1841-45, 1.8 percent; 1841-45 to 1871-75, 4.9 percent; 1871-75 to 1891-95, 0.25 percent; and 1891-95 to 1911-13, 5.0 percent. In the Stalinist era, over the period 1926-28 to 1936-38, there was an average annual *decrease* in foreign trade of almost 9.0 percent. In the post-Stalinist period, the trend reversed dramatically, yielding an increase of 10.3 percent *per annum* from 1948-52 to 1970-74. See M. T. Florinsky, *Russia: A History and Interpretation,* vol. 1 (New York, N.Y.: Macmillan, 1954), p. 564, vol. 2, pp. 710, 789-790, 1230; Ministerstvo Vneshney Torgovli (MVT)SSSR, *Vneshnyaya torgovlya SSSR, 1818–1966* (Moscow, 1967), pp. 8-9, 62; MVT, *Vneshnyaya torgovlya SSR za 1974 god* (Moscow, 1975), p. 10.

tive of deterrence. Moscow would still want a strategic sea-based reserve, complete with protection forces, but the accent might be on its straight military potential rather than its value as an intra-war deterrent and bargaining instrument. In the long run, strategic arms limitations would be difficult to maintain, and there would presumably be substantially greater allocations to strategic defense, regardless whether or not a real technological breakthrough occurred.

I am inclined to think, however, that the Soviet commitment to Third World naval diplomacy might be weakened by a reversal of current trends. Moscow has been able to cut a figure in underdeveloped regions in the post-Stalinist period because of its willingness to compromise with nationalism and strike quid-pro-quo bargains with non-Communist governments. If ideology creeps back into Russian calculations, there might be a revival of interest in Communist movements rather than in government-to-government relations. Soviet military involvement would become less important, unless more ideologically compatible groups come to power.

The Military-Naval and Technological Effect. One of the most profound yet enigmatic questions about the Soviet navy in the year 2000 is: What impacts on the art of naval warfare can we expect from technological improvements and advances in the next twenty-five years? One can only discuss this question, not pronounce, and even then with the full expectation that the real world will unfold surprises. The discussion is divided into three sections: (1) strategic strikes and sea-control support; (2) strategic defense; and (3) peacetime naval diplomacy and local war.

Strategic strike and sea-control support. Military as well as political requirements dictate that the U.S.S.R. will maintain the maximum permissible force of sea-based ballistic-missile platforms out to 2000. Presumably substantial effort will be made to reduce platform noise and to ensure that all missiles will be of sufficient range to permit launching from home waters. Sea-control support will have to be given all platforms in the nonnuclear phase of a war, but only to those withheld from the initial strikes during the nuclear phase. This was indicated some time ago by a Soviet theoretician, speaking elliptically and using Western fleets as a surrogate for his own. He pointed out that, if ballistic-missile submarines are held back from a strategic strike, they will have to be in the reserve, since they have a narrowly specialized mission that precludes their use for nonstrategic tasks. To survive in the reserve, they will have to be protected; this requirement has accelerated the development of general-purpose forces, especially submarines. By emphasizing that ballistic-missile submarines will "always" be in the reserve if the war starts out nonnuclear, he evidently meant to imply in the context that in some cases, but not always, they will also be in the reserve after escalation, which is why "they are not capable of fully realizing their potential even in a nuclear war without the appropriate support of other forces." [70]

One can only speculate how the support mission would be carried out. In a period of threat, missile submarines will probably be directed to local sanctuaries, such as the Barents Sea (Northern Fleet) and the Sea of Okhotsk (Pacific Ocean Fleet). The sanctuary concept has been hinted at by Soviet authors, as usual employing a Western surrogate. According to one writer,

> arming submarines with long-range missiles enables them to operate . . . at a significant distance from the shores of a probable enemy, reliably screened by surface ships and aviation. These submarines can launch their missiles both when transiting and when leaving their own bases, and even from points along the shores of the American continent. . . . Arranging launch areas close to one's own shores appreciably simplifies the organization of control and communications, and cuts down on the expenditure of fuel and the time spent on ocean transits. [71]

Other authors, after indicating by the typical method of indirection that U.S. submarines are not now intended for the first strikes, go on to assert that, when the U.S. Navy acquires the long-range Trident missile, its launch vehicles will evidently be sited in home waters; around them will be concentrated "the principal ASW forces, which will be assigned a new function—guarding the strategic missile forces." [72] In each of these cases the surrogate character of the U.S. example is glaring. No one in the United States has advocated putting Trident in a local sanctuary and guarding it; it needs the security of neither, but Soviet submarines can use both.

The Barents and Okhotsk sanctuaries would presumably be heavily mined and equipped with fixed underwater acoustic surveillance systems. Additionally, one would assume submarine barriers at all entrances to inhibit penetration by Western hunter-killer submarines. It would be

---

[70] N. Aleshkin, "Certain Tendencies in the Development of Naval Forces," *MS,* no. 1 (1972), p. 25.

[71] Engineer Capt. 2nd Rank V. Erofeev, "A Replacement for 'Polaris' and 'Poseidon,'" *MS,* no. 1 (1972), p. 89.

[72] G. Svyatov and A. Kokoshin, "Sea Power in the Plans of American Strategists," *Mezhdunarodnaya zhizn,* no. 3 (1973), pp. 80-81.

to the U.S. advantage, thanks to the superior stealth of its submarines, to handle the encounter as a duel of platforms employing passive sonar. However, for the next decade or so—and I emphasize the time limitation —the Russians will probably continue to detect with active sonar,[73] attempting to transform the encounter into a duel of weapons systems (missile-thrown torpedos and depth charges).[74] To be sure, active sonar has a beaconing effect for enemy ASW air overhead; this may be the explanation for Soviet insistence that today "command of the sea has become unthinkable without command of the air," [75] and for the current Soviet emphasis on producing flight-deck cruisers of the Kiev class, which can provide air defense and interceptor cover for submarines, surface ships, and aviation engaged in barrier operations.

By the end of the century, if the theoretical promise of submarine-towed passive acoustic arrays proves out in eliminating the interference of self-generated noise, the underwater encounter could again become a duel of platforms, assuming both superpowers are successful in developing a submarine weapons system that can exploit the potentially greater detection ranges of towed arrays. If no such weapon solution is found, the requirement for air power to prosecute submarine contacts becomes even more crucial; but even with an underwater strike solution, the need for ship-based air would be merely reduced, not eliminated. If one air-capable ship is put out every other year (a conservative projection), the Soviet navy could have thirteen by the year 2000, with several hundred fixed-wing V/(S)TOL aircraft in addition to the helicopter complement. Follow-on carriers would be larger than the current Kiev class, and their aircraft vastly more effective—with greater interceptor ranges and higher speeds—than the YaK-36 Forger now aboard the *Kiev*.

Strategic defense. Clearly there will be an urgent *military* requirement for combating U.S. ballistic-missile submarines in the year 2000. However, from today's perspective, a practical solution to the strategic-defense problem even at that late date probably still seems remote to Soviet scientists. The U.S.S.R. is bound to continue its efforts in that direction, especially on the theoretical-research side, but until there is a technological breakthrough, Moscow must strike some balance in its hardware programs between avoiding possibly futile investments and having platforms available should the large-area sensor and weapons problems be resolved.

---

[73] For this hypothesis, I am wholly indebted to discussions with John Thompson and John Underwood of the Center for Naval Analyses.

[74] K. J. Moore, "Antisubmarine Warfare," in MccGwire and McDonnell, *Soviet Naval Influence*, p. 193.

[75] Bystrov, "Winning Command of the Sea," p. 20.

Clearly, by the year 2000, when Polaris and Poseidon have been fully replaced by long-range Trident and follow-on missiles, the large-area sensor obstacle will have become immense, extending to millions of square miles of ocean. Even if the satellite nonacoustic detection problem is solved, which seems doubtful by the year 2000, detection and destruction—presumably using land- or sea-based missiles—would have to be executed in rapid order, since satellites are vulnerable to enemy action.

For area search with naval air, simply assuming an extrapolation of current procurement trends, the Soviet Union could very well expand the number of fixed-wing open-ocean aircraft by 50 percent, possibly replacing current land-based models (Bear-F, May, Mail) with long-range wing-in-ground (WIG) vehicles. State of the art by the year 2000 might permit their equipment with wake and electromagnetic detection devices for rapid high-altitude search;[76] if not, they could perhaps be used to set out recoverable acoustic arrays. WIG search vehicles could prosecute their own contacts, using advanced sonobuoys and weapons systems, or this function could be turned over to submarines and perhaps ship-based aircraft, assuming it is available in the forward area.

Clearly control of the air, or at least air denial, in the forward area would be crucial in this hypothetical approach. For this reason, it is difficult to find a viable place for strategic ASW air in the initial nonnuclear phase of a war. Aside from the risks of provoking escalation, there would be an overwhelming land- and sea-based air threat on the open ocean and its approaches; under the circumstances, ASW air might be more safely and productively employed in sanctuary sea control. After escalation and the destruction of land-based air, the threat would be reduced but probably not eliminated, because of surviving carrier air. If perfected satellites are still available for reconnaissance and targeting on behalf of improved submarines with longer-range cruise missiles, the Soviets could decide to mount an extensive ACW effort in the forward area during the nonnuclear phase. Surely there will be such an effort in the Mediterranean, but in the Atlantic one would expect their cruise-missile submarines to be located mainly in the Norwegian Sea for use in conjunction with land-based missile-armed aircraft. Thus, our Atlantic carriers might survive, if the United States is conservative in committing them against Soviet strong points in the conventional phase. To prosecute strategic ASW, then, the Soviet navy might have to break out some of its own carriers to fight the battle for command of the air above the ocean. Whether this course is taken will depend on a number of factors, including the availability of carriers after conventional-phase attrition,

---

[76] Moore, "Antisubmarine Warfare," pp. 190-192, 195.

the higher priority allocation of carriers to sanctuary sea control, and Soviet ability to cope with the emerging threat from large numbers of U.S. antiship cruise missiles by the year 2000.

One can also expect substantial Soviet investment in hunter-killer submarines. Assuming no expansion in either cruise-missile or ballistic-missile submarines, only upgrading replacements maintaining strategic arms limitation levels, Moscow could triple the present number of nuclear-powered torpedo-attack submarines without further exploitation or expansion of existing capacity. These platforms would be shared primarily between the sea-control and strategic-defense missions, with the allocation edge in favor of the latter. They would be quieter and possibly equipped with advanced sensors of longer range. To take advantage of increased detection distances, the Soviet navy would need longer-range ASW missiles having a terminal undersea acquisition capability, as well as more advanced torpedoes and, perhaps, antiship cruise missiles that could be launched from the same tubes.

I would not expect substantial forward deployments of platforms during the conventional phase of the war. Leaving aside escalation sensitivity, the counter-ASW environment would not be favorable and, given a perceived withholding strategy for the United States, it should not be necessary for the Soviet navy to prosecute strategic ASW immediately upon entering the nuclear phase. These factors may explain Admiral Gorshkov's insistence that sea control is necessary for strategic defense as well as strategic offense. Command of the sea also includes command of the air and, to a certain extent, the underwater environment, which requires "coordinated operations for the destruction of enemy basing points, and his airfields and command, control and communications centers." [77] Until escalation occurs, then, the bulk of strategic ASW submarines would be held north of the Greenland-Iceland-United Kingdom gap and in contiguous closed seas in the Pacific. After escalation, with the vitiation of Western choke-point and other air capabilities, Soviet submarines could be broken out with the assistance of shipboard air and surface support.

Even safely out in the open ocean, however, it is difficult to see how hunter-killer submarines alone can do the job, if only because of the large area to be searched.

Peacetime naval diplomacy and local war. If the Soviet armed forces are to have a political role in the Third World, particular military requirements have to be satisfied to make the mission credible. Ultimately—and I stress the word "ultimately"—the main Soviet opponent in the year 2000 will still be the United States, and the main U.S. instru-

---

[77] Bystrov, "Winning Command of the Sea," p. 20.

ment will still be the carrier; hence, Moscow will have to concentrate on anticarrier warfare first of all. The ACW function is also a principal component of the Soviet sea-control mission, but the allocation of forces is somewhat different in principal sea-control areas such as the Norwegian Sea. There land-based aircraft can be drawn upon, in addition to submarines and surface ships. This is not normally the case, however, for peacetime politico-military tasks in the forward area; here the main reliance has to be on the cruise-missile submarine, supported by surface ships and torpedo-attack submarines. To some extent this approach reduces credibility, for which the Soviets have attempted to compensate by adopting the crisis tactic of the "close embrace" of the U.S. carrier by Russian surface ships, to get around the carrier's long-reach advantage.[78]

From the standpoint of the Soviet navy's professionals, this tactic might not be an entirely satisfactory solution. It is too situation-dependent; the U.S. carrier could decide to lose its tattletale and maintain an advantageous distance from the Soviet fire-control and launch platforms. Moreover, by the year 2000, a carrier task group will probably have much greater antisubmarine detection ranges. While the Soviets may more than offset this development with the use of satellites for reconnaissance and targeting, in conjunction with submarine cruise missiles with ranges on the order of several hundred miles, I do not believe this will eliminate a Soviet requirement for forward air. At a minimum, forward air would still be needed for sea- and air-control support of an ACW task group, if not for use as a principal standoff strike platform against the U.S. carrier.

Moscow might hope that, by the year 2000, a "satisficing" solution could be reached by installing forward land-based air on the territories of friendly countries. But this would put the task at the mercy of political vagaries; surely the Soviet navy would prefer globally mobile sea-based air, a requirement that could be met by the continued production of air-capable ships beyond the needs of sea control. Still, despite the military requirement, I am not persuaded that the political authorities will take this course on behalf of the Third World ACW effort alone. Soviet ACW task groups can give a good account of themselves without air-capable ships; and if Moscow continues to select occasions for confrontation with prudence—when its client (rather than Washington's) is in support of the status quo or when Washington is not firmly committed to the status quo—then experience suggests that Soviet strength of will from this source will more than compensate for deficiencies in Soviet capabilities.

[78] Zumwalt, *On Watch*, pp. 300-301.

However, the ACW effort is not the only requirement that Moscow has to consider in Third World coercive diplomacy. Confrontation in the Third World is first of all between client and client; after that, between a patron and an opposing client; and only ultimately between patron and patron. The Soviet navy, as presently constituted, can credibly meet the requirements for the first and third aspects. It can police the sea and, to some extent, the air lines of communication that maintain the flow of arms and other supplies to clients, at least until war breaks out. It is also credible in confining U.S. intervention from the sea, against the land, to defensive ends. However, the Soviet navy has only a limited capability for intervening against an opposing client on land. As already pointed out, this has not yet proved a severe handicap. If time is not of the essence, as it was not when the U.S.S.R. intervened in the Arab-Israeli war of attrition in 1970, Moscow can rely on the sea- and air-lift of strategic reserves from other branches of the armed forces to the forward area, using the Soviet navy to protect the lifeline back to the U.S.S.R. If rapid reaction is crucial, as it was in the June and October wars, Moscow could resort to airborne troops, again relying on the navy to secure lines of communication, this time in the air over the sea. However, geography works against the U.S.S.R. as a global air power even more than it does as a sea power. To reach the forward area, Moscow needs overflight rights from nonbloc countries that, in turn, have to be sympathetic with Soviet Third World goals. To acquire an independent, rapid-reaction intervention capability, Moscow would have to expand its naval infantry component, and to back it up with sea-based aircraft.

Thus, the Soviet drive to forward sea-based air might not be motivated primarily by the need to counter the United States in the Third World. Because its vital interests are not at stake, Washington is likely to respect the credibility of Soviet ACW task groups, as long as Moscow is on the side of the status quo. On the other hand, Moscow could not expect that the mere addition of sea-based air to ACW task groups would sufficiently tilt the balance in strength of will to force Washington's acceptance of breaches of the status quo by the U.S.S.R. or its clients. The Soviet Union would still consider such a use of force an unacceptable risk. By contrast, precisely because the vital interests of U.S. clients are often at stake (for example, Israel), Moscow has to be concerned about its intervention credibility; and the future could bring political developments along overflight routes that might jeopardize air lines of communications. In addition, even airborne troops could use maritime air for support of its land operations. These considerations, together with the usefulness of shipboard air in carrying out forward sea-control ACW in general war, might lead to Soviet production of carriers for forward deployment, especially in the Mediterranean.

Of course, I am not predicting that the Soviet Union will actually take this course. The advantages may not justify the additional costs and risks. Power-projection capabilities are politically potent and militarily usable primarily when the target is a large-scale domestic opposition against an established client government or a Western client engaged in a successful offensive against a Soviet client. Almost all of these situations could be handled by small-scale naval action in coastal regions or large-scale recourse to other branches of the armed forces for action in the interior. Up to now, quick reaction in the interior has proved to be a Soviet requirement only in support of Syria and Egypt against a victorious Israel; and Moscow may continue to feel that the airborne solution will be adequate for similar situations in the future. In all other international crises, the Soviet client or ally was victorious or taking the offensive—for example, in the Jordanian crisis of 1970, the Indo–Pakistani War of 1970, and the mining of Haiphong in 1972. The target, therefore, was the U.S. Navy and the Soviet objective was to limit the scope and reduce the political impact of American intervention or threatened intervention. Interior power projection was not a requirement; the crucial problem was credibility at sea. Moscow may well be sanguine enough to think that this will be the typical scenario of the future, that history is on its side, and that the main task ahead will be inhibiting U.S. reversals of gains by Soviet clients, rather than protecting Soviet clients against Western clients.

COMMENTARIES

Frank Uhlig, Jr.

We have heard two excellent papers. As an editor I envy those who will have the privilege of publishing them. Interestingly, both speakers show the roles of the navies under examination as mirror images one of the other. Admiral Crowe, quoting Admiral Holloway, sees the main tasks of the U.S. Navy as being "sea control and power projection." By power projection, Admiral Crowe means a number of things but mainly, he tells us, it "consists of a broad spectrum of offensive actions from strategic nuclear response by fleet ballistic missile submarines to surgical air strikes mounted by carrier-based aircraft." Among the other items included in projection, he mentions amphibious assault and naval bombardment.

Mr. McConnell tells us that the Soviet navy sees its main assignment as being "operations against the shore" by ballistic missile submarines. Associated with that is a sea control mission for the protection of submarine-launched ballistic missiles which, Mr. McConnell says, are apparently to be withheld from the initial strikes even in general nuclear war. The Soviet navy also has what it now describes as a "secondary" mission—the "strategic defense of the homeland against sea-based strike systems." Once a more important mission in the Soviet navy, this one seems to be fading for lack of the technology needed to make it successful. For much the same reason the U.S. Navy never did put much effort into such a mission.

However, while the Soviets appear to put first the role of striking at the foe with ballistic missiles, leaving sea control in a supporting role, the Americans reverse those priorities. They view sea control (or the more attractive term Mr. McConnell reminds us of, "command of the sea") as, in Admiral Crowe's words the "preeminent function of the U.S. Navy because it is a prerequisite to the successful conduct of other types of naval operations and to the support of U.S. military forces deployed overseas."

One of the main concerns in Western navies in recent years has been that of the protection of shipping, called by our writers, "the sea lines of communication." Mr. McConnell, however, does not believe the Soviets will make any serious attack upon that shipping. Why not? Because (1) the Soviets believe that ballistic missiles when launched against the harbors and shipyards where merchant ships normally are found and to which they must always return, will do that job; and (2) even if the war begins in a nonnuclear fashion, any Soviet forces deployed against allied shipping will not be available to control the sea in which lurk their ballistic missile submarines. That is, Mr. McConnell tells us, the Soviets find it more important to protect their missile submarines than to attack our tankers and freighters.

One gets the impression that Admiral Crowe agrees with this analysis of the Soviet navy's priorities.

Since Mr. McConnell is quoting the world's greatest authorities on the Soviet navy, their own admirals, there is good reason to share his view. Moreover, those Soviet admirals belong to a navy which has fought three important wars in the twentieth century, the two world wars and the bloody, disastrous contest with Japan in 1904–1905. In none of those wars was attack on hostile shipping an important part of Russian naval activity, though it might have been.

However, some people are made uncomfortable by these views. Keeping in mind the idea of the primacy of sea trade expressed by Captain Mahan and Sir Julian Corbett or—perhaps more accurately, the primacy of sea logistics—they harken back in their minds to the three great submarine campaigns of the twentieth century which, more than any single thing, brought down one huge empire and twice came close to destroying another. They are aware of the small size of NATO's supply dumps in Europe, and of the dependence both Europe and our own country place upon imports from overseas—a dependence not only for the waging of war, but also for the ordinary business of keeping society going—and they are concerned. Let us assume that these people's views carry some weight, and that the U.S. Navy and the navies of our allies hasten, when war comes, to protect shipping.

Let us also assume that Mr. McConnell's views are accurate and that the Soviets intend to do very little in the way of attacking U.S. and allied shipping at sea, and very little more about NATO's naval forces except when they threaten the Soviet Union's ballistic missile submarines.

Does this mean that, in war, a large part of the U.S. fleet will be busy protecting ships which are not in danger? Does it mean that a large part of the U.S. fleet will be operating in one part of the ocean while most of the Soviet fleet will be in another? Does it mean that those ships which we so employ will have no useful role to play?

The answer to all those things is "perhaps." It is not a new kind of situation with which we are faced, nor is it necessarily bad. Let me give some examples to show why.

Most navies had submarines before World War I, and they knew how they intended to operate them: against the fighting ships of the foe. And so they did, during World War I, for a short time. Then the Germans found that their submarines were excellent ships for use—not indirectly against enemy shipping, as Mahan counseled naval forces should be used—but directly against shipping. The British, of course, knew in a general way before the war what the Germans' intentions were with regard to their submarines. But when the Germans did something else they were unprepared. And because the German submarines were attacking the shipping upon which Britain's very existence depended, the British very nearly lost the war.

But unrestricted submarine warfare against shipping was so repugnant to the Americans, among others, that between the world wars, the U.S. Navy planned to use its submarines solely against warships. Its submarines practiced solely at attacking warships. It designed the magnetic exploders of the submarines' torpedoes solely with that employment in view. Yet, on the first day of war in the Pacific, those submarines were ordered to do something they had never intended to do, had never practiced doing, and were not well armed for doing: to conduct unrestricted submarine warfare against shipping. At first they did not do it very well, partly for the reasons already given, but eventually they destroyed the merchant marine upon which the existence of the Japanese empire and its armed forces depended. Like the British in the previous war, the Japanese navy was little interested in the protection of shipping. When the need to do so became evident, it was already too late.

Interestingly, at the same time, the U.S. Pacific Fleet expected the Japanese to conduct unrestricted submarine warfare against our shipping. Accordingly, it employed a large portion of its meager destroyer force in escort work. Happily, the threat did not materialize and the destroyers were then released for other work.

The point of this is that it seems unwise to bind one's plans too tightly to what we know our enemy sincerely intends to do. He may just find himself doing something very different from what he thought he would. Since he—and certainly we—do not know what he really will do, the wisest thing is to be prepared to protect that which we value most.

In the Soviet case, that is their ballistic missile submarines. In our case, such submarines are already fairly safe. So it is shipping, and that includes amphibious forces and their supporting carriers, which we should value most highly.

Is it conceivable, then, that the opposing fleets would seldom be in contact with each other? Yes. It is conceivable. Let me give two examples. In World War II while the slender Axis naval forces in the Black Sea were busy escorting supplies to Axis troops advancing along the Soviet Union's southern shore, the much larger Soviet Black Sea Fleet was equally busy bringing in supplies to Soviet troops beleaguered at Odessa and in the Crimea. Why did the Soviets use their superior naval force in that fashion? Why not attack the enemy's sea communications? Partly it was because the Axis also had overland means of communication. The loss of their sea communications would merely have inconvenienced them, not beaten them. Partly, also, because the Soviets had lost their overland means of communication. If the Black Sea Fleet chose to attack enemy supplies rather than bring in friendly supplies, the defenders at Odessa and the Crimea soon would have no supplies. Did the Black Sea Fleet do wrong?

But the best known example of what we might call "pacific war" occurred in World War I when the Grand Fleet, anchored at Scapa Flow, rarely ventured into the southern half of the North Sea while the German High Seas Fleet, anchored in the Jade, seldom entered the northern half of that sea. Yet each of the two fleets, though they met only once in battle, played a major role in that war. Just imagine what would have happened if one of those fleets had existed and the other had not.

While we are on the subject of the protection of shipping, it is necessary to discuss the proviso one often hears—Admiral Crowe mentioned it—that it will be necessary to protect reinforcements to our armies and allies overseas "in a protracted conflict." In a short war, the proviso goes, forces suitable for the protection of shipping would have no influence. We are also told, a short war is the way to go.

Of course, when a war starts, one does not know how long it will last. In August 1914, the Kaiser promised his troops they would be home before the leaves turned. Two wars later, in Korea in the fall of 1950, General MacArthur promised his troops they would be home by Christmas. We have had similar promises since. No matter what anyone says on this line, do not count on it.

The ability and readiness to protect the U.S. and allied shipping can be just as important in a war which really turns out to be short as in one which does not stop on some astrologer's schedule. Of course, if

Europe is overrun in a week or so and the United States says "we quit," it will not matter. But consider what will happen if the defenders in Europe succeed and throw back the Soviet assault. Unless the United States and its allies can provide and protect the shipping Europe will need to continue supporting and defending itself, it will still be in danger of being cut off—even by a fleet which really did not intend to do that. It would be ironic if, after having achieved a notable triumph on the ground, the Western maritime nations were forced to surrender anyway because they could not protect the shipping they needed to continue their successful defense.

Here is another point to consider: the Soviets need not even make any attacks on Western shipping; the West must merely perceive it is unable to protect that shipping. The surrender will then come because it must.

Above all then, we must be ready and able to protect our shipping. But how are we to do it? We are not bound to use the methods and instruments which once worked for us just because they once worked. And Admiral Crowe has warned us that the speed, endurance, and firepower of nuclear powered submarines have rendered obsolete many traditional concepts of convoy protection, including some of the evasive tactics pursued by convoy commanders. Against a foe who has such submarines, supported by satellite reconnaissance vehicles, long-range reconnaissance aircraft, and long-range missile-armed aircraft, convoy, the savior of the allied cause in 1917 and as Captain Roskill called it, "the linch-pin of our maritime strategy" in the Atlantic in World War II, may no longer serve our purpose.

We must use the time we have, time whose length we do not know, to work in the war colleges and in the laboratories ashore, and to exercise with ships at sea, until we find out how under the foreseeable conditions we can carry out the U.S. Navy's ancient purpose.

Herschel Kanter

I want to compare and contrast these two papers. In particular, I would point out that the missions of the U.S. and Soviet navies as related by the two papers are not only different, as we might expect because of differences in geography, alliances, technology, and history of the two countries, but also that the naval missions of the two countries, again as related by the papers, have little to do with each other. This is true despite the fact that U.S. and Soviet naval leaders have developed their navies as instruments to control and oppose each other's navy, or at least have sold much of their naval forces to their respective political leaders on that basis. After contrasting the missions as presented, I will examine whether or not McConnell's view of Soviet missions, in particular his emphasis on strategic antisubmarine warfare, is a reasonable one. Then I will suggest why consideration of these missions is important for U.S. naval force planning and for predicting future Soviet behavior. Finally, I will finish with some discussion of future missions, again contrasting the two papers.

I should point out before going on, that I consider Admiral Crowe's approach and mission emphasis typical of naval and defense spokesmen, who discuss the rationale for U.S. naval forces, and McConnell's approach typical of those who study and observe the Soviets, including their military writings, naval forces and characteristics, and peacetime operations. I admit in both cases to be overlooking a number of subtle distinctions between the two writers and their respective colleagues.

U.S. and Soviet Mission Comparisons. Admiral Crowe, in reviewing naval missions beginning in the early 1950s, emphasized (1) forward deployments to project tactical air and amphibious forces, and (2) contribution to massive retaliation with aircraft carriers, and later with ballistic missile submarines. McConnell reports that the Soviets' major investments in the last twenty years are the following: (1) ballistic missile submarines, accounting for 40 percent of the value of all combatants, both major and minor; (2) antisubmarine warfare forces to be used against our ballistic missile submarines, accounting for 20 percent of the Soviet combatant investment; and (3) another 15 percent on the antiship, mainly anticarrier function. Thus 75 percent of the Soviet shipbuilding investment has been earmarked for what we would call strategic missions. Their other major interest after strategic warfare is in protecting state interests by countering the U.S. Navy in local conflicts. I will return to this last mission later on.

Up to this point the two speakers' descriptions are complementary. The primary purpose of the Soviet buildup, outside of a strategic offensive mission, was the strategic-defensive one of countering both our carriers, which were considered to be strategic weapon systems capable of delivering nuclear weapons against the Soviet Union, and our ballistic missile submarine force. Then, when they developed their own fleet of ballistic missile submarines, their antisubmarine warfare forces could be used either to counter our ballistic missile submarines or to protect their own from our nuclear attack submarines.

Unfortunately, the complementarity of the papers ends at this point. Admiral Crowe goes on to describe a Soviet navy designed to challenge Western supremacy, not as reported by McConnell in the strategic warfare area, but against our sea lines of communication in a conventional war. The U.S. Navy exists to oppose the Soviet naval mission that, according to McConnell, is barely mentioned by the Soviet strategists and then only in the broken-back phase of a general nuclear war.

Strategic Antisubmarine Warfare Missions. Naval force planners, in both the U.S. Navy and the Office of the Secretary of Defense (OSD) pay little attention to Soviet strategic antisubmarine warfare in sizing our naval forces. They seem to feel that the two missions described by McConnell—threatening our ballistic missile submarines and protecting theirs—are not reasonable missions for the Soviets to pursue. It is not reasonable, they say, for the Soviets to buy forces to threaten our ballistic missile submarines because these submarines are invulnerable, and the Soviets have no need to buy forces to protect their own ballistic missile submarines because we do not threaten them. According to this argument, not only do we not threaten them, but, because of our strategy of mutual assured destruction, it is in our interest that the Soviets should possess the secure second-strike capability represented by their ballistic missile submarine force.

First, let me discuss the impossibility of destroying our ballistic missile submarines. Why should the Soviets spend large amounts of money on an impossible task? I am not sure why, but I am sure that a government might spend hundreds of millions, or even billions, of dollars on systems that have a seemingly impossible task. In this country there are numerous examples of this, in both the defense and the nondefense areas. Taking but one example from our navy, the surface missile systems of the late 1950s and early 1960s probably never worked very well and may not have been very useful for defending the fleet. But there was a willingness to spend great amounts of money on unworkable systems because they were the only ones around. It may even be rational; perhaps experience is the only way to develop systems that will eventually work. The Soviets have a long view and they may feel that a capability against ballistic missile submarines can be developed only by having a large antisubmarine force now and betting on future breakthroughs.

Let us look at the other Soviet use of antisubmarine forces: to protect their ballistic missile submarines from our forces, primarily our nuclear attack submarines. Do the Soviets have any reason to think we might wish to threaten their ballistic missile submarine force; that is, that we are pursuing a strategic antisubmarine warfare mission that could endanger part or all of their ballistic missile submarine force? If so, it is quite rational for them to buy forces to protect their own forces. First, we have substantial antisubmarine warfare forces and complementary sensors for barrier operations at choke points as well as for open ocean search. Second, our navy, through both the Advanced Research Projects Agency and the Office of Naval Research, is developing more acoustic and nonacoustic knowledge on the physics of the ocean and on the anomalies created by large objects in the ocean, taking measurements over finer and finer grids and shorter time periods, and is processing that information on large computers. This research, if successful, would be used to locate submarines, probably both attack and ballistic missile submarines, or so the Soviets must assume. Our undersea and satellite area surveillance systems, which we say are aimed at nuclear attack submarines in wartime, are vulnerable and would probably not be available to protect our sea lines of communication in wartime. Thus the Soviets could easily view our whole area antisubmarine warfare capability as aimed at locating their ballistic missile submarine force in peacetime. Their deployment of only one in six Yankee-class submarines and their recent development of the Delta, with a SS-N-8 missile that can hit the United States from the Barents Sea, indicates some fear on the part of the Soviets. Since the Soviets stress war fighting over deterrence even in the context of a thermonuclear war, a damage limiting strategy for the United States against their ballistic missile submarines must seem reasonable. Mutual assured destruction and secure second strike may seem to them merely propaganda concepts that have no real relevance to policy.

Intentions and Capabilities. What difference does it make if we think that the Soviets' major interest is in strategic forces and that that is the major planned use of their navy? Perhaps we should look only at capabilities, not at intentions. If they have a large submarine force that is not capable of finding our ballistic missile submarines but could attack our merchant shipping and cut our sea lines of communication to Europe and Asia, maybe they will use it for that, and maybe we ought to prepare for such a contingency.

Two major problems with overlooking the Soviet emphasis on a strategic navy are:

(1) We as a nation probably spend too little on the short war that will probably escalate to nuclear weapons if it cannot be terminated quickly, and too much on a long war that the Soviets may not let happen.

(2) We may ignore a threat to our ballistic missile submarine force when it finally comes, as we did for a long while with the cruise missile threat to our surface ships.

76

By ignoring what our experts on the Soviet navy tell us, we spend too much on some threats and too little on others. Further, we are poor at predicting Soviet force developments. Finally, although I have not discussed it because I have no direct evidence, I suspect that our operational plans are not appropriate to deal with the real Soviet threats.

Beyond these problems, if we are spending money on a damage limiting mission against Soviet ballistic missile submarine forces, then the public presentation of the U.S. strategic force posture by the Department of Defense has, for the past fifteen years, been misleading if not deliberately deceptive.

Local Conflicts. Now I would like to go on to the nonstrategic mission area that McConnell and other Soviet naval experts discuss: the use of the Soviet navy to confront the United States in crises and local conflicts. Admiral Crowe fails to emphasize this mission for the U.S. Navy, probably because it has always been considered, by both navy and OSD planners, to be a mission for which one would not buy forces. These planners assume that if forces have been bought for a major war then those forces are more than enough for crises confrontations. The particular capabilities or characteristics of the forces that were bought for other purposes are not important.

There have been a number of crisis confrontations with the Soviets at sea in the past fifteen years. Although the stakes are usually not as high as they would be in a direct NATO confrontation, the dangers of war are at their highest in these confrontations. Crisis scenarios such as the October War ought to loom large in our force planning. The purposes of a navy include deterring war, and terminating war quickly with minimal damage if deterrence fails or, if the war fails to terminate quickly, before the war escalates. We therefore ought to have forces that can perform these functions in such crisis confrontations, or we ought to have a foreign policy which avoids these confrontations altogether.

The aircraft carrier, particularly as it is operated today, threatened by cruise missiles, does not appear to be the appropriate force for handling crises. It is a high value target that is vulnerable to surprise attack. Once attacked there is a high probability of losing a large percentage of our force. Moreover, since our best antiship weapon system is the carrier-based aircraft, we are not in a position to retaliate in kind.

Future Missions, Forces, and Technology. What are our naval planners thinking about for the next ten to twenty-five years? The Soviets will be our major adversary and will be looking for ways "to counter the U.S. Navy." Admiral Crowe mentions the major missions of protecting sea lines of communication and nuclear retaliation but gives little attention to this latter mission. He mentions the "regular or periodic presence of U.S. naval force," to counter military intervention by the Soviets or one of its client states, and says we will have forward deployments, but since we may lose bases suddenly we should seek off-shore solutions for logistics support. We should seek arms control agreements, but they will be difficult to conclude, so we should not count on them.

Admiral Crowe expects that increasing tension between the northern and southern hemispheres will leave us with the missions of safeguarding lives and property, protecting ships and aircraft in international commerce, and containing local or regional instabilities. As for technology, he expects faster ships, stand-off missiles, and improved antisubmarine ships and aircraft. V/STOL technology will replace our current carrier-based aviation. He expects both the United States and the Soviets to improve their capability to locate ships and aircraft. The Soviets would have stand-off weapons, which we hope to counter with tactical aviation. Radars will improve, and laser-beams will be used for target interrogation and acquisition. We must hedge against a Soviet breakthrough in antisubmarine warfare. Admiral Crowe's navy of the future sounds to me like the navy of the present, and of the past twenty-five years, in missions, forces, and tactics, with a handful of technical innovations added.

Turning to the Soviets, McConnell expects them to protect their ballistic missile submarines in sanctuaries and to develop the technology to contest for air superiority in order to look for and destroy our ballistic missile submarines. For peacetime intervention, McConnell suggests that the Soviets will use carrier aircraft and will continue to use various elements of air, surface, and subsurface forces to counter our carriers.

Future Problems. If the U.S. Navy's major concern will be countering the Soviet navy, then Admiral Crowe's paper is an example of neglect of what McConnell and others, including in-house navy experts, say about the Soviet navy. Although it does not in itself matter why the Soviets got to where they are, such information along with information about operations and technology can provide clues to what will deter the Soviets from war, to what the Soviets might do in a war, and to the missions they might undertake and the forces they might buy in the future.

If the Soviets continue to emphasize the strategic mission in all three forms and if their other major mission is facing us in a political role in local conflicts, then we might at least consider the possibility that our two major naval problems in the next ten to twenty-five years will be: (1) protecting our ballistic missile submarine force, if the oceans become transparent; and (2) finding a way to protect our political interests with different hardware and tactics—in particular, avoiding the "close embrace" of our carriers by Soviet cruise missile surface ships, which makes the carrier so vulnerable to a first strike.

Perhaps many small, relatively cheap submarines operating in noisy high traffic areas would be the solution to the vulnerability of our ballistic missile submarines. Alternatively a large number of submarines and surface ships might be equipped with strategic cruise missiles. Admiral Crowe mentions early in his paper that sea control contributes to the protection of our ballistic missile force. Following this, we should at least consider, in sizing sea control forces, how these forces contribute to protection of our strategic forces if they become vulnerable.

The problem of the "close embrace" of our aircraft carriers might be solved by changing our deployment policy to one in which the carriers are not deployed forward on the current rigid basis. Alternatively they might withdraw from the direct confrontation in a crisis, leaving a less highly valued prize, but one with projection capability, such as an air capable amphibious ship, or a sea control ship, or a vss, or a through-deck cruiser, or a Kiev, to confront the Soviets. This would hold the carrier in reserve to strike back.

Further, if protecting the sea lines of communication is as important as Admiral Crowe and others tell us, then perhaps we should be looking for better ways to perform the mission. Equipping merchant ships with antisubmarine and antiair warfare equipment might be a way to increase protection of sea lines of communication. Other innovations ought to be sought rather than just more of what we do now. Also, no mention is made in the paper of what we would or could do about protection of the sea lines of communication if the Soviets disabled or destroyed our area surveillance sensors.

Other Innovations. Other omissions in Admiral Crowe's paper include dealing with the short war/long war problem mentioned earlier and dealing with the use of tactical nuclear weapons. Although McConnell did not mention it, he and other observers of the Soviets find that the Soviets do not see the sharp distinction that we see between nuclear and nonnuclear war, and therefore consider a long nonnuclear war to be unlikely. 215370

79

Other important problems include political command and control of our ballistic missile submarines and countering and incorporating the new technology weapons, such as precision-guided weapons, including cruise missiles and remotely piloted vehicles. The use on a large scale of land-based aircraft, such as the land-based multipurpose naval aircraft, ought to be considered. Finally, as a substitute for forward bases that we are told by Admiral Crowe we may continue to lose, we should examine the use of very large stable seagoing platforms.

Concluding Comments. None of these ideas is original, but I mention them because it is important to consider radical departures in planning for the navy of the future, rather than continuing to do what we have been doing. We should also, in planning for the navy of the twenty-first century, consider a more realistic view of the Soviets and ourselves. Finally, because of the contribution of sea control and especially anti-submarine forces to protecting and destroying ballistic missile submarines, we should drop the artificial distinction between strategic and general purpose forces that bedevils our thinking about naval forces.

John Moore

The question of manpower was mentioned briefly by Admiral Crowe. I think it is a point that could be lost in the extreme complexities of whether or not people will protect their strategic ballistic missile submarines and the other things that have been discussed. I am sure that the future for the Soviet navy on the manpower front is a very difficult one. There is a declining population in western Russia and, therefore, the future sailors of the Soviet navy will be drawn increasingly from the less educated areas to the east. The Soviets have acknowledged their problems in educating the draftee. If we examined the training pattern of the Soviet sailor, we would see the enormous strain that is being put on their officers and the resultant channeling of ideas by those officers.

When the core of the fleet—that is, the senior enlisted men—come up for their chief's rating at the age of twenty-one, that is a problem. We do not have that problem at the moment, but the Soviets certainly have. It is a problem that Admiral Gorshkov himself has acknowledged on more than one occasion. The frame of mind of officers is immensely important. With increasingly advanced technology in the next twenty-five years, it is not likely that this problem will diminish.

As far as Western navies are concerned, and particularly the U.S. Navy as Admiral Crowe has made clear, the problems center on not knowing what the economic situation will be, what the manpower expenditure will have to be. One line we must take is to look at what is the greatest single expenditure in the naval budget. When we refer to a ship's cost over its whole life, 50 percent of it, at least, is spent on the people who man it. The reduction of on-board manpower ought to be one of our major priorities for the future. In the Royal navy, manpower reductions have been realized in the new ships. Interestingly, it was a commercially designed ship, the type-21 frigate, that made the biggest reduction, cutting manpower 50 percent more than the ministry-designed ships did.

The business of command and the flexibility of mind of the ship's officers are vital to naval diplomacy and to the use of ships in furthering political aims. In such situations reaction time may be very short, and officers may have to make decisions for themselves on the spur of the moment.

James McConnell spoke of the status quo in various areas where tension might develop. I suggest that the status quo could easily be manipulated by a force as large as the KGB. The KGB is perfectly capable of brewing up a crisis that the Soviets might resolve, given the growing potential of Soviet ships, with a force of not very great size, but of great efficiency. The *Kiev* is a possible candidate for such a task. Although people have said this is absolute nonsense, I still think that this ship has two of the necessary attributes—the command structure and the air power—on board, backed up by strategic amphibious forces which might well not be needed. It could be a method of using a bludgeon on a recalcitrant government that has been infiltrated and has requested assistance. In the United Kingdom today, the infiltration of a few dissident members of the community into high places has been disastrous in certain spheres, and such infiltration could take place in other parts of the world.

One part of the world where this sort of infiltration could take place is the Indian Ocean. It has attractions for the Soviet Union. It is as far from the United States as it can be, and it is the source of raw materials that are essential to the West and to this country in particular. The Soviets have already established certain safe havens in the area where they can anchor and maintain their ships. Now that Britain has opted out of its bases east of Suez, the only remaining sources of support are Australia and Diego Garcia. Consequently, I believe the Indian Ocean is of enormous strategic importance.

Our present attitude toward South Africa is virtually denying us the strategic use of that essential part of the world. And as a result, the Soviet Union is probably better placed for deploying its ships to that area than the West. At this point one wonders why we think of the Tropic of Cancer as the southern boundary of NATO. NATO's interests are worldwide, and that is one of the more important points we must consider over the next twenty-five years.

As far as sea lines of communication are concerned—and I hope James McConnell will excuse me for quoting his favorite author Gorshkov—who said that the significance of naval operations, in carrying out such traditional missions as interdicting the sea communications of the enemy, and protecting one's own communications, had changed. These operations are now a most important integral part of naval efforts aimed at under-undermining the military economic potential of the enemy.

Sea lines of communication do exist today. There are now about 4,000 merchant ships in the Atlantic. They are bringing astonishing quantities of raw material to the NATO countries, as Admiral Crowe has pointed out. Is there any reason why disruption of sea lines of communication could not take place in what is rather euphemistically called peacetime? It could be accomplished by processes other than actual war—for example, by harassment, by declaring danger areas, and by various other options wide open to the Soviet Union. Apart from the Soviet fleet, the largest single fleet in an area like the Indian Ocean is usually that of the French. I suggest that World War III started when the military mission of the Soviet Union moved into Greece in 1944–1945. There are many activities in which the Soviets might indulge, without ever firing a shot, that could be extremely embarrassing to us.

DISCUSSION

ADMIRAL CROWE: Mr. Kanter said that the future navy I described looks, in certain respects, a lot like today's navy. There is a lot of truth in that, and I must admit that, in reading my own paper, this impression at first distressed me a little. The more I thought about it, however, the more sure I was that this statement is not as alarming as it sounds.

First, we are talking about a period that is not very long, and, second, we are talking about shipbuilding times that are long. I was discussing not the character of the navy but the character of ships. That will remain the same. I do see a tremendous continuity in functions and missions and roles. Mr. Kanter recommended that we examine new tactics and new ways to do our business. The U.S. Navy is doing that, but it requires money and support. Seminars like this help the people make wise and informed decisions. Those who deal with naval affairs have to make their needs and requirements known.

ROBERT W. HERRICK, Ketron Corporation: I am now engaged in a year-long study of Soviet naval missions from the Soviet perspective for the chief of naval operations. In regard to the comments of the anti-SLOC (sea lines of communication) mission, Frank Uhlig gave us a very timely reminder, using some glaring historical examples, of instances where the navy has found itself performing, or not performing, anti-SLOC missions. I think the Soviets might possibly be in that position, too.

I would like to mention briefly two relevant factors that have not come up in general discussions.

First, James McConnell mentioned, but did not stress, Admiral Gorshkov's comment that antishipping, or anti-SLOC, has now become a part of the battle against the land. What this means is very clear. If the Soviet Delta submarines of the Golf or Hotel classes can take care of our shipping terminals, then the Soviet Union will not have to field a large force or use its SSBNs (nuclear-powered ballistic missile submarines) and large force of diesel submarines for anti-SLOC missions. It could then carry out missions that it would not otherwise have enough

83

ships for, including the very important mission of cover and gunfire support of tactical amphibious landings of their armed forces, particularly in a push to the Atlantic. The Soviets themselves stress the importance of their coastal sea communications for support of the army, a mission that eats up a lot of their forces.

The second factor is the Soviet army. Even though the Soviet navy might intend to take care of the anti-SLOC mission—largely by hitting our terminals—there is a very important point in the 1968 edition of Marshal Sokolovskiy's *Soviet Military Strategy*. He stresses that the navy must launch an anti-SLOC campaign on the very first days of the war. The army still is rather influential in the Soviet military setup, and if it says it wants an anti-SLOC campaign in order to keep us from supporting our forces in Europe, it will probably get it.

I would also like to suggest how the Soviets might carry out the missions that McConnell described so well. Soviet writers for many years have talked about zones of defense. The Soviets hope to command the sea within a couple hundred miles of their coasts. In these zones, they could use all their small fast craft, surface ships, and PT boats, and even their expensive missile artillery. Beyond these zones—which would include their peripheral seas—the Barents, the Baltic, the Black, and the Sea of Japan—they have an area in which they hope to contest us for command of the seas. And beyond that, there is what they call the open-ocean zone, where they have to practice sea denial, because they cannot support their submarines with surface forces until they have more carrier-based aircraft.

In my analysis of Soviet naval strategy, there has been a constant effort since World War II to push out into the second zone, where they have a good chance to fight for command of the sea. I would suggest that by the year 2000, we may see them well south of the Greenland, Iceland, United Kingdom gap, east of the entrance to the Sea of Japan, and into the Western Mediterranean.

MR. NITZE: I am surprised that all of the speakers seem to assume that the Soviet naval forces, including the Soviet naval air force, are all we have to worry about. I would have thought, for instance, that in an all-forces approach, the Soviets would use other components of their air force. Backfire is not necessarily assigned to the naval air force. Floggers and all kinds of instruments could be used to take out ports, making our depots and other facilities vulnerable. Therefore, we are not looking adequately at the air defense of the points in the NATO area to which these lines of communication lead.

WILLIAM STOKES, Army Staff: The vital sea lines have drawn a lot of attention, and I certainly appreciate Mr. Uhlig's views.

One thing that has not been brought up is what SLOC implies in terms of the maritime forces needed to reinforce Europe. More specifically, no one addressed what might be in the wings, in terms of rationalizing the use of the shipping available within the initial alliance. From an army perspective, the lift matter should be addressed.

ADMIRAL CROWE: We are giving quite a bit of attention to lift capability. In the navy, the party line is that we need more modern ships. We would like to see increased emphasis on the merchant marine in the United States, particularly, a merchant marine that includes and incorporates developments that will make it compatible with naval operations. I see some improvements coming in that area, but I am not so sure we can satisfy all of the army's preferences. Our major problem will be the availability, accessibility, and control of shipping in the time we would like. In my opinion, the coordination between the civilian side of our government and our naval organization is not as good as it should be. Incidentally, that is not a Soviet problem; unlike us, they have a very good handle on the problem.

WILLIAM RUHE, General Dynamics: Admiral Crowe quoted Admiral Holloway as saying that the United States would have the edge in all of the important scenarios being used today. I would address the question, then, to Mr. McConnell, How do you feel about the present force-planning scenarios for the next ten years? Are they valid or how would you regard them?

MR. McCONNELL: To tell you the truth, I don't look at them. I have mainly concentrated on what the Soviets say. I hope, sometime, to look at our responses to these situations, but I have not done that yet.

ADMIRAL JERRY MILLER: In the discussion about roles and missions, we have talked a lot about sea control, sea denial, and sea projection. In his position as the head of navy strategy, policy, and operations, did Admiral Crowe have difficulty with those terms? Did he find them too restrictive? He referred to the law, Title 10, that says the mission of the navy is to conduct combat at sea. I don't know whether the law breaks this mission down into convenient terms for systematic analysis for preparing a budget. Are these terms—sea denial, sea control, sea projection—limiting? Maybe it would be a good idea to abandon them, to focus on the law, and not to restrict ourselves. Don't we

85

give up something of what navies can really do by trying to classify roles and missions in budgetary terms rather than combatant terms?

ADMIRAL CROWE: We probably do give up something in terms of imaginativeness and innovation. You are absolutely correct, we are victims of our syntax. Crossing over from the bureaucracy to a group like this, whose vocabulary is somewhat different, is sometimes a little taxing. Some of the things we write in the navy are not necessarily understandable.

I am a little curious about your general comment. The terms "sea control" and "power projection" seem to allow a lot of leeway. We can be awfully sinful inside of those general categories, especially when we break them down into various tactical functions, evolutions, maneuvers, and so on. Admiral Holloway uses a rather broad definition of sea control. Anything that would help us either to deny the sea, to control the sea, or to command the sea comes under that definition. I don't find the vocabulary nearly as limiting as our own minds. The press of everyday business—the routine work of the Joint Chiefs of Staff and the navy bureaucracy—has a deadening effect on imagination. From that standpoint, participation in seminars of this kind is valuable. But I don't think it is the vocabulary that bothers us.

ADMIRAL MILLER: Let me be more specific. Let's take the term "sea projection." In the academic community, where I have lived since my retirement, that term always brings an adverse reaction. A force that will project itself is considered a bad thing. A force that will fight at sea is fine, but the minute I say that this force may be drawing a projection, I am in trouble. My programs could get a lot further, whether they are involved with strategy or the forces themselves, if I didn't have to use the word "projection."

ADMIRAL CROWE: In that respect, I would agree totally. Admiral Holloway is trying to develop some other terms that are not loaded down with adverse historical or traditional connotations. You are right; the term "sea projection" carries a lot of emotional baggage that sometimes makes our task very difficult.

MR. NITZE: The word "projection" is not in the language of the law you quoted, Admiral Crowe.

ADMIRAL CROWE: No, I said I distilled that law, Mr. Nitze.

NORMAN POLMAR: About fifty years ago, I used to wear a funny army green suit, and I was forced to read Title 10. As I recall, it gives the navy three missions: protection of merchant shipping, antisubmarine warfare, and reconnaissance. That was refined in the 1947 statement of missions to include a number of other things. But I think it might be interesting to look at the actual wording of Title 10 and one or two of the other key documents. The words are somewhat restrictive, if one goes back too far.

MR. UHLIG: Well, it is sort of like a family tree. [Laughter.]
   Admiral Crowe commented that sea control and projection involve the same ships, which is something we tend to forget. Amphibious ships can be used both for sea control and for projection; so can aircraft carriers and all the enormous number of supporting and screening ships of one sort or another. We should not allow our words, our terms, to lead us astray. I think that is one of the problems Admiral Miller was leading up to.

MR. KANTER: I would like to make a comment with respect to one of the points made in the last part of Mr. McConnell's presentation. In looking out to the year 2000, he said that one of the variables might be whether or not Soviet dedication to the idea of peaceful coexistence continued and strengthened, or whether it was abandoned in favor of a war-winning attitude. Isn't that correct?

ADMIRAL CROWE: Right.

MR. KANTER: My recollection is that the rate of Soviet defense expenditures began to increase at the time Moscow adopted the policy of peaceful coexistence, and that the rate has been expanding ever since. From less than 3 percent, it has probably grown to 5 percent or 6 percent, despite the emphasis on détente and peaceful coexistence. Therefore, it strikes me that the term "peaceful coexistence" is just something the Soviets *say* to the world at large for cosmetic effect, in contradistinction to what they *do* when they increase their military capabilities. Would you like to comment on that?

ADMIRAL CROWE: Yes. The expression "peaceful coexistence" should always be put in quotation marks. Nevertheless, I think the term has some meaning. For example, back in the Stalinist era, in 1928, the real burden of defense on the Soviet economy was something like 2.5 percent—not very significant. By the early 1950s—assuming we have been underestimating the real burden for that period at the same rate as we did five years ago—it was probably more like 30 percent of the gross national product (GPN). The latest estimates—even though they doubled during the period we are discussing—turn out to be something like 11 percent or 13 percent. So, it does seem that peaceful coexistence has some practical meaning in terms of priorities in allocations.

MR. NITZE: Bill Lee is an expert on the translation of the Soviet program into either ruble or dollar equivalence. His 1970 figures for Soviet military expenditures was right when the CIA was totally wrong; the CIA finally came to agree with him on that. Lee says that the CIA method is quite wrong. For one thing, it grossly overestimates Soviet expenditures on defense in the late 1950s and early 1960s. Lee says that the Soviet Union was spending much less at that time than the CIA suggests. It is hard to demonstrate which figure is right. I happen to agree with Bill Lee's computations rather than the CIA computations, because it is unbelievable that they were spending 30 percent of their GNP on defense in that period.

DOV ZAKHEIM: The discussions on the meaning of power projection and sea control and on Soviet defense expenditures point up a very important caveat about terminology, whether it is naval terminology or any other. When we read Shakespeare in the eighth grade, it meant something very, very different from what it meant when we read it at nineteen or twenty, because Shakespeare is full of double meanings. The same, I think, applies to just about every language. One runs into a lot of difficulty focusing solely on intention and ignoring capability. That is not to say we should ignore intention, but I think the navy overlooks Soviet intentions to the point that it hurts some planning. Nevertheless, no one has yet spoken about the dangers of focusing solely on naval terminology. For instance, Mr. McConnell said that the cyclical pattern of Soviet naval development has a lot to do with whether the internal political domain of the Soviet Union is conservative or not. It is true that in the early Stalinist years, there was a radical shift in the Soviet Union. If we look at the period after 1937, we notice that the regime became extremely conservative internally. To say that the regime has been radical is to belie a full assessment of the way the Soviets have been behaving. Since 1964, they have been extremely conservative.

On the other hand, in regard to the expansion of Soviet defense as a percentage of gross national product at the time when Moscow was talking about peaceful coexistence, one should remember that Krushchev was premier at the beginning of the peaceful coexistence period. He talked about it as early as 1956. Furthermore, if we look at the intentions of people in the political context, we should look not at what happened but at what could have happened if Zhukov had won in 1957 and Khrushchev had been sent packing. With a land general running the Soviet Union and naval plans already under way since 1954, would we have the Soviet navy acting today as it does? The question is not would there be a Soviet navy, but would the Soviet navy be behaving in the same way? I submit that it would not with a land general running the Soviet Union. Therefore, when we look out to the year 2000, we must be careful about terminology, because even if the Soviets mean what they say, it may not matter in five years. And I am not sure they mean what they say.

I think people like Mr. McConnell are crucial to the defense effort of this country, because somebody has to know what the Soviets are saying. They just might mean it, but their words must be taken with some caution. I don't think the navy takes what they are saying with enough caution.

MR. NITZE: I take it you are not suggesting that we ignore such wisdom as we can get from what they say. As Mr. McConnell said, it is the earliest indicator. Often we have no idea what they are about, and their words help to put one together. We have to be flexible, isn't that right?

MR. ZAKHEIM: Right, I would agree with that. No one, however, has mentioned that there is no either/or choice between intention and capability. The capability is unchanging as long as they have the forces, particularly naval forces. But the intention must be looked at first and then questioned.

MR. NITZE: Yes?

WALTER ASH: John Moore noted that only one of the two major speakers commented on manpower and that he loaded his comments toward Soviet manpower. The army released a statement on West Point cadets, indicating that they need a sense of humor, training in ethics, sex education, and victories in football games. If they hadn't admitted women last year, they wouldn't need sex education this year. [Laughter.] Maybe not ethical training, either.

The navy has had manpower problems for ten years now. To what extent are the navy's manpower problems a major element of naval capability for the next ten years?

89

ADMIRAL CROWE: I addressed that question in my paper, but not in my remarks because I was trying to be brief.

Yes, manpower is a very serious problem. In the future, it may become one of the three or four most important problems. We have both a long-term and a short-term problem. For the short term the question is whether we can attract, in an all-volunteer environment, the quality of people we need. While we understand demography pretty well, we do not yet understand the relationship between the all-volunteer force and the economy. I am not quite sure what the future holds in that respect, but I would say that we will have a tough problem with the economic factor.

In the long-term, I think John Moore was wrong about our compensation programs, our policies—that whole area. It has not been given enough attention, and we do not fully appreciate the impact it will have on our effectiveness in the long term. Yet, it is a critical element.

We do not have the kind of manpower problem the Russian navy is facing, which John Moore described. First of all, I believe our manpower is vastly superior to Soviet manpower. One reason is the technical orientation of American youth; another is the independence with which they come into the navy—and into all the armed services. This is a tremendous advantage, and I see no diminution in that. I am not so confident about attracting the required supply of manpower, particularly in an all-volunteer environment.

MR. UHLIG: It appears that in manpower the American navy probably has its biggest problem for the rest of this century. Our birth rate has been declining since 1960. That means seventeen-year-olds are fewer this year than last year; next year, there will be fewer still. And each successive year there will be fewer and fewer people to be attracted into this navy. Those who are available seem to be poorly educated. The navy has reported on problems of its young men being unable to read, and on the damage they have done to their equipment. The navy also has a severe desertion rate, compared with that of other services. Recently, it was reported that the desertion rate was about 3 percent in the navy, less than 1 percent in the other services. I don't know the causes for this. Perhaps it is the demands we place on our engineers. The engineers have always faired less well than others, and it may be worse now than ever. Whatever the reason, personnel is the main problem in our navy. When we speak of wasting money on people rather than on hardware, we have our priorities backwards. It is people who make things go. Hardware does not work by itself.

MR. NITZE: I want to support our speaker on the importance of the political background. A Russian admiral was once being quite frank with me and admitted that they did not want to build all those Y-class submarines and Delta-class submarines, and so forth. This was a decision forced by higher authority, and the Soviet navy did not know how to recruit and maintain the number of crews necessary to keep all of these nuclear power plants going. They have the same problem we do. It is not only a question of quantity of manpower, but also of the quality of manpower needed to keep these things in operation.

PART TWO

AREAS OF CONFLICT

While the subject of naval missions is important, any discussion of the future of sea power must ultimately come around to potential areas of conflict. Most analysts would agree that except for possible conflict along the sea lines of communication, the days of battles on the high seas are gone forever. For indications of where conflict may arise, we must therefore look to the flanks, and the most likely candidates are the Mediterranean, Europe's northern flank, the Indian Ocean, the Western Pacific, and the Caribbean. Of these, the Mediterranean is of most immediate concern.

As Lieutenant Commander Bruce Watson points out in his paper, there has been an American presence in the Mediterranean Sea since the end of World War II, with at least one aircraft carrier since 1947. The Soviet navy started deploying a permanent group to the area in 1958. However, it was not until 1967 that U.S.–U.S.S.R. rivalry became a dominant Mediterranean theme. Commander Watson traces the events of the past thirty-odd years, pointing out the problems the Soviet navy has had in establishing a presence, first in Albania and then in Egypt. He also notes the reactions of the two superpowers to conflicts that have arisen in the area, such as the various Arab-Israeli wars and the Lebanon crisis.

Looking toward the twenty-first century, we see that both super-powers face major problems. As Commander Watson notes, the ultimate goal of controlling the Suez Canal still eludes the Soviet Union. It does not yet exert a dominant influence over any of the exits from the Mediterranean, and the U.S. Sixth Fleet continues to pose a strategic and political threat. He indicates that the Soviet Mediterranean force level is currently declining but warns us that it can be reinforced quickly from the Black Sea fleet. Finally, he notes that the political value of the

Soviet fleet is presently underutilized, which should cause Moscow great concern.

The outlook for the Sixth Fleet is not very sanguine. As Bruce Watson states, the declining force level of the U.S. fleet may cause difficulties in the future, and the changing balance of power is affecting— and could even undermine—the cohesion of NATO and the security of Israel. The Sixth Fleet is also much more vulnerable to geopolitical changes than is its Soviet counterpart. Finally, the problem of supporting the Sixth Fleet could become more difficult. In short, both the Soviet and the American fleets face some important and potentially crippling problems as we approach the twenty-first century.

As Vice Admiral Steinhaus points out in his paper, those who think of NATO's northern flank as a small, relatively insignificant area may be surprised to learn that it consists of the Greenland Sea, the Norwegian Sea, the North Sea, the Baltic Sea, and the English Channel, with a ratio of 90 percent water to 10 percent land, and that it has the highest density of shipping in the world. Another disturbing fact is that our Western allies in this area are resource poor; thus their survival depends on open sea lines of communication. Their Communist-bloc counterparts, on the other hand, are not so dependent on imported raw materials, thanks to the mineral resources of the U.S.S.R.

The strategic importance of the northern flank cannot be over-estimated. The Soviet northern fleet, which until World War II was the smallest of the Russian fleets, is now the largest, and Admiral Steinhaus reminds us that the American Second Fleet deployed in the area is the smaller of the two big U.S. fleets. Thus, the Western forces in the northern flank will have to accomplish a "typical" sea control mission, while the Warsaw Pact nations will have only to conduct a sea denial mission. He also reminds us that the problem is not simply control of the northern flank; the outcome of a fight in this area would decide whether the vital sea link between Europe and America could be maintained, even under "blitzkrieg" conditions, and for that reason, whether it would be decisive for the fate of Europe as well. If this area were taken by a blitzkrieg operation, the whole of central Europe would be threatened. It seems that as we look into the future the West will simply have to place more emphasis there. Admiral Steinhaus urges an increase in the naval forces on the northern flank.

In his essay on the Indian Ocean, Dale Tahtinen traces the importance of this area back to 1498, when Vasco da Gama set out in search of spices. For a great part of the nineteenth and twentieth centuries, the ocean was considered a British lake. Today spices are no longer important, but, as Dr. Tahtinen points out, almost three-quarters of the free world's oil is transported across this important body of water. In discussing existing and potential conflict areas, he includes almost every part of the littoral region, from Indonesia and Australia to the Horn of Africa, southern Africa, and the Middle Eastern countries around the Persian Gulf and the Red Sea.

Dr. Tahtinen's paper goes into detail on the Soviet challenge in these parts, which has been growing steadily for fifteen years or so. The Soviet Union normally keeps a small task force in the Indian Ocean but frequently augments it to fleet size with cruisers, destroyers, escorts, submarines, and even one of their large 18,000-ton helicopter carriers. The Soviet navy has several anchorages in the area and makes port visits to many countries. In response to this challenge, the American navy maintains a small permanent force of two destroyers and a flagship, which also is frequently augmented with task forces that have included an aircraft carrier. And, of course, the United States has a new naval facility at Diego Garcia.

One of the interesting aspects of the Indian Ocean area is the role played by outside powers other than the United States and the Soviet Union. Particularly intriguing is the presence of a French naval squadron that has at times numbered twenty ships. As we look to the future, one of the most interesting events may be the deployment of ships from the People's Republic of China, which would have far-reaching effects—not just for the indigenous states, but for the United States, the United Kingdom, France, and the Soviet Union as well.

The Western Pacific, according to Commander Soverel of the Naval War College, is in a state of flux. Interestingly, it is one of the few potential conflict areas in which there has been a reversal of usual relationships. With the seemingly pro-American attitude of the People's Republic of China, the Soviet Union may, for the first time, be facing a "two-front" war. The Sino-Soviet conflict has introduced much uncertainty about the future of the Western Pacific. This situation has given the United States some option, since, according to the paper, we no longer have to think about intervention in "continental" terms of requiring an intervening force. Rather, the role of American naval forces could be negative, that is, simply to carry out a denial mission. In that case, Western forces could actually be reduced, although this might be unwise, according to Commander Soverel. He suggests that the key to the American mission in the Western Pacific may well be Japan. Without our commitment to defend Japan, the U.S. naval mission could change from sea control to sea denial.

The last potential conflict area under discussion is the Caribbean. During the Cuban missile crisis of 1962, the U.S. Navy boarded and searched a Soviet merchant ship, marking the first such U.S.–U.S.S.R. confrontation in time of tension. Despite this famous incident, it was the appearance of a seven-ship Soviet naval squadron in the Caribbean in 1969 that, according to Ambassador Theberge, signaled a new chapter in U.S.–U.S.S.R. political-military competition. Since the Caribbean is not an area of "vital" interest to the Soviet Union, this deployment into a forward area was of some interest to the United States. More interesting was the Soviet attempt to establish a strategic submarine base in Cienfuegos, Cuba, which we rebuffed by applying political pressure. While Soviet naval activity in the area has lessened since the early 1970s, there has still been the occasional deployment of Soviet surface ships and submarines. There is always the possibility, however, that Moscow will try to establish a permanent Caribbean base and use it as a "bargaining chip" for U.S. withdrawal from Polaris bases in Rota or Holy Loch or for a corresponding reduction of U.S. surface forces from an area of comparable Soviet sensitivity, according to Ambassador Theberge.

Maritime Problems in the Mediterranean Sea As We Approach the Twenty-First Century

Bruce W. Watson

Soviet Strategy, Tactics, and Goals

The predominant theme of the current maritime context in the Mediterranean Sea is a Soviet-American naval rivalry which has existed since 1967. The scope of this rivalry has increased steadily and the problems attendant to it are likely to influence Mediterranean affairs into the twenty-first century, becoming increasingly critical as the rivalry expands.

The United States has maintained a naval presence in the Mediterranean since shortly after the end of World War II. At least one aircraft carrier has been present since 1947, and operations by a second carrier task group began in 1951. Since then, the force level of the Sixth Fleet has remained fairly constant, except for escalations during crises and periods of exercise activity. The mission of the fleet has been to provide "relevant military power" (to borrow Admiral Zumwalt's terminology) to contain Soviet influence and to support those aspects of American foreign policy aimed at influencing the affairs of the littoral Mediterranean nations. The mission has been both defensive (protecting NATO's southern flank) and offensive (posing a threat to the southwestern sector of the Soviet Union) and primarily political in orientation. Initially enjoying a position of absolute strategic and naval superiority, the Sixth Fleet has gradually been losing this advantage and now must vigorously compete with the Soviet navy for a position of superiority in the Mediterranean.[1] This shift in the balance of power stems from our inability to contend with two problems:

- Containing the expansion of Soviet naval power into the eastern Mediterranean—the United States had no way of preventing the

The opinions expressed in this paper are those of the author and do not necessarily represent those of the Department of the Navy, Department of Defense, or any other government agency.

[1] Horatio Rivero, "Why a U.S. Fleet in the Mediterranean?" *U.S. Naval Institute Proceedings,* vol. 103 (1977), p. 88; Elmo R. Zumwalt, Jr., *On Watch* (New York: Quadrangle/The New York Times Book Company, 1976), pp. 344-346.

Soviet Union's aggressive naval construction program that eventually led to global expansion of Soviet naval capabilities.

- Maintaining a dominant American naval presence in the Mediterranean—an inadequate U.S. naval construction program and worldwide American commitments have kept the Sixth Fleet at a static force level; given the expansion of Soviet naval power, a relative shift in the balance of naval power in the Mediterranean was inevitable.

Among the reasons motivating Soviet naval operations in the Mediterranean are: to offset the influence of Western naval power; to protect the southern flank of the U.S.S.R.; and to extend Soviet influence over the Suez Canal. These purposes are integrally related to the Soviet long-range strategy goals of: providing for the defense of the Soviet Union; advancing the Soviet Union's international position; establishing a preponderance of strength in the international balance of power; and exercising military power to effect changes in the international political system by transforming the maximum number of the world's social systems into communist systems conforming to the Soviet model.[2]

The Soviet naval goal of neutralizing the influence of the U.S. Sixth Fleet is related to the navy's missions of defending the Soviet Union and of working in support of Soviet foreign policy aspirations. With respect to the first mission—national defense—stationing the U.S. Sixth Fleet in the eastern Mediterranean has posed a significant threat to the southwestern sector of the Soviet Union, particularly its Black Sea ports, the oil fields at Baku, and the region's industrial complexes. The second, or political mission is intimately related to both the political value of Soviet military forces and the Soviet perception of the postwar international balance of power.

Prior to the end of World War II, the Soviet Union's immediate, Messianic aims centered on Europe and East Asia, and the relevant military power was the Soviet army, which proved its political utility in two ways: by occupying Eastern Europe, which enabled the Soviet Union to transform several European political systems into communist systems conforming to the Soviet model, and by guaranteeing the security of its own eastern borders. In the postwar period, a latent Soviet-American rivalry became the dominant theme, and as Admiral Gorshkov has stated, the Soviets perceived that the primary threat to their political aspirations was posed by the maritime alliance of NATO, of which the American navy was the key force. In 1956, the Twentieth Party Congress

---

[2] Joseph Schiebel, "The U.S.S.R. in World Affairs: New Tactics, New Strategy," in *The Soviet Union: The Seventies and Beyond,* ed. Bernard W. Eisenstat (Lexington, Mass.: Lexington Books, 1975), p. 74.

affirmed the decision of Soviet leadership to construct a modern navy that could actively compete with the United States for influence and adequately provide for the nation's defense. The objective of subsequent operations by the Soviet Mediterranean fleet was to neutralize the political value of the U.S. Sixth Fleet, eventually forcing the cessation of American naval operations in the Mediterranean.[3]

The Soviet Mediterranean fleet has also been part of a concerted effort to extend Soviet influence over the Suez Canal—a program that has consisted of political, economic, and cultural initiatives as well as military aid to Egypt. After consolidating its gains in Eastern Europe and Northeast Asia in the late 1940s and early 1950s, the Soviet Union focused its attention on the Third World. Under the guise of "peaceful coexistence," Moscow initiated a tactical reorientation aimed at exploiting the traditional antagonism between colonial powers and their colonies as a means of extending Soviet influence in the Third World. Its primary emphasis was on the Middle East, Africa, and South Asia. The Suez Canal was crucial, both as a link in the Soviet supply route to the Indian Ocean and as a route in deploying naval power. Soviet influence over the canal might not only deny or restrict use of the waterway for Western purposes, but, if the influence was sufficiently great, guarantee its use for Soviet purposes. Thus, Soviet designs on the Suez Canal are a second key to an accurate understanding of both Soviet naval operations and Soviet-American naval rivalry in the Mediterranean.

In attempting to accomplish its missions, the Soviet navy has had to resolve four problems:

- Developing the logistical capability to support a Mediterranean naval force, which, initally, was solved by using Albanian ports and, subsequently, by constructing a modern auxiliary force and by making use of Egyptian ports.

- Establishing a force sufficiently potent to successfully confront the Sixth Fleet, which was solved by constructing a fleet of modern combatants.

- Increasing the strength of the Mediterranean naval force to the point of being sufficiently powerful to diminish the influence of the Sixth Fleet and, ultimately, to effect an American naval departure from the area.

---

[3] Sergei G. Gorshkov, *Morskaya Moshch Gosudarstva* (Moscow: Voennoe Izdatelstvo Ministerstva Oborony SSSR, 1976), pp. 257-263, 266-270, 275-276, 278-279, 344-345, 380-386, 407; Sergei G. Gorshkov, "Okeanskiy Shchit Rodiny," *Kommunist Vooruzhennykh Sil,* vol. 14 (1975), pp. 12-13.

- Maximizing the political value of the fleet by actively participating in the maritime affairs of the Mediterranean littoral nations—conducting port visits; gaining access to Mediterranean port facilities; and carrying out politically motivated operations in support of Third World clients.

The Execution of Soviet Strategy

Although Soviet ships had operated in the Mediterranean for several decades, it was not until 1958 that Moscow established a permanent naval presence. The U.S.S.R. staged an impressive naval response to the Arab-Israeli war of June 1967, by stationing approximately seventy ships in the eastern Mediterranean. This action indicated that Moscow had solved two monumental problems in the intervening period: developing the ability to station a fleet in the Mediterranean, and insuring that this fleet possessed sufficient military and political power to challenge the U.S. Sixth Fleet.

Current Soviet naval operations on the high seas originated in 1956 when the Communist party decided to construct a modern navy. Given that the purpose behind the initial operations in the Atlantic and Pacific oceans was primarily to establish a defense perimeter around the U.S.S.R., the commencement of operations in the Mediterranean marked the first Soviet attempt to use their navy to influence affairs in the Third World. These operations began shortly after the Suez crisis of 1956, which involved a joint British, French, and Israeli military operation to seize the Suez Canal. The American response was characterized by an adroit use of naval power, in which U.S. forces were moved into the eastern Mediterranean and Arabian seas, generally converging on Suez. During the incident, the Soviet Union was unable to prevent Western naval operations and had to limit its opposition to protests through diplomatic channels. This incident must surely have reinforced the Soviet policy decision to initiate significant naval operations in the Mediterranean.

The Soviet navy's crucial task from 1956 until 1964 was to develop the ability to maintain a constant presence in the Mediterranean. The Montreux convention of 1936, which established rights of passage through the Turkish straits, prohibited submarines from using this waterway—the only exit from the Black Sea to the Mediterranean. Thus, Soviet submarines destined for Mediterranean operations could not be based in the Black Sea ports. From 1956 until the Lebanon crisis in 1958, Soviet Mediterranean naval operations were characterized by an intermittent rather than a constant force presence, highlighted by port visits to Albania, which presaged the future use of Albanian facilities by Soviet submarines.

Because of the limitations imposed by the Montreux convention, Moscow was unable to deploy sufficient naval power to influence the outcome of the Lebanon crisis of 1958. At the request of the Lebanese government, U.S. Marines were landed, and Lebanese political stability was reestablished. The Soviet naval response to these operations consisted only of publicizing regularly scheduled Black Sea naval exercises with an abnormal degree of fanfare. Possibly as a result of the 1958 crisis, the Soviets began stationing a naval force in the Mediterranean. Operating out of Vlonë, Albania, Soviet submarines began patrolling the Mediterranean. As shown in Tables 1 and 2, the annual number of ship/days spent in the Mediterranean by the Soviet navy increased from only 100 in 1956 to 5,600 in 1960; by 1960, Soviet naval ships spent almost three out of every four days in the Mediterranean.

In June 1961, as a result of the Sino-Soviet dispute (perhaps also because of Albanian fears concerning Soviet designs on their nation), Albania expelled the Soviet naval forces from Vlonë, seizing two Soviet submarines in the process. The loss of these facilities hampered Soviet

Table 1

Soviet Naval Presence in the Mediterranean: Ship/Days per Year, 1956–1977 [a]

Year	Number of Ship/Days	Year	Number of Ship/Days
1956	100	1967	8,800
1957	600	1968	11,700
1958	1,000	1969	15,400
1959	4,100	1970	17,400
1960	5,600	1971	18,700
1961	2,300	1972	17,700
1962	800	1973	20,600
1963	600	1974	20,200
1964	1,800	1975	20,000
1965	3,700	1976	18,600
1966	5,400	1977	16,300

[a] Data are based on official U.S. Navy statistics. The figures for the years prior to 1969 have been extrapolated from approximated information and are not considered as valid as those for the years 1969–1976.

Table 2
Geographical Distribution of Soviet Naval Presence on the High Seas: Percentage of Ship/Days per Year, 1956–1977 [a]

Year	Mediterranean Sea	Indian Ocean	Atlantic Ocean	Caribbean Sea	Pacific Ocean
1956	13	0	62	0	25
1957	26	0	65	0	9
1958	31	0	41	0	28
1959	58	0	29	0	13
1960	72	3	20	0	5
1961	44	0	42	0	14
1962	12	2	65	0	21
1963	10	2	59	0	29
1964	20	0	58	0	22
1965	32	0	47	0	21
1966	39	0	40	0	21
1967	48	1	31	0	20
1968	51	5	26	0	18
1969	44	12	27	1	16
1970	40	11	31	2	16
1971	42	9	33	2	14
1972	36	18	30	4	12
1973	41	18	26	3	12
1974	38	20	26	2	14
1975	42	15	27	2	14
1976	39	15	30	2	14
1977	34	14	33	3	16

[a] Data are based on official U.S. Navy statistics. The figures for the years prior to 1969 have been extrapolated from approximated information and are not considered as valid as those for the years 1969–1976.

naval activities, as evidenced by the reduced naval presence during the next few years.[4]

The Soviet Union's first problem—sustaining a large presence in the Mediterranean—was soon solved, thanks to the naval construction program initiated in the latter 1950s. With new cruisers, destroyers, submarines, and supply ships joining the fleet in the early 1960s, the Soviet navy was able to begin expanding its Mediterranean operations by 1964.

[4] George S. Dragnich, *The Soviet Union's Quest for Access to Naval Facilities in Egypt Prior to the June War of 1967* (Arlington, Virginia: Center for Naval Analyses, 1974), pp. 17-18.

For the next decade, the Soviet naval presence in the area continued without interruption; from a low of 10 percent in 1963, it had increased to 42 percent of the total Soviet presence on the high seas by 1975.

Having solved the primary problem of establishing a naval presence in the Mediterranean, Moscow's next immediate problem was the strengthening of its Mediterranean naval force sufficiently to pose a challenge to the U.S. Sixth Fleet, militarily and politically. The Soviet solution was to station numerous modern combatants in the Mediterranean. With the exception of ballistic-missile, nuclear-powered submarines (which fulfill a strategic mission targeted against the West and, therefore, must operate in the Atlantic and Pacific oceans), the most sophisticated Soviet combatants—*Kara, Kynda,* and *Kresta I* and *II* guided-missile cruisers; Charlie-class nuclear-powered cruise-missile submarines; and both Moskva-class guided-missile helicopter ships—have conducted the overwhelming majority of their fleet operations in the Mediterranean. The force level averaged about five ships daily in 1964 and increased yearly from 1965 through 1967.[5]

Having solved the problem of projecting naval power in the Mediterranean through the construction of a modern navy, Moscow was able to maintain an increased naval presence in 1964 without access to Mediterranean ports. Realizing the political and logistical value of such access, the Soviet navy attempted to gain entry into Egyptian ports shortly after its expulsion from Albania in 1961. This effort was highlighted by several diplomatic visits to Egypt by Premier Khrushchev, Premier Kosygin, Marshal Grechko, and Admiral Gorshkov as well as by naval port visits to Port Said and to Alexandria. In his extensive study of this effort, George Dragnich concluded that in June 1967, the Soviets still had not gained access to Egyptian facilities, in spite of substantial military aid, economic assistance, and an aggressive diplomatic barrage. He suggested that it was the June 1967 Arab-Israeli war that finally turned the tide of resistance, since fighting this war had so weakened Egypt's and Syria's strategic positions vis-à-vis Israel, that they had to succumb to Soviet demands.[6]

The Arab-Israeli conflict of June 1967, was a landmark on several other accounts. Although it enabled the Soviet Union to greatly increase its position of influence in Egypt—thus dramatically increasing the political use of the fleet—the gain was more than offset by the closing of the Suez Canal—whose control was the ultimate Soviet goal.

[5] Norman Polmar, *Soviet Naval Power: Challenge for the 1970's,* rev. ed. (New York: Crane, Russak and Company, 1974), p. 66; Office of the Chief of Naval Operations, *Understanding Soviet Naval Developments* (Washington, D.C.: Government Printing Office, 1975), p. 11.

[6] Dragnich, *Soviet Union's Quest,* pp. 21-22, 29, 44.

It significantly affected Soviet naval operating patterns and merchant shipping. In the case of naval patterns, there is considerable evidence to indicate that the Soviet Union intended to establish a standing naval force in the Indian Ocean in the late 1960s, to home-port most of this force in the Black Sea, and deploy it to the Indian Ocean via the Suez Canal. With the canal closed, it had to base these ships in the Pacific. To sustain such operations, the navy had to transfer additional ships from the Atlantic, which resulted in a fragmentation of Soviet naval power, isolating several combatants, thus precluding their timely participation in crises in the Atlantic or in the Mediterranean.

With respect to merchant shipping, closure of the Suez Canal occurred during the height of the Soviet logistical effort in support of North Vietnam. Since a significant portion of Soviet-supplied materials were transported to North Vietnam on merchant ships from Black Sea ports, the loss of the Suez waterway essentially doubled the distance of each voyage. Assuming that Vietnam assistance took priority over other merchant-fleet commitments, one could reasonably assume that Moscow curtailed deliveries of arms and supplies to the Third World in order to sustain the Soviet effort in Southeast Asia. Furthermore, the merchant fleet's role in world commerce would also have been curtailed, resulting in a loss of revenue for the Soviet Union.

The war in Vietnam also impacted on Soviet and American naval operations in the Mediterranean. In contrast to its minimal performance in the 1956 Suez and the 1958 Lebanon crises, the Soviet Union augmented its Mediterranean fleet during the 1967 war in the Middle East. The resulting force numbered over seventy ships, including two cruisers, fifteen destroyers, and ten submarines. The United States, which had made strong responses to the 1956 and 1958 crises, maintained a low profile during the 1967 crisis. It was the first indication of our yielding to pressure from the Soviet Union and the Third World. As opposed to its decisive 1956 and 1958 operations, U.S. actions in 1967 reflected American desires to convey a measured response. According to Admiral Wylie, the restrictions on American operations could be inferred from the fact that during that war, scheduled port visits in the Mediterranean were neither canceled nor curtailed; American amphibious forces were in Malta, considerably away from the arena of hostilities; and the U.S.S. *Intrepid,* en route to Vietnam and in the Mediterranean in early June, was not subordinated to the Sixth Fleet but remained independent and left the area shortly before the war began.[7]

---

[7] J. C. Wylie, "The Sixth Fleet and American Diplomacy," *Soviet-American Rivalry in the Middle East,* ed. J. C. Hurewitz (New York: Frederick A. Praeger, 1969), pp. 57-60.

Admittedly, the crisis of 1967 was different from those of 1956 and 1958. The American response to the Arab-Israeli war was tailored to meet the demands of a situation in which Israel was scoring a decisive victory and American involvement was not mandatory. However, the response was considerably less deliberate than those of 1956 and 1958, and we must conclude that in 1967, for a variety of reasons—including Soviet policy and deployed Soviet naval power—American naval operations would hereafter be conducted in consideration of both Soviet and Third World desires, and that the Soviet Union was making progress toward achieving a naval balance of power in the Mediterranean. With respect to the Soviet Union, its response indicated that it had solved the problem of being able to project sufficient naval power in the Mediterranean to confront the United States, at least politically. However, Soviet gains in that conflict were more than offset by the adverse impact effected by the closure of the Suez Canal and the subsequent failure of Soviet policy, which, from 1967 until 1973, was directed at creating an Egyptian military force capable of defeating Israel and recapturing the Suez.

Since 1967, the shift in the Mediterranean balance of naval power has been in favor of the Soviet Union. The force level of their interwar Mediterranean fleet increased considerably, averaging between thirty-five and forty ships daily: from ten to fifteen major surface combatants, from eight to ten submarines, and from ten to fifteen auxiliaries. This presence rose to a peak of 18,700 ship/days in 1971, amounting to a daily average of fifty-one ships. Relative to its global naval activity, however, the Mediterranean presence declined rather consistently, from 51 percent in 1968 to 36 percent in 1972, reflecting that the Mediterranean represented only one element of Soviet naval operations on the high seas; Soviet fleets were also operating in the Atlantic, Pacific, and Indian oceans and the Caribbean Sea.[8]

Between 1967 and 1973, Mediterranean naval operations were highlighted by the Soviet presence in Egypt. Soviet ships operated out of Alexandria, Port Said, and Matruh, and a territorial anchorage in the Gulf of Sollum; Soviet naval aircraft were staged from Egyptian bases. The presence of Soviet ships and aircraft resulted in obvious benefits for both the U.S.S.R. and Egypt. For the Soviet Union, use of Alexandria for repair and logistical support facilitated the fleet's supply problem. The presence of Soviet personnel in all the major Egyptian ports along the Mediterranean coast also enabled the Soviet Union to monitor, and probably even to actively participate in Egypt's naval and

---

[8] Polmar, *Soviet Naval Power,* p. 66; Office of Naval Operations, *Understanding Soviet Naval Developments,* p. 11.

commercial maritime affairs. In addition, use of Egyptian airfields extended Soviet surveillance over the eastern Mediterranean. For Egypt, the presence of Soviet ships and aircraft afforded additional security for its military and commercial facilities, since fear of Soviet retaliation may have discouraged Israeli attacks. At any rate, these operations represented only two aspects of the total Soviet involvement in Egyptian political, economic, cultural, and military affairs—a concerted action that represented unprecedented Soviet influence over another nation not within the Soviet bloc or contiguous to its borders.[9]

The outcome of the June 1967 Arab-Israeli war enabled the Soviet Union to exercise a long-coveted degree of control in Egypt but not to achieve its ultimate goal—extending its influence over the Suez Canal. From 1967 until 1973, Soviet efforts to improve Egypt's military capability were the means to one specific end—recapturing the Suez Canal and exercising further influence in Egypt. In 1971, Moscow's attempts to extend influence backfired as Egypt began to curtail Soviet involvement. In 1972, access for Soviet naval aircraft in Egypt was terminated. Over the next few years, the Soviet advisers were expelled, and in 1976, Egypt denied the Soviets further naval access to Alexandria.

In attempting to improve the Egyptian military capability, the Soviets were more successful. The Arab-Israeli war of October 1973 marked the first time that Egypt was not overwhelmingly defeated. At the war's conclusion, Egypt held a portion of the east bank of the Suez, and, after postwar negotiations, gained possession of both banks. The Suez later was reopened under Egyptian control.

The prolonged 1973 Arab-Israeli conflict required more active involvement from both the Soviet Union and the United States than had the 1967 war. In response to the outbreak of the hostilities, the Soviets almost doubled the force level of their Mediterranean fleet—from fifty to almost one hundred ships. The United States also expanded the Sixth Fleet up to a force level of approximately sixty-five ships. Further augmentation of the fleet was difficult. Between American commitments to Vietnam and the retirement of many older combatants, the United States had little or no naval power to spare. Initially, the U.S. Sixth Fleet continued routine operations except for the U.S.S. *Independence* task group which sortied from Athens and joined the Sixth Fleet flagship in a holding area to the south of Crete. Subsequently, the U.S.S. *Kennedy* and three escorts were ordered to proceed from the North Sea to a holding area west of the Strait of Gibraltar. Within the Mediter-

---

[9] Office of Naval Operations, *Understanding Soviet Naval Developments,* p. 11; J. C. Hurewitz, *Middle East Politics: The Military Dimension* (New York: Frederick A. Praeger, 1969), pp. 99-100.

ranean, U.S. amphibious forces were ordered to remain in Soudha Bay, Crete, and the U.S.S. *Roosevelt* task group was ordered not to proceed into the eastern Mediterranean. This action represented a compromise between military posture and political expediency.[10]

The prolonged conflict exhausted Egyptian and Israeli supplies, and both the Soviet Union and the United States began airlifts to rearm their respective allies. On October 24–25, when it was obvious that, if left unchecked, the Israelis would recapture recent Egyptian territorial gains, the Soviet-American confrontation climaxed. Moscow suggested that both nations deploy forces to man the cease-fire lines. Secretary Brezhnev further stated that, should the United States reject the proposal, the Soviet Union would consider undertaking a unilateral action. The United States responded by ordering the Sixth Fleet to accomplish several contingency operations: moving the *Kennedy* task group into the Mediterranean; directing the *Roosevelt* to proceed eastward in the Mediterranean and join the *Independence;* and ordering U.S. amphibious forces to sortie from Soudha Bay and proceed to an area south of Crete. The Soviet Union decided against sending troops into the Middle East and the tension gradually subsided.[11]

Current Soviet Operations

Current Soviet operations in the Mediterranean reflect a continuation of previous trends. The total naval presence has declined slightly each year since 1973, presently consisting of a force that will log from 16,000 to 18,000 ship/days annually—an average daily presence of from forty-four to forty-nine ships. Although its force level has increased by several hundred percent since 1958, the Soviet fleet remains concentrated in the eastern Mediterranean, with only a moderate presence in the central and a nominal presence in the western portions of the sea. This suggests the preeminence of the fleet's foreign policy mission of influencing affairs in the maritime approaches to the Suez Canal. The defensive mission of providing for the security of the Soviet Union seems to have taken a secondary rank since if Moscow considered the defensive mission more important, it would have extended the naval presence westward to keep the area of potential conflict farther from the Soviet border.

At present, as before, Soviet naval activities consist of routine operations, surveillance, fleet exercises, and port visits. Routine opera-

[10] Zumwalt, *On Watch,* pp. 435-437. It should be noted that the U.S.S. *Hancock* and escorts transited the Arabian Sea and provided the United States with a preponderance of power along the southern coast of the conflict area.

[11] Zumwalt, *On Watch,* pp. 439-449.

tions involve prolonged periods of immobility in several Mediterranean anchorages, reflecting a weak Soviet resupply capability, an absence of an underway replenishment capability, and an inability to maintain sustained operations at sea.

The anchorages used by the Soviet navy coincide with several normal Soviet patrols and stations and are ideally located for surveillance of Mediterranean maritime activity. In the western Mediterranean, a few ships are normally at anchor in the Alboran Basin, where they can monitor merchant and naval movements through the Strait of Gibraltar. In the central Mediterranean, Soviet ships are stationed in the Gulf of Hammamet, just south of the Strait of Sicily, where they can monitor all transits into and out of the area. In the eastern Mediterranean, Soviet ships are stationed just north of the Gulf of Sollum, northeast of Crete, and near the Greek island of Kíthira. From the Kíthira and north-of-Sollum anchorages, the Soviets can accurately monitor all movements into the eastern Mediterranean, and from the Kíthira and east-of-Crete anchorages, they can monitor traffic moving in and out of the Aegean Sea. In addition, Soviet ships in the north-of-Sollum and east-of-Crete anchorages are able to monitor traffic to and from the Suez Canal. Finally, the ships in the area east of Cyprus enable the Soviets to maintain a presence in the far eastern Mediterranean, in proximity to the Syrian, Lebanese, and Israeli coasts.

Soviet naval exercises are frequent and generally of short duration, hardly ever lasting more than a few days. Participants generally sortie from eastern Mediterranean anchorages, exercise, and return to the anchorages. Exercise scenarios are realistic, encompassing both anti-aircraft carrier and antisubmarine warfare scenarios.

In addition to the type of monitoring conducted from the aforementioned anchorages, the Soviet navy can accomplish more active surveillance using intelligence collectors that conduct patrols off the U.S. naval base at Rota, Spain, and until recently, off the Syrian and Israeli coasts. Soviet ships also conduct fairly constant surveillance of U.S. aircraft carriers operating in the eastern Mediterranean.[12]

The operating patterns of the Soviet navy vary with the type of ships involved. Surface combatants and amphibious ships spend the majority of their Mediterranean deployments in the anchorages while auxiliary ships transit to and from Mediterranean and Black Sea ports with fuel and supplies for deployed combatants. We know the least about the deployment of Soviet submarines, but it is generally believed that they spend the majority of their time on patrol, with periodic interludes at anchor for crew rest, ship upkeep, and repair of equipment.

---

[12] Office of Naval Operations, *Understanding Soviet Naval Developments,* p. 29.

Problems Confronting the Soviet Navy

The operations of the Soviet Mediterranean fleet in 1977 stand as a vivid testament to Moscow's success in overcoming two extremely difficult problems—establishing a standing naval force in the Mediterranean and equipping this force with sufficient power to challenge the U.S. Sixth Fleet. Resolving these problems has enabled the Soviet Union to challenge U.S. naval hegemony in the Mediterranean and has provided it with a means of fulfilling its long-range policy aspirations. However, the Soviet Union has not fulfilled its maximum goals in the Mediterranean; to achieve success it must overcome several problems of which the five discussed in the sections that follow seem of paramount importance.

Control of the Suez Canal. To reiterate, the June 1967, Middle East war enabled the Soviet Union to exert great influence over Egyptian affairs, but interdiction of the Suez prevented Moscow from extending the same influence over the canal. The 1971–1973 period brought a curtailment of Soviet influence, while events after the October 1973, Middle East war allowed for the reopening of the canal under Egyptian auspices. Thus, the Soviet-Egyptian relationship of 1977 had reverted to the 1966 situation, to the extent that the Soviet Union was hoping to extend its influence to the canal, and an independent Egypt was trying to limit Soviet influence in its internal affairs.

Other aspects of the 1977 Soviet-Egyptian context were decidedly different from those of 1966. For example, Soviet influence with respect to the Arab-Israeli relationship was extremely low. Joseph Schiebel has observed that, tactically, Soviet foreign policy operates through the exploitation of existing adversary relationships, or through the creation of such relationships when none exist, in order to gain concessions it could not otherwise obtain. The evidence is that Soviet policy in the Middle East has operated through exploitation of the Arab-Israeli adversary relationship, and Soviet success in Egypt was, until 1973, directly related to both Egypt's losses in its war with Israel and its alienation from the West.

Egyptian success in the October 1973 war went far toward erasing the national disgrace incurred in June 1967, and its regained national pride and the economic benefits of continued peace have done much to moderate Egypt's position vis-à-vis the Soviet Union. Consequently, negotiation, rather than war, has become the preferred vehicle for the further resolution of existing Arab-Israeli animosity. When this trend toward a negotiated settlement is viewed in light of the current American role as principal arbitrator between Egypt and Israel, Soviet influence on the Arab-Israeli relationship appears even less significant. Thus, although the ultimate Soviet aim of extending influence over the Suez Canal remains unchanged, the more immediate Soviet goal of gaining a foothold in Egypt has been frustrated by changes in Israeli-Egyptian relations—changes that are adverse to the Soviet Union but favorable to the United States. The outlook for Soviet Middle East policy will remain pessimistic as long as Egyptian political and economic conditions do not deteriorate dramatically. To make that outlook optimistic, Moscow would have to create a force or movement capable of reversing current trends and of precipitating a change in Egyptian leadership. The Soviet Union apparently rejects the idea of assassinating President Sadat or of a *coup d'état* by radical Egyptian officers as optimal methods of reestablishing influence—at least for the immediate future. Furthermore, since we are in the unique position of being able to influence Israel and to moderate its desires, the Soviet Union has a slim chance of replacing the United States as the primary arbitrator in the dispute. Based on recent Soviet arms deliveries to Libya, current Libyan-Egyptian tension, and current Egyptian aloofness to Soviet overtures, it appears that the Soviet Union has chosen manipulation of the adverse Libyan-Egyptian relationship as the optimal method of exerting pressure on Egypt.

Although positing future Soviet manipulations of the Libyan-Egyptian relationship is conjectural, one could readily identify several benefits for the Soviet Union should such a policy prove successful. First, Egypt's current independent position, which is based largely on its prestige within the Arab world and the political popularity of President Sadat, would be adversely affected should the current animosity between Libya and Egypt erupt into general hostilities. Such a conflict would further fragment the cohesion of the Arab world and reduce President Sadat's prestige as a foremost Arab leader. Second, a Libyan-Egyptian war would be unpopular with factions interested in maintaining a united Arab front against Israel. Third, the cost of conducting such military operations would surely have a negative impact on Egyptian economic growth. Rather than risk such a situation, Egypt may be willing to come to terms with the Soviet Union, and accordingly, the Soviet Union would be in a better position to influence Egyptian affairs.[13]

Access to the Mediterranean. The fact that the Turkish straits, Suez Canal, and the Strait of Gibraltar are controlled by nations potentially hostile to the Soviet Union not only would restrict the use of Soviet naval

---

[13] Schiebel, "U.S.S.R. in World Affairs," pp. 74-75.

power in wartime but also would drastically affect current Soviet naval operations in the Atlantic and Indian oceans and the Mediterranean Sea.

In the case of the Turkish straits, much has been written about Soviet circumvention of the provisions of the Montreux Convention governing the passage of warships through the Bosporus and the Dardenelles. One commentator, for example, recently argued that "the Articles of the Convention were written primarily to protect those nations with Black Sea coastlines and to provide an uncancelable 'ticket to the Mediterranean.' "[14] Easily interdicted in time of war and diplomatically restricted in time of peace, the straits provide a very real strategic problem for the U.S.S.R. As a result, Moscow has maintained an inflated Soviet Mediterranean fleet to prevent a "bottling up" of Soviet naval power in the Black Sea. This use of the fleet coupled with the use of contingency or false Turkish strait declarations has facilitated Soviet access to the Mediterranean from the Black Sea. However, development of alternative naval facilities capable of supporting the majority of the Soviet combatants now based in the Black Sea is the only completely acceptable long-range solution. Such facilities—preferably along the Indian Ocean or, possibly, the Mediterranean—not only would assure the movement of Soviet ships between the Indian Ocean and the Mediterranean Sea but also would further guarantee the presence of adequate naval power in both areas.

With respect to the Suez Canal, the present state of Soviet-Egyptian relations has had a decided effect on Soviet naval operating patterns. Only a few Soviet combatants have passed through the Suez since its reopening, and no regular augmentation of the Soviet Indian Ocean squadron from the Black Sea fleet should be anticipated until such time as Moscow perceives that use of the canal for combatant transits is reasonably secure. Minimum requirements for such security would probably be a resumption of Soviet influence over Egypt and a decline of the Israeli military position sufficient to ensure that Israel would be incapable of militarily interdicting the canal. At present, Soviet Indian Ocean operations require the stationing of significant numbers of major surface combatants in the Pacific, where they are so geographically isolated they cannot easily be deployed for crisis management in the West. Consequently, future Soviet policy will be directed at guaranteeing the security of Soviet warships passing through the Suez Canal.

The Gibraltar strait also poses a potential barrier to the Soviet Union. Passage through the strait can easily be influenced by the British, who control Gibraltar, as well as by Spain and Portugal. The importance

---

[14] John A. Gregoire, "The Montreux Convention . . . A Perennial Soviet Ticket to the Mediterranean," *U.S. Naval Institute Proceedings,* vol. 103 (1977), p. 177.

of Gibraltar is sure to increase in the future, as the Soviet Union continues to increase its presence along the West African coast. Ships operating off Africa are currently staged from the Black Sea, Baltic, and northern fleets. Should the Soviet presence in West Africa continue to increase as expected, then the use of Gibraltar strait by the Soviet navy will become crucial. Thus, Moscow may augment the Soviet naval presence in the western Mediterranean and initiate diplomatic overtures to Morocco and Great Britain (or Spain if proprietorship of Gibraltar reverts to that country) in order to assure continued Soviet use of the strait.

Threats Posed by the Sixth Fleet. Although there has been a relative shift in the Soviet-American balance of power in the Mediterranean, the Sixth Fleet continues to pose a unique and potent threat to the Soviet Union. From the eastern Mediterranean, it is continually prepared to launch timely strikes against Soviet forces, and its extremely fast response time, among other outstanding attributes, cannot be overstated. Admiral Zumwalt tells us that in crises that have arisen since World War II, the "relevant power" has been naval power in almost all cases, and that naval power will continue to be the relevant power in all future crisis situations except for those involving nuclear attacks. As principal Sixth Fleet scenarios, he listed the defense of NATO's southern flank and response to Middle Eastern conflicts.[15] Admiral Rivero has posited a similar argument, maintaining that the Sixth Fleet "must be counted as an essential component of NATO defense of the land," and that a reduction of the fleet's aircraft-carrier strength in peacetime "could only have disastrous consequences for the wartime scheme of defense in the southeastern sector."[16] The Sixth Fleet also provides the only relevant power in Middle Eastern conflict situations, as periodic Arab-Israeli wars have so often demonstrated.

Currently, the Soviet Mediterranean fleet is not, in itself, a sufficient threat to prevent American operations in the area, and U.S. commitments to NATO and Israel necessitate the continued presence of the Sixth Fleet over the next several decades. The Soviet response to the threat posed by the Sixth Fleet appears to be both military and diplomatic in nature.

Militarily, the force level of the Soviet Mediterranean fleet has declined in recent years. Nevertheless, it is the most concentrated Soviet presence on the high seas, and Moscow continues to deploy the most modern surface combatants as fleet entities. The concentration of Soviet

---

[15] Zumwalt, *On Watch*, pp. 344-346, 526-527.
[16] Rivero, "Why a U.S. Fleet?" p. 86.

naval forces is not expected to change in the next several years, although the present trend of a slightly declining force level will probably continue.

With respect to diplomacy, the Soviet Union has publicly been a proponent of naval-force reductions in the Mediterranean. In 1971, Brezhnev proposed that naval deployments to the Mediterranean Sea and the Indian Ocean be limited, and in 1974, he proposed that ships carrying nuclear weapons be withdrawn from the Mediterranean. While the implementation of this latter proposal would require significant concessions from the Soviets, it would call for even greater concessions from the United States. For the Soviet Union, denuclearization of the Mediterranean would drastically reduce the utility of the Black Sea ports, since many classes of major Soviet surface combatants are assumed to be equipped with nuclear weapons and, thus, would be prohibited from operating in the Mediterranean while carrying these arms. Restrictions on the Black Sea Fleet, would mean that the Soviet Union would have no facilities for staging nuclear-weapons-equipped combatants along the entire area from its Baltic to its Pacific ports—a situation that would considerably increase the Soviet navy's logistics and deployment problems. Furthermore, the current situations in the Middle East and in southern Europe offer great potential for the use of Soviet naval power, and it is doubtful that Moscow would want to deny itself a significant portion of combatant naval power while these political opportunities remain.[17]

However, the denuclearization of the Sixth Fleet would afford the Soviet Union the following advantages. First, it would remove the strategic threat against the Soviet Union; second, it would significantly reduce the security of the southern NATO flank; and third, it would drastically reduce American influence in the Middle East. The concessions on the part of the Soviet Union—primarily, the curtailing of the use of the Black Sea for naval purposes—might not be as prohibitive as they first appear, especially if alternative bases are established. Some commentators are critical of the value of the Black Sea bases. Admiral Stansfield Turner and Commander Thibault, for example, recently noted that the lack of adequate air cover for Soviet surface combatants operating in the eastern Mediterranean is such a liability that if hostilities were imminent, such combatants would probably not be deployed from the Black Sea. The Soviet leadership probably perceives this vulnerability and will direct future Soviet policy toward a solution. In this context,

---

[17] Anne M. Kelly and Charles Petersen, *Recent Changes in Soviet Naval Policy: Prospects for Arms Limitations in the Mediterranean and Indian Ocean* (Arlington, Virginia: Center for Naval Analyses, 1976), p. 1.

it is conceivable that the Soviets are advocating force reduction merely to keep this option open and intend to further emphasize it when greater Soviet benefits can be accrued from its implementation.[18]

Declining Force Level. As shown in Table 1, the fleet's force level reached an apex in 1973 and has subsequently declined; Table 2 indicates that since 1968, the Mediterranean fleet has accounted for a rather steadily declining percentage of the total Soviet naval presence on the high seas, and in 1977 the Soviet fleet logged approximately 16,300 days in the Mediterranean, amounting to 34 percent of the total Soviet naval presence on the high seas. The declining force level may reflect a Soviet perception that the current naval force in the Mediterranean is more than adequate to fulfill its assigned missions, and that a curtailment of the fleet's size can be accomplished without serious detriment to Soviet national security or to Soviet foreign-policy initiatives.

The declining percentage of the Soviet Mediterranean presence relative to the total Soviet presence on the high seas, is the result of increased Soviet operations in the Caribbean Sea, along the west coast of Africa, and in the Indian Ocean, and it may reflect merely a more efficient use of available naval power. On the other hand, the decline may reflect an overextension of existing naval power, in which case Moscow may have curtailed the force level of the Mediterranean fleet to enable operations in other ocean areas. The greater declines in 1976 and 1977 may reflect both an overextension of naval power and an inability to sustain a larger fleet in the Mediterranean without adequate access to Mediterranean port facilities.

If the decline in Soviet Mediterranean forces since 1973 stems from an overextension of Soviet naval power, then it should be noted that this problem has by no means reached criticality. Further, given the current Soviet construction programs and the ratio of ship/days on the high seas to the total Soviet naval order of battle, the availability of Soviet ships for deployment to the several ocean areas should not become a critical problem for at least several years. However, in view of the increasingly high cost of constructing combatant platforms and the expected expansion of the Soviet naval presence in the South Atlantic and Indian oceans and the Caribbean Sea, it is conceivable that the Soviet Union will eventually find it difficult to maintain an adequate

---

[18] Stansfield Turner and George Thibault, "Countering the Soviet Threat in the Mediterranean," *U.S. Naval Institute Proceedings,* vol. 103 (1977), p. 31.

presence in the Mediterranean. The impact of such a development would be benign if it attenuated the aggressiveness of Soviet actions in the area; on the other hand, if the Soviet Union were deeply involved politically in the Mediterranean or the Middle East and without adequate naval power and had to pose a strategic threat to achieve its aims or honor its commitments, the impact could be rather sinister.

The availability of Mediterranean port facilities may prove to be a more immediate Soviet problem. Having the use of Albanian port facilities furthered Soviet naval operations in the Mediterranean from 1958 until 1960; termination of this courtesy led to a hiatus in Soviet operations. Thanks to its active naval construction program, the Soviet navy was able to resume Mediterranean operations in 1964, and access to Egyptian ports after June 1967 enabled it to maintain a much larger presence in the area. At the time, most commentators believed that access to Egyptian facilities, while a great convenience, was not mandatory for successful Soviet operations in the Mediterranean. However, after the Soviets were expelled from Alexandria in April 1976, there was a significant decline in the force level of the Soviet fleet. Since this decline coincided with the general curtailment of the Soviet presence that began in 1973, it may indicate that although the navy can certainly maintain a Mediterranean fleet without access to Mediterranean port facilities, it may be experiencing difficulty in conducting operations on the 1968–1975 scale. Thus, although Moscow may have decided to curtail Mediterranean operations, it may also have plans to significantly augment the fleet in the event of crises, making greater use of its Turkish straits contingency declarations than it has in the past. Since Soviet ships can deploy from their Black Sea bases to the eastern Mediterranean in as little as forty-eight to seventy-two hours (subject to the provisions of the Montreux Convention), the Soviets need very little forewarning to order a massive force into the area. Yet, as the unexpected outbreak of the October 1973 Arab-Israeli war has demonstrated, Middle Eastern crises can erupt with almost no warning. Thus, Moscow probably considers the present curtailment of Mediterranean forces less desirable than the larger naval presence previously maintained.

Soviet actions since their expulsion from Alexandria support this hypothesis. The Soviets have recently made greater use of Syrian facilities; but, located in the far eastern Mediterranean and extremely congested, they are less than ideal for Soviet purposes. Consequently, the Soviets seem to be actively seeking access to alternative ports. A recent prolonged visit to Yugoslavia by Fleet Admiral Gorshkov apparently failed to elicit significant concessions, and Soviet use of Yugo-

115

slavian ports has not noticeably increased. Moreover, the restricted waters leading to Yugoslavian ports would offer only a partial or stop-gap solution. Recent port visits to Tunisia and Algeria may also reflect Soviet attempts to gain access to facilities in either or both of these countries.

Denial of access to Alexandria has certainly made logistical support and ship repair more complex for the Soviet navy. Although it is too early to state conclusively that the denial of such facilities is preventing the Soviets from maintaining a force on the scale of that previously seen, recent Soviet naval and diplomatic actions seem to reflect Soviet hopes of gaining access to port facilities elsewhere in the Mediterranean. This problem, which will probably dominate Soviet actions for years to come, could be alleviated by access to the ports of several Mediterranean nations, such as Syria, Yugoslavia, and possibly Algeria or Tunisia. Should this occur, the Soviets would no longer be dependent on any one port or nation, and a denial by any one nation would not present the massive logistical problem incurred through the loss of Alexandria in 1976.

Underutilization of the Fleet's Political Value. The political value of the Soviet navy was most significantly realized during the 1967–1972 period, when the fleet had access to Egyptian ports and Soviet naval aircraft were staged from Egyptian airfields. Political utilization of the navy has since declined, suffering an additional setback in 1976, when the fleet was expelled from Alexandria. The Soviet navy's political tasks at present seem to be limited to maintaining a presence in the eastern Mediterranean and carrying out a moderate program of port visits. Thus, it would be valid to state that the political value of the Soviet fleet consists of exerting a broad-scale global influence by its rather innocuous presence; a more focused influence on certain countries via port visits; and a clearly defined influence only in Syria and Yugoslavia, where the Soviets have considerable access. Given the political mission of the fleet and the inherent messianism of Soviet communism, it seems logical that Moscow will continue its attempts to exert influence on selected littoral Mediterranean nations. Gaining access to port facilities appears to be the ideal means of achieving this influence, and Algeria, Tunisia, and Libya seem to be the most likely targets. By gaining access to a target nation, the Soviet Union could exert greater influence over its maritime affairs and, in the context of a general Soviet offensive, it could perhaps extend that influence to the internal affairs of both the country and the region.

116

Problems Confronting the Sixth Fleet

For the United States, as for the U.S.S.R., the year 1977 continued the contrasting trends that have prevailed since the inception of large-scale Soviet naval operations in 1964. One of these trends is the relative decline in the prestige and influence of the U.S. Sixth Fleet. Our Mediterranean naval force is plagued with a host of difficult problems that will govern American actions for the next several years, if not decades. Of these problems, the four described in the sections below seem to be the most critical.

Static Force Levels. Public response to the threat posed by the rise of Soviet naval power and Congressional measures to modernize the U.S. Navy have been insufficient to guarantee any dramatic change in the military strength of the Sixth Fleet for at least several years. Two factors make this outlook even more pessimistic. First, since American commitments are global in scope, the Sixth Fleet must compete with other forces for available naval resources; for example, with the projected withdrawal of American forces from Korea, U.S. naval power may become the most important element in guaranteeing the security of Northeast Asia. Second, given the expanding Soviet naval presence on the high seas, within the next several years we may see tremendous increases in the level of Soviet forces in the Indian Ocean and along the West African coast. Barring an unexpected Soviet-American rapport reversing the current trend of Soviet naval expansion on the high seas, we may also see, within the next several decades, a constant presence of naval combatants in the Caribbean Sea and along the littorals of the Latin American coast. Such scenarios imply that American naval forces should be available to meet not only existing but also future American maritime commitments. Paramount among the various foreseeable demands for naval power are maintaining the security of the sea lanes leading from the Persian Gulf to both Europe and Japan, which are heavily trafficked by oil-laden supertankers, and guaranteeing the security of the American coasts and the North Atlantic sea lanes to Europe.

If American naval construction continues at its present rate, there will be only a minor increase in the force level of the U.S. Navy, although the firepower of the new ships will be greater. Thus, it is reasonable to assume that the United States will find it increasingly difficult not only to significantly augment the Sixth Fleet (except in crisis situations) but also to maintain the fleet at its present force level.

The balance of naval power in the Mediterranean will be heavily influenced by Soviet actions. If the U.S.S.R. commits additional re-

117

sources to naval construction and deploys a significantly greater number of surface combatants and submarines to the Mediterranean, then the Soviet threat to the Sixth Fleet in the future will probably be greater than it is at present.

It should be noted that the recent increase in Soviet Mediterranean naval power has been partially offset by astute American diplomacy, which has elevated the United States to the position of primary arbitrator in the ongoing Arab-Israeli dialog. However, the Arab-Israeli wars of 1967 and 1973 demonstrated that the Middle East is too volatile, and Soviet policy too aggressive, for the United States to rely solely on diplomacy in influencing Middle East affairs. Crisis situations calling for timely naval responses by an adequate fleet of modern American surface combatants and submarines are sure to arise. U.S. confidence in its ability to respond to such situations rests on the most astute employment of available American naval resources. The remaining problems confronting the Sixth Fleet are all tied to this fundamental problem, the importance of which cannot be overstated.

Changing Balance of Naval Power. To a great extent, the thrust of the balance of power problem lies in the ability of the United States to fulfill its commitments. At present, the crux of the issue is the American commitment to Israel. If the United States refuses or is unable to guarantee Israeli security and to honor its stated commitments, the ensuing loss of American credibility will almost certainly result in a weakening of NATO. As Philip Mosely has astutely observed, the ultimate Soviet goal in the Middle East is to expel American influence and to establish Soviet control, possibly through a confederation of communist-oriented Arab nations. In such a scheme, Israel might "come under some form of Soviet protection" and be urged to assist in the industrialization of the region. Should this actually occur, then the credibility of the American commitment to NATO would be fatally undermined not only diplomatically but also strategically. Without access to the eastern Mediterranean, and with the Soviets asserting a dominant influence over the Suez Canal, our ability to defend southern Europe would be practically impossible.[19]

In any case, our ability to defend southern Europe will be questionable—at least for the next several decades. The current capability of the Sixth Fleet relative to that of the Soviet Mediterranean fleet demonstrates that the Soviets have already made significant progress. The

---

[19] Philip E. Mosely, "Soviet Search for Security," in *Soviet-American Rivalry in the Middle East,* ed. J. C. Hurewitz (New York: Frederick A. Praeger, 1969), pp. 216-217.

consensus is that, in contrast to its previous position of absolute superiority in the Mediterranean, the Sixth Fleet could not today conduct immediate operations against Soviet forces invading southern Europe, but it would first have to establish an acceptable level of sea control in the Mediterranean. The length of time needed to do this would depend on the magnitude of American casualties in the initial Soviet strikes. Significant damage to an aircraft carrier, for example, not only would neutralize an extremely significant weapons system but also would create a tremendous liability, in that many craft would have to be detailed to protect and to repair the damaged ship. In general, it can be said that if American losses during initial strikes are low, then the period necessary to establish an acceptable level of sea control will be short. However, if American losses are so great that the Sixth Fleet has to await reinforcements before taking the offensive, the delay could be considerable.

In a confrontation between American and Soviet Mediterranean forces the fate of southern Europe would depend on the ability of the Sixth Fleet to defend itself in a Soviet-initiated, preemptive strike situation. Any additional shift in the Mediterranean balance of power would make the fate of southern Europe even more uncertain. If the balance of power were to continue to shift toward the Soviets, left unchecked it would most certainly contribute to a weakening of the NATO alliance.[20]

Geopolitical Vulnerability. With respect to geography, the Gibraltar and Turkish straits, the Suez Canal, and the straits of Sicily and Messina are critical choke points that govern traffic into and out of the western Mediterranean. In 1964, when Soviet large-scale naval operations resumed in the Mediterranean, all choke points, with the exception of Suez, were controlled by nations friendly to the United States. In essence, the Soviets have since operated under adverse geopolitical conditions. The Soviet reverses in Albania and Egypt notwithstanding, the changing geopolitical context in the Mediterranean, although moderate, has been in favor of the Soviet Union. While geopolitical balance is still moderately in favor of the United States, there are three reasons for concern about the future. First, unlike Soviet operations, current Sixth Fleet operations rely greatly on a favorable geopolitical context, and any adverse change in this context could force a revision in or a curtailment of American naval operating patterns. Second, the littoral nations, in adjusting their policies to accommodate the growing Soviet naval presence, are more apt to make decisions favorable to the Soviet

---

[20] Rivero, "Why a U.S. Fleet?" p. 86; Turner and Thibault, "Countering the Soviet Threat," p. 26.

Union than to the United States. Finally, except for current American prestige in dealing with the Arab-Israeli question, the outlook for a geopolitical context favorable to Americans seems particularly uncertain, and an anti-American trend may accelerate considerably in years to come. In this context, changes could occur among the European or the African littoral states. In Europe, changes adverse to the United States could occur in Greece or Turkey as a result of the Cyprus issue; in Yugoslavia, should Tito die; in Italy, because of increasing Communist party gains; and in Spain, as a consequence of realignments in the post-Franco era. In Africa, changes adverse to the United States could occur if recent Soviet overtures to Libya, Tunisia, and Algeria meet with success, particularly in light of significant radical elements in both Algeria and Libya. Pro-Communist gains in Italy and Tunisia could facilitate Soviet naval transits through the straits of Messina and Sicily and, perhaps, restrict American passage. Finally, a reversion of Gibraltar to Spain coupled with a movement toward the left in Spain could deny the United States the use of Rota and discourage—if not threaten—American access to the Mediterranean via Gibraltar. In summary, any of these presumed geopolitical changes could make Sixth Fleet operations more difficult, and if they do not occur, the geopolitical context of the Mediterranean would not be any more adverse for Soviet naval operations than it is at present.

Logistical Support. Unlike current Soviet logistical operations, the Sixth Fleet logistical effort relies heavily on the U.S. naval base at Rota, Spain, and the naval support facility in Naples, Italy. In addition, the fleet makes heavy use of a host of ports throughout the Mediterranean for crew rest, ship upkeep, and procurement of fresh provisions. Obviously, the facilities at Rota and Naples are vulnerable to political changes in Spain and Italy, and, should Communist parties come to power, it is possible that the United States would be denied access to these facilities. If the American Mediterranean presence is reduced, and a strong Soviet presence remains, it is conceivable that the Sixth Fleet would be permitted access to fewer and fewer Mediterranean ports, as the host governments become more sensitive to offending the Soviet Union.

Conclusion

In the current context of the Soviet-American naval rivalry in the Mediterranean, neither fleet is omnipotent. Rather, each is vulnerable to threats posed by the other as well as to possible political changes in any of several littoral nations. It is evident that naval power will continue to play a major political role in the area into the twenty-first century, and the Soviet and American naval forces will continue to provide the military power to implement the foreign policies of their respective governments and to react to crises in the Third World.

With respect to crises, the increased Soviet naval presence since 1964 is particularly alarming for three reasons. First, the Soviets could increase the level of their standing Mediterranean naval forces. Second, barring a change in current American policy, there will be no significant increase in the force level of the Sixth Fleet in the foreseeable future. Third, Soviet actions since 1967 have shown that the degree of Soviet response to a crisis situation is directly related to the distance between the crisis arena and the nearest Soviet home fleet area. Given the proximity of the eastern Mediterranean to the Black Sea, the Soviets have been able to muster unusually large naval responses to Middle Eastern crisis situations—much larger than their responses to crises in the Atlantic, Pacific, or Indian oceans. The Soviet crisis-response capability is even more alarming since it has increased (in terms of numbers of naval units) with each succeeding Arab-Israeli conflict.

If we do not significantly accelerate our naval construction program to allow for increases in the force level of the Sixth Fleet, then we should consider augmenting the force level of our Sixth Fleet, using existing naval forces. This, of course, would require a fundamental reorientation in American policy. To arrive at such a policy decision, the United States would have to examine its worldwide commitments in terms of available military strength and to identify commitments that are crucial to our defense or our foreign policy aspirations. Surely our commitments to NATO and Israel would rank high on such a list. This would resolve the dilemma arising from our ambivalence over the past decade. On the one hand, we have continued to affirm our commitments to both NATO and Israel; on the other, we have failed to maintain sufficient naval power to ensure the future defense of these commitments. Thus far, this dichotomy has not precipitated a crisis in our Mediterranean policy. However, we are finding it increasingly difficult to muster the requisite naval power to respond to such crises—as implied by our response to the October 1973 Arab-Israeli war.

If the present naval trend continues, and we fail to alter our foreign policy to reflect a realistic assessment of our naval strength, we may soon experience a Mediterranean crisis situation in which we are confronted with a Soviet naval force of sufficient magnitude and power to prohibit the successful accomplishment of American policy objectives. In 1973, we were able to honor our commitments by setting a strategic defense condition. However, current Soviet-American strategic parity makes the use of this option extremely risky and a dangerous substitute for the

121

display of naval power. Therefore, a prudent U.S. Mediterranean policy, based on an astute understanding of our current naval power, is the only reasonable solution to our dilemma. Such a policy would involve the difficult decision of either augmenting the Sixth Fleet by reassigning naval power from other fleet areas (and possibly weakening our ability to defend other portions of the globe) or of reducing our commitments to Israel and NATO to a manageable number that can be defended with existing Sixth Fleet naval power. Such a reorientation—although it entails some difficult decisions by responsible American leaders—would enable optimal and intelligent use of Mediterranean-based American naval power into the twenty-first century.

The Indian Ocean: A Region of Potential Conflict

The Indian Ocean, the third largest on the globe, is assuming a position of increasing interest and concern among the world's major powers. The region has always been commercially important, and valuable resources have been transported across the ocean's waters for centuries. In 1498, when Vasco da Gama established a sea route to India, spices from South Asia and the Near East were in great demand in Europe. By the nineteenth century, many of the raw materials needed to sustain Europe's developing industrial revolution came from littoral Indian Ocean and other Asian states via the Indian Ocean. Europe imported such items as rubber, jute, indigo, tea, teak, copra, and coconut oil and exported manufactured goods to the largely colonized littoral region.[1]

In recent times, the key commodity shipped across the Indian Ocean is petroleum, destined mainly for Western Europe, Japan, and the United States. However, there is a vast difference between Indian Ocean commerce today and during the era of colonization. Indeed, the last remnant of the old British imperialism disappeared in 1968 with Great Britain's announcement of its intent to withdraw from "east of Suez." For many decades, the Indian Ocean had been essentially a British lake, and perhaps for that reason the rest of the Western world tended to minimize the importance of the region—that is, until the energy crisis.

Interest in the Indian Ocean will surely increase in the near future, primarily because nearly three-quarters of the free world's petroleum is supplied by the littoral states, and that proportion may soon be larger if explorations in the Indian Ocean (beyond the two-hundred mile economic exploitation zones) prove successful. Even so, interest in the

---

The views expressed are those of the author and do not necessarily reflect the views of the American Enterprise Institute, where he serves as the assistant director of foreign and defense policy studies.

[1] The term *Indian Ocean states* (or *littoral region*) refers to those countries along the coast of the Indian Ocean as well as along its appendages, such as the Persian Gulf, the Arabian, Red, and Anadaman seas, the Bay of Bengal, the gulfs of Aden and Oman, and the Mozambique Channel.

123

region is not limited to petroleum, nor to the hundreds of millions of people accessible by the Indian Ocean. The independent Indian Ocean states control vast reserves of many other key mineral and organic resources that will continue to be of keen interest to the more developed world.

Not surprisingly, since Britain's historic withdrawal east of the Suez, the competition between the two superpowers for influence over the formerly British-dominated area has intensified—in the economic, political, and military sectors. American and Soviet military activities range from deploying sizable task forces in the Indian Ocean to selling arms to many of the indigenous states, which includes supplying them with advisers and other skilled manpower. It is, therefore, most appropriate to commence this essay with an examination of regional conflicts that could involve exogenous powers, particularly, the U.S.S.R. and the United States.

Potential Conflict Areas

The number of conflicts that could erupt between various littoral states is legion, and any shooting hostilities could result in superpower involvement. Ideally, the United States and Soviet Union should be exerting maximum efforts to achieve an agreement, whereby neither power would keep combatants in the Indian Ocean, or, a more likely alternative, an agreement to limit the number and type of combatants deployed in the region. Without such an agreement, it is highly probable that competition between the two superpowers will intensify, and the likelihood of a showdown in the Indian Ocean will increase. This paper is based on the pessimistic premise that the opportunity for such an agreement is rapidly diminishing.

Before dealing with more specific U.S. and Soviet activities in the Indian Ocean area, I should discuss some of the issues or situations in the littoral region that could incite local conflict among the various states. The examination of such conflict scenarios is particularly important since disagreements between Third World states tend to attract foreign intervention to both sides of the dispute.[2]

One issue that could affect nearly every littoral state associated with an outside power centers on rights to the 200-mile economic exploitation zones in the Indian Ocean. Because these zones are often ill-defined, arguments frequently arise over efforts to establish sovereignty over such

---

[2] For a more extensive treatment of potential conflict scenarios, see Dale R. Tahtinen, with John Lenczowski, *Arms in the Indian Ocean* (Washington, D.C.: American Enterprise Institute, 1977).

a protected area. Contending interpretations might even hinge on how large an offshore rock must be to qualify as the baseline from which to measure a country's limits or whether a national claim should be based on non-island coastline. Such disagreements will undoubtedly become more intense with increasing world demand for scarce mineral resources and food—and increasing regional awareness of the handsome profits to be realized by those in possession of the desired resources.

Although petroleum is at present the most lucrative export (and is likely to be in the near future), the littoral region contains significant amounts of other valuable resources, such as manganese nodules (which also include some iron, nickel, cobalt, and copper).[3] In addition, the hot brines of the Red Sea, though located at depths of some 6,000 feet, contain potentially significant amounts of zinc, copper, lead, silver, vanadium, molybdenum, and iron. Another factor of great importance in an increasingly food-short world is the area's great potential for fish production. Since a large percentage of the fish are found within the economic exploitation zones, access to this important resource could also lead to conflicts over proprietary rights.

A recent situation on the Horn of Africa illustrates how easily the superpowers could become involved in local conflicts. In the territorial dispute between Ethiopia and Somalia, the United States initally supported Ethiopia, while the Soviet Union was the patron of Somalia. After an Ethiopian coup in which a Marxist government came to power, Moscow began supporting Ethiopia and, a short time later, Washington's position began to shift toward Somalia. Even such a seemingly minor change could have had serious ramifications, since the Somali claims are not limited to the Ogaden and Haude regions of Ethiopia and the territory of the Issas and Afars, but also include the northern frontier district of Kenya. Somali success in seizing some of their long-standing claims may have led to intervention in Kenya, which in turn would have placed the United States in an awkward position, since Washington considers Kenya to be a friendly Third World state. Furthermore, any American effort to assist their Kenyan friends in such a situation would almost certainly have been met by hostility on the part of the Somalis, and the Soviet Union would probably have been more than willing to fill the breach. Yet, neither could Washington easily disregard the Somali expulsion of the Soviet Union.

Elsewhere on the Horn, a newly independent Eritrea may be the scene of intense competition among exogenous powers, including the

---

[3] For more detailed discussion of the resource potential of the Indian Ocean area, see *Indian Ocean Atlas* (Washington, D.C.: Central Intelligence Agency, 1976), especially pp. 15-17.

125

United States and Soviet Union. The Sudan could very easily become involved in the local hostilities between Somalia and Ethiopia or in a conflict with Saudi Arabia over ownership of the Red Sea hot brines and other mineral-rich sediments. Although the cost of exploiting these resources is presently uneconomical, an increasingly mineral-short world might be willing to pay greater amounts for minerals like silver, vanadium, molybdenum, iron, and lead. The Red Sea sediments also represent potential wealth in terms of the large concentrations of potassium chloride, sodium, calcium, and sulfate that can be extracted from the brines.

The Red Sea area could also become embroiled in another Arab-Israeli war. Indeed, the actions of the principal contenders leave little doubt about this eventuality. Already, both sides have increased their naval preparations, and the Israelis fly frequent patrols over the Red Sea.[4]

There is potential for conflict, too, on the Arabian peninsula. Conflicts could arise from disputes between the two Yemens, which might also involve Saudi Arabia; from the Dhofari rebellion in Oman; or from the territorial disputes among the various Persian Gulf states, including Iran, a country that has serious potential for separatist movements inside its own borders.

Iran, in turn, is likely to become involved in any disputes centering around Pakistan. The shah has been very specific in indicating that his government will not be an idle witness to the dismemberment of Pakistan. Consequently, Pakistan's disputes with Afghanistan and India could lead to a widening of the conflicts in the Indian Ocean littoral region. Furthermore, separatist activities inside Pakistan could easily become more serious, in which case outside states would probably be accused of aiding and abetting the dissidents.

Farther to the east, India and Bangladesh are at odds over water rights to the Ganges River, which is presently being diverted at a point some eleven miles inside India. In Southeast Asia, communist groups are busily exploiting various discontented minorities in Burma, Thailand, and Malaysia, and the danger of warfare is constant. In these conflicts, whether in Southeast Asia or on the Indian subcontinent, the possibility of foreign intervention is not restricted to the two superpowers. The People's Republic of China might also try to exert its influence, and any Chinese action is sure to elicit strong superpower reaction.

To the south, Indonesia figures in a number of other conflict scenarios, in which there is a strong potential for intervention. The government there is trying to build a cohesive state out of the many ethnic and

---

[4] See Robert J. Pranger and Dale R. Tahtinen, *Implications of the 1976 Arab-Israeli Military Status* (Washington, D.C.: American Enterprise Institute, 1976).

religious groups inhabiting the country's numerous and geographically widespread islands. Indeed, Indonesia's potential wealth and strategic location might tempt an exogenous power to support dissident groups. For similar reasons, the likelihood of outside intervention in a racial war in Rhodesia or South Africa should not be dismissed. While the potential for conflict in southern Africa is serious, a purely racial war would probably not be fought with the same level of intensity as one involving exogenous powers.

American Concerns

What national interests does the United States presently have in the Indian Ocean, and are these interests likely to remain relatively constant in the future? Does the Soviet Union pose a real threat to the area now? Is it likely to represent a greater threat in the future? Does the United States need a large naval presence in the area? These are a few of the important questions that must be examined when considering the possibility of conflict in the Indian Ocean.

Perhaps the basic question centers on the nature of U.S. interests in the littoral region over the coming years. We can assume that our future interests will change little from our present interests—namely, access to the region's resources, petroleum in particular. Beyond the immediate years, other regional resources may well join the list of critically needed raw materials. American interests will undoubtedly also include equal access to the Indian Ocean for our Western allies and Japan.

Another element of future U.S. policy will be the continuation of a favorable environment for private American investments in the area. This interest is of particular importance because of its vulnerability to inevitable political, economic, and social changes. Consequently, U.S. cognizance of regional developments, will be an essential element in making astute policy decisions.

In the region around the Indian Ocean, as in any part of the globe, the United States will want to project a positive image and to improve its standing throughout the Third World. This, too, is an important objective since there will be mounting reliance on international forums to reduce conflict and improve relations in what will be an increasingly interdependent world. Not surprisingly, Washington will, at the same time, try to prevent the Soviet Union from realizing any significant political or economic gains in the littoral region. In the absence of any limitation agreement, it is virtually certain that the United States would

127

strongly oppose any attempt by an Indian Ocean state to provide the Soviet Union with naval or other military facilities.

The United States should guard against changes that are likely to elevate anti-American regimes to power. For instance, if a communist or pro-Soviet government were to take over in South Africa, the Soviet Union would probably be given access to the outstanding naval facilities in Simonstown. While it may not be essential for the United States and its European allies to have use of the South African facilities, it would be a serious blow if the Soviet Union were to have them at its disposal.

Soviet Challenge

Having outlined the major U.S. current and future interests in the Indian Ocean and its littoral state, I will discuss the question: To what degree, if any, does the U.S.S.R. threaten those interests? In that context, let us briefly consider the balance of superpower forces in the Indian Ocean littoral region.

At present, whenever an American carrier task force is in the Indian Ocean, Washington has a naval advantage over Moscow's forces. The Soviet Union seems to be trying to keep a small force in the Indian Ocean that could easily be increased during a crisis period.

During the last decade, Moscow has steadily increased its naval presence in the Indian Ocean, but the number of combatants has varied. Generally, there have been fewer than ten; however, Soviet warships require a much larger number of support ships than their American counterparts. Any sizable increase in the number of Soviet ships deployed in the area has usually been in reaction to an increase in the strength of American forces. For example, in 1971, about three weeks after a United States show of force during the Indo-Pakistani war, the Soviet presence increased to six surface combatants and six submarines. The one major exception to the reaction-sponsored increase in the Soviet presence was operation Okean—a naval exercise. On this occasion, Moscow sent additional combatants into the area to test the fleet's capabilities in carrying out military operations on a global basis. Undoubtedly, it also intended to display that capability for whatever political benefits might be forthcoming.

The usual composition of the Soviet fleet includes cruisers, destroyers, destroyer escorts, and attack submarines, which are sometimes augmented by the *Leningrad,* an 18,000-ton helicopter carrier. During visits by these units, the Soviet navy uses various Indian Ocean facilities, including those at Vishakhapatnam, India; Chittagong, Pakistan; the islands of Mauritius and Madagascar off the east coast of Africa; and

Mogadiscio, Somalia. It has also utilized anchorages at Socotra Island, a protectorate of Aden, and the Seychelles, British islands in the ocean. In the Persian Gulf, it has used Umm Qasr, and for access to the Red Sea, naval facilities at Aden, Hodeida, and Berbera.

During the last two or three years, the Soviet Union has enlarged its naval presence by the deployment of long-range reconnaissance aircraft over the Indian Ocean. Although often less sophisticated than comparable American reconnaissance patrols (which are accompanied by better antishipping and antisubmarine forces), these additional forces have been a source of great concern to the Western powers. Still, the fact that the Soviet Union has entered an area that has previously been essentially the exclusive domain of the Western powers should not be surprising. One must analyze the significance of Moscow's Indian Ocean presence in the context of a new and growing power that may not always be seeking immediate control of a region but, at a minimum, to deny dominance to any other state. At the same time, the Soviet toehold in the region puts Moscow in a position to take advantage of any mistakes made by the West—a situation it has been highly successful in exploiting during the past several decades.

It is difficult, of course, to discern the Kremlin's real motives. As the world's number two superpower, they could merely be attempting to achieve parity, near parity, or dominance. However, in the absence of at least a limitation agreement, one can make certain predictions relative to Moscow's future behavior with a reasonable degree of certainty.

The Kremlin will probably increase the size of its amphibious forces in the Indian Ocean and deploy additional units to the region at more frequent intervals, generally maintaining a greater presence, with increased emphasis on aerial reconnaissance and antishipping, and submarine patrols. It will justify the increased naval presence as necessary to counter the possibility of Western intervention. The Soviet Union is not going to cease supporting liberation forces within the Indian Ocean countries. Of course, one will hear the usual argument that Moscow is merely responding to the Western military presence, in general, and the U.S. forces, in particular. The U.S.S.R. can be expected to continue to avail itself of the use of littoral facilities. To avoid the political mistake made by the United States, it will not establish bases in the region.

Superpower competition is not the only reason behind the Soviet Union's desire to maintain a significant presence in the Indian Ocean littoral region. Probably the most important is related to Russian worldwide fishing interests. As Moscow is faced with restrictions in other areas, the Indian Ocean will become increasingly attractive. These fishing interests might be further intensified by the nearby potentially rich

Antarctic waters. It is possible that as the Russians improve their technology for extracting seabed minerals, they will become increasingly involved in the exploitation of such regional resources. Indeed, the Kremlin has demonstrated its astuteness with respect to scarce resources by relying on imports whenever possible in order to conserve its domestic supplies —another lesson perhaps learned from American mistakes. In any case, the Kremlin will want to be prepared for the possibility that someday a littoral state may attempt to seize a Russian economic exploitation ship; in other words, the U.S.S.R. will be prepared for gunboat diplomacy in the Indian Ocean.

Another reason for Moscow to increase its naval capability in the area is to offset the qualitative and quantitative growth of Peking's fleet and, possibly, to compete with the Chinese for alliances with the different liberation groups operating in the littoral states. Russian condemnation of the Americans for possessing base rights has even extended to the mainland Chinese with such statements as, "The imperialists can now count on Peking in Asia and can also count on the forces of internal reaction in several countries." Such commentaries have been highly critical of the Chinese for "not taking part in the campaign against bases in Asia." [5] Similar criticism can be expected in the future, but that is not to say that Peking will do anything to help the United States, unless the leadership deems it to be in their national interest.

In general, the Soviet Union appears to have learned what the great powers of history have long known—that a powerful navy, despite its high cost, can reap economic and political as well as military benefits. Consequently, the Kremlin can be expected to continue competing with American naval activity in the Indian Ocean, but it can also be expected to continue avoiding confrontations that might lead to a nuclear exchange.

American Military Activity

American naval activity in the Indian Ocean has been far more impressive than that of the Russians. U.S. carrier task forces carry a wide array of power, and the presence of a significant U.S. base at Diego Garcia enhances the American potential for an increased military presence in the region. In the absence of a carrier group, any addition to the American presence is usually limited to a task force spearheaded by a guided-missile cruiser, with destroyer escorts and, frequently, attack submarines. When neither type of task force is present, a much smaller Middle East

---

[5] A. Leontyev, "The Bases in the Indian Ocean," *Krasnaya Zvezda,* May 30, 1976, as reported by the Foreign Broadcast Information Service on June 4, 1976, p. B6.

force assumes responsibility for the area. Utilizing facilities in Bahrain, the smaller U.S. force consists of a command ship and two destroyers.

Why does Washington maintain such an extensive presence? Will the United States continue to do so in the future? Will the size of American forces in the Indian Ocean increase? Answers to these questions should prove useful in determining the kinds of situations the United States is likely to face in the coming decades.

In the recent past, we have justified our increasing activities in the Indian Ocean in several ways. First, American spokesmen have argued that the British withdrawal from the area created a power vacuum that Washington had to prevent Moscow from filling. Some have contended that if the U.S.S.R. were to become the dominant power in the region, it would try to intimidate neighboring states into giving them a warm-water port and/or an overland route to the Indian Ocean. A more recent argument is that the Kremlin is planning to be in a position to interfere with shipments of petroleum from the Persian Gulf—an action that would have serious consequences for our European allies and Japan. A related concern has been that if the Russians were to gain a superior military position in the area, many of the littoral oil-producing states might be less inclined to resist Soviet influence.

Portions of these arguments may be used in the future, and variations will probably arise, including those related to Soviet ambitions for a global posture. In reality, it is unlikely that the Soviet Union will attempt to disrupt oil supply lines on the ocean because of the high risk of nuclear war and the tremendous amount of naval power such an action would require. If Moscow did decide to interfere with petroleum shipments to Europe, it would be far more likely to attack the sources in the Persian Gulf.

United States interests in the area will continue to focus on oil and other key mineral resources as well as on the protection of American business investments in the various littoral states. Not surprisingly, Washington will also continue to thwart any type of economic and/or political gains by Moscow.

Having suffered significant political costs in the building of Diego Garcia, the United States will probably have more frequent deployments into the area, utilizing the facilities on that island base. Indeed, in the absence of a limitation agreement, the familiar action-reaction cycle between the superpowers will continue, and the size of the forces each country deploys will begin to be limited only by the respective naval budgets; little effort will be made to call off the race.

131

Other Outside Powers

Any discussion of potential conflict in the Indian Ocean would be incomplete without considering the role of exogenous powers other than the United States and the U.S.S.R. The principal outside states with interests in the littoral region are France, China, Great Britain, and Japan. Of these, France presently has the most important military presence in the area. It has been reported that Paris would, for an "indefinite" period of time, "maintain a fleet of some twenty warships in the Indian Ocean." [6] Early in the 1970s, the French created an Indian Ocean command and have strengthened their units in the area by deploying a helicopter carrier and naval patrol aircraft. In fact, during the past several years, the French naval presence in the region has generally exceeded that of the Soviet Union.

In terms of the future, there is little to indicate that France will significantly decrease its military activities. Indeed, one may even expect more frequent deployments by nuclear-capable submarines. Why do the French maintain such a large presence in the region? The reason appears to be of an economic nature. France has considerable investment interests in the littoral region and is trying to increase the markets for French products as well as to develop and/or retain access to the most dependable and least costly sources of raw materials. These interests will undoubtedly continue and may even intensify in the coming decades.

Meanwhile, British economic involvement in the Indian Ocean area is still very strong, even though their military presence has largely disappeared. Great Britain's withdrawal from the area was motivated by a variety of reasons ranging from sheer domestic-political considerations to more urgent domestic conflicts such as the need for a naval presence in home waters during the recent "cod war" with Iceland and to protect North Sea drilling rigs and other offshore resources. However, London has maintained a limited capability to deploy forces outside of Europe, although it is unlikely to send any to the Indian Ocean, barring a serious challenge to Western (including British) interests in the region.

By the advent of the twenty-first century, the country most likely to enter the Indian Ocean in significant force is the People's Republic of China (PRC). Initially, Peking may deploy units, including submarines with nuclear-tripped missiles, primarily to counter Russian activities. If stationed in the northern Indian Ocean, their strategic submarines would represent a serious threat to the heartland of the Soviet Union. Another motive for PRC involvement in the region might be to establish

---

[6] Desmond Wettern, "French Keep 20 Ships in Indian Ocean," *London Daily Telegraph,* April 15, 1976.

the perception among most of the littoral states that, as an Asian power, it does not intend to allow the United States and the Soviet Union to enjoy unfettered military dominance of the area. Underlying this presumed PRC challenge of the two superpowers might well be the tremendous potential for economic and political influence among the littoral states.

Japan, the fourth exogenous power with Indian Ocean interests, realizes significant economic benefits from the area, even though it has not had a military presence there since World War II. Any Japanese military activity in the future would be limited to occasional naval training visits on the eastern periphery of the Indian Ocean. However, there is always the possibility that if the United States abandoned the Far East, Japan might decide to allocate more of its budget to defense, which could include a presence in the Indian Ocean. Such an action would be fraught with numerous political problems and would be taken only under rather dire conditions. After all, Tokyo has enjoyed tremendous economic benefits without spending very much of its resources on defense and recognizes its unique advantages.

Indigenous States

A significant fact in considering the strengths and future roles of the indigenous Indian Ocean countries, is that some have amassed a large amount of military power. The most impressive arsenals are those of Australia, South Africa, Indonesia, India, Pakistan, and the Persian Gulf states of Iran and Iraq. In total, the littoral nations have more than 2,600 combat aircraft, 800 helicopters, over 850 naval craft, thousands of tanks and armored personnel carriers, a variety of air-defense systems, and military forces in excess of three million individuals. Of course, there is great disparity in quality of weapons and in ability to use them. Nevertheless, the quantitative statistics are significant in that they reflect the importance these littoral states attach to being prepared to resolve national problems by military means and/or a lack of confidence in the possibility that other states would pursue diplomatic alternatives in settling disagreements.

It is not surprising that the acquisitions trend among these littoral states seems to be in the direction of weaponry well-suited to protecting territorial claims within their respective 200-mile economic exploitation zones. Of course, they are not restricting their arms inventories to weapons that are useful only for such efforts, nor are they limiting their military capabilities to defensive actions.

In some cases the power of a littoral state has increased to the point

133

of precluding any type of takeover except by one of the world's few major powers. One need only briefly examine the forces of the most powerful regional states to realize that they could effectively conduct offensive operations. For instance, Iran already possesses an impressive, highly sophisticated air force and, if present plans are brought to fruition, will in the coming decades, have a long-range navy capable of becoming a significant regional force. In addition, its modern, sizable, armor forces would be an important factor in any war on the subcontinent.

India's forces, though lacking the same quality of aircraft, are combat-tested. It already has an impressive fleet, including an aircraft carrier, and will be increasing the size and quality of its naval, air, and ground forces.

Pakistan and South Africa will also continue to increase the size of their military forces. There is little reason to doubt that by the year 2000, several more littoral states will be joining India as nuclear powers, for example, Iran, Pakistan, South Africa, Iraq, and possibly, Saudi Arabia. It is also likely that, as we approach the twenty-first century, some of those states may no longer be pro-Western.

Meanwhile, Australia, with its sophisticated military forces, and long-range air and naval capabilities, might also decide to develop nuclear weapons. However, the country's geographic location plus its long, close ties with the United States make it less likely that the Australians will rush to develop nuclear weapons. Over the next couple decades, Australia's only conceivable regional threat would come from Indonesia; at present, however, relations between the two states are relatively smooth. Canberra has even been providing Jakarta with military assistance, most recently delivering a pair of 51-foot patrol boats.[7] Even if relations were to deteriorate, Indonesia might find it difficult to move against its southern neighbor, since it faces serious problems with its armed forces. Its domestic difficulties are significant enough to preclude any effective military operations beyond home waters for at least a decade—despite the fact that the country has a potential long-range capability, with frigates, corvettes, and submarines presently part of its naval inventory.

Conclusion

As this presentation has indicated, there is a myriad of potential conflict situations within the Indian Ocean region, and there are ample

---

[7] "Australia: Two More Patrol Boats for Indonesia," *Defense and Foreign Affairs,* September 1977, p. 43.

weapons in the hands of various littoral states to conduct open hostilities should fighting erupt. Any local conflict could easily involve exogenous powers, particularly the United States and Soviet Union. As history manifests, it is frequently the case that when one superpower supports one side in a local conflict, a competing superpower will come in on the side of the other.

If there is no limitation agreement, we can expect that the United States and the Soviet Union will eventually maintain fleets in the Indian Ocean. As a result, the danger of superpower intervention in local disputes and, perhaps, of nuclear confrontation will increase. However, the exorbitant cost of deploying large, permanent fleets to the Indian Ocean may be a mitigating factor. Neither the United States nor the Soviet Union is in a position to spend billions more on defense. Washington is now, and will continue to be, in a disadvantaged position, since the American people appear to be increasingly reluctant to spend huge sums of money on military expansion. Of course, it must be noted that seemingly localized conflicts or confrontations sometimes serve to convince domestic populations of the necessity of allocating additional resources to defense.

An American or Russian buildup could also be occasioned by the action of a belligerent regional power in dissonance with the interests of either superpower. Certainly, the fact that exogenous states have been supplying sophisticated weapons to the littoral region has done little to encourage a movement away from the reliance on force to settle disputes. In the case of the resource-hungry West, the policy of improving balance-of-payments statistics by selling arms may prove to be short-sighted, especially if it contributes to disruptions in the supply of needed raw materials.

Nevertheless, it would appear that Moscow and Washington will continue to compete in the Indian Ocean region. For the United States, the key questions are, Will our response bring seemingly short-term benefits while courting long-run disaster? Or will we be able to recognize that we must find new approaches to regional problems, especially those that deemphasize military competition? This is not to argue that the age of projecting military power has passed; rather, it is meant to suggest that armed force should not be brandished when there is little intent of using it. It is particularly important to recognize the sensitivity of former colonial nations to any reminder of Western military prowess. A display of force merely provides our adversaries with an opportunity to gain influence, since pride and concern may prompt many of the relatively new independent littoral states to take surprising measures in order to offset reminders of the old colonial days.

The Northern Flank

Rolf Steinhaus

Apart from the fact that the Soviet Union and the United States have reached nuclear strategic parity, one of the most momentous changes in the postures of the two big military blocs is undoubtedly the U.S.S.R.'s transformation from a traditional continental power into a world sea power. This development has enabled the Soviet Union to pursue its political, social, and economic objectives not only in the Eurasian landmass but far beyond its continental borders. The recent history of the noncommitted world provides several examples in point.

Even more decisive than the global impact of Soviet maritime expansion is the U.S.S.R.'s influence on East-West relationships. The military threat to the free West is no longer directed at Western Europe alone but at the vital link between the United States and Europe—the Atlantic Ocean—as well. This new threat emanates from the desolate and remote reaches of the Greenland and Norwegian seas, where Soviet bases are concealed, far from the Mediterranean and African areas of crisis on which public attention is focused. Although the threat raised by Soviet sea power is not as widely publicized as the nuclear threat, it does exist. It is a reality and a menace to peace and the liberty of the West.

In his book *Sea Power and the State,* Admiral Gorshkov defines the extensive mission of the Soviet naval forces as follows:

> The sea power of our state serves to provide favorable conditions for the building of communism, for a vigorous growth of our economic potential, and for an incessant strengthening of the defense capability of this country.

Geographical Features

Those who regard the northern flank as an area confined to Norway, Denmark, and the Federal Republic of Germany (FRG) are bound to be surprised at the region's vast expanse. Most of it consists of water—the Greenland Sea, the Norwegian Sea, the North Sea, the Baltic Sea, and the English Channel; the ratio is about 90 percent water to 10 percent land, most of which consists of islands or peninsulas. Svalbard, the North Cape, the island of Bornholm in the Baltic, the Elbe estuary, the narrowest passage of the English Channel between Dover and Calais, the Shetlands, and Iceland are prominent landmarks of this northern flank area which is comparable in size to the United States minus Alaska.

The most northern parts of the area are lost in long, polar nights and perpetual ice, restricting the capabilities of man to narrow limits, in spite of modern technology. Only on Svalbard has man succeeded in wresting from nature a small base for the exploitation of the rich coal fields. By international agreement, military activities are prohibited on these islands, including the interception of electronic emissions from the Russian-controlled Barents Sea.

To the south, between Norway and Iceland, is the Norwegian Sea, with an average depth of 500 meters. It is notorious for its frequent storms and days of fog. The meteorological conditions and the ruggedness of the coastal areas impede reconnaissance and surveillance, thus favoring clandestine transit. South of these desolate expanses are the comparatively narrow, shallow, land-rimmed waters of the Baltic and the North seas, with their high density shipping and heavily populated, highly developed littoral states.

Like a long, narrow shield with a longitudinal axis of 2,000 nautical miles and a transverse axis of 1,000 nautical miles, the northern flank juts out between the bases that support the Russian maritime forces and the Atlantic, forming a bulwark between the Atlantic Ocean and the Communist-bloc navies: the Soviet northern fleet based on the Kola peninsula to the north and the Baltic approaches to the south, where the united Baltic fleets of the Warsaw Pact nations, the Russian red banner fleet, and the German Democratic Republic (GDR) and Polish navies are deployed. Apart from land lines of communication, these two major bases are linked by the White Sea–Baltic Sea waterway, which runs from Leningrad to Belomorsk. During the ice-free season from May to October, combatants of destroyer size can be towed across this waterway in a painfully slow process that takes two weeks. While the Warsaw Pact nations have direct access to Atlantic waters from the north, between North Cape and Svalbard, access from the south is impeded by the Danish straits, which enjoy the status of international waters in peacetime but would have to be forced or seized in wartime.

This is the area we must consider in discussing the problems of the northern flank. So far, Western strategists have failed to give it the prominence it warrants as a major contributor to the strength and capabilities of Soviet sea power.

Historical Background

Seafaring and sea power are two factors that have governed the history of this area and its nations and have given momentous impetus to developments in the rest of the world.

From southern Scandinavia, the Vikings set out in their long, open ships around 500 A.D. They pillaged the English, French, Spanish, and Mediterranean coasts, settled Iceland, and ventured farther toward the west. They were the first Europeans to set foot on the American continent, long before Columbus, around the year 1000; they founded principalities on many European coasts and for three centuries remained the masters and the terror of northern waters. In the course of their long plundering raids and conquering expeditions, they learned to appreciate the usefulness of commerce, gradually settling down as traders throughout northern Europe. The Hansa followed in their footsteps. In a contemporary context, the Hansa would be defined as a multinational cartel that controlled the capital market and the exchange of commodities over large parts of the continent through monopolies and mutual arrangements.

With the advent of the era of great discoveries, the flow of commerce and centers of power began to shift.

Russia's role in these activities was relatively minor for two particular reasons.

First, the Russian colossus had been absorbed with its own problems for thousands of years, especially with the task of consolidating its power. It did not emerge as a factor in international history until the control of the world's oceans had long been settled, limiting its involvement in international activities to the continent. Second, and perhaps equally decisive, Russia lacked bases from which to exert maritime influence. Given their climate, primitive hinterland, and low technological state of development, the endless Siberian and Pacific coasts were unsuitable as bases from which to project global sea power, and the exits to the largely enclosed Baltic and Black seas were controlled by foreign powers. Several Russian attempts to break the Baltic barrier of the Danish Isles failed. Thus, Russian aspirations for sea power were confined to the Baltic and Black seas, and later to the Sea of Japan, with the objective of denying third powers any influence in those waters.

This state of affairs underwent a radical change in the current century. The Soviets, in particular, realized that their claim to world power (which is still based almost exclusively on military strength) was worthless without a worldwide naval presence. Direct access to the Atlantic Ocean became a high-priority strategic objective. On the Kola peninsula, they established the largest of the four Soviet fleets.

139

Political and Economic Structure

With the exception of Sweden and Finland, the non-Baltic countries bordering the northern flank are members of the North Atlantic Treaty Organization (NATO); five of them—Denmark (5 million inhabitants), the Federal Republic of Germany (61 million inhabitants), the Netherlands (13 million inhabitants), Belgium (10 million inhabitants), and the United Kingdom (55 million inhabitants)—are also members of the European Economic Community (EEC). Sweden (8 million inhabitants), although traditionally neutral, has formidable armed forces that would present a great challenge to any aggressor. The geostrategic situation of a neutral Sweden is advantageous to both power blocs. It relieves NATO of the responsibility of defending more than 1,000 kilometers of Norwegian border, and the Swedish airspace provides the Warsaw Pact nations (Communist-bloc counterpart to NATO) additional protection against air and missile attacks. Therefore, Sweden's neutrality would probably not be immediately in jeopardy in the event of a war. Finland (5 million inhabitants), however, is in a different situation. Under the Russo-Finnish treaty of friendship, the small country with its negligible armed forces is, in wartime, obliged to put its territory and resources at the disposal of the Soviet Union.

The role played in NATO by Denmark, Norway, and Iceland has its peculiarities. In deference to their overwhelming Soviet neighbor, Scandinavian solidarity, and neutral inclinations, these Scandinavian countries joined NATO with a set of reservations. They will not store nuclear weapons or station foreign troops on their soil in peacetime. Iceland does not make a military contribution to NATO and tolerates only reluctantly the maintenance of a U.S. air base at Keflavik.

The NATO countries on the southern border of the northern flank— the Federal Republic of Germany, the Netherlands, and Belgium—are primarily concerned about the superior ground forces of the neighboring Warsaw Pact nations, giving only second thoughts to the maritime threat to the flank. As for the United Kingdom, it has yet to find its bearings as a European power; economic problems have led to major reductions in its maritime assets.

The countries on the northern flank are comparatively poor in natural resources, and their economies are geared to the production and distribution of high quality industrial goods. Therefore, all of their economies depend to a high degree on imports and exports. On average, the northern flank ports handle 750 million tons of goods annually. In accordance with their economic structure, these countries have sizable merchant fleets and efficient shipbuilding industries. Norway, Denmark, the Federal Republic of Germany, the Netherlands, Belgium, and the United Kingdom together operate merchant fleets of 82.5 million gross registered tonnage (GRT). This amounts to 22 percent of the world's tonnage, compared with 15 million GRT or 4 percent of the world's tonnage for the United States, and 20.7 million GRT or 5.5 percent of the world's tonnage for the U.S.S.R. In 1975, these NATO countries built ships totaling 6.7 million GRT.

It is not surprising, then, that the northern European waters carry the highest density of shipping in the world. On any day, 300 ships pass through the English Channel, and 325 pass the Baltic Straits. While many of these ships are part of the merchant fleets of the northern flank countries, quite a few sail under flags of convenience or those of the Warsaw Pact countries. The GDR and Poland rely exclusively on their Baltic ports.

It is true that the countries in the Communist economic bloc (COMECON), thanks to the vast Russian mineral resources, are not as dependent on imported raw materials as their NATO counterparts. In addition to the 20.5 million GRT of the Russian merchant fleet, 3.3 million GRT belong to Poland, and 2.5 million GRT belong to the GDR. The shipbuilding capacity of these countries is another noteworthy fact. In 1976, their Baltic shipyards alone built merchant ships totaling about one million GRT and almost one hundred warships. This is more than twice the number of warships the NATO alliance collectively commissioned over one year and more than three times the number of ships produced by the other Soviet shipbuilding centers combined. The bulk of these vessels were small units of large series, such as minesweepers and fast patrol boats, but they also included large, sophisticated ships, such as Kresta-class missile cruisers and Krivak-class missile destroyers.

Two other factors of economic importance to the northern flank are the petroleum and natural gas fields in the North Sea and the fishing industry. Natural gas fields have been exploited in the North Sea area since the late 1960s. Starting off the Netherlands and southeast English coasts, a chain of drill and production rigs has since moved steadily northward on either side of 5 degrees eastern longitude. As to the order of magnitude of the North Sea oil fields, we do not yet have reliable figures, but the fields discovered to date would supply 40 percent of the projected Western European requirements for fuel until 1985. Norway is now self-sufficient, and the United Kingdom hopes to be by 1980. One thing seems to be certain: for some decades Western Europe will be less dependent on overseas energy resources. However, the same cannot be said about other raw materials.

Allocation of the continental shelf in the northern flank region has long been settled by treaties and is generally not a matter of contention— except for the border between Norway and the Soviet Union, where once again the potential for oil plays a part.

The situation is different where fishing is concerned. By tradition, fishing in northern European waters is an important economic and nutritional factor. Unfortunately, centuries of overfishing are at last beginning to take their toll. The herring, for instance, once the staple diet of the coastal population, is extinct in the Baltic and threatened by the same fate in the North Sea. Iceland, whose main industry is fishing and fish processing, is trying to conserve its remaining stocks by setting fishing quotas. Recently, Iceland, Norway, and the EEC countries have established protective zones. Although necessary in the long run, these restrictions impose immediate sacrifices on local populations.

Fish is also an important foodstuff for the Soviet Union, the GDR, and Poland. These countries all have large fishing fleets. The Soviet fleet is larger than the combined size of the next nine in size. Because of their large fleets and the scarcity of fish in the coastal waters, the Warsaw Pact countries have been honoring the protective zones; they are also prepared to open up new fishing grounds in the remaining free zones or to negotiate agreements on fishing quotas.

Strategic Factors

The military problems of the northern flank stand out in relief when viewed against the backdrop of the change in the balance of power and the divided interests within the NATO alliance.

As long as it could be assumed that the allied naval forces—in particular, the U.S. and British navies—were sufficiently superior to the Russian northern fleet, we could accept the regional inferiority of NATO forces in Norway, Denmark, and Schleswig-Holstein, and the absence of local forces in Iceland. Given the offensive capabilities of carrier-borne air forces and the ability to deploy reinforcements by sea at any time, we could quickly offset such weaknesses. Even in case of temporary territorial losses, we would not have to anticipate serious consequences to the NATO alliance, since the Warsaw Pact countries lacked the capabilities that would have allowed them to take strategic advantage of a local initial success. While this state of affairs lasted, deterrence would remain a credible northern flank strategy and would be consonant with preserving peace.

The fact that this estimate of the situation, which had been quite correct for the 1950s, remained the baseline of NATO defense planning well into the 1970s can only be understood today in light of the events of the past decade. During this time the leading power of the alliance, the United States, was involved in the Vietnam campaign; the Soviets were attaining nuclear parity; and the chances of arriving at worldwide stabilization through détente were overestimated.

The U.S. diversion in Vietnam together with our misappraisal of the motives behind Soviet maritime expansion and of the inherent capabilities of tactical surface-to-surface missiles, gave Moscow almost ten years in which to activate its naval forces. During this decade, Soviet naval capabilities increased to a point that surpassed by far what was required for national defense, while the West failed even to try to counterbalance these forces.

The Soviet northern fleet, until World War II the smallest of the Russian fleets, is now the biggest. This significant change has simply been ignored by the United States. The U.S. Second Fleet has remained the smallest of the big American fleets. This fact is inexplicable. The ratio of opposing forces in the North Atlantic is disproportionate to the relative force capabilities of the two superpowers in the Mediterranean or in the Pacific. In light of President Carter's affirmation of the priority of the American commitment to NATO, a shift in the ratio of North Atlantic forces appears an urgent necessity. By way of contrast, the most sizable of the U.S. land and air forces stationed in foreign territories are those deployed on the European continent.

As for our NATO allies on the northern flank, there is a risk of their giving in to temptation and putting overall military security second to the protection of maritime resources in their respective 200-nautical-mile economic zones—a choice that places high demands on their naval and naval air forces.

Early in the 1970s, the NATO Supreme Allied Command Atlantic (SACLANT) had to face the fact that the ratio of Soviet-bloc to allied naval forces had shifted so drastically that NATO was no longer able to retain its established concept of operations. It was no longer possible to take NATO's absolute superiority in the Atlantic for granted, an assumption that had been the basis of NATO's previous plans for the support of land operations in central and northern Europe and for the assured provision of logistic support to Europe in case of war. Nowadays, the task of gaining this superiority in the first line is the crux of the strategic problems of the northern flank. In the past, the threat was to the territorial integrity of the northern flank countries of Norway and Denmark; at present, the threat is extended to the North Atlantic.

The decisive question for the alliance as a whole is whether NATO is strong enough to maintain control of this vital link between America and Europe. If the North Atlantic were no longer able to provide this link, an essential element of deterrence would be lost. In that case, the Soviet leaders might reckon that, if they were to invade Western Europe, they could prevent reinforcements from the United States and Canada from arriving in time to stop them.

In the past few months entirely different speculations have emerged regarding the strategy the Warsaw Pact countries would use in an aggression against Europe. Current thinking favors the idea of a blitzkrieg, in which the main thrust would be directed against the central front of Western Europe, while a defensive course would be pursued on the flanks. The objective of such a move would be to reach the French Atlantic coast early, before effective reinforcements could be deployed from overseas, and thus to establish a decisive strategic fait accompli. In such a situation, the overriding task of our overseas augmentation forces, in particular their air component, would be to intervene directly to relieve the threatened forces in central Europe. I would not dare hazard a guess about how effectively or for how long the augmentation forces would be able to do so.

The blitzkrieg strategy would undoubtedly carry high risks for the attacker, especially that of losing the race against time. However, even in the unlikely event of success, the battle in and for Europe would not be over. The task of interrupting, or at least permanently disrupting, the Atlantic lines of communication would remain. NATO's maritime strike forces would have to face a formidable task, the details of which are beyond the scope of this paper.

In the event of a war, the instruments the Soviet Union and its allies would use to interrupt the Atlantic lines of communication are the northern fleet, based on the Kola peninsula, and the united Baltic fleets, based on the Baltic coastline from Wismar to Leningrad. The Russian Pacific and Black Sea fleets would be included in this disposition only indirectly. One is based too far from the area of operations to be capable of direct intervention, although it could contain substantial forces of the U.S. Navy in the Pacific area. The other would first have to fight for superiority in the Mediterranean and to force the Strait of Gibraltar in order to penetrate the Atlantic.

An analysis of forces must therefore concentrate on the strategic positions of the various deployments in the North Atlantic and in northern European waters. All of these forces, with the exception of the Second Fleet, are stationed in the northern flank area. Any attempt to present the actual relative force capabilities in this region by tabling the opposing forces is bound to fail. What would happen here is not a direct duel between two fleets in a spectacular battle for the control of the

144

Atlantic but, rather, the execution of two highly dissimilar missions through dissimilar forces, which would presumably not be employed in the same stage of an armed conflict, but it should be kept in mind that naval forces are flexible and their deployment can shift at any time.

In the Barents and Norwegian seas, NATO has a classic sea-denial mission: to prevent the Warsaw Pact nations from successfully employing their forces in the following tasks:

- Protecting nuclear ballistic missile submarines deployed in that area.
- Screening the transit of its attack submarines into the Atlantic.
- Outflanking the left wing of defensive operations in Europe.
- Seizing strategic positions in northern Norway, Svalbard, and Iceland.
- Preventing NATO forces from attacking the Soviet naval base on the Kola peninsula.

The Warsaw Pact forces in this region are: elements of the attack submarine fleet; the blue-water component; the land-based naval air forces; the amphibious forces of the northern fleet; the civilian sea-transport capacity; and the air offensive, airborne, and ground forces stationed on the Kola peninsula.

NATO forces in the Barents and Norwegian seas are: the attack submarines of the commander in chief of allied naval forces in the Eastern Atlantic (of which the U.S. contingent must be deployed across the Atlantic); the surface and naval air forces of the same command; and the local air and land forces of Norway. In addition, NATO could count on reinforcements from the Striking Fleet Atlantic, and land and air forces from the strategic reserve of Supreme Allied Commander Europe (SACEUR), for instance the Allied Command Europe Mobile Force, the Canadian striking brigade, British or Netherlands marines, and elements of the U.S. Marine Corps. Reinforcements for the land and air forces have not been completely programmed for the northern flank, but there are several operational options. Since these reinforcements would have to take along their heavy equipment and supplies, they would be dependent on sea transport. Unless high attrition rates were acceptable, they could only be counted on if they were deployed either before the outbreak of hostilities or after superiority had been gained in the Norwegian Sea. The maritime ratio of forces would be determined by the Striking Fleet.

If the Striking Fleet were able to operate in the waters east of Iceland before the outbreak of war, there would be a marginal, but perhaps decisive, balance in favor of NATO. This would be especially true if additional land-based, air-offensive forces were flown to air bases in the area (that is, to Scotland, Iceland, and northern Norway) and if American attack submarines were deployed into the area early. If the Striking Fleet were not able to operate near Iceland, the Norwegian, Greenland, and Barents seas would soon be controlled by the Soviet northern fleet. If that were to happen, it is hard to believe that NATO would hold the strategic positions in northern Norway and Iceland.

In the southern part of the northern flank region—the Baltic and the Baltic approaches—NATO would have to protect the territories of Schleswig-Holstein, Denmark, and southern Norway, and to bottle up the Warsaw Pact united fleets in the Baltic.

As for the Warsaw Pact forces, they would have to seize the Danish main isles in order to gain control over the Baltic approaches and carry out the following tasks:

- Commit the ocean-going maritime assets of the Baltic coast base (forty cruisers and destroyers and thirty submarines) in support of the Soviet northern fleet in the North Sea and in the Atlantic.
- Disrupt the continuity of defense at the boundary between central and northern Europe and outflank NATO's forward defense in central Europe.
- Use the Baltic as the line of communication for an attack against central Europe.

Defense of the Baltic approaches is not merely a problem of naval warfare. Since the aggressor would seek to occupy and hold coastal strips and islands in a very confined area, integration of operations among the three services would be of high importance. NATO allows for this need by unifying its land, air, and naval forces in the Baltic Approaches Command. The regional ratio of forces must also be seen in this light. As far as land and air forces are concerned, the Warsaw Pact forces are so clearly superior that successful, sustained defensive operations do not hold out any promise, unless local land and air forces were effectively augmented with reinforcements. To do this, NATO has developed quite a number of options in its contingency plans.

At first sight, the ratio of naval forces might seem unfavorable to NATO too, but any such comparison should make allowance for the fact that many of the Baltic fleet's major surface units and the bulk of its submarines are unsuitable for warfare in the Baltic sea, having been designed for operations on the high seas in combination with the Soviet northern fleet. Moreover, the shallow waters of the Baltic are well suited for defensive mine warfare. The Baltic units of the German and Danish navies have been developed specifically for anti-invasion operations in these waters. The German fast-patrol-boat component alone possesses 120 surface-to-surface missile launchers at present. If you also consider the combat power of the fighter bomber units integrated with the German navy (which will, in the near future, be converted to the multi-role combat aircraft (MRCA) armed with standoff air-to-ship missiles) plus the combat power of the Danish and German coastal submarines (which are optimized for Baltic operations), the quantitatively negative picture changes into one that is satisfactory from a mission-oriented perspective.

The two vital areas of naval operations on the northern flank are linked by the North Sea. If its waters were controlled by NATO, it would help maintain continuity between the two main areas of operation. Moreover, it would allow NATO to shift forces in response to new developments in the northern flank and to deploy reinforcements from overseas, without which the overall defense of Europe could not succeed. Thus, NATO would have to accomplish a typical sea-control mission in the North Sea as well.

The Warsaw Pact navies would, in turn, strive to deny NATO the use of the North Sea, particularly to prevent deployment of reinforcements by sea to the two vital areas of operation—northern Norway, the Baltic approaches and the central region. In addition, they would surely have a special interest in cutting off the flow of supplies from the United States at the terminals, namely, the major North Sea ports. They could not wait to do so until they had seized the Baltic approaches, so they would have to employ suitable forces for this purpose at the outbreak of hostilities. Such forces would be bombers of the naval air forces of the Baltic fleet, submarines of the northern fleet, and mines. A massive deployment of surface combatants and submarines from the Baltic into the North Sea prior to the outbreak of hostilities is conceivable, but it would sacrifice the advantage of strategic and tactical surprise.

The significance of the North Sea in the defense of NATO's northern flank and central Europe has obviously not yet been fully realized. Current force allocations are inadequate, and there is no unified command. The three major NATO commanders share responsibility for the North Sea, and this results in no consistent planning for the area as a whole.

With respect to geographical location of naval bases, then, it would seem that the Warsaw Pact countries are in a geostrategically unfavorable situation, while NATO holds strategically important northern flank positions. NATO's problems are the weakness of its local forces; the extensive and rugged nature of the area, and timely deployment of external reinforcements from all three services over distances of thousands of miles.

147

It should hardly be an exaggeration to say that the accomplishment of SACLANT's mission depends vitally on events on the northern flank. At the same time, however, the northern flank is the left wing of the defensive front in Europe; a breakdown on this front would shatter the capability of forward defense in the central region, which would be the heart of the land and air operations in Europe. As long as the northern flank is controlled by NATO, it would be possible to preserve the continuity of overall operations in northern and central Europe and across the Atlantic Ocean.

Future Developments

Nothing in the overall political climate indicates that the Soviet Union is going to (or will have to) modify its strategy in the next few years. This implies that Moscow will continue its efforts to retain or to achieve military superiority. If we assume that the second round of strategic arms limitation talks (SALT II) and the mutual balanced force reductions (MBFR) negotiations will restrict the margin of change in nuclear capability and in central European force levels, we must expect the flanks and the high seas to be the areas for future Soviet activities. These areas offer the Soviet Union chances for expanding its sphere of influence without risking a direct military confrontation with the West. Such activities would tend to improve its military strategic position. The northern flank provides a number of opportunities in this respect. In practice, Moscow would aim at a continuation of the purposeful expansion of the maritime capabilities of the northern and Baltic fleets and an improvement of its geostrategic positions in that region.

If that objective is to be attained without brute force—that is to say, without the seizure of territories—the Soviets will have to concentrate on weakening the Western position by ways and means that fall under what Moscow calls "peaceful competition of ideologies." This would not be an entirely new course of action but a continuation of a process that has been under way for some time. For years the Soviet Union has sought to dislodge Denmark and Norway from the Atlantic Alliance, and it is likely that it will continue to pursue this goal by various methods.

One approach toward this end would be to exploit the solidarity of the Scandinavian countries. To many people in the area, the idea of a northern European neutral zone, protected by a collective defense, continues to be highly attractive. The example set by Sweden and hopes that Scandinavian neutrality might serve to release Finland from total dependence on her overpowering neighbor, the Soviet Union, are con-

148

tributory factors. It is small wonder that the Soviet Union is eager to take advantage of this trend, encouraging it wherever possible. It will certainly continue its recent ruthless demonstrations of military power off the Danish and Norwegian coasts if such displays impress rather than antagonize the countries in question. Moscow will also continue to support Scandinavian groups that are dissatisfied with the social and economic situation in their countries as well as the strong Icelandic Communist party.

In parallel with this political and psychological offensive, the Soviet Union will energetically continue its efforts to strengthen its position in the Barents Sea. For example, the Soviets obstinately insist on a continental shelf agreement that would provide for a division by sectors instead of the internationally accepted equidistance principle. Such a division would enlarge the Soviet share substantially, expand the size of the Russian community on Svalbard, strengthen Soviet claims to Bear Island (Bjornoya), and lead to frequent territorial restrictions over extensive areas for the conduct of naval maneuvers and missile-firing exercises.

Northern Norway—more accurately, its fjords and air bases—are regarded as the potential objective of a limited Soviet military action, since the seizure of advanced submarine and air bases farther to the west would be of substantial military advantage. The remoteness of the area would make it easy to launch a surprise action, using forces stationed in the Kola area. Such an aggression would result in a fait accompli that the West could hardly prevent by the application of military force. The military advantages to be gained from such an action would be both defensive and offensive in nature, since Moscow could deploy nuclear-powered submarines and long-range bombers in that region. The Norwegian fjords and bases would provide protection from naval and air forces threatening the Kola peninsula base and make it easier to force the bulwark formed by Greenland, Iceland, the Faeroes, and the Shetlands, which block Soviet access to the Atlantic. The assumption that the Soviet Union considers these advantages so important as to make acceptable the risk of a military conflict must remain open to doubt. Clearly, it would not carry out such an aggression as long as it were convinced that NATO is prepared to defend this area (as well as others), and that the alliance will not tolerate isolated actions against the northern flank.

As far as the southern part of this region—the Baltic and the Baltic approaches—is concerned, the Soviet Union will wait for the outcome of the third law of the sea conference to see whether the special arrangements on enclosed and semi-enclosed seas will provide new momentum

149

for its old project, which is sold under the label of "Sea of Peace." The object of this project is to deny the Baltic to the navies of nonlittoral countries. In view of the strong superiority of the Warsaw Pact navies, this outcome would assure Russian hegemony in the Baltic.

Although a limited military action with the objective of seizing the Baltic approaches is well within the limits of the Warsaw Pact nations' military capabilities, it is highly improbable. Apart from the the fact that the ratio of forces in the Baltic is not as unfavorable to NATO as it is in the far north, the escalation of any such action into a European war would be inevitable, given the immediate adjacency of the central region.

It is beyond doubt, however, that one of the Soviet efforts in the northern flank will be directed at strengthening its maritime capabilities and expanding its bases. In pursuing this objective, the Kremlin seems to assume that although the pace of buildup in force levels will slow down, the balance of power will remain in its favor. The reasoning is that first, Western shipbuilding programs—in particular the U.S. program—initiated in response to the Soviet maritime expansion, will begin to register from 1980 onwards, and second, the numerous older Soviet units are obsolescing rapidly and will have to be replaced. The large series of Whisky- and Foxtrot-class submarines, Sverdlov-class cruisers, Skory- and Riga-class destroyers, OSA-class fast patrol boats, and Badger bombers have reached, or will soon reach, the end of their service life. (Finding itself in a similar situation during the last decade, the U.S. Navy reduced its inventory of ships almost by half.) All the same, there is no indication of a reversal of trend in the ratio of forces, provided the Russians intend, and are able, to maintain their present construction rate. The Soviet potential will continue to grow, and its ocean-warfare capability, in particular, will improve. A second Kiev-class carrier has been commissioned, and by 1985 four others may have followed, although probably not all of them will be deployed with the northern fleet. When the number of Soviet nuclear ballistic missile submarines fixed in the SALT I agreement is reached, or when the respective number of submarines have been modernized, the Soviet navy's fleet of nuclear-powered attack submarines might increase through the introduction of a new class. For the time being, the Kresta II-class cruisers and the Krivak II-class destroyers will continue to be delivered at the customary rates. There are no indications as yet of a new class, but in light of Soviet procurement procedures, the possibility of new construction cannot be ruled out. It is a certainty that we shall soon identify Backfire bomber units stationed on the Kola peninsula base as we did on the Baltic coast base as long as one year ago.

As for the amphibious component, the Ropucha-class will have a longer range, and air-cushion craft of higher capacity will reduce considerably transit times in the Baltic. Thus, the Soviet forces will improve their capability of achieving tactical surprise. It remains to be seen whether their difficulties with the missile-equipped patrol hydrofoil craft can be overcome. In any case, continued Soviet deployment of additional major auxiliaries will markedly increase their underway replenishment capability.

In NATO naval forces, the most marked change over the next few years will be the introduction of long-range, surface-to-surface missiles of high-hit accuracy. Their deployment will lessen the inferiority of the Western navies in a surface duel.

To sum up, it may be said of foreseeable developments on the northern flank that the Soviet Union will continue to strengthen its posture in the Barents and Baltic seas and to undermine NATO's position in Norway, Iceland, and Denmark. To achieve their political ends, the Soviets will make use of a great many ways, means, and methods. However, they will hardly resort to military power—not even for actions with limited objectives—unless the Atlantic alliance's will to resist and defensive capabilities were to ebb so much that the Soviets could consider the risk of military action acceptable.

To counter this political objective, the West would have to continue to assure the Scandinavian NATO members that their security in the alliance is guaranteed. In the foreseeable future, Norway and Denmark will hardly abandon their reservations with respect to peacetime stationing of foreign troops and storage of nuclear weapons. Nevertheless, NATO's ability to reinforce important strategic positions early in an emergency could be improved through appropriate plans, prepositioning of heavy material, and the construction of additional airfields. Although the West's current naval construction programs will prevent the kind of rapid shift in balance of power toward the Warsaw Pact nations that occurred during the past ten years, the NATO alliance will have to continue to reckon with the acute threat to its vital lines of communication across the Atlantic. In this respect, strengthening the Second Fleet by redeployment of units—for instance from the Pacific Fleet—would be an urgent requirement. Permanent deployment of a carrier group around Iceland would be the best solution.

Prospects for the Rest of the Century

In considering the prospects for the northern flank to the year 2000, one should bear in mind that the time frame is just half that since World

War II. Moreover, the epochal change in the international situation wrought by World War II and postwar events has resulted in a situation in the Northern Hemisphere that—whether one likes it or not—has a comparatively high degree of inherent stability. Fundamental changes are not to be expected in the short run. This applies more to NATO's northern flank than to its southern flank, with its higher sensitivity to crises. In the decades to come, we will continue to see fluctuations in the noncommitted world, although we should not expect a new center of power to crystallize in that area. But, even the northern flank is likely to be influenced by a number of factors that are not foreseeable but are implied by the following questions:

- What will develop out of the détente between East and West which, besides defense, is the second pillar in the preservation of peace? Will SALT, the conference on security and cooperation in Europe (CSCE), and the MBFR negotiations result in a balance of Eastern and Western forces in central Europe and in a mutually advantageous atmosphere of peaceful cooperation?
- Will the instability of the noncommitted world be exploited with greater intensity by the Soviet Union and its allies in order to extend their sphere of influence and control the resources on which Western prosperity is largely dependent?
- How will the West respond to the growing superiority of the Soviet military capabilities—by remaining inactive or by increasing its efforts?
- What frictions will result from the new law of the sea? From the extension of territorial waters out to twelve nautical miles and economic zones out to two hundred nautical miles? What forces will be required for the protection of these extended rights?
- What are the risks to international peace from the conflict between Israel and the Arab countries and from the racial problems in South Africa?
- Who will replace the superannuated leaders in the Kremlin?
- Will naval materiel and naval warfare undergo drastic changes as a result of new technologies?

These are but a few of the many questions that nobody can answer with any degree of reliability. Moreover, the interval between now and the next century is too short to realize ultimate results in many fields. In discussing prospects for the remaining years of this century, one can rely only on a few basic assumptions that seem to be comparatively certain. In my opinion they are:

(1) Communist ideology being what it is, the East and West will continue competing for political, military, and ideological power. Soviet policies will continue to be motivated by Moscow's desire to maintain, and even to expand its position of international power and by its craving for prestige in its relations with the United States. The policy of détente, provided it continues successfully, will merely serve to check that competition to some extent.

(2) The Soviet Union will continue its efforts to secure the territorial gains and power position won in Europe during and after World War II. It will continue to concentrate its political and military powers toward achieving this objective, seeking at the same time fully to exploit any NATO weaknesses, for instance, on the southern flank.

(3) The Warsaw Pact countries will continue their efforts to expand their influence in the noncommitted countries at the expense of the West, stopping—or at least impeding—the supply of raw materials to NATO countries. Success in these efforts will, however, be limited, because of the political instability of the noncommitted countries. (The Soviet Union has just learned that the hard way in Egypt and Somalia.) Western economic and financial assistance to developing countries and options for diversifying their raw material imports and developing their own resources will also reduce communist success.

(4) The Soviet Union and its allies will seek to avoid a military conflict with NATO as long as such a conflict would threaten their existence, which will be the case at least for the rest of this century.

(5) Revolutionary breakthroughs in technology are not anticipated until the turn of the century, but the development and refinement of capabilities now in their infancy will continue. As a result, there will be certain shifts in the weight given to naval weapon systems, inter alia, in favor of the flying components of the most varied versions.

Given these five basic assumptions, the northern flank and the maritime capabilities of the Warsaw Pact nations will play an important part in future developments. The overriding objective of the Soviet Union will be to secure what it now possesses, ideally by forming a neutral protective belt, on the model of Finland, around the area under Warsaw Pact domination. In this respect caution is indicated in the MBFR negotiations, inasmuch as a special arms-control zone covering the Federal Republic of Germany might be a first step in this direction. This overriding objective suggests that Soviet political and diplomatic activities relative to the Scandinavian countries will continue to be aimed at dislodging these countries from NATO and, if possible, to commit them, by agreements, to the support of the Soviet Union or to disable them, politically, from concluding other alliances. Improvements in the maritime capabilities of the forces confronting NATO's northern flank will also continue. This is one facet of the Soviet objective of achieving and maintaining military superiority in Europe. The Soviets will continue to regard the northern flank as a steppingstone toward their goal of interrupting the lines of communication between the United States and Europe and of improving their own offensive capabilities. The enhancement of Soviet-bloc maritime capabilities should be seen in two perspectives.

First, they will have to improve and expand the infrastructure of the Kola peninsula base. To that end, there will be industrial expansion, in particular, shipbuilding capacity, of which 40 percent is, at present, located in the Baltic; an increase in the population of the peninsula; and an improvement in the transport system, with the objective of embedding the base, which, at present, is exposed to the environment. There are indications of such efforts. It cannot be ruled out that such a transfer of resources would, in the long run, be at the expense of the Baltic coast base, given its unfavorable conditions for deployment of naval forces. The Kola base would also accommodate ocean-going units, in particular submarines, which have no combat value in the Baltic because of its shallow depth. The Warsaw Pact nations have not, so far, emulated the German type-206 submarines, whose small dimensions (450 tons) are more suited to the Baltic Sea. In consequence, the strategic importance of their Baltic approaches position will diminish. It should, however, be borne in mind that the Baltic is the natural maritime gateway to the Soviet homeland, so that the Soviet claim to hegemony over that sea will change as little as the Soviet desire to control its approaches or exits. In addition, the Baltic offers much better training opportunities than the Barents or Greenland seas, whose considerable disadvantages include adverse weather conditions, short daylight hours in winter, and lack of training facilities. The military threat to the Baltic approaches will continue even after the Kola peninsula base has become efficient enough to provide for all forces involved in posing a direct threat to NATO's Atlantic lines of communication. The Baltic forces will remain an instrument of national security to the Warsaw Pact nations and, at the same time, serve as a potential threat to central Europe.

The second perspective from which to view the growing maritime threat is the changing ratio of naval forces as a result of new constructions, with particular reference to technical improvements of weapon systems. As indicated earlier, it will be difficult for the Soviet Union to step up substantially its construction rates. Moreover, given the trend toward replacing large numbers of old vessels designed primarily for inshore missions with bigger units capable of blue-water operations, the high rate of change in the quantitative ratio of forces will be further slowed down, unless the West resumes its previous practice of offsetting high construction costs by reducing the number of new units constructed. As it is, such compensation is subject to close restriction, particularly with respect to antisubmarine warfare elements, which are so important in opposing the Soviet threat. The protective qualities of water against any kind of sensors will continue to necessitate a substantial quantitative effort, although less than in World War II when on the allied side, each enemy submarine was confronted by 25 antisubmarine units and 100 aircraft. Having said this, I could go on and say that for the rest of this century the changes governing the maritime ratio of forces on the northern flank will indeed be characterized less by numbers of units than by technological progress in the field of weapon systems.

It is a certainty that in the next twenty-five years the Soviet northern fleet will commission, in addition to improved submarines carrying strategic weapons, new nuclear-powered attack submarines that will be faster, quieter, and better equipped, especially with improved sensors. As far as ordnance is concerned, the subsurface-to-surface missile of longer range and high-hit accuracy will come to the fore. Submarines will continue to be the main threat to the lines of communication between the United States and Europe, appearing in the northern flank region mostly in transit.

It may be assumed that the Backfire bomber will be the mainstay of the naval air components of the northern and Baltic fleets in the decades to come. That bomber will extend the air umbrella for surface forces operating far to the west, beyond Iceland. It will be armed with long-range air-to-ship missiles of improved accuracy. The disadvantage in the range of the Soviet flying air defense component relative to that of the bomber might be compensated, to some extent, by the deployment of more Kiev-class carriers. In case of war, it would be fully compensated by early seizure of air bases in northern Norway and Iceland and redeployment of high-performance fighters to those bases.

The Russians will have to improve their shipborne surface-to-air missile systems to counter the threat to their major surface units from the deployment of the Harpoon missile—to be followed by the Tomahawk—in the NATO navies. The number of major naval units is likely to depend, inter alia, on the Soviet carrier concept, which is not yet discernible. Moscow will certainly have to fill the gap in supply ships. After its experiences with bases in foreign countries, the Soviet navy may place more emphasis on underway replenishment and nuclear propulsion. Moscow will continue to improve the quality of its anti-submarine warfare capabilities, because it has to assume that NATO's attack submarines will remain the main threat to its forces in the Barents and Norwegian seas, even if Soviet forces were able to gain superiority in those waters.

The Soviet amphibious component, too, will undergo marked qualitative changes. Application of the air-cushion principle and con-struction of bigger landing ships—inter alia, for the transport of air-cushion craft—will permit the Baltic navies to execute faster short-range operations at lower risk, especially in the mine countermeasures field, and to plan for long-range operations—for instance, against Iceland. The area of amphibious operations is the only one to which the navies of Poland and the GDR make a substantial contribution to the Soviet maritime offensive capabilities. Poland also constructs landing ships for the Soviet Union (for instance, Polnocny-class units). Otherwise, the two navies concentrate on inshore forces. It may be assumed that, in this respect, there will be no change in the future.

Combined operations of naval and naval air forces, integrated with land-based command-and-control systems, is a combat development that both the East and the West seek to perfect. The West German navy is responding to this trend by the development of new classes of fast patrol boats and frigates, equipped with tactical data-processing systems, and by the construction of a new computerized naval headquarters that will, inter alia, help to compensate the inevitable weakness in the sensor capability of their smaller units. In coastal waters, the air-cushion craft is likely to take over the functions of the present small craft in the long run, provided stabilization problems in the weapons platform can be effectively solved.

The surveillance and control of extensive maritime areas require great efforts. Attempts to employ satellites for this task are even now evident on both sides. If it were possible to develop satellites capable of transmitting reliable information directly to naval forces for immediate tactical evaluation—for instance as standoff target-acquisition informa-tion for long-range missile weapons systems of high accuracy—there would be a decisive change in naval warfare capability on the northern flank, as well as elsewhere. Such a development would initially provide a significant advantage to the side first making use of it—which might happen well within the current century.

Conclusion

NATO's principal defense problem was a territorial one as long as the Warsaw Pact had but one option for aggression. Apart from the irrational possibility of a deliberate nuclear strike, that option was the occupation of Western Europe by land. By its development into a maritime power, the Soviet Union has provided itself with an instrument that allows it to deploy naval forces wherever it needs them in support of its policies in the noncommitted world and, what is even more aggravating, has extended its spectrum of threat considerably.

In case of an armed conflict in and for Europe, the Soviet Union's two north European fleets would become the instrument for interrupting the lines of communication between Europe and the United States. The implications of this fact for NATO's defensive capability and, hence, for the credibility of deterrence, are obvious.

Even if NATO succeeded in deploying the immediately available resources of the United States to Europe before the outbreak of hostilities, these reinforcements together with the European forces would, in fact, not be able to take advantage of their definitely improved capabilities to conduct a sustained defense, unless they could rely on the continuous support of logistic assets from the American continent beyond the period of initial operations.

The battle for the lines of communication in the North Atlantic will be decisively influenced by military operations in the northern flank. If the Warsaw Pact navies succeeded in extending their control beyond the Baltic and Barents seas to the Norwegian and North seas and succeeded in seizing key control positions in these areas, the result would be a collapse—not only of the left wing of the defensive front in Europe (with ensuing adverse consequences for the central front) but also of the bulwark that protects the North Atlantic link.

This danger is by no means a new one—fleets cannot be built up in a few years, nor can they be built up clandestinely—but the realization of the existence of this danger has too long been repressed. It is high time we gave it due attention, looking it squarely in the face.

Problems of Sea Power in the Western Pacific As We Approach the Twenty-First Century

Peter W. Soverel

Writing a paper entitled "Problems of Sea Power in the Western Pacific As We Approach the Twenty-First Century" is a formidable challenge. The uncertainty of the future may be seen in the contrast between the region as it is today and as it was a quarter century ago. In laying a course to the twenty-first century we might draw from our navigational experience on the premise that knowledge of the past and present will provide some references with which to establish a dead reckoning. The shortcomings inherent in this approach are obvious to all navigators: while we have a chart of the past, there is no hydrographic office edition for the future.

The problem in the Western Pacific is only indirectly associated with sea power and navies. U.S. difficulties relate more to defining the nature and extent of American interests in the region. The object of this paper is to discern the nature and extent of American interests in East Asia during the period 1985–2000 and to relate maritime strategy to those interests, recognizing that strategy is the organized direction of military power toward achievement of national policy objectives.

Before discussing maritime strategy, we should understand the policy framework within which the strategy is to be operative, so I will start by discussing the nature of U.S. interests in East Asia. When discussing a nation's international objectives one should keep in mind that those objectives can be threatened by the actions or the countervailing interests of other nations. We shall consider how a nation's interests might be threatened, and how the exercise of sea power might contribute to securing or defending those interests. This examination of the relationship between sea power and national interests may shed light on the kind of sea power (that is, the force structure of navies) and on the maritime strategic concepts of both the United States and the Soviet Union. Finally, I shall develop the process of threat analysis in some detail to illustrate that strategic options must be considered in terms of a broad policy perspective, with an appreciation of the linkages between policy choices and strategic consequences.

Sea power does not exist for its own purposes. Rather, it is one of several instruments of state power that may be employed in pursuit of political objectives. The utility of this particular instrument is a function of objectives and environment. Under certain circumstances it may provide a means to an end. Sir Julien Corbett, one of the first commentators on naval affairs to establish the proper relationship between sea power and political objectives, suggested that sea power is a means of securing the use of the seas for national purposes while denying similar use to one's adversaries.[1] To paraphrase Clausewitz, the first duty of maritime strategists is to understand the nature of sea power, neither misconstruing it nor trying to turn it into something alien to its nature.[2]

This paper attempts to clarify three points: U.S. objectives in East Asia; the use of the seas for national purposes; and the relationship between naval forces and national purposes. In other words, it is about U.S. global interests, regional Pacific interests and naval power in the Western Pacific. It discusses the following five potential uses of naval forces. First, such forces may be employed for the purpose of denying an adversary the use of the sea as a medium for the transportation or exploitation of its resources. Naval power may be dedicated to preventing use of the sea as a base from which an opponent could project military power, including strategic nuclear force, against the United States. In a positive sense, sea forces can secure for the United States or allies use of the sea as a transportation medium and/or for the exploitation of its resources. Fourth, American naval forces might be used both to secure use of the sea as a base from which to project military power ashore and to project combat power for the purpose of compelling an adversary to modify its international behavior. Finally, naval forces might be thought of as the earnest of U.S. political involvement in East Asian security affairs. As can be seen, except for their use as earnest, these potential uses of naval forces are combat functions and are not conducted during peacetime.

---

[1] Sir Julien S. Corbett, *Some Principles of Maritime Strategy* (London: Longman, Green, 1918), pp. 12-14.

[2] More exactly, Clausewitz stated, "The first, the supreme, the most far-reaching act of judgement that the statesman and commander have to make is to establish by that test the kind of war on which they are embarking; neither mistaking it for, nor trying to turn it into, something that is alien to its nature." Carl Von Clausewitz, *On War*, Michael Howard and Peter Paret, eds. and trans. (Princeton: Princeton University Press, 1976), pp. 88-89.

American Foreign Policy: 1950–1960

Until the war in Korea, U.S. policy makers proceeded in the sound belief that expansion of Soviet control in Europe and Japan would pose a direct threat to American security.[3] American strategy involved a combination of military pressure to prevent direct Soviet aggression in Europe and massive economic assistance. Sound European economies, it was believed, would establish political stability which, in turn, would forestall indirect Soviet aggression through domestic Communist parties.[4] These initiatives implied an extension of U.S. security frontiers. The preceived threat to American security that motivated the containment strategy was the expansion of Soviet—as distinct from Communist —power. Unfortunately, the policy was justified to the American public in ideological terms.[5]

The North Korean attack on South Korea had the effect of extending the U.S. policy of containment. The policy had centered on the European balance of power but now it became a global, anti-Communist crusade in which Moscow was regarded as the head of a tightly controlled international Communist movement. Thus, Communist gains anywhere in the world represented Russian gains and American losses.[6] It is clear now that this assumption was fallacious in 1950 and grossly inadequate by the middle 1960s. First, it led to an undifferentiated perception of interests, in which South Vietnam and Japan might be considered in the same category. Second, it greatly constrained the United States by gratuitously identifying certain nations as U.S. enemies and Soviet tools, without any objective analysis of the actual interests and policies of those nations. The result of this kind of thinking was

---

[3] Report of the Department of State Policy Planning Staff of November 6, 1946, "Resumé of the World Situation." This resumé prepared by George Kennan was accepted with minor changes by the secretary of state and forwarded to the President. *Foreign Relations of the United States, 1947,* vol. 1 (Washington, D.C.: U.S. Government Printing Office, 1973), pp. 770-777.

[4] Harry S. Truman inaugural address delivered on January 20, 1949. *Department of State Bulletin,* vol. 20, no. 500, pp. 123-126.

[5] Ibid., p. 123.

[6] The consensus of the U.S. top leadership was that the North Korean attack was being supported by the Soviets as a part of some larger plan to overthrow the United States, that the larger Soviet effort would be in Europe, and that the danger in making a military response in Korea was that the United States would become mal-deployed for the expected Soviet effort in Europe. See John W. Spanier, *The Truman-MacArthur Controversy and the Korean War* (New York: W.W. Norton, 1965), pp. 23-30.

an open-ended security perspective, supported by an active, indeed interventionist, foreign policy on a global scale.[7]

This U.S. policy was to have unfortunate consequences because it did not differentiate among or rank American interests. Even a nation as powerful as the United States does not command unlimited resources. Foreign policy that fails to recognize that this (or any other) country cannot "pay any price, bear any burden"[8] (except for the most fundamental interests) may lead to disaster. In the 1950s and early 1960s, the United States seemed to act on the assumption that, because the Soviets and their fellow travelers desired to overcome the United States, it was also their intention to use all means (including military) to fulfill this desire. Threat analysis under these conditions tends to center on an analysis of military capability.

U.S. Policy Alternatives

Before progressing further, we may find it useful to examine methods of threat analysis and to compare capabilities analysis with an alternative process. Capabilities analysis is often associated with the armed forces or military postures. It starts with the collection of hard intelligence concerning a potential enemy's force structure—determining how many and what type of tanks, aircraft, ships, and troops the enemy has and how they are deployed and arrayed. This assessment leads to conclusions about what the enemy could do if it so desired. Military threat analysis is done in bilateral terms, on the presumption that the adversary can devote all its resources to operations against our own forces.

The process so far described is similar to the so-called worst-case analysis, and, in making policy, it is important that responsible military

---

[7]The consistency of the view is apparent in the public statements of successive administrations equating U.S. interests with the containment of communism. Compare, for example, Vice President Nixon's remarks to the press in 1954: "The United States as Leader of the Free World cannot further retreat in Asia. It is hoped that the United States will not have to send troops but if this government cannot avoid it, the Administration must face up to the situation and dispatch troops" (*New York Times,* 17 April 1954, p.1) with those of President Johnson in 1965: "we fight [in Vietnam] because we must fight if we are to live in a world where every country can shape its destiny . . . we do this to convince the leaders of North Vietnam and all who seek to share their conquest of a simple fact. We will not be defeated." (*Department of State Bulletin,* vol. 52, no. 1348, pp. 607-608.)

[8]"Let every nation know, whether it wishes us well or ill, that we shall pay any price, bear any burden, meet any hardship, support any friend, oppose any foe to assure the survival and success of liberty." John F. Kennedy inaugural address delivered on January 20, 1961. *Department of State Bulletin,* vol. 64, no. 1128, p. 175.

experts and intelligence analysts illuminate the worst case. The process of viewing military operations in terms of meeting the worst-case threat, while protecting the full range of national interests from other potential adversaries, tends to drive the required force level upward. Although desirable and necessary, the described process is inadequate for a national threat assessment.

An alternative method would involve examining the armed forces an adversary could use in worst-case operations and then seeking means of reducing the threat by altering the political environment. This kind of civilian or political analytical process begins rather than culminates with the enemy order of battle and poses a different set of questions. The first step is to take the analysis out of a bilateral context and set it firmly in an international framework. The determination of what an enemy is likely to do depends on two considerations: what it might theoretically be capable of doing, and what its neighbors may do in response.

In this analytical context, there are two implications. The first is that national interests may be ranked by preference, but they are pursued on the basis of cost. For every interest a nation pursues, there are *counterbalancing national interests* that, under the circumstances, are not being actively sought.[9]

The second implication, linked to the first, is that the degree of international political enmity is relative. In battle, forces must be expected to fight at full fury, regardless of the nature of the national decision to commit forces to combat. Political enmity, however, is qualitatively different in that it is rarely unequivocal; therefore, it may provide an opportunity to influence national behavior through a choice of alternative policies or an appeal to the adversary's counterbalancing national interests.

The process of conceptualizing alternative national goals and policies adds important dimensions to threat analysis. It implies that a nation chooses its enemies by its choice of policies and that a modification of policy may alter the constellation of enemies. Changing the scheme of analysis forces an examination of factors other than a strict order of battle and results in an assessment that combines three factors:

(1) *Capability*. On the basis of order-of-battle information, can a nation take action inimical to our own interests?

(2) *Intention*. Does that nation have reason to take such actions?

---

[9]For a more detailed examination of this concept see, Frederick H. Hartmann, "A Difference of Perspective," *Naval War College Review,* Spring 1976, pp. 65-74.

(3) *Circumstances.* Is that nation likely to be successful; what might its neighbors do; what might we do to reduce the likelihood of enemy success through modification of policy with respect to that enemy's neighbors?

Fundamental to such a conceptual framework is a belief in a range of American interests, differentiated by importance and cost. As a corollary, the formerly held belief in an international Communist movement operating in response to and on behalf of the Soviets has been supplanted by a belief that nations seek to promote their own interests. Thus, there exists the presumption that national behavior can be manipulated by an appeal to a nation's counterbalancing national interests. As stated above, for every policy or interest a nation pursues, there is a range of policies and interests that are not being pursued but could be. From a policy perspective, these alternative national interests are of the greatest importance in the formulation of strategic options.

Applied to East Asia this conceptual framework was to have important consequences since it questioned the very foundations of existing policy. If American interests were differentiated by cost and related to worth, U.S. policy in Vietnam was clearly an inversion of means and ends. In objective terms, if the Chinese and Soviets share more differences than mutual interests and it is presumed that nations seek their own interests, the American choice of East Asian policies will have an important impact on Sino-Soviet relations as well as U.S. military needs in the Western Pacific. In this context, it is apparent how the Sino-American rapprochement, begun by the Nixon administration and expanded by subsequent administrations, has revolutionized U.S. strategy and priorities both in East Asia and in the rest of the world. The effect of the Kissinger-Nixon initiatives and the policies of the Carter administration has been to restore American international freedom of action with an attendant reduction in Soviet flexibility.

Sino-Soviet Relations

As in the preceding decades, the Soviet Union is still identified as the one nation that can threaten the United States with direct attack. Prevention of such an attack remains the most important objective of U.S. foreign policy. A closely related objective is the prevention of Soviet domination of Western Europe and Japan.

The new U.S. policy toward China—the so-called China card—has permitted Sino-Soviet relations to be affected by the competing interests of China and the U.S.S.R. in East Asia. The aggressive anti-Chinese stance of the United States throughout the 1950s and 1960s, backed by the forward deployment of powerful forces all along the eastern and southern Chinese frontiers—including three-fourths of a million men engaged in hostilities in Vietnam—tended to constrain Sino-Soviet hostility. China submerged its long-standing enmity with the Russians in the face of the more active American threat.

Sino-American hostility did not serve U.S. interests, particularly in light of the greater importance the United States has attached to Western Europe. The coincidence of certain American and Chinese security interests is apparent here. Chinese preoccupation with the growing Soviet military menace encouraged China to improve its relations with the United States so that Chinese forces could be concentrated along the Soviet frontier. Such a redeployment of Chinese military formations would clearly reduce Soviet flexibility, which was and remains of some considerable interest to the United States. Both the United States and China had mutually beneficial alternatives to an adversary relationship.

Predictably, as Sino-American hostility declined, Sino-Soviet relations became more hostile. Improved Chinese-American relations, in turn, forced substantial redeployment of Soviet armor and air forces to East Asia with the result that Soviet power available for use in Europe declined. The shared interest that made this new Sino-American relationship possible was the desire to constrain Soviet aggression. There seems little doubt that this basic Sino-Soviet hostility will persist.[10]

U.S. cooperation in West Germany's *ost politik* has increased Western influence in Eastern Europe, where the Soviets—as a result of the growing "security threat" posed by China—were already operating at a serious handicap. These difficulties have increased dramatically as a result of the interpretations—both in the West and in the Soviet constituencies in Eastern Europe[11]—of the Helsinki Accords and the Carter administration's emphasis on human rights. Soviet ability to respond effectively to these challenges is severely constrained and is unlikely to improve. In any case, there can be little doubt that the Soviets would be exceptionally nervous about the reliability of Eastern European nations in the event of hostilities with either NATO or China. Even without actual combat, the margin of usable Soviet power, in a global as

---

[10] Following Mao's death there had been speculation that China and the Soviet Union would reconstruct their relationship. China's recent behavior and the statements of the new leadership provide no evidence to that effect.

[11] A major development of the Helsinki Accords has been to undermine the domestic legitimacy of East European regimes and complicate their already delicate relationships with the Soviets. The determined efforts of the East Germans, for example, to use the Accords for legitimate emigration efforts is well known. See *New York Times*, January 12, 1977, p. 3, and February 2, 1977, p. 4.

well as in a regional sense, has declined as a result of the altered international context.

The altered international environment compels the Soviet Union, to a far greater degree than it does the United States, to divide its attention and limited defense resources between powerful potential enemies in both Asia and Europe. The new Sino-American relationship requires the Soviet Union, rather than the United States, to contemplate, even plan for, the two war scenarios so familiar to American planners of the late 1960s.

The United States is not "playing" China against the Soviet Union, but it is not impeding the natural development of their differences either. It would prefer to see Sino-Soviet differences develop within limits that exclude actual hostilities. Nothing, however, would be likely to undermine the Sino-American rapprochement more quickly or surely than Chinese perceptions of U.S. attempts to use China to further American interests. Both nations need to appreciate their shared interest in constraining Soviet behavior. However, barring American actions that either threaten China directly (such as a return to the anti-Chinese policies of the 1950s and 1960s) or increase the threat posed by the Soviet Union, the intensity of Sino-Soviet rivalry seems to be largely independent of American action.

The congruence between American and Chinese security requirements vis-à-vis the Soviet Union has revolutionized the American security perspective in East Asia and is likely to have far-reaching consequences for U.S. naval forces in the Western Pacific. For the United States, the main problem in East Asia—if indeed it is a problem—is how to cope with the favorable circumstances brought about by the altered perceptions of the threat to U.S. regional and global interests.

American security policy in East Asia must now be viewed as part of an overall attempt to constrain the Soviet Union globally through, at least in part, a cooperative security relationship with China that acts as a counterweight to the Soviet threat. In contrast to our former view of the People's Republic as a militarily aggressive, expansionistic, and revolutionary nation, the United States today shares a de facto, anti-Soviet security relationship with China. The current U.S. perception is that China is preoccupied with both defense and internal development and, therefore, is much less of a threat to U.S. interests than previously believed. While the future role of U.S. military forces in the Western Pacific is not well defined, improved Sino-American relations have led to a dramatic shift in the orientation and planned use of American military in East Asia.

166

Relations with East Asian Allies

The former U.S. relationship with China and its alliance system required, even demanded, the forward deployment of powerful intervention forces capable of frustrating anticipated Chinese or client aggression. American security interests in East Asia were conceived in continental and regional terms that linked U.S. security to that of numerous Asian states perceived as threatened by China. To enhance the security of these nations, and thus American security, the United States extended military guarantees and economic assistance to offset any domestic tendency toward revolutionary movements and military assistance to help them deal with internal subversion or external aggression. U.S. military capabilities in the Western Pacific and the assistance programs to East Asian states were designed to secure U.S. regional interests against a perceived threat by China, North Korea, and North Vietnam against their mainland neighbors.

The definition of U.S.-East Asian interests, in continental terms, required a military capability to project power onto the Asian mainland for the purpose of compelling China, North Vietnam, and North Korea to adjust their behavior to accommodate U.S. interests. These power projection requirements emphasized the need for U.S. bases along the periphery of Asia.[12] In other words, the definition of U.S. interests necessitated the availability of military bases and influenced U.S. relations with its Pacific island allies. The American view of its interests on the Asian continent demanded the maintenance of strong intervention forces along the periphery of Asia to contain Chinese expansion.

Since it was a perceived Chinese military threat to U.S.-Asian interests that initially justified the major American involvement in regional security affairs (including the forward deployment of coercive intervention forces), any reduction in U.S. perceptions of threat was likely to produce a sharp decline in U.S. military involvement as well. If China, Japan, and NATO had common security interests vis-à-vis the Soviet Union, the United States would have no reason to maintain substantial intervention forces in East Asia. In short, the international environment that had spawned and sustained the previous U.S. rationales

---

[12] The war in Vietnam illustrated the importance of base and support facilities in the Philippines to sustained combat operations. However, when the ability to conduct sustained power projection operations in Southeast Asia is not required, the net worth of Philippine bases to the United States declines sharply. On the other hand, should the Soviets acquire naval basing facilities in Vietnam, Philippine air and naval bases would be most useful. The point is, without the political intention of projection of power against the Asian mainland, Philippine bases are of little importance. See *New York Times,* April 10, 1977, p. 7.

for forward deployment and combat use of intervention forces in the Western Pacific has now been radically, probably irreversibly, altered. It is not that the United States is less interested in East Asia, but that it no longer perceives a threat by regional powers to these interests.

As a result of reorienting its security interests in East Asia, the United States has restructured the nature of its interests in regional allies. Except in Japan, it no longer needs island bases for the projection of power. United States forces have taken on a defensive rather than offensive role. As long as the Soviet Union does not obtain base rights in Taiwan or the Philippines and South Korea remains nonhostile toward Japan, the United States can satsify its basic military interests in its Asian allies. This negative nature of U.S. interests is consistent with allied defensive needs and it avoids conflict arising out of the use of host country bases for offensive operations that might involve our allies in situations they would rather avoid.

At the same time, U.S. allies in the Western Pacific, with the exception of South Korea, are island nations and, excluding Taiwan, have no major conflict of interest with China. Each has significant defensive military capabilities. The combination of island or peninsular geography and strong defensive systems provides adequate capabilities for self-defense, so there is no need for active American combat support. The rate of economic and industrial development in the allied nations indicates continued improvement in their defensive military capabilities, which further reduces their objective dependence on the United States for conventional defense.

In the larger policy context, the question facing the United States is how to extend credible nuclear guarantees to these Asian countries without the presence of substantial U.S. conventional forces. Indeed, the economic and industrial strength of these allies simultaneously reduces their dependence on the United States and introduces tensions with respect to U.S. policy on nuclear proliferation. In the absence of some form of credible U.S. nuclear protection, it is fair to presume that Taiwan and South Korea will soon develop their own nuclear capabilities.

Relations with Japan

U.S. relations with Japan differ from the negative or defensive U.S. orientation toward other Asian allies. The United States is interested, not in simply defending the Japanese islands or in denying them to the Soviets, but rather in using them as a base from which to destroy, or at least to contain, the Soviet Pacific fleet and dominate the approaches to and egresses from the Soviet maritime provinces. The Japanese are rightfully sensitive to the implication that these U.S. military interests could involve Japan in a war with the Soviets. This delicate political situation complicates meaningful Japanese-American discussions concerning U.S. contingency uses of Japanese bases. Potential limitations on U.S. use of Japanese bases raise questions about the utility of Japanese-American security links. Japan is acutely aware of its dependence on the United States for security and the limited U.S. role in East Asia may threaten Japanese defenses. For reasons similar to those inhibiting discussion of U.S. contingency uses of Japanese bases, Japan is not likely to engage in candid discussion with the United States on the limits of American protection or about cooperative action in support of mutual regional interests. The issue of cooperative action is of particular importance to Japan in light of U.S. retrenchment in the Pacific.

Indeed, the recent provocative Soviet behavior vis-à-vis Japan[13] has had the effect of calling into question the utility of Japan's ties to the United States. Soviet-Japanese fishery disputes, Soviet air and naval units patrolling close to Japan, and Soviet military buildup in the Far East are all matters of considerable Japanese concern, largely independent of and unrelated to U.S. force levels in the Western Pacific or the American security treaty.

Up to now, Japanese confidence stemmed from American willingness to use force in East Asia and a very broad interpretation of U.S. regional interests to secure Japanese interests. The current U.S. narrowing of Western Pacific interests clearly implies a decline in the relative security of Japanese regional interests. This has been particularly evident in Japanese concerns over U.S. policies regarding, for example, Taiwan and Korea. In both cases, the United States appears to have placed greater emphasis on American interests than on Japanese concerns for their own interests.[14]

The Japanese still smart at the U.S. failure to discuss President Nixon's visit to China with them. The recent willingness of the Carter administration to modify the disengagement rate of U.S. troops in Korea

---

[13] Japanese sensitivities concerning their vulnerability to Soviet pressures have not been ignored by the Soviets, who have taken to referring to Japan as the Finland of the East, leaning on them in fishery negotiations and patrolling in the vicinity of Japan (*New York Times,* April 21, 1977, p. 12). In part, at least, this suggests that in addition to their advantages, basing rights also have disadvantages in that they may give the appearance of obligation. The fact that the United States can do nothing about provocative Soviet behavior further calls into question the advisability of Japan's continued reliance on the United States for security. The question of bases and political liability is examined in greater detail in Ken Booth, *Navies and Foreign Policy* (New York: Crane, Russak & Co., 1977), pp. 90-92.

[14] *New York Times,* June 13, 1977, p. 7.

after talking with the Japanese (and also after disclosing withdrawal schedules without prior Japanese consultation), may be a hopeful sign for the Japanese.[15] However, this positive turn must be balanced by what Japan considers bad faith in the U.S. decision concerning President Carter's opposition to Japanese control of nuclear fuel reprocessing.[16] Japan is also nervous about U.S. plans relative to Taiwan.

In balance, the lesson for Japan may be that the security treaty and cooperative Japanese-American relations are of exceedingly limited utility across a very wide spectrum of Japanese interests. From the American viewpoint, however, the lesson appears to be that political confidence, at least relative to Japan, is only indirectly related to U.S. force levels, but depends upon Japanese conclusions as to the permanence of future U.S. involvement in East Asian security affairs. As a result of the altered international environment, Japan may look to securing her own interests. The Japanese-American relationship is unstable because Japan's inability to deal with strategic issues inhibits any surfacing of conflicting interests. Such a relationship is hardly designed to foster mutual confidence. Japanese-American problems are essentially independent of U.S. force levels; Japan's concerns center around the extent of American political, not military, retrenchment in East Asia.

Military Intervention Alternatives

The altered U.S. attitude toward the People's Republic of China greatly affected our perception of the threat to U.S. interests in East Asia and our relations with East Asian countries. In the new Sino-American environment, the mission of U.S. armed forces in the Western Pacific shifted from intervention on the continent as a means of containing China to emphasis on sea power as a means of containing the Soviet Union and maintaining the security of U.S. regional allies. The economic and industrial development of these allied nations makes them largely independent of the United States for conventional defense. Thus, U.S. future military requirements in the Western Pacific may be significantly reduced in the years ahead.

Quite apart from the altered strategic considerations outlined above, the utility of intervention forces—particularly naval and amphibious forces—as instruments of policy has declined and will probably continue to do so. In the abstract, military power is used to compel a

---

[15] *New York Times,* June 6, 1977, p. 1.
[16] *New York Times,* May 18, 1977, p. 3.

nation to accept one's will. Whether coercive or punitive, the application of power serves the same purpose—to force another nation into accommodating one's interests.

At one violent extreme are punitive or reprisal military operations against value target sites. Short duration, high intensity attacks in reprisal for specific activities are launched to preclude retaliation rather than to diminish an adversary's capacity to persist. When confronted by a determined adversary, such punitive military operations may be insufficient. The ability to enforce one's will may require coercive military operations to limit or destroy the adversary's military and political capacity to resist. While an adversary's acceptance of one's will is the objective of a military operation, the application of force is directed at reducing an opponent's capacity to resist.

The utility of coercive or punitive intervention forces as a means of achieving policy ends depends—as does any use of force—on the consistency of ends and means as well as of costs, benefits, and risks. Until recently, Western nations, particularly the United States, accepted almost as a given the utility of navies as instruments of intervention. As pointed out by MccGwire among others, a number of recent developments make the future utility of sea-based intervention forces questionable.[17]

The first and probably the most important such development is diffusion of technologically advanced weapons systems that threaten the actual military viability of both punitive and coercive intervention operations against militarily advanced nations and greatly increase the military and the political risk of intervention against all other nations. Sea-based intervention operations against advanced nations have always been exceedingly risky because they are incredibly difficult and dangerous to carry out. However, the spread of increasingly lethal precision-guided munitions of considerable reach puts U.S. sea-based intervention forces at risk in future operations, even against lesser powers. It may be possible to conduct one-time reprisal air strikes without excessive danger to sea-based forces, although the North Vietnamese air defenses demonstrated that such an operation can jeopardize attacking forces. In any case, sustaining coercive intervention forces over any extended time frame clearly risks destruction of naval elements. The point is not that combat carries risks, but that the risks may not be consistent with the objectives, including the desire to limit hostilities.[18] Sinking U.S. naval vessels of any description, much less capital ships, is not conducive to limiting hostilities.

---

[17] Michael MccGwire, "Changing Naval Operations and Military Intervention," *Naval War College Review,* Spring 1977, pp. 3-25.
[18] Ibid., p. 23.

A second development is the recognition that use of military force against lesser powers has not been, is not now, and most probably will never be favorably received internationally or even domestically. In and of themselves, unfavorable political dispositions do not rule out the use of force, but they do increase the cost of military operations.[19] As in the case of Vietnam, such costs can be considerable and are impossible to ignore.

In some situations, the resort to arms may be the only remaining option, but in many circumstances the political costs—domestic as well as international—are sufficient to warrant adjustment to an unpleasant situation. When considered in light of the current East Asian context of limited U.S. interests on the mainland, the imbalance between potentially exorbitant political and military costs and limited political objectives is hard to reconcile as long as nonmilitary options are available.

Consider, for example, the unsuitability of a military response to restrictions on unimpeded use of various international straits in Southeast Asia. Access to these waterways does reduce transit time between the Pacific and Indian oceans, but the archipelagic nations clearly have important environmental and sovereignty interests in restricting or regulating their use. If the use is commercial, it might be wise either to submit to regulation or to reroute traffic. In the case of military transits, world opinion may question the "innocent" nature of the transit and, if there is a risk of damage to transitting forces, rerouting remains an attractive option. In both cases, the potential hazards and costs—political as well as military—associated with forced transit in the face of opposition by precision-guided munitions may render military options unattractive.[20]

Developments in weapons technology, the availability of advanced offensive and defensive systems, and altered international and domestic attitudes regarding use of force against secondary powers do not necessarily rule out U.S. use of intervention forces. However, the utility of coercive intervention seems exceedingly low. Punitive intervention, in those cases where U.S. objectives are clearly defined and sharply limited, may retain its utility, but the risks associated with such action can be considerable.

---

[19] Stanley Hoffmann, "The Acceptability of Military Force," *Force in Modern Societies: Its Place in International Politics,* Adelphi Paper No. 102 (London: International Institute for Strategic Studies, 1973), p. 2.

[20] Booth, *Navies and Foreign Policy,* pp. 221-223. This line of reasoning should not be overdrawn, Booth points out, because the perceived decline in the utility of force as an instrument of policy is largely a Western phenomenon. There is, of course, a cost for not having forces available when necessary.

Containment of the Soviet Threat

In summary, the restructuring of American security perspectives in East Asia from containment of the People's Republic of China toward containment of the U.S.S.R. and the simultaneous, but unrelated, decline in the utility of military intervention as an instrument of policy have transformed the East Asian environment, U.S. perceptions of threat, and U.S. relations with allies. The altered strategic considerations and the reduced utility of intervention forces suggest the logic of a partial U.S. military disengagement from regional security affairs, with continued emphasis on stable, friendly relations with Japan and mutually beneficial security perspectives with China.

An offshore island position anchored on Japan maximizes U.S. advantages in air and naval power—which is particularly appropriate given the restricted nature of U.S. interests in East Asia—and at the same time reduces the potential for misunderstanding with China and inadvertent involvement in regional conflict on the mainland.[21] As the United States moves toward an offshore island position supported by fewer American forces and a restricted definition of regional security interests, the emphasis of its military power in the Western Pacific is likely to be on the Soviet Union and not on China or lesser Asian powers.[22]

The upshot of these developments is an offshore, defensive American strategy that envisions only limited participation in regional security affairs, with little or no involvement on the Asian mainland. This position differs substantially from our former policy of active American participation in the full range of regional security affairs, including potential military involvement on the continent. Where our former strategy provided for substantial intervention forces, the current redefinition of American East Asian interests substantially reduces demands for forward deployment of major intervention forces. In the future, the principal mission of U.S. forces in the Western Pacific will not be to cope with regional conflict but to help deter aggressive Soviet behavior in Europe or in Asia. The deterrent effect of these forces would seem to depend

---

[21] Ironically, this offshore position is very similar to that proposed after World War II but later abandoned in the face of the Korean and the Cold wars. Documents prepared for presidential consideration by the National Security Council in 1948 outlined a strategy for disengagement from the Chinese civil war on the premise that the United States should not continue to remain involved (National Security Council Report 11/2, December 12, 1948) and a proposal for an offshore defensive position in East Asia to facilitate concentration of resources against the Soviets in Europe (National Security Council Report 20, July 12, 1948).

[22] *New York Times,* May 1, 1977, section 4, p. 4.

173

on two factors: (1) the extent to which U.S. forces can cause or increase damage to Soviet interests, protect U.S. interests, or reduce Soviet ability to threaten U.S. interests; and (2) the extent to which U.S. forces contribute to sustaining an international environment that constrains Soviet behavior. In both cases, Japan's geographic location is exceedingly important to the United States.

American forces along the periphery of Asia, particularly in Japan, command the sea approaches to the Soviet maritime provinces. They threaten the vulnerable Soviet sea and land lines of communications to the Far East as well as the Soviet Pacific fleet. United States air and naval capabilities aimed at isolating Soviet maritime provinces and the Soviet Pacific fleet complement Chinese and Japanese security interests. However, these American forces neither threaten China nor encourage either Japan or China to modify their relationship with the Soviets. Our ability to isolate the Soviet Far East clearly jeopardizes fundamental Soviet interests and, presumably, moderates Soviet behavior.[23]

The necessity for the United States and its Asian allies to secure the sea for transportation and to deny the sea as a base from which to project power—submarine-launched ballistic-missile strikes—adds to the importance of the Japanese islands. Given the length of the various allied lines of communication and the geographic expanse of the Pacific, the destruction of the Soviet Pacific fleet or its containment within the Sea of Japan at the very outset of hostilities becomes a necessity if U.S. and allied escort requirements are to be kept within achievable bounds.

The foregoing discussion raises the serious issue as to the availability of Japanese bases during hostilities. If Japan should deny U.S. use of these bases for combat operations in the event of a Korean crisis or U.S.-U.S.S.R. hostilities, the effect would not be to complicate but to simplify military considerations. Since U.S. interests in Korea are related to Japanese security, Japan's refusal to grant such operating rights would put U.S. interests and priorities in the region in an entirely different perspective. Moreover, any uncertainty about the availability of Japanese bases to U.S. forces would only increase Korea's incentive to acquire a national nuclear capability, which would further complicate Japan's security problem. In short, by denying U.S. use of its bases to support

---

[23] The boxing in of Soviet flexibility as suggested could have the undesirable effect of encouraging irresponsible Soviet behavior. It is not inconceivable that the Soviets, caught between deteriorating military situations in both Europe and Asia, could conceptualize both their problems and the resolution of their problems in military terms. The situation the Soviets increasingly find themselves in is not unlike that of Imperial Germany in 1914, in that even minor adjustments to the status quo can become extremely threatening when the slope of the general trend is not favorable.

combat air and naval operations during Korean hostilities, Japan would in effect remove the major U.S. incentive for any involvement in Korea.

Japan's refusal to support the United States in a war with the Soviet Union or to permit American use of Japanese air and naval facilities for offensive combat operations against Soviet facilities—especially the Soviet Pacific fleet—would drastically alter U.S. naval requirements in the Pacific, particularly securing the commercial sea lines of communications to the Western Pacific and thus to Japan. While the United States would retain an interest in destroying Soviet Pacific naval assets in order to secure its own use of the central and eastern Pacific and to deny Soviet nuclear power projection capabilities, it would no longer be concerned in any immediate sense with the vulnerable sea lines to the Western Pacific.

Making provisions to destroy the Soviet Pacific fleet from a central and eastern Pacific basing line is a formidable but by no means impossible undertaking. In the absence of Japanese cooperation, the fundamental nature of U.S. interests in the Western Pacific would shift from sea control to denial of the Pacific as a base for Soviet power projection. However, it is questionable whether U.S. aircraft carriers would be able to conduct sustained successful power projection operations against the Soviets in the Western Pacific—particularly toward the end of the century. The alternative of a submarine or a mine offensive from a central or eastern Pacific basing line is probably more consistent with the limited nature of American interests.

The naval imperatives affecting the Soviets in East Asia are fundamentally different from those affecting the United States. American use of the Pacific to support the Japanese economy and to conduct power projection operations puts the Soviet Union at a serious disadvantage. In wartime, Soviet forces would have to isolate Japan and deny U.S. use of the sea as a base from which to launch attacks. To accomplish these tasks, Soviet naval forces would have to focus primarily on the navy and secondarily on allied use of the sea for transportation. Furthermore, except in the case of preemptive first use, Soviet forces would be of limited utility and, given the geographic location of base facilities, extremely vulnerable. Soviet power projection capabilities are not significant now, nor are they expected to be, particularly in light of the diffusion of advanced technology. Under these circumstances, the utility of the Soviet forces deployed against China would be reduced, and the presence of limited U.S. air and naval forces in the Western Pacific would not complicate Chinese security problems. Moreover, given the dual nature of its security problem in East Asia, the Soviet Union would have to divide its assets, thus further enhancing Chinese, Japanese, and American security.

Future Force Levels

One of the great hurdles facing the United States in the years ahead may well be the task of convincing our Asian allies that the altered American security perspective in the Western Pacific is in their interest as well as our own. The difficult question is, How can the United States extend credible nuclear guarantees and assurances of continued access to weapons and technology and at the same time reduce its forward deployed forces? Without the actual presence of substantial U.S. conventional forces, it may be exceedingly difficult to convince our allies of a continuing interest in Asian affairs and, even more important, continuing political support.

Over and above their role in potential wartime missions, U.S. forward deployed forces have been widely assumed to have significant deterrent value. All nations tend to view such forces as visible evidence of American concern for and involvement in regional affairs. Furthermore, U.S. force levels are often thought to be notional or shorthand indicators of the level of U.S. interest and, as such, to increase the credibility of U.S. nuclear guarantees. Without the presence of conventional forces, it may be exceptionally difficult either to extend believable nuclear guarantees or to reassure allies of continued U.S. political support.

As already mentioned, the current U.S. trend toward modification, even retrenchment, of security interests coupled with substantial force reductions is likely to continue. If U.S. forces are to be deployed on the basis of military requirements, future levels in the Western Pacific could be quite low. From the perspective of U.S. allies, neither the ultimate bottom line for U.S. forces nor the extent of future political retrenchment is known. The tensions resulting from this uncertainty center on the outcome of two questions: To what extent should these Asian countries rely on the United States for their security needs? and How can the United States credibly communicate its continuing interest in and commitment to Asian allies—either in the absence of or reduction in forward deployed military forces—without jeopardizing other national interests, such as our security understanding with China? In other words, sustaining a strategic environment favorable to the United States depends on actions that do not encourage our allies or friends to seek other security arrangements. What those actions are depends in turn on satisfying two different sets of customers for American security assurances: first, Japan and China, and second, our lesser allies in East Asia.

In the case of Japan and China, success in sustaining a cooperative security arrangement seems to depend most heavily on their confidence that the United States will continue to serve as a counterweight to the Soviet Union. To do so the United States must maintain some kind of military equivalence with the Soviet Union on a global scale, but these forces need not necessarily be located in East Asia to counterbalance Soviet forces. Confidence can be sustained only in part by the forces actually deployed to the Western Pacific, whose purpose would be essentially to contain the Soviet Pacific fleet within the Sea of Japan. China in particular needs assurances of a general U.S.-U.S.S.R. military balance. A severe imbalance, with the Soviet Union enjoying a significant military advantage, would place China in some considerable jeopardy, unless it sought some form of political and military accommodation with the U.S.S.R. Under these circumstances such an accommodation would of course be especially dangerous to U.S. interests.

In the case of the lesser Asian allies, success in sustaining a cooperative security arrangement depends on their confidence in the United States as a source of weapons and continued political support. These nations have no strong incentive to acquire national nuclear weapons or to seek alternative political arrangements for their security. If they did, the strategic environment so favorable to the United States would be threatened. United States failure to resolve credibility issues would also encourage these nations to exercise alternative security options. In short, lesser American allies must have confidence in continued U.S. political and military support if they are to be dissuaded from providing their own security needs either by developing national nuclear capabilities or altering their political relationships with the U.S.S.R. Since these allies are not presently threatened by China or the Soviet Union, their security does not depend directly on U.S. forces in the Pacific, as was the case in the past; however, it does depend on U.S. political support. At issue is how the United States will assure these allies of continuing political support without the earnest of forward deployed forces.

Clearly, the United States has modified its definition of interests and future military involvement in the Western Pacific. However, until future levels of U.S. interest and involvement are known, there will continue to be considerable uneasiness in East Asia. While uncertainty is only partially related to U.S. forward-deployed force levels, the potential for sustaining an international situation that so clearly restricts Soviet freedom of action may be of sufficient merit for the United States to consider maintaining larger force levels in the Western Pacific than strategically required. Although it is not altogether certain that the Soviet position would be improved by a rearmed Japan or a nuclear-capable Taiwan or Korea, or even that these conditions would result from U.S. force drawdowns, the downward trend of U.S. forward deployment would tend to encourage our East Asian friends and allies to examine alternatives to continued dependence on the United States for future security needs. More importantly, neither a rearmed Japan nor a nuclear capable Taiwan appears to be consistent with U.S. interests.

To resolve the dilemma posed by the limited U.S. military requirements versus the credibility requirements of our allies in the Western Pacific, the United States could maintain more forward deployed forces in East Asia than indicated by objective military needs. Presumably, these forces would assure friend and foe alike of continued U.S. involvement in East Asian security affairs. In time of military crisis elsewhere, Western Pacific forces could be withdrawn and deployed where needed. Thus it might not be necessary to maintain the overall U.S. force structure at levels higher than global military needs. What must not happen —and this the United States should guard against—is to compromise the political objectives sought through such a stratagem by allowing U.S. forces to assume a life of their own, independent of their political purpose. Thus, for example, the United States might continue to maintain substantial naval forces forward deployed in the Western Pacific, but with the clear understanding in U.S. policy circles that these forces are in excess of requirements in that theater. In view of the high visible-power quotient, intervention forces might also be included, as long as the limited utility of intervention as a policy instrument is recognized. In each case the forces would be deployed to support an advantageous political environment, considered to be both dependent on the United States and of sufficient importance to justify the cost of deployment.

Because of their inherent mobility, naval forces are often thought to be particularly relevant in this kind of application. However, reliance on naval forces as evidence of U.S. credibility has a significant drawback. Their very mobility and low visibility—in contrast to other, more permanent forces—may substantially lessen their usefulness as the earnest of American commitment. Thus, even though the focus of U.S. military needs in the Western Pacific is naval, credibility may be better served by relying on shore-based forces.

The major drawback to purposeful maintenance of excess forces as part of an effort to pacify East Asian allies and avert nuclear proliferation is the possibility of rapid force drawdowns. Requirements for U.S. forces in the Atlantic or the Persian Gulf may be particularly urgent in the period 1985–2000 and could demand immediate drawdowns of

Pacific forces. Rapid, unannounced reallocation of these forces could precipitate instability at precisely the moment the United States would desire stability in East Asia above all things. Instability in East Asia threatens the evolving American strategic concept, which attaches great importance to China as a counterweight to the Soviet Union as well as a stable Japanese-American security relationship. Rapid redeployment or substantial drawdown of U.S. Pacific forces to meet European contingencies may be a good deal more unsettling to this kind of international environment than a gradual reorientation of U.S. forces in peacetime.

An alternative approach to the East Asian dilemma would be to continue with Pacific force drawdown for the purpose of making deployed force levels consistent with objective military requirements. As noted above, this erosion of its force levels under way since 1970 creates anxieties concerning the actual extent of U.S. interests and involvement in East Asia. Such a policy, of course, risks the possibility that our allies, and possibly even China, will conclude that the United States ultimately intends to withdraw from Asia and Asian affairs. Such a conclusion might encourage all concerned to make new arrangements for their security.

The net effect of the altered strategic environment—characterized by narrower U.S. security interest in East Asia; diminished threat to U.S. interests; modified relationships with U.S. allies; and declining utility of intervention forces—would be a reduction in future military needs for forward deployed American forces in East Asia, particularly naval intervention forces. This is not to say that these forces should be reduced or redeployed to areas of greater objective military need, such as the Atlantic, but it does suggest that forces will be available for such reassignment. On the other hand, a stable East Asian environment that contributes significantly to the diffusion of Soviet power is of such importance to the United States that it clearly justifies maintaining peacetime forces in the Western Pacific in excess of military mission requirements, assuming such forces are necessary in sustaining the desired international environment.

Soviet Naval Presence in the Caribbean Sea Area

James D. Theberge

The Soviet navy's primary mission for over half a century has been to defend the homeland against attack from the sea. In the first post–World War II decade, the principal maritime threat was perceived by Moscow to be a seaborne invasion launched by the West. But, as the United States acquired a seaborne strategic-strike capability, the Soviet Union reordered its priorities and gave paramount importance to deterrence and to countering the Western strike fleet. It invested heavily in naval nuclear technology and built up a large modern fleet of warships and auxiliaries, which expanded Soviet capabilities for long-range warfare and politico-military activity.

By the early 1960s, Moscow had adopted a policy of forward naval deployment to counter the increased weapons range of the American carrier strike force and the Polaris submarines. This involved a series of measures designed to counter seaborne strike aircraft and missiles as close to the launch area as possible. Thus, Western carrier strike forces are kept under continuous surveillance by Soviet naval forces, and strategic submarines are tracked, to the extent possible, by aircraft and submarines. In wartime, the objective would be to destroy as many Western seaborne strategic launch platforms as possible before Soviet ships were lost to counter action.

Moscow started to establish a significant naval presence outside of home waters in 1964, when surface naval units were deployed to the Mediterranean on a regular basis. After 1967, this distant-seas deployment rose sharply but was still concentrated in the Mediterranean. A continuous Indian Ocean naval presence followed in 1968, and regular cruises to the Caribbean began in 1969. By the end of the decade, the forward deployment began to serve political as well as strategic defensive and offensive purposes. Moscow developed and practiced ways of employing its naval forces in peacetime to support its interests on distant seas and oceans.

In the Mediterranean, the primary purpose of Soviet naval operations is strategic defense, but Moscow stresses its political mission of

181

neutralizing or inhibiting Western intervention capabilities (mainly the U.S. Sixth Fleet) against its Arab clients. It did, in fact, deter Israeli air strikes against Port Said and Alexandria by establishing a permanent naval presence in those Egyptian ports. On more distant seas—the Gulf of Guinea, the Caribbean, and the Indian Ocean—Soviet naval units have been used politically in various ways: in 1968, to pressure Ghana into expediting the release of two impounded Soviet fishing vessels, the Soviet navy staged a display of force in the Gulf of Guinea; in 1969–1970, to probe U.S. reaction to a forward submarine anchorage in Cuba and to show support for the Castro regime; and in 1970, to intervene in support of Somalia's military government, Moscow prolonged an official naval visit until an alleged revolutionary plot was defeated. Also in 1970, Moscow established a regular combatant patrol off the Guinea coast to prevent a recurrence of a seaborne attack on Conakry, Guinea, in which President Sekou Touré sought to prove Portuguese involvement.

The increased number, mobility, and readiness of Soviet naval forces in distant waters will undoubtedly lead to additional opportunities for long-range politico-military actions in support of Soviet interests other than primary naval tasks. These will range from "flag showing," to establishing areas of political-military influence, and exploiting weak points in the Third World and Western zones of influence.

New Caribbean Chapter

The appearance of a seven-ship Soviet naval squadron in the Caribbean–Gulf of Mexico in early July 1969, signaled a new chapter in U.S.-Soviet postwar political-military competition. Such a deployment obviously could not be explained in terms of "natural" interests, which might apply to waters close to the Russian landmass, such as the Mediterranean Sea and Indian Ocean. The Caribbean is not by any stretch of the definition an area of "vital" interest to Moscow—the high priority it gives to the preservation of "socialist" Cuba notwithstanding. It is not marked by a Russian legacy of longstanding political and economic relationships with local countries. Moreover, it is geographically remote from the Soviet landmass and extremely vulnerable to U.S. power. Nevertheless, Soviet surface warships and submarines have been continuously active in Caribbean waters since 1969, for a number of political-military reasons, as discussed below:

- The U.S.S.R. has been interested, at least until recently, in acquiring a submarine facility in Cuba in order to reap the tangible benefits of greater operational efficiency for its Yankee-class strategic submarines, which now cruise the Atlantic near Bermuda and Nova

Scotia. It demonstrated this interest in 1970 by attempting to establish a strategic submarine facility in the Cuban port of Cienfuegos but was rebuffed, at least temporarily, by the United States.

- During 1971–1974, the U.S.S.R. began to escalate the deployment of submarines (from November-class nuclear-powered attack submarines to Golf-class diesel-powered strategic ballistic missile submarines in 1971–1974) to probe the limits of the U.S. "understanding" (announced by President Kennedy in 1962 following the Cuban missile crisis) that the U.S.S.R. will not establish a strategic base in Cuba or in the Western Hemisphere. The evidence suggests that the U.S.S.R. has not entirely abandoned its interest in a strategic submarine facility in Cuba and hopes to establish incremental precedents and test U.S. resolve on the issue.

- The U.S.S.R. has used naval deployments to the Caribbean as a means of cementing closer political-military ties with Cuba and of reassuring Castro of the seriousness of the Soviet commitment to protect his "loyal, socialist" ally.

- The existence of an accessible "socialist" client in the Caribbean has provided the Soviet navy with a convenient justification for friendly visits and winter training cruises in warm waters.

- Soviet naval calls in the Caribbean serve to emphasize Russia's coming of age as a superpower. In the 1960s, the U.S.S.R. launched an unprecedented peacetime naval construction program that resulted in a surplus naval capacity presently available for flag-showing expeditions and similar activities in support of Soviet global interests.

- Through the establishment of a submarine facility or frequent surface-warship visits to the Caribbean, the U.S.S.R. may have hoped to acquire a bargaining chip that it could use for trading U.S. withdrawal from Polaris bases in Rota and Holy Loch or for a corresponding reduction of U.S. surface warships from an area of comparable Soviet sensitivity, such as the eastern Mediterranean.

Naval Activities since 1969. A review of the pattern of Soviet naval operations in the Caribbean area since July 1969, reveals the complex and shifting political-military reasons behind these deployments. The conclusions drawn in this paper, while tenuous at best, are based on publicly available data. Although incomplete, these data were sufficient to reconstruct the general pattern of Soviet surface-ship and submarine deployments to Cuba and the Caribbean area.

From July 1969 to May 1978, Soviet warships have called in the Caribbean nineteen times on visits to Cuba. The nature and frequency of these deployments are detailed in Table 1. Until 1975, the average

Table 1
Soviet Naval Deployments in the Caribbean Sea, 1969–1978

Deployment Dates	Total Warships[a]	Tender	Submarines	Surface Vessels[b]
July 11–August 12, 1969	9	yes	2 Foxtrot, 1 November	1 Kynda, 1 Kashin, 1 Kilden, 1 AGI
May 8–June 3, 1970	8	yes	2 Foxtrot, 1 Echo	1 Kresta, 1 Kanin, 1 AGI
September 3, 1970–January 8, 1971	9	yes	—	1 Kresta, 1 Kanin
November 30, 1970–January 8, 1971	3	no	1 Foxtrot	1 Kashin
February 10–March 17, 1971	6	yes	1 November	1 Kresta, 1 Kanin, 1 AGI
May 22–June 11, 1971	3	yes	1 Echo	1 AGI
October 31, 1971–January 23, 1972	8	no	2 Foxtrot	1 Kresta, 1 Kashin, 1 AGI
March 7–May 11, 1972	4	no	1 Foxtrot	1 Kanin
April 27–May 15, 1972	2	yes	1 Golf	
November 26, 1972–February 21, 1973	7	yes	1 Echo	1 Kresta, 1 Kanin, 1 AGI
August 2–October 16, 1973	5	no	1 Echo, 1 Foxtrot	1 Kresta, 1 Kanin
April 29–May 30, 1974	5	no	1 Golf	2 Kresta, 1 AGI
September 24–November 12, 1974	6	yes	1 Foxtrot	2 Kresta, 1 AGI

February 25–April 5, 1975	3	no	—	2 Krivak
May 23–June 6 ,1976	3	no	—	2 Kanin
August 16–September 21, 1976	3	no	—	2 Krivak
June 27–July 22, 1977	4	no	—	1 Kresta, 2 Krivak
December 17, 1977–January 15, 1978	4	no	1 Foxtrot	2 Krivak
March 20–May 6, 1978	3	no	—	1 Kashin

a Includes oilers and tenders.
b Does not include oilers, tankers, tugs, landing and similar craft.

composition of the deployed squadrons was about 40 percent submarines (diesel and nuclear-powered) and 60 percent surface ships (frigates, destroyers, cruisers, and AGIS). Submarines were normally accompanied by tenders, surface ships by oilers.

In mid-June 1969, two Foxtrot-class diesel attack submarines, a November-class nuclear attack submarine, and an Ugra-class tender were observed departing the area around the Soviet base in the White Sea. On June 18, they rounded North Cape, steaming south into the Norwegian Sea.[1] At the same time, a surface force comprising a Kynda-class missile cruiser departed the Black Sea area, passing through the Turkish straits into the Mediterranean on June 23. The surface warships entered the Atlantic on June 28. The submarine and surface groups rendezvoused off the Azores on July 3 and, after refueling from two tankers, steamed westward on separate courses, joining off Bermuda on July 9. The flotilla, armed with nuclear missiles, entered the Gulf of Mexico and Caribbean, calling at Cuba July 20–27 (minus the November-class nuclear attack submarine and oil tanker). After a visit to Port de France, Martinique (August 5–8) and Bridgetown, Barbados (August 10–12), the flotilla departed the Caribbean on an easterly course. It had included some of the most modern warships afloat, with the Kynda- and Kashin-class ships especially noteworthy for their advanced designs.

The first Soviet naval visit clearly had a military-training mission, including the familiarization of personnel with navigation in the Caribbean area, the sonar environment for both offensive and defensive operations, and the electronic environment of the area. Such familiarization missions are regularly undertaken by major navies in potential operating areas. This demonstration of distant-seas naval deployment was followed in November 1969 by a nine-day visit to Cuba by Marshal Grechko, the Soviet defense minister. Prominent Cuban military leaders, including Raul Castro, Cuba's minister of the armed forces, returned the visit in February 1970.

The second deployment of Soviet naval power in the Caribbean occurred in conjunction with Okean, the Soviet worldwide naval maneuvers. The Okean operation, consisting of some Soviet surface warships, submarines, and support ships from all four fleets, was carried out in a series of exercises in several seas. During the height of Okean activities in the North Atlantic, a pair of TU-20/95 Bear-D naval re-

---

[1] For a detailed description of Soviet naval visits to the Caribbean, see U.S. Congress, House of Representatives, Subcommittee on Air Defense of the Southeastern United States, Committee on Armed Services, *Air Defense of Southeastern United States* (HASC No. 91-39), 1970.

connaissance aircraft took off from a Soviet northern fleet base in the White Sea area, flew around Norway, over the Soviet ships operating in the Iceland-Faeroes gap area, and then continued nonstop to Cuba, landing on April 18, 1970.[2] This flight of more than 5,000 nautical miles marked the first time that Bear aircraft had landed outside Soviet-bloc nations.

In addition to this naval reconnaissance flight, a flotilla of surface ships broke away from the North Atlantic phase of the Okean exercise late in April 1970 and made for the Caribbean, being joined en route by a submarine group. This seven-ship flotilla arrived at Havana on May 14, 1970. For the second time in less than a year the Soviets had projected a powerful, multipurpose force into the Western Hemisphere. This second deployment to the Caribbean and Cuba may have been intended to augment the level of deployed forces—first a nuclear attack submarine and then a nuclear antiship missile submarine. The next logical step would be deployment of a strategic missile submarine and the establishment of support facilities in Cuba.[3]

Strategic Submarine Base in Cuba. The force that operated in the Caribbean during May 1970 called at Havana and Cienfuegos on the southern coast of Cuba. The visit of the nuclear Echo-II to Havana is believed to be the first by a Soviet nuclear attack submarine to a non-Russian port.

In September 1970, a third Soviet squadron was sighted en route to the Caribbean. It included a Kresta-class guided missile cruiser, a Kanin-class guided missile destroyer, submarine and tender, merchant tanker, and Alligator-type landing ship. The missile cruiser and destroyer, submarine tender, and tanker entered the Caribbean through the Mona Passage on September 5, preceded a few days earlier by a buoy tender and ocean-going rescue tug. The cruiser, destroyer, and tender did not stop at Havana but rendezvoused outside Cienfuegos on September 9. The landing ship is the Soviet version of the U.S. Navy's LST, especially designed to transport wheeled and tracked vehicles as well as general cargo that can be unloaded by bow and stern ramps or crane. The *Alligator* transported two large nuclear submarine support barges, which were towed into Cienfuegos.

[2] TU-20 is the naval designation and TU-95, the bureau designation. The latter generally is used by U.S.-NATO for identification purposes. The Bear-D is the only variant of this aircraft flown by the Soviet navy.

[3] Russia's attempt to operate strategic submarines from Cuban support facilities was frustrated in 1970 by U.S. reaction, but Moscow finally sent its first strategic submarine (G-II-class) to Cuba in May 1972. The G-II diesel-powered ballistic-missile submarine carries three Serb (SS-N-5) solid-fuel missiles, each of which is fitted with a one-megaton warhead and has a range of 650 miles.

The arrival of the Ugra-class submarine tender at Cienfuegos made clear Moscow's intention to use the port to replenish nuclear-powered submarines. The facilities in Havana, already available for port calls and courtesy visits, were not sufficient or secure enough from prying eyes for Moscow's purposes, which apparently embraced extended submarine operations in the Caribbean Sea and the Atlantic Ocean. The arrival of the submarine tender and barges—reportedly capable of receiving radioactive effluents from Soviet nuclear-powered submarines—in Cienfuegos led the White House, on September 25, 1970, to warn the U.S.S.R against building a strategic submarine base in Cuba. The same day a Pentagon spokesman announced that construction of a base for Soviet Y-class Polaris-type submarines "could not be ruled out."

The U.S.–U.S.S.R. "Understanding"

In early September 1970, Washington became seriously concerned about the expanded Soviet naval activity in Cuba, especially in Cienfuegos. Particularly disturbing were the extended deployment of a 9,000-ton Ugra-class submarine tender; intense naval construction activity in Cienfuegos that included rest, recreation, and communications facilities; the anchoring of two barges capable of receiving radioactive effluents; and emplacement of a submarine net inside the harbor.[4] The construction activity, which first caught the attention of U.S. intelligence in August, continued throughout the fall of 1970. On September 25, Dr. Henry Kissinger, assistant to the president for national security affairs, warned the Soviet government against construction of a strategic submarine base in Cuba, reminding it of Khrushchev's promise to President Kennedy to keep "all weapons offensive systems" out of Cuba and the Western Hemisphere. Dr. Kissinger added: "The Soviet Union can be under no doubt that we would view the establishment of a strategic base in the Caribbean with the utmost seriousness."[5] Dr. Kissinger also referred to a passage in President Kennedy's speech of November 20, 1962, immediately after the Cuban missile crisis: "If all offensive weapons are removed from Cuba and kept out of the Hemisphere in the future, under adequate verification and safeguards, and if Cuba is not used for the export of aggressive Communist purposes, there will be peace in the Caribbean."[6] This restatement of the U.S. position

---

[4] According to U.S. intelligence and other sources, as reported in the *New York Times* on November 15, 1970.

[5] *New York Times*, September 26, 1971.

[6] President Kennedy's speech to the nation of November 20, 1962, the text of which is included in Robert F. Kennedy, *Thirteen Days: A Memoir of the Cuban Missile Crisis* (New York: W.W. Norton, 1969), pp. 216-218.

was followed by a series of somewhat confusing public exchanges between Washington and Moscow. On October 9, the Soviet Union denied reports that it was planning to build bases for guided missile submarines in Cuba. *Izvestia* called the U.S. allegations "groundless" and said Moscow would honor the 1962 agreement with President Kennedy to remove offensive weapons from Cuba as long as the United States honored its pledge that there would be no invasion of Cuba.[7]

On October 13, Moscow said in a statement distributed by *Tass:* "The Soviet Union is not building its military base on Cuba and is not doing anything that would contradict the understanding reached between the governments of the U.S.S.R. and the U.S. in 1962."[8] On December 2, Secretary Laird indicated that the accord would not preclude the servicing of strategic submarines outside the Caribbean waters.[9] A month later, on January 4, 1971, President Nixon stated that he would consider the servicing of nuclear submarines "either in or from Cuba" as a violation of the Kennedy-Khrushchev understanding of 1962 and of Moscow's October 13 statement.[10] On the following day, an aide to Dr. Kissinger clarified President Nixon's statement and interpreted the "understanding" to rule out servicing of nuclear submarines "anywhere at sea"[11] by a submarine tender operating from Cuba.

These confusing declarations of White House and Pentagon spokesmen over the precise meaning of the so-called U.S.-Soviet understanding suggest strongly that no clearly specified limits were established concerning the placement of offensive seaborne weapons systems in Cuba or the hemisphere. Most likely, there was a tacit understanding, with a margin of uncertainty as to what the U.S. reaction might be under various contingencies. Whether the "understanding" is oral or written, Washington officials decline to say, and the details have been held in strict secrecy by the few top officials, aside from the president and Dr. Kissinger, who know the facts.[12]

Soviet–Cuban Relations

A key factor in the Soviet decision to send a flotilla to Cuba in July 1969 appears to have been the rapprochement that followed Castro's endorsement of the Soviet-bloc intervention in Czechoslovakia. Relations

---

[7] *Izvestia,* October 9, 1970.

[8] *Tass,* October 13, 1970.

[9] *New York Times,* December 3, 1970.

[10] *New York Times,* January 5, 1971.

[11] *New York Times,* January 6, 1971.

[12] *New York Times,* November 15, 1971.

between the Soviet Union and Cuba were strained and marked by mutual recriminations in late 1967 and throughout most of 1968. This was observable in the Escalante affair,[13] in Cuba's boycott of the Soviet-sponsored meeting of Communist parties in Bucharest, and in the tightening of Soviet economic assistance in early 1968. Facing an erosion of hemispheric leverage after Guevara's failure in Bolivia, Castro attempted to force a redefinition of Soviet-Cuban ties. His August 23, 1968 speech on the Czech crisis expressed displeasure over Soviet-bloc internal developments and relations with Cuba. He argued that the intervention, while a "flagrant" violation of Czechoslovakia's sovereignty, was justifiable politically in view of the fact that "Czechoslovakia was moving . . . into the arms of imperialism."[14] Basing his argument for intervention on ideological grounds, he demanded that the same Soviet-bloc protection be extended to North Vietnam, North Korea, and Cuba.

The speech appears to have been a major turning point in relations with Moscow. By 1969, mutual recrimination and tension had given way to rapprochement. The Soviet naval visit to Cuba in July 1969 was one of several signs of mutual concessions and closer political, economic, and military ties observed in 1969 and 1970, and was evidently a response to the demand for a Soviet commitment to defend Cuba against any threat of U.S. aggression.[15] Castro's delegate at the June 1969 conference in Moscow again raised this question, asserting that Havana would support the Soviet Union in the event of a war or if the Soviet Union were to take action against imperialist attempts to foster counterrevolutions in communist countries. The Cubans also supported Moscow in its conflict with the People's Republic of China.

The 1969 naval visit served to demonstrate Moscow's growing capability to operate in distant waters and to assist Cuba, thus helping to reassure Castro. In his report to the Supreme Soviet on July 10, 1969, the minister of foreign affairs, Andrei Gromyko, said: "The Soviet Union is doing everything to help the Republic of Cuba and its people to withstand pressure and provocations. We attach great importance to the future strengthening of friendship and cooperation with Cuba. . . ."[16]

---

[13] The old-line Communist Anibal Escalante, ex-executive secretary of the defunct pro-Soviet Popular Socialist Party (PSP) and thirty-four other ex-members of the PSP were tried and sentenced in January 1968, for operating a so-called microfaction to oppose Castro's economic and foreign policies and urge his replacement by trustworthy old-line Communists. For full details see Edward Gonzalez, "Castro: The Limits of Charisma," *Problems of Communism,* July–August 1970, pp. 21-22.

[14] *Granma,* August 25, 1968.

[15] For details, see Gonzalez, "Castro: The Limits of Charisma."

[16] *Pravda,* July 11, 1969.

Moscow, however, did not give Castro a formal commitment to defend Cuba.

It is likely that the Soviet leaders waited to see how the Cubans would act at the Moscow conference before deciding on this gesture of support. The intended naval visit was announced only on July 7. The visit was timed to coincide with the July 26 national celebration in Cuba, thereby simultaneously providing a justification for the visit and giving both countries the best conditions for propaganda exploitation. According to a comment in *Red Star*, "The friendly visit to Cuba this July by Soviet warships was a graphic illustration of the combat unity between the Soviet and Cuban armed forces." [17] As for Castro, he had been effusive in his greeting of the Soviet ships and, as one observer writes, had gone ". . . into raptures about the superior naval skills, unequalled revolution qualities of the Red sailors."[18] In a speech, Castro noted that the beginning of the 10 million-ton sugar harvest and the Soviet fleet visit were ". . . two very important things, and two symbols of progress, of great progress." [19]

De-escalation of Naval Calls

The naval visit to Cuba in September 1970, coincided with various unofficial reports that Cienfuegos was being prepared as a nuclear submarine base. This step was probably encouraged by the failure of the United States to react publicly or privately to the two previous visits, and by U.S. reluctance to acknowledge, up to then, the possibility of the construction of a Soviet submarine facility at Cienfuegos. In fact, considerable congressional and public pressure on this question developed before Washington issued its warning on September 25. In its response, the Kremlin made a particular point of the U.S. warning against the construction of "Soviet bases" in Cuba. Moscow argued that it had always opposed the existence of military bases on foreign soil and, therefore, would not build its "own" base in Cuba.

The statement did not exclude the right of Soviet submarines to use ostensibly Cuban bases. Furthermore, the Soviet Union did not specifically comment on or agree to the U.S. expansion of the "understanding," which now included a prohibition on the servicing of nuclear submarines at sea by tenders based in Cuba. Soviet submarine tenders have been demonstratively kept in the Caribbean since September 1970,

---

[17] *Red Star,* December 2, 1969.

[18] K. S. Karol, *Guerrillas in Power* (New York: Hill and Wang, 1970), p. 514.

[19] Luis Baez, "Friendship, Fraternity, Affection for Soviets," *Juventud Rebelde,* Havana, July 27, 1969, p. 3, cited in JPRS *Translations on Latin America,* No. 224 (September 5, 1969), p. 43.

and they continue to visit Cuban ports. Since the U.S. prohibition on the use of submarine tenders is rather vague, it is difficult to ascertain violations. This makes it easy for the Soviet Union to probe the limits of toleration and to erode the U.S.-Soviet "understanding."

Between 1971 and 1974, the Soviet Union upgraded its submarine deployments to Cuba, moving from Foxtrot-class diesel-powered attack submarines to a Golf-class diesel-powered strategic ballistic missile submarine. Instead of establishing a Yankee-class strategic submarine base at once, as attempted in 1970, the U.S.S.R. appeared to be bent on establishing precedents over a protracted period of time. If the United States failed to react, the result would ultimately be the establishment of an operating submarine base in Cuba. Because each step in the escalation was a small one, the United States did not consider it important enough to warrant a protest. Nonetheless, the pattern of Soviet submarine visits during this period represented an important modification of the 1970 "understanding," which one might have expected to continue.

The problem this series of submarine visits to Cuba might have posed for U.S. foreign policy has diminished in the period since November 1974. In this period, only one Soviet submarine has made a port call to Cuba; naval deployments have largely consisted of surface warships. Moscow's encroachment on its "understanding" with the United States appears to have been halted, if only temporarily.

A number of reasons may be adduced for de-escalation of Soviet submarine calls and for the decline in surface warship visits to Cuba and the Caribbean since the end of 1974.

(1) The growing Soviet military involvement in Africa, particularly in Angola since 1974 and Ethiopia since 1977, may explain the reduced level of surface naval deployments. The increased requirement for additional warship deployments off West Africa and around the Horn has limited the availability of ships for lower priority missions in the Caribbean.

(2) The decline in submarine calls to Cuba may reflect the strength of the Soviet desire for a Cuban-American rapprochement, which the U.S.S.R. has been encouraging discreetly but persistently since the early 1970s with the aim of legitimizing the Castro regime and reducing Moscow's burdensome subsidy of the stagnant Cuban economy. Further efforts to erode the "understanding" with the United States prohibiting the establishment of a Soviet submarine base in Cuba would endanger the process of Cuban-American détente, which began to be explored directly by the governments of Cuba and the United States in mid-1975.

(3) The bold and increasing use by Moscow of Cuba as a proxy military combat force in Africa and the delicate U.S.-Panamanian negotiations over the U.S. withdrawal from military facilities in the Canal Zone, together with the transfer of complete control of the Canal and Canal Zone to Panama by the end of the century, may have inhibited a more visible Soviet naval presence in recent years. The Soviet Union may have wished to avoid arousing fears which could be used against Cuban-American détente and the new Canal Treaties, both favored strongly by the U.S.S.R.

As Soviet conduct is characterized by considerable complexity and ambiguity, it is impossible to know whether the decline in Soviet submarine visits to Cuba is temporary or permanent. If the primary Soviet interest is to smooth the way for Cuban-American rapprochement, then it is possible that the policy of self-denial will continue until the normalization process is far advanced and appears irreversible. At that time, Moscow may reassess the risks of further encroachment on the "understanding," and it is possible that it will resume submarine port calls of increasing political significance. There is no reason to believe that this recent step backward—the virtual halting of submarine visits to Cuban ports—implies an abandonment of the Soviet objective of establishing a base in Cuba. It may be merely a tactical retreat, to be followed by renewed efforts of a gradual and cautious kind.

Except for its relations with Cuba, the Soviet navy has maintained a notably low profile in the Caribbean Sea area since 1969. It has made only a few dozen port calls (if the available data are reasonably accurate) in the Caribbean basin since mid-1969—to Mexico, Martinique, Barbados, Colombia, Jamaica, and perhaps one or two other countries. Visits of Soviet surface warships to Caribbean ports are rare. The U.S.S.R. has carefully and successfully avoided arousing any sense of threat by its naval visits to the Caribbean islands and rimland states. In fact, the perception of a Soviet naval presence in the Caribbean is, for all practical purposes, absent outside of Cuba.

Soviet naval behavior suggests that the primary interest during this current phase of naval involvement in the Caribbean is Cuba—strengthening Soviet-Cuban relations; reassuring Castro of Soviet commitment to its defense; bolstering Cuban morale; and transforming Cuba into a more useful support base for Soviet naval-air operations in the Western Hemisphere and a more effective proxy combat force for operations in the Third World.[20]

---

[20] In March 1978, there were rumors circulating in London and Washington that the Soviet Union has resumed construction on a strategic submarine base in Cienfuegos, but they were denied by the U.S. government.

COMMENTARIES

Gene La Rocque

Mr. Nitze's plea that we need to look at all the other forces in order to decide on the needs for NATO forces highlights one of the real problems with this conference.

When I was a young commander in the Pentagon, Vice Admiral Nells Johnson put me and three of my colleagues in a room and told us he would let us out only after we determined what the navy should look like in 1977. When at last we were let out, we told him we couldn't do it because we didn't know what our national objectives would be. We did not know what forces the army, air force, or marines would have, either.

It is difficult to discuss cogently war at sea, much less the kinds of conflict situations that would call for the use of naval forces in one geographic area. The authors of the papers presented in this section did a magnificent job.

The matter of naval missions reflects on everything we do, and I have noticed considerable confusion in this conference as to just what our navy's mission really is. Some mention was made of Title 10 of the U.S. Code, but I was unfavorably impressed that none of my active naval colleagues seemed to know what it said. Title 10 is extremely important. It says that the navy shall be organized, trained, and equipped primarily for prompt and sustained combat incident to operations at sea. It goes on to say that the navy is responsible for the preparation of forces necessary for the effective prosecution of war, except as otherwise assigned, and is generally responsible for naval reconnaissance, anti-submarine warfare, and protection of shipping.

Unfortunately, the various chiefs of naval operations have now come along and devised their own missions. Admiral Zumwalt had four, Admiral Holloway has three, as I read them. We have all totally ignored the Key West agreements, which set forth the missions of the naval forces as well as of the other services.

195

In 1940, when I first came into the navy, we were very proud to be the first line of defense, because we pushed for freedom of the seas. Now where are we? We are talking about sea control, sea denial, and power projection. One of the problems with the term *power projection* is that it is absolutely unpalatable anywhere; it conjures up a vision of dropping bombs and killing Africans, South Americans, or Indonesians. Yet when we look at the globe and try to figure out where we will bomb from our aircraft carriers today, we find it difficult to pinpoint a target other than the Soviet Union.

What we have been trying to do in the navy for the last thirty years is to define a mission that will fit our existing and future naval forces. Thus, we have had huge navy budgets and poor morale resulting from the fact that the men don't really know what is going on. We have a navy that is ready to fight World War II all over again rather than to counter Soviet strategic and attack submarines, which constitute the major naval threat to the United States. The navy has already gone on record as saying that, in the event of a war in the Pacific, it can't ensure the support or the safe arrival of our military or other ships. Admiral Steinhaus's paper suggests that we cannot do this in the Atlantic either.

Since I am among friends, let me make a harsh statement and perhaps a judgment: I think the navy is in violation of Title 10 of the U.S. Code, and that it has been derelict in its duty to defend the United States. I think, too, that the navy's building program is making a mockery of our NATO commitments. We cannot continue to build and operate a navy based on power projection and aircraft carriers, and still provide the reconnaissance, the antisubmarine warfare, and the protection of shipping that are required by Title 10 of the law.

Changing the nomenclature won't do it. That is the easy way out. We have done that over the years, but it is no longer possible.

Admiral Crowe said this morning that Admiral Holloway is working on changing the nomenclature on missions to make it a little more palatable, but I do not think that is the solution. Rather, I suggest that we look at the problem a little more carefully

At present, our navy has 160 surface antisubmarine warfare escorts to deal with 120 Soviet nuclear-attack submarines and nuclear strategic submarines. Those figures always alarm me. If we give our escorts the job of protecting aircraft carriers, we can forget about escorting merchant ships, amphibious ships, or anything else. There just aren't enough escorts.

Lieutenant Commander Bruce Watson's paper addressed our naval presence in the Mediterranean since World War II. It may surprise him that there is no written mission for the Sixth Fleet in that area. At least there wasn't when I was flying my flag on the carrier *Saratoga*. Commander Watson indicated that our objective in the Mediterranean has been to contain the Soviets and to exercise hegemony over the littoral nations. It is clear that we have not been successful in that.

Commander Watson pointed out that the primary purpose of the Sixth Fleet is political. I disagree. We seem to have forgotten that our job is to go to war and fight. I think we have become too enmeshed in politics. It seems to me that the Sixth Fleet has become a kind of garrison force. It violates the most fundamental aspects and attributes of a naval force—to be able to move into a place and move out again. It is not only a garrison force; it has become pretty well tied to bases over there, much more than I think is wise.

When I commanded Task Group 60.2, we tried to determine what the primary job of the Sixth Fleet should be. If its job is political, then, we determined, we ought to split up the whole Sixth Fleet and send it to a lot of ports to influence a lot of people. If, on the other hand, its job is to go to war against the Soviet Union or another country, we ought to keep our forces close together so that they can be mutually supportive.

Our solution, finally, was to split the force up 50 percent of the time and keep it together 50 percent of the time.

When I returned to the Pentagon, the first stop I made was at the office of Paul Nitze, then secreteary of the navy, and I told him that those aircraft carriers and our whole force was terribly vulnerable to the OSA and Kolmar boats, to the submarines, and to the aircraft. It is now ten years later, and they are still vulnerable. I am sorry to see that.

Commander Watson pointed out that the Soviet navy's primary role is defending the Soviet Union. That is a reasonable role, and we can't fault the Russians for it. I just wish our own navy would make U.S. defense a primary role. All the time Admiral Zumwalt was chief of naval operations, I never once found any reference to the fact that the navy had a role in defending the United States. Since the aircraft carrier no longer has a role in defending the United States, that may be the reason we don't talk about it.

I think Watson gives too little emphasis to the critical constraints on the Soviet Union's Black Sea fleet in entering and leaving the Mediterranean via the Sea of Marmara and the Dardanelles. Many people have forgotten lately that the Soviet Black Sea fleet has to go under a Turkish bridge to get into the Dardanelles, and it wouldn't take much for a precision guided munition (PGM) to knock that bridge down and bottle up the Black Sea fleet; a few mines in the Dardanelles might also help.

Also, Watson treats the absence of Soviet bases too lightly. He makes is sound like lots of fun for the Soviet navy to hop around anchoring at various places without a base to operate from. He also plays down the vulnerability of our aircraft carriers. At one time, I was on the carrier *Saratoga*, which had four propellers. We had some problems with it, and eventually it could only operate with three. With just one propeller out, we couldn't operate our aircraft in a combat mode. Now, we have homing torpedoes, which will give us a lot of trouble as well.

Watson's conclusion implies that increasing the size of the Sixth Fleet would solve all of our problems. It is my opinion that even doubling the size of the fleet would not have an impact on the problems. What we need in the Mediterranean is a clear-cut statement of mission, a recognition of the problems—sonar problems in particular. We ought to get away from the garrison concept and permit the Sixth Fleet to move in and out of the Mediterranean.

Dale Tahtinen's paper on the Indian Ocean is, on the whole, logical and in tune with the times. Tahtinen makes the suggestion, though, that we ought to make a major effort to help the Japanese and the Germans build up their military forces. Well, the Japanese are spending less than 1 percent of their gross national product on military forces; while we spend around 6 percent. Our European allies, too, are spending a good deal less of their GNP than we are. So, I am not too enthusiastic about getting raw materials for our allies, particularly Europe and Japan.

Tahtinen suggests that we need to prevent the Soviet Union from making any significant political and economic advances in the Indian Ocean region. This is an important point, but where we need more political clout is on the land, not on the sea. We don't really care what happens near Diego Garcia, but we do care what happens on the land masses.

On the importance of keeping the Soviets out of South Africa, I agree with Tahtinen. But, as a retired strategic planner, I don't think it makes much sense for the Soviets to send their submarines to the Indian Ocean, or even down to the Cape, in order to sink merchant ships carrying oil. They should stay up near the focal areas such as Great Britain, Germany, and Japan, where they can do the same job with half the submarines. In the littoral states, the Soviet Union is having a rough time. It has begun to pursue imperialist policies very late in the game, and does not know how to do it well. They are not sophisticated in this sense. Its position in the Indian Ocean is weak, and its status regarding Somalia and Ethiopia is unclear. It has been kicked out of many places, including Egypt and Albania.

198

Tahtinen seems to agree, however, with my view that the establishment of a full-fledged base on Diego Garcia was a mistake. It will drain our naval efforts to defend and supply Diego Garcia, and will encourage the Soviets to establish a similar base. I remember that an assistant secretary of the navy said a few years ago that the base at Diego Garcia was self-sustaining. I couldn't believe it. There is not a thing on that island; it is self-sustaining only if equipment is brought in from somewhere else.

Tahtinen thinks it unlikely that the Soviets will attempt to disrupt the supply lines on the Indian Ocean, and I agree. It would be much easier to be disruptive in other ways.

He also points out that the British are doing extremely well economically in the Indian Ocean littoral, even though they have almost no naval or military forces. Maybe we could learn a lesson there. Japan, too, has enjoyed economic benefits without anything except self-defense forces. We ought to pay attention to this, particularly in view of our poor balance of payments, our huge deficits, and our enormous federal budgets.

Tahtinen is absolutely right when he says that the addition of sophisticated weapons in the area increases the likelihood of conflict. Both the United States and the Soviet Union are guilty of increasing the likelihood of conflict. More weapons in the area are likely to disrupt the supply lines for the raw materials we need.

Vice Admiral Steinhaus's paper presents a fascinating view of the northern flank. I think it is true that most of us don't know much about the area. I concur in his assessment that it is a very dangerous area because of its close proximity to the Soviet Union. But our approach to it cannot be based on increasing the number of conventional forces. Let us remember that about 60 percent of the major U.S. warships today, are equipped with nuclear weapons or—more properly put by the navy—are capable of carrying nuclear weapons.

I concur with Admiral Steinhaus that the U.S. shipbuilding programs will make a major register in about 1980. The U.S. Navy now has about 120 major warships under construction, or funded, for a total of about $25 billion, and I think it will make a significant contribution. Steinhaus concludes by saying that the Soviets can interrupt the lines of communication between Europe and the United States. I agree. It is high time we gave due attention to that fact.

Commander Peter Soverel, a "professor of strategy," gave a paper on the Western Pacific. In the early 1950s, when I was on the staff of the Naval War College, we were called "staff officers," and probably rightly so. But judging from the quality of Commander Soverel's work,

199

he is entitled to be called professor of strategy. He properly started with a question of what will be our interests in the Western Pacific towards the end of this century, but I was disappointed that he concluded his analysis with an examination of the enemy order of battle. As military men and naval officers, we ought to start by looking at the enemy order of battle and at enemy capabilities in precise terms.

Commander Soverel is still a little hung up on the idea of containing the Soviets. He would have us in an alliance with China, which, in the long run, may be a powerless force. He still shows a lot of this old business of trying to contain the Soviets.

He suggests that we can begin moving out of the Western Pacific, with the exception of Japan. Except for Japan, he says, the United States no longer needs to use island bases for projection of power. Well, I wonder why we need 55,000 troops in Japan today. If we are still thinking of going ahead with a land war in mainland Asia, maybe it makes some sense. But I don't think that will happen in this century.

Commander Soverel does clearly conclude, though, that we do not intend to wage war on the mainland of Asia and that we should fall back to a central or eastern military position in the Pacific. That is very logical, and I am delighted to hear a member of the Naval War College express that. In this technological era of nuclear weapons, nuclear submarines, ICBMs, and cruise missiles, and the continuing advance of technology, we ought to give more attention to threats against the United States and we ought to provide for the defense of the United States against weapons that will go over, under, or around our deployed forces in the Far East.

I certainly subscribe to Commander Soverel's conclusion that there is a major decline in the use of military forces to ensure the supply of raw materials. The first time we drop bombs from carrier-based aircraft and kill several hundred Muslims, I suspect we will see all the Arab oil wells shut off at the wellhead. By the same token, if we attack Accra, the capital of Ghana, and kill several hundred Africans, we will probably have difficulty getting raw materials from Africa. I think President Carter echoed Commander Soverel's sentiments when he spoke at the United Nations recently. He said that the old adage— war is a continuation of politics by other means—is passé.

That was the commander in chief talking, and I think he was right, at least with respect to the United States and the Soviet Union. The adage may have had some applicability in the past, but it certainly is not applicable for superpowers in a nuclear era.

The subject of Jim Theberge's paper is the Caribbean. It goes into great historical detail, but I am afraid the historical facts of the Caribbean are about as useless to us today as Alfred T. Mahan's nineteenth century writings. Forgive me, Alfred. [Laughter.]

I have two conclusions that pertain to all the foregoing papers. First, we have downplayed, almost ignored, nuclear weapons. This is an important area which only Mr. Tahtinen addressed. It is inconceivable that we will fight a nonnuclear war with the Soviet Union, but that is what we seem to be pretending.

Second, the usefulness of military forces in supporting our foreign policies and maintaining our high standard of living is rapidly declining. U.S. naval forces should be oriented to the major mission of defending the United States and supporting our NATO commitments.

Michael MccGwire

First of all, I want to reassure everyone that, despite what John Moore said, the British government is not penetrated, and it is still quite reliable as an ally.

We are looking at the role of navies in the face of many developments: The Soviet Union has substantial naval forces in distant parts parts of the globe; China has had a steady buildup of forces, with about eighty submarines of its own and others for sale to Korea; sophisticated weapons systems proliferate in coastal states; regional navies have emerged; European navies have withdrawn from a worldwide role; and there has been a shift in the balance between the relative capabilities needed to prevent the use of the sea and the capabilities required to secure that use.

I don't understand the problem with defining the navy's mission. The mission has always been the same—to prevent the use of the sea to one's own disadvantage, and to secure the use of the sea for one's own purposes. We do that in both peace and war. That is what navies are all about, the maritime forces as well as the land-based forces. That mission, of course, includes securing the use of the sea and projecting military force against targets ashore when necessary.

Most of the papers focused on the Soviet navy. According to Admiral Gorshkov, a new Soviet navy started in 1955. What he will not admit is that the Soviet navy underwent drastic changes in 1957, 1958, and 1961. This is an important fact which helps to explain the diversity of Soviet tactics.

I would like to highlight a point James McConnell mentioned, that the Soviet emphasis on fighting wars may have diminished. This seemed to come through in 1969 and 1971, as a result of the SALT negotiations. In other words, SALT may have been an educational process during which

Moscow began to play down the threat of war with the West. This is important. If the Russians feel that, in the event of an encounter with the West, it would not be advantageous to escalate to nuclear war, they can concentrate on using their ships in a peacetime role.

I won't go into why the Western sea-based systems are so important. It has to do with the fact that Europe would be held in hostage.

There have been frequent statements in all the papers that the Russians have more forces than they require. Is this really so? If we take the time to think through the 1960s and 1970s, it will be apparent that ours is the side to be on. I can sum this up by referring to a recent statement by the Supreme Headquarters Allied Powers Europe (SHAPE), which said that the Russians on the central front are finally getting the forces they need to discharge their missions. In other words, the Soviet forces have always been short. I think they are still short.

We can compare our situation to the race between the tortoise and the hare, with the Western powers representing the hare. We frequently fall behind, sleep behind bushes, and so on. But as long as we don't fall asleep, we will come out ahead. In the West, naval building is entirely cyclical. It has to do with budgetary factors, as well as diversions in other parts of the world. And the old Soviet tortoise plods on. But the Soviet Union has been outflanked so often by U.S. technology that it has reason for concern. The Sovietologists say that the Russians are not worried about trying to get superiority. Rather, they are worried about retaining parity.

If we compare shipbuilding programs over the last twenty years —which is a good indicator of a government's support for its navy—we can see that, on the whole, the West has built two to three times as many ships as the Communist nations recently. If we compare tonnages, it is even better than that, in terms of our capability. I am not talking about the Soviet push toward air supremacy which people keep mentioning to frighten us. I am talking about 1,000-ton ships that can go to sea.

It is best to think of navies in terms of wartime and peacetime. The Russians talk in those terms and I think it clarifies it.

In a wartime situation, the Soviets would have two quite different potential problems: a NATO war and a China war. If they became involved in a NATO war, they would probably observe the general task priorities that McConnell suggested this morning. I would be very surprised, however, if a certain number of submarines were not deployed for antishipping purposes. Regardless of the Soviet priorities, we must expect their submarines to be deployed to stop our ships; it fits with their basic policy of not giving anybody a free ride. It is just common sense to complicate the enemy's problem.

A NATO war would be a war of attrition, a matter of "catch as catch can." We will have a real problem if we get into that kind of conflict.

From the Russian point of view, a war with China would be more likely, and less disastrous, than a war with the West. In such a war, the Soviet Union would be faced with a problem of sea lines of communication to the eastern front, because the trans-Siberian railroad would no longer be available. The Chinese have said this and the Russians would have to supply the eastern front by sea, using the Indian Ocean as a link in their sea line of communication. I think this explains the second phase of the Soviet move into Berbera after 1972. If necessary, they would use the Persian Gulf as a supply route, just as we did when we supplied them during the two world wars.

There is a general concern to overjump our enemy as he comes around our flank; the same thing happened in 1955 when we overjumped into Egypt.

Let us not underestimate the time it takes the Russians to develop an operational capability somewhere. It took a tremendous amount of time for them to get something going in the Mediterranean. It wasn't until they got access to the bases and port sides that they had any effective operational capability. That was the first time they managed to have a year-around deployment; the first time they managed to have effective forces on station. Only two to four submarines were sustained on a station prior to that—terrible.

Certainly, once they are there, they will be used for political purposes. But we are looking for the primary determinants.

The question facing us now is, How important does the Soviet leadership rate the role of naval forces in overseas policy in peacetime? Admiral Steinhaus remarked that the Soviet influence is based exclusively on military power. The facts, however, contradict that. There are many other areas of Soviet influence: a well-entrenched ideology; a developmental model; some weak, yet selective forms of economic power; and a whole range of other instruments.

When we look at the role of oceans in the Soviet Union's foreign policy, we find that the primary maritime instrument is, in fact, its merchant fleet. This is an instrument of overseas influence-building, and of force projection. The way the Russians project force is by using airlift, sealift, and the cutting edges provided by revolutionary forces. If we examine the various components of their oceans policy, we do not find any organized policy in terms of setting objectives. Not surprisingly, what we find are extensions of domestic policies, just as we find in any other country.

The question is, What do the Russians think about the role of force? How useful is it? The answer is debatable. They have been watching us use force, sometimes successfully, sometimes unsuccessfully, since 1945. I have the impression that there was an argument among Soviet leaders between 1969 and 1972 about the role of force, or, precisely, about putting Soviet forces overseas. The argument came to a head during the war of attrition in Egypt, after the Russians had committed substantial forces to Egypt. There was a big debate inside the Kremlin about this. Eventually, they decided to withdraw.

It appears that the debate arose again over the costs and benefits of putting those forces in. And then, of course, there was a possibility that they would use bases in the Mediterranean for their ships and airfields. But again they withdrew. I think they, in fact, set up a situation for withdrawal because it seemed to be in their interest to be invited to go. By then, they had already moved on to Berbera, just as the British, who couldn't get anywhere in the Suez in 1948, moved on to Kenya.

It is interesting that they downgraded the importance of their naval base at that time. I think this relates to the policy shift between 1969 and 1971, the shift from a concern about war readiness to, possibly, a belief in deterrence. Consequently, there was a downgrading of the Soviet navy's role in the Mediterranean. Originally, its primary role had been to counter Western strategic strike forces there. The Mediterranean, as you know, is closer to Moscow than the Barents Sea and there are much more interesting things south of Moscow than north.

There is still the matter of whether or not they will use the naval strength they have in the area. My answer is, Of course they will use it, if there are opportunities. I think, though, that they are running out of opportunities. The good old colonial days of stirring up trouble against the imperalists are vanishing. Now, they find themselves picking sides in old-fashioned interstate wars, as they are doing in Korea. It makes life very difficult.

Will the Russians allocate resources to a deterrence role, as opposed to a war-preparedness role, as we do? It is my guess that something like 30 percent of our assets are put into this peacetime role, though I do not know for certain. The present evidence is that they are not doing what we are doing. They are still building for the general war role. Incidentally, the Soviet navy still has to work within very tight budgetary and resource allocations. When the navy had a completely new mission given to it between 1961 and 1964, changing to operational concepts, it had to do it all within the same yard capacity, remembering, of course, that the increase in nuclear submarines had been authorized in 1957 and 1958. This brings us back to the fact that the Soviet navy doesn't work in a vacuum. It operates in an army-dominated political-military environment. Paul Nitze said earlier that the Soviet navy was *forced* to take the Yankee, just as the Royal Navy was forced to take Polaris, and so on. A navy, in fact, does things for the central government and not for itself.

This brings us back to this prognosis. Are we, in fact, going to go into a worse situation in the future? Jamie Theberge's prognosis is that the cycle is going to go downwards. I would argue not, because I think he has drawn on the wrong basis. It is not a cyclical thing; it is a reaction to a series of threats.

The Soviet naval building program of 1945 was the last of a series of long-term building programs. Others occurred in 1888, 1910, 1926, and 1945. Each time, the Russians were trying to rebuild a navy that had been shattered in war. But the 1945 program has survived.

I think the interesting thing to note is that, when the Soviet Union shifted its threat assessments in 1954, it did, in fact, cut back allocations to naval shipbuilding and shifted funds into a merchant and fishing fleet, which indicates they saw the value of using the sea.

We cannot predict what will happen in the future, but I do warn you against the puberty theory of sea power, that is, that the Soviet Union must have a navy because it is becoming a certain size. Rather, it will be a question of whether or not shipbuilding is the most cost-effective way of allocating resources.

Unlike Western navies, the Soviet navy has usually been viewed as an expensive necessity, and quite a lot of money has been put into it. Thus, it is the third or fourth largest in the world, most of the time. But this doesn't necessarily mean that the Russians see it as a very effective instrument of policy.

I would like to make one point about the antisubmarine problem. I think we should not be concerned just with the escort role. Sea lines of communication can be hit anywhere between the factory and the front; similarly, submarines can be hit anywhere between the base and the engagement area. I know we think about that problem, but we need to talk more frequently about how we intend to deal with it. Our sea lines of communication are vital, and threats to them constitute a deliberate attack on our interests.

In his paper, James Theberge wisely brought out the problem of incrementalism. The Soviet gradual advance is one thing we must be very careful about.

Also, we have a habit of seeing everything in terms of military power in peacetime, which is dangerous. Let me give a classical example of this. We were told that we could lose our bases in South Africa. Well,

I would far prefer to lose the bases in Simonstown than to lose the whole of black Africa. It is that kind of problem. I don't want us to end up in Africa as we did in the Mediterranean, on the side of the smallest nation, losing the other littorals.

Another problem we need to be conscious of is the action–reaction syndrome with the Russians. If we allow that the Soviet navy was drawn forward by Polaris, then we must consider whether or not the final balance is in our interest. Why does the long-range Trident missile have to cruise all over the world's oceans if the Russians are going to go after it? It would be more useful to bring the Trident missile back into home-protected waters, and thus deescalate. It would be cheaper and would provide more security. It would also deny the Soviet navy of a budgetary argument for escalation.

This brings me to the subject of Soviet surplus capability. The Russians have built up their navy in order to react to the U.S. Navy. If we were to throw away half of our carriers, we would give the Soviet navy a sudden surplus of capability over requirements, and that surplus would be used to our disadvantage. So, what we do is just as important as what we do not do.

Finally, let us remember the political battle in the Kremlin. The Gorshkov series is considered evidence of the navy's part in a very large debate that has been going on in the Soviet Union for three or four years. There are arguments about allocation of resources, about the role of the navy, and so on. We must be careful not to feed the wrong side of that argument. On the one hand, we have to deny the Soviets opportunities; on the other hand, we must not build up the kind of frustration that leads them to think they must escalate.

DISCUSSION

ADMIRAL STEINHAUS: Concerning my alleged statement that Soviet influence is based only on military power, let me say that the outstanding characteristic of any superpower is its vast military power. As far as the Soviet Union's economic influence is concerned, it should be noted that the Federal Republic of Germany gives more help to the underdeveloped world than the Soviet Union and its allies do. That is why, to me, its economic offensive does not seem very big. But I did say in my paper that the Soviet Union supports communistic parties and unsatisfied groups in the NATO population, as part of its ideological fight. So I did not mean to suggest that the Soviet Union is only working by military means.

REAR ADMIRAL MARK HILL: I wish to comment on the statements my old friend, Gene La Rocque, made. I spent two years on the *Saratoga*. After three months on the Mediterranean, we had lost one shaft because of a design deficiency in the turbine. We launched and recovered every airplane we had on three shafts. I later verified the design of those ships, when I had command of the *Independence*. I discovered that it is possible to make 25 knots on two shafts and launch and recover an entire air wing, and that is what we were able to do.

I also wanted to ask Ambassador Theberge to comment on the possibility that the Soviet Union has reduced its image and presence in the Caribbean of late in order to help the Panamanians secure a favorable Panama Canal treaty. It is possible that, if that treaty is concluded as President Carter wishes, we will see a vigorous resumption of the Soviet presence, not only in Cuba but in Panama as well.

AMBASSADOR THEBERGE: That is a very good question. I don't really think that the decline in Soviet naval activity in the Caribbean in the last three years, particularly in port calls to Cuba, is directly related to the treaty negotiations with Panama. I think, rather, that it is bound up with this détente process in the Caribbean—the normalization of relations between Cuba and the United States, and the strong Soviet desire for this normalization to be successful, so as to relieve its economic burden.

The Soviet Union has been keeping a pretty low profile throughout the Caribbean generally. I don't think that the fewer Soviet port calls in Cuba and the fewer surface ships going into the Caribbean in recent years is directly related to Panama. At least, that is my feeling.

I tried once to collect statements made by Soviet leaders or by political analysts that might explain their interests in the Panama Canal, and there is really very little literature on the subject. What I collected, though, suggested that they viewed the canal as something outside of their control, and that it would be very dangerous to challenge the United States by somehow trying to get a foothold there. I know a lot of people would not agree, but that is the conclusion I came to from a quick look at the Soviet literature a few years ago. Maybe the situation has changed in the last few years, but I doubt it.

PART THREE

THE FUTURE OF SEA-BASED AIR POWER

One of the most intriguing questions that will be facing navy decision makers over the next few years towards the twenty-first century is the future of sea-based air power. Will the large aircraft carrier finally become obsolete, will V/STOL airplanes and carriers be the wave of the future or will land-based air power take over the sea-control function? As Norman Polmar points out in his paper, the death of the aircraft carrier has been predicted since the end of World War II. He also points out that aircraft carriers seemed doomed during the McNamara era only to be quickly resurrected when the secretary saw their utility during the Vietnam War.

Despite the great utility of the large carrier and its cost-effectiveness per ton compared with smaller ships (as Norman Polmar, an advocate of sea-based airpower, points out), sea-based aviation is increasingly expensive and may even be reaching the prohibitive stage. While he advocates building one more Nimitz-class large nuclear carrier, Polmar suggests that we must also pursue the quest for good V/STOL aircraft and ship carriers.

Dov Zakheim of the Congressional Budget Office, however, while seeing a definite role for carriers, also sees a definite role for land-based aircraft options for sea control. He also notes the expense of a new large Nimitz-size carrier and foresees that the navy might be forced to use land-based aircraft in certain situations because of the unavailability of sea-based aircraft. One of the most obvious areas, according to Zakheim, is in the Greenland-Iceland-United Kingdom (G-I-UK) gap where planes operating out of Iceland could be used for sea control in the northern area. He does not, however, see a use for land-based aircraft for the larger oceans.

Thus, Zakheim sees land-based aviation as a "complement" rather than as a "full alternative" to sea-based aviation. He recommends building a large plane for this purpose. This plane, called an LMNA (for land-based, multipurpose naval aircraft) or "Big Momma," would be a follow-on to the present P-3 maritime patrol aircraft; however, it would have an extensive offensive weapons system, such as the Phoenix antiair missile system or a Harpoon or Tomahawk for antiship missions.

The Case for Sea-Based Aviation

Norman Polmar

Sea-based aviation is increasingly expensive. With reduced fleet size, with alternatives to big carriers becoming available, and with modern technology making carriers more vulnerable, the future of sea-based aviation requires reexamination. There are substitutes for large aircraft carriers. However, the question should not be whether carriers are still viable, but rather what the options are for improving U.S. naval capabilities in view of a still-declining fleet, constrained budgets, and advanced technology. What options could change the "rules of the game" to provide U.S. naval forces with a significant advantage over potential adversaries, the U.S.S.R. and certain Third World nations?

Sea-based air power still appears to be a vital part of any effort to change the "rules of the game" in favor of the United States.

Perspective

The case for sea-based aviation is a difficult one to make. To provide a bit of historical perspective, fifty years ago a distinguished and forward-looking military aviator wrote:

> As airplane carrying vessels are of no use against hostile air forces with bases on shore, and as they can only be of use against other vessels or hostile fleets that are on the surface of the water, and as these fleets will be supplemented by submarines, there is little use for the retention of airplane carriers in the general scheme of armaments.[1]

General Mitchell was wrong. During World War II aircraft carriers in the Pacific—both those of the United States and those of Japan—*always* defeated land-based enemy aircraft. And, in fleet actions they were the most significant warship, regardless whether or not submarines were present. In the comparatively restricted waters of Europe and the Mediterranean, British aircraft carriers were often trounced by German

---

[1] William Mitchell, *Winged Defense* (New York: G. P. Putnam, 1925), p. 125.

land-based aircraft. But even in the European theater no fleet carriers were sunk by land-based aircraft. That is particularly significant when one considers the very small numbers of aircraft on British carrier decks—half the number of planes on comparable U.S. and Japanese carriers—and that the British planes were obsolete by comparative standards.

Even so, no British carriers were sunk by land-based aircraft, and British carrier aircraft were instrumental in such successful operations as sinking the *Bismarck* and running convoys to Malta, the latter a key factor in the German defeat in Africa.

On a less dramatic note, in World War II the U.S. and British escort of "jeep" played a major role in the battles of the Atlantic. Aircraft were the principal "killer" of U-boats. Considering the delays in the availability of capable land-based aircraft and jeep carriers, the effectiveness of aircraft and, in the later stages, carrier-based aircraft in the anti–U-boat war is impressive.

Despite the effectiveness of aircraft carriers in World War II, there appeared to be little need for tactical sea-based aviation in the postwar period: the U.S. monopoly in nuclear weapons and delivery systems was perceived to provide the "final word" in any future conflicts; carrier-capable aircraft were too small to carry nuclear weapons; and there was no fleet afloat—either allied or potential enemy—to challenge even a minimal U.S. naval force.

The overall U.S. Navy, including the carrier forces, was severely reduced in the postwar period. Efforts by the navy to initiate construction of a new class of very large carriers were devastated in 1949 when the prototype supercarrier the *United States* was canceled five days after the keel-laying ceremony. The navy was further trounced in the B-36 versus carrier controversies of that period. The admirals fought for sea-based aviation, and the so-called air power advocates fought for emphasis on strategic bombers—at the cost of any carrier program.

Not only were the leaders of the newly independent U.S. Air Force opposed to carriers, but so were other American and foreign defense leaders. Edward Teller, the "father of the H-bomb," declared:

> Looking at [an aircraft carrier] . . . it looked to me like quite a good target. In fact, if I project my mind into a time when not only we, but also a potential enemy, have plenty of atomic bombs, I would not put so many dollars and so many people into so good a target. Come to think of it, I would not put anything on the surface of the ocean—it's too good a target.[2]

---

[2] Edward Teller, "The Nature of Nuclear Warfare," *Air Force* magazine, January 1957.

Table 1
German Submarine Losses in World War II

Destroying Weapon	Number Destroyed
U-boats lost to allied forces	
All aircraft	356 (46%)
Carrier aircraft	43
Surface ships	246 (31%)
Surface/Air [a]	46 (5%)
Submarines	22 (2%)
Other [a]	109 (14%)
U-boats lost to U.S. forces	
All aircraft [a]	112 (70%)
Carrier aircraft	29
Surface ships	36 (23%)
Surface/Air [a]	10 (6%)
Submarines	2 (1%)

[a] Includes several sunk with carrier-based aircraft participation. In addition, several surface ship successes resulted from land- and carrier-based aircraft detections.

Source: S. W. Roskill, *The War at Sea* (London: H.M.S.D., 1954–1961); and H. T. Lenton, *German Submarines* (London: Macdonald, 1965).

Britain's leading general, Field Marshal Viscount Montgomery, was equally critical and, from the viewpoint of this AEI conference, more to the quick of the issue:

> It seems to me that the day of the large warship on the surface of the sea is over. The emphasis in the future is likely to be on the smaller type of vessel and on underwater craft. If it is true that the seas will in the future be controlled mainly from the air, then it is for consideration whether this control would not be best exercised by national air forces and not by naval forces. If this is the case, then navies will not in the future require their own air forces. That time has not yet come. But in my view it will come eventually. If this is true, then we should not build any more expensive aircraft carriers. . . . What it amounts to is that new weapons have not yet rendered the aircraft carrier obsolete, but they are likely to do so in the future. And I see control of the seas eventually passing to [land-based] air forces.[3]

[3] Field Marshal Viscount Montgomery, "A Look Through a Window at World War III," *Royal United Services Institution Journal*, November 1954.

These statements plus innumerable other criticisms of aircraft carriers came shortly after the Korean War (1950–1953). Yet, it was at the start of that conflict, with airfields available to the United States in Japan and Okinawa, that carrier-based aircraft again proved their worth. Only carrier-based aircraft that could operate effectively over the North during the early period of the conflict because of the loss of all air bases in the South and the limited range of tactical aircraft based in Japan and Okinawa. Even after tactical aircraft could again be based in the South, carriers still were employed in the conflict. In part there were political reasons for continued carrier participation in the latter stages of the war; but there also were valid operational reasons.

And, as the U.S. defense leadership considered the action in Korea as only the distraction from a pending Soviet attack in Europe, U.S. forces in Europe were reinforced, with the capabilities of the carriers continuously deployed in the Mediterranean being increased (with nuclear weapons embarked in the carriers from 1951 onward).

This emphasis on carriers in the Mediterranean is interesting in view of the availability during the 1950s of major air bases in North Africa and Spain, as well as France, England, and West Germany. Again, it was partially political, as U.S. administrations sought to maintain certain "balances" in the defense establishment, but carrier deployments were based principally on realistic requirements that could not be effectively met by land-based aircraft. The Lebanon crisis and Marine landings of 1958 demonstrated the effectiveness of sea-based aircraft when land-based aircraft could not provide effective and timely support.[4] (The British and French had learned the same lessons at Suez two years earlier, when two French and five British carriers supported the ill-fated Anglo-French assaults.)

The rapid-response characteristics of aircraft carriers were again demonstrated soon after the Lebanon crisis of July when, in August 1958, the Communist Chinese began pressing against Nationalist-held offshore islands. This crisis, halfway around the world, also was countered by a rapid deployment of U.S. carriers to the scene, including one flattop that had been in the eastern Mediterranean, had transited the Suez Canal, and then had crossed the Indian Ocean to arrive off the Taiwan straits.

But these operations were secondary to senior U.S. defense planners. The principal role of forward-deployed carriers in the Mediterranean and Western Pacific in this period was nuclear strike. Large

---

[4] The problems of employing land-based tactical aircraft in the Lebanon crisis is detailed in Colonel Albert P. Sights, Jr., "Lessons of Lebanon," *Air University Review*, July-August 1965.

turboprop AJ Savages and then turbojet A3D Skywarriors provided a long-range nuclear strike force on the carriers, while numerous fighter and light attack aircraft were fitted to deliver nuclear weapons at shorter ranges in daylight conditions. During some periods of tension a forward-deployed carrier would offload her fighter and reconnaissance aircraft and carry some eighty nuclear strike aircraft.

The demonstrated versatility and capabilities of carriers in non-nuclear conflicts and crises, and their potential for nuclear strike, led to supercarriers being authorized in every annual defense budget from fiscal years 1952 through 1958. One of these seven ships, the *Enterprise*, was nuclear propelled. Long-lead funds for another carrier were authorized in FY 1960 but were not spent. There was another *conventional* carrier authorized in FY 1961, the eighth postwar flattop.

Modern Technology. Modern technology overtook the aircraft carrier in the 1960s. First, the Kennedy-McNamara administration emphasized strategic missiles fired from underground silos and submarines while cutting back land- and carrier-based bomber programs. Missiles were more effective in military terms and more cost-effective in McNamara terms. By 1962 the carriers were no longer a primary component of the single integrated operational plan (SIOP), the nuclear attack plan. Strategic missiles could perform a mission that had been a major justification of carrier programs for two decades.

The second technological development was the extensive Soviet development of antiship (cruise) missiles. By the 1960s these weapons were being carried by large numbers of Soviet aircraft, surface ships, and submarines. They were the harbingers of a viable anticarrier capability.

Recall the World War II attacks against major surface ships? Dive bombers were the most effective ship killers, and scores would go into screaming dives over their targets, with each releasing one, two, or more bombs. Hits were generally few . . . if there were any. Most ships were sunk by near-misses that shattered their hulls by underwater concussions. But carriers could be sunk or at least knocked out of action for days, if not weeks and months, by one or two small bomb hits among armed and fueled aircraft on their flight decks. The Japanese lost four carriers at Midway in that manner.

Cruise missiles present the potential of small, high-speed, highly accurate antiship missiles that can be fired at long and short ranges from aircraft, surface ships, and submerged submarines. Although defenses could be developed against cruise missiles, as they were against the manned kamikaze "missile" during World War II, the incremental cost of adding cruise missiles to an attacking force is far cheaper than attempting to develop and construct platforms to defend against them. The subsequent development of tactical ballistic missiles and highly accurate aircraft bombing systems has further increased the vulnerability of aircraft carriers.

Thus, modern technology (1) replaced the aircraft carrier in the key strategic mission and (2) significantly increased the carrier's vulnerability to various forms of aircraft and missile attack. By the mid-1960s the end of the carrier appeared within sight. The U.S. Navy had fourteen attack carriers and nine ASW carriers immediately prior to the escalation of the Vietnam War; in 1965 Secretary of Defense McNamara had made the decision to allow the number of carriers to decline without replacement.

Just as the Korean War had turned around the views of the nation's defense leaders, so did the Vietnam War. Despite the availability of tactical air bases in South Vietnam and the Philippines, and subsequently in Thailand, aircraft carriers were heavily employed, from the Gulf of Tonkin incidents in 1964, through the entire war, to the final evacuations in 1975.

The few efforts to attack aircraft carriers ended in total losses for the attackers. While thousands of aircraft were damaged and hundreds destroyed on land bases by Communist guerrillas, the carriers steamed in the Gulf and South China Sea with complete immunity. Further, carriers built during World War II and the Korean War found useful employment, while no U.S. land bases used in those conflicts were within tactical air range of Vietnam. In addition, when the war was over several major airfields, complete with fuel, bombs, and aircraft, were abandoned to the communist enemy, while the carriers simply steamed away.

Even before the conflict came to its traumatic ending, Mr. McNamara decided that the "flattops" were cost- and mission-effective. In 1967 he approved the construction of three nuclear-propelled, *Nimitz*-class "supercarriers."

The lesson was there again; there is no substitute for sea-based tactical aviation.

The supercarrier *Nimitz* was commissioned in 1975, and the second, the *Eisenhower*, was commissioned in 1977. The third carrier of the class, the *Vinson*, is under construction. That ship will give the navy four modern nuclear and eight conventional carriers suitable for service into the late 1980s, if not beyond. The question is where do we go from here?

Current Issues

The following issues appear significant in this context: (1) Should the current carrier force be maintained? (2) Are additional aircraft carriers warranted? (3) Are there alternatives to aircraft carriers? and (4) What is the potential for v/STOL aircraft at sea?

Should the Current Carrier Force Be Maintained? The twelve carriers can permit forward deployments of four ships on a continuous basis, with increases on a "surge" basis for brief periods. (History shows that normal carrier forward deployments have significantly exceeded the 1-in-3 ratio.)

Aircraft carriers today are primarily "political" instruments. They present the national leaders with a number of options beyond "backing down" or all-out thermonuclear war. Obviously, land-based aircraft and other naval forces have significant capabilities in this regard. However, history and analysis indicate that land-based aircraft traditionally have been too short ranged and require foreign bases to be effective in crisis areas; submarines lack visibility (although the Soviet navy certainly uses them for political presence), while surface warships lack visible and in some cases real striking power compared to an aircraft carrier. Further, as noted above, the modern flattop is more survivable than any other surface warship.

For example, consider the relative striking power, endurance, and vulnerability to guided weapons of a large missile boat compared to a modern aircraft carrier. A destroyer or cruiser may fare better than the smaller missile craft, but the aircraft carrier has more striking power, endurance, and survivability than any other surface ship.

These characteristics have led the United States national leadership continually to "send a carrier" during periods of crisis: the waters between Turkey and Cyprus, the Persian Gulf, the Indian Ocean, the eastern Mediterranean, and the South China Sea have been among the areas to which carriers have been dispatched.[5] We must remember that for many of the nations bordering those areas the free use of the seas is vital to their economic survival and future growth; they recognize that

---

[5] A Brookings Institution study of the period 1945–1975 identified 212 "incidents," to which the United States responded with aircraft carriers in 106—60 percent of those that involved naval forces and 50 percent of the total incidents. See Barry M. Blechman and Stephen S. Kaplan, "The Use of the Armed Forces as a Political Instrument," The Brookings Institution, 1976 (sponsored by Defense Advanced Research Projects Agency). The British use of carriers in this role as well as U.S. operations are detailed in Polmar, *Aircraft Carriers: A History of Carrier Aviation and Its Impact on World Events* (New York: Doubleday & Co., 1969).

the nation that can project naval forces into the region is the nation they want as an ally and trading partner.

Even against the Soviet Union the modern attack carrier with its eighty-plus high-performance aircraft seems to present a viable threat. This is obvious in Soviet reactions to carriers operating in certain areas; in analyses of Soviet exercises, especially the multiocean Okean 1970 and 1975 maneuvers; and in the continued modernization of Soviet anti-carrier forces, the most recent manifestations being the SS-N-12 long-range cruise missile, the Backfire strike aircraft, and the Charlie I/II classes of missile submarines.

Although expensive to maintain, the current twelve-carrier force represents a largely "sunk" investment (no pun intended), and has a demonstrated *political* effectiveness. Although the force has become increasingly vulnerable, for the foreseeable future its capabilities for sea control and projection missions will remain high. At the least, the twelve existing carriers should be retained in full commission. (Later in this paper some alternative concepts of operations will be suggested.)

Are Additional Aircraft Carriers Warranted? If twelve aircraft carriers are a valid force, would thirteen or fourteen or fifteen be justified? The answer obviously would be "yes" on a mission-effectiveness basis. Interestingly, the answer would probably be "yes" on a cost-effectiveness basis as well, especially in comparison with other types of warships.

Aircraft carriers are good investments in comparison with other warships on a tonnage basis. Although such ships as frigates (FFG) and destroyers (DD/DDG) are considerably cheaper than aircraft carriers on an individual hull basis, the cost per ton of a conventional supercarrier (such as the *Kennedy*) is one-half that of a 3,500-ton frigate, while a nuclear carrier (such as the *Nimitz*) costs about two-thirds as much per ton.

Thus, with a fixed budget for surface warships of about $4 billion per year, we could annually construct thirty-three frigates or two *Nimitz*-class carriers or three and a fraction *Kennedys*. Thus, a twenty-five-year building program could provide a fleet of 825 frigates or 80 *Kennedy*-class carriers or 50 *Nimitz*-class carriers![6]

Imagine what a JCS planner could do with a carrier force of that size! One could literally escort one big carrier with another, or two for antiair and antisubmarine defense, with one carrier concentrating its aircraft on defense while the others concentrate on offense. Obviously, the above concept does not include operating and aircraft costs; but

---

[6] For a full discussion of this trade-off concept, see Norman Polmar, "A Fleet for the Future: Some Modest Suggestions," *Sea Power* (Navy League), April 1976.

those have always been secondary in budgetary and congressional considerations. The number of flight decks has always been the key issue. Also, existing wings could be reduced in size when the ships are not forward deployed, reserve squadrons could be used, and Marine tactical squadrons—which all fly carrier-capable aircraft—could be employed to help provide air wings for these ships.

However, it is exceedingly unlikely that the U.S. Navy will increase its carrier force beyond the current twelve ships . . . primarily because of political reasons. But I would argue for the construction of a fifth nuclear carrier at this time. The alternatives of a midsize carrier, either nuclear or conventionally propelled, or another *Nimitz* would provide twelve deployable carriers through the 1990s while one ship is undergoing long-term SLEP (service life extension program) modernization.

Although some arguments could be made for constructing a less-expensive, and less-capable, midsize ship to provide a twelve-deployable carrier force, *if* only one more "fleet" carrier is to be constructed it would be less costly to build to the already-designed *Nimitz* configuration rather than to go to the expense of designing a new ship. Remember, in a carrier the vast number of equipment interfaces and other specialized problems would drive the cost of building a single, new-design ship probably higher than building one more *Nimitz*.

To recapitulate, at this time, in order to maintain twelve deployable large carriers for the foreseeable future, one more *Nimitz*-class carrier appears to be warranted.

Are There Alternatives to Aircraft Carriers? The answer to this certainly is yes. Alternatives include using sea-launched cruise missile (SLCM) for certain missions now assigned to carrier aircraft, using land-based aircraft, and using VSTOL/VTOL aircraft.

Cruise missiles provide the opportunity for frigates, destroyers, and cruisers to have the long-range striking power previously associated only with aircraft carriers. Similarly, both the Harpoon sixty-mile missile and the longer-range, three-hundred- to six-hundred-mile Tomahawk, can be launched from submarines.

These weapons are limited, however, by the target acquisition systems of the launching ships. It is conceivable that at some time in the future reconnaissance satellites could be fitted with the resolution, data links, and other features necessary to permit them to undertake targeting and guidance that would permit ships or submarines independently to launch and guide missiles beyond their radar, ELINT, and acoustic "horizons." However, these systems appear to be some years away and to be relatively costly, and have the limitation of relying on some degree

219

of data processing in the satellite. Aircraft—manned or unmanned drones—appear to be the more reasonable approach to over-the-horizon targeting.

The man in the cockpit has a number of advantages. He can ascertain the nature of targets visually, he can process data, and he can perform other functions, such as general reconnaissance and observation. The drone aircraft, or RPV (Remotely Piloted Vehicle) in the current vernacular, in turn is less costly than either the manned or unmanned satellite or the manned aircraft and can have a very long time on station (that is, several hours or, at some time in the future, days). However, the data links between the ship and RPV make the system more vulnerable and susceptible to detection than does employing a manned aircraft, and the RPV tends to be a single-purpose vehicle while manned aircraft can be more multimission configured.

However, there can be no doubt: the cruise missile is here to stay. Astute employment of the SLCM will provide the U.S. Navy with many opportunities in the sea control and projection missions, *some* of which will be in place of carrier-based aircraft. Indeed, once strike versions of the Tomahawk are at sea, the missile airframe and power plant should be considered for adoption to antisubmarine, reconnaissance, and possibly other missions as well. But for several missions, especially strike in the sea control and projection missions, the SLCM will be dependent upon the use of manned aircraft for certain reconnaissance and targeting support.

Land-based aircraft can obviously perform certain missions now assigned to sea-based aircraft. Here one must, however, exercise extreme caution. U.S. national interests are largely in overseas areas, far distant from air bases on U.S. territory; foreign bases, as we have learned from experience in North Africa, France, Vietnam, Thailand, and elsewhere, are precarious at best. We are still learning this lesson in Spain, Japan, and the Philippines. Indeed, the 1973 conflict in the Middle East demonstrated that even our staunch NATO allies will not permit us to use their bases for noncombat and tanker aircraft under many conditions (some U.S. military leaders had already learned that lesson in earlier Middle East crises).

Thus, if we are to discuss land-based aircraft to support naval operations as a realistic alternative to sea-based aircraft, we must discuss very long range aircraft. In the context of future national interests, we should consider the need for deployments in the Middle East, Indian Ocean, east and west African coasts, and possibly even South American coasts.

Current and near-future land-based aircraft simply cannot undertake such missions with meaningful payloads on a realistic basis. Perhaps three existing aircraft could be modified for such missions: the C-5 and C-141 transports, and the B-52 heavy bomber. The numbers of the large transports are too small and their current commitments are too large to consider them seriously for the maritime role. The B-52s would make suitable platforms, but they are dated (the last B-52s were delivered fifteen years ago) and, at this time, most of those available are committed to strategic offensive forces. With the cancellation of the B-1 bomber they will be unavailable for the foreseeable future.

The development of a new long-range maritime aircraft with a comparable range would be an expensive undertaking. This is especially true for a multimission aircraft, that is, one that could perform in the naval strike, reconnaissance, antisubmarine, early warning, and intercept roles that are now performed by sea-based aircraft.

Finally, there is the issue of the practicality of long-range, land-based aircraft to support missions. By practicality I mean (1) mission time and (2) vulnerability. Aircraft mission time is expensive. An aircraft with a range of 500 miles costs far less (or can carry considerably more payload) than a plane with a range of 5,000 miles. Why carry that fuel several thousand miles to the operating areas if there are ships nearby that could launch the aircraft to fly a fraction of the distance? Regardless of the mission, the aircraft trade-off will favor the sea-based aircraft at significant distances from the U.S. coast. (Certain foreign bases may initially appear attractive, but indirect costs, military and political vulnerabilities, and other factors make them generally much more expensive than either U.S. bases or even carriers; again, Secretary McNamara determined this after the most exhaustive cost-effectiveness studies in Department of Defense history.)

The second major argument against land-based aircraft centers on vulnerability, both to mechanical failure and to enemy action en route to the operating area. For example, the number of aircraft required to generate a given number of sorties is highly dependent upon distance to station, because it takes time to fly to and from the station. Remember, this is necessary but nonproductive time for the land-based aircraft. It is less for aircraft operating from ships in the region.

Assume that an aircraft must fly six hours to reach its operating objective. If, after five hours, it suffers a mechanical failure or is shot down, and a replacement aircraft can be launched *immediately,* the objective will be "uncovered" for at least five hours. The time that the objective area is uncovered—that is, the delays until the target area can be reached—increase with distance or with planned mission time

221

on station. A ship-launched aircraft closer to the operating objective or target area can reduce time-to-station and reaction times significantly. Of course, if the mission is short-range ASW (ten to fifty miles from a ship or force) or air patrol or airborne early warning over a ship or force, then the time the objective or station is uncovered because of time en route is virtually nil in the case of sea-based aircraft.

And if, for example, twenty land-based aircraft and a lesser number of sea-based aircraft are required to keep two aircraft on station, sea-based aircraft can be added on station more rapidly in a crisis situation and can provide more "aim points" over the objective more quickly in time of attack.

Again, the less the distance to the objective area for the aircraft, the more effective the use of resources and the more flexibility.

What is the Potential for V/STOL Aircraft at Sea? Vertical and Short Take-Off and Landing (V/STOL) or simply VTOL aircraft provide another consideration for this conference. The V/STOL/VTOL concept is not new for sea-based aviation; during World War I several nations employed fighter and spotter aircraft launched from small decks attached to battleship and cruiser gun turrets. The turrets simply pointed into the wind and the light, wood-and-fabric aircraft simply sailed off. These planes were replaced eventually by carrier-based aircraft (and to some extent by catapult floatplanes). The carrier plane, with its *short* take-off and landing capabilities, was far superior to the turret-launched aircraft (which had to come down at sea or land ashore at the end of its mission).

I believe it fair to say that today and for the foreseeable future the modern carrier aircraft—the F-14 Tomcat, A-6E Intruder, E-2C Hawkeye—and their successors will be far more capable than V/STOL or VTOL aircraft. But we are being driven to alternatives because more carriers simply are not *politically* acceptable. In that context V/STOL and VTOL become more attractive.

The V/STOL/VTOL technology is certainly available. Second-generation aircraft are now in service, the Anglo-American Harrier and the Soviet Yak-36 Forger (the unsuccessful U.S. Navy XFY-1 and XFV-1 "tail-sitters" of the early 1950s could be called the first generation). The current Harrier is based on the Hawker Siddeley P.1127 Kestrel, which first flew in 1960! Today we have several U.S. aerospace firms ready to begin advanced development of the third generation of V/STOL aircraft, especially Grumman, McDonnell Douglas, and Rockwell International. To date, however, the U.S. Navy has not expressed sufficient interest in V/STOL—the aircraft, ships, or operating concepts—for these

222

firms and others to apply the proper initiative to the effort. The recent congressional decision to fund an air-capable *Spruance*-class destroyer for v/stol aircraft, the navy's asking for preliminary data prior to awarding design contracts for the so-called Type B v/stol, and the Soviet development of the *Kiev*-class aircraft carriers may provide the proper incentive to the U.S. Navy and to the secretary of defense.

Looking now at specific uses of v/stol/vtol aircraft at sea, the "jump jet" concept could permit the deployment of improved-performance aircraft to sea aboard ships smaller than "fleet" carriers. In particular, carriers as small as 25,000 tons are considered capable of operating about twenty-five v/stol fixed-wing aircraft and helicopters with a reasonable speed and certain other features considered necessary for effective fleet operations. Recalling the effectiveness of aircraft at sea, I believe that the v/stol Support Ship (vss) could become second in importance to the larger supercarrier in naval operations. Future v/stol fighter, attack, asw, aew, and reconnaissance aircraft could provide the vss with more versatility and capability than any cruiser or destroyer in the fleet today or on the drawing boards. Further, application of the twin-hull swath (Small Waterplane Area Twin-Hull) design could provide a most stable platform that would be superior to any other surface warship afloat in rough seas, permitting the vss to fly planes in weather that would prevent other surface ships from operating effectively.

For today I see the v/stol aircraft providing over-the-horizon targeting, asw, and aew functions far superior to that possible with helicopters. Under current planning, a third-generation (Type A) v/stol could be at sea for these functions in the early 1990s. That schedule could be accelerated and, in view of certain congressional actions, I am certain that funding could be made available to an accelerated and forward-looking program for sea-based v/stol.

Where does one base these aircraft? Certain v/stol aircraft could supplement conventional aircraft on the big carriers. The larger ship's ability to concentrate large numbers of aircraft and provide comprehensive support for them is equally valuable to v/stol aircraft and conventional aircraft. Next, the v/stol carrier or vss of about 25,000 tons must be reexamined. I use the term "reexamined" because in the early 1970s the tentative Five-Year Defense Plan actually provided for seven ships of this type. Somehow, they got lost in the shuffle and in our on-again, off-again interests in v/stol.

Next, let's look at destroyer-size vtol platforms. A design has been developed for providing four vtol aircraft of about 45,000 pounds on a *Spruance*-class destroyer without any changes to the propulsion machinery, and retaining the gun-missile armament and all sensors forward. A prototype could be built with the $300 million provided by Congress for an air-capable *Spruance* in the fiscal year 1978 budget, and the thirty standard *Spruance*-class destroyers could be modified at their half-life point, starting about 1990. If the development of the *Spruance* air-capable ship were to be accelerated, Congress probably would fund on the order of one to two ships per year for the next few years. Assuming that perhaps ten of these V/STOL-capable missile destroyers were to be constructed, and just half of the thirty standard *Spruances* are modified for the Type A V/STOL aircraft, those twenty-five ships could provide up to two hundred antisubmarine, early warning, reconnaissance-missile targeting aircraft to the fleet. Unfortunately, an extremely conservative approach has been taken with the "air capable" *Spruance,* now being planned as merely a conventional, all-gun/ASW destroyer with space for four helicopters in place of the normal two.

Of course, various amphibious ships could tomorrow accommodate VTOL aircraft, and the planned Arapaho helicopter facility for merchant ships is readily adaptable for VTOL aircraft.[7]

Beyond ships that can operate and support V/STOL/VTOL aircraft, we must keep in mind that other ships can be used as touchdown and refueling bases. For example, a VSS could provide one or two VTOL aircraft to a number of cruisers, destroyers, and even frigates that do not have hangars or support facilities, but simply flight decks. The aircraft could then fly one or two missions, for missile guidance, ASW, or AEW, and return to the V/STOL carrier (or regular carrier) for maintenance, rearming, and crew replacement. This enhances the total force capabilities; it provides more targeting problems for an enemy; it can increase response time; and it has other advantages.

The planned Type A V/STOL, employed in a task force with cruise missiles and possibly RPVs, could be a considerable "force multiplier," that is, it obtains more force capability for a finite number of ships.

Courses to Steer

The U.S. Navy's "track record" in the post-Vietnam period has not been encouraging. From a viewpoint of force levels, the navy is significantly smaller than in the pre-Vietnam period. For example, in the early 1960s, before the Vietnam buildup, the navy had over 800 ships in commission.

---

[7] See James J. Mulquin, "The Navy Begins a New Approach to Modern Maritime Defense," *Sea Power* (Navy League), March 1976.

Today the fleet has 460 commissioned ships, plus a number of civilian-operated auxiliary ships. The goal of 600 ships has been dropped; there is some talk of requiring 550. I submit that unless there is a long war or sustained crisis, a 500-ship fleet will not be seen again. Indeed, I doubt if the U.S. fleet in 1990 will number more than 450 ships in commission; 300 to 350 is more probable. Anyone who does not accept my predictions of a *maximum* fleet size of 450 ships—and that estimate may be optimistic—need only to look at the record of the past decade. We have been constructing significantly fewer ships than have been proposed in the annually revised five-year shipbuilding plans; the recent Department of Defense decisions against the CVN-71, the strike cruiser, the nineteen planned mine-countermeasure ships, and the eight dock landing ships, and the opposition to the PHM missile hydrofoil program and cutting weapon system development for the 3,000-ton SES reflect only a part of the opposition to major changes in fleet size.

Of course, the quality of U.S. warships has improved. Today's ships are, in most respects, far superior to their predecessors. But they are more difficult to maintain because of the sophistication of equipment and the problems of an all-volunteer force, and for a number of reasons they cost more to build and operate than their predecessors.

At the same time, the nation's need to use the seas for political, economic, and military reasons is increasing. The Soviet Union today has a major oceangoing fleet, which continues to expand and improve, and several Third World nations have coastal naval and air forces that can effectively challenge the U.S. Navy in certain regions.

What, then, are our options for the 1980s and 1990s, and beyond? Obviously, tactical air power will be an essential element of future U.S. naval operations. The number of ships cannot be increased, nor can radical changes be made in the composition of the fleet, in part because of the slow rate of change possible when warships have an effective life of some thirty years, and, again, because of opposition to such concepts as a fifty-carrier surface navy or an SES fleet or even an all-submarine fleet.

But something must be done. The navy simply cannot continue along its present course: a 450-ship fleet, with perhaps ten aircraft carriers in the 1980s, and even fewer ships and flattops in the 1990s. *Conventional* fleets of those sizes will not be able to support U.S. interests effectively in a world that is highly dependent upon use of the sea.

What is to be done? James Woolsey, the under secretary of the Navy Department, has astutely addressed this problem:

> Military breakthroughs . . . come by approaching things from a new perspective, by devising a different way, for example, to exploit the effect of mass or shock, a way to use surprise or concealment to accomplish what was previously accomplished by ponderous force, or a way to disperse and then concentrate for battle that confounds the enemy's planning. . . . The real breakthrough occurs when a man of vision has the intellectual audacity to shatter the conventional wisdom, often . . . in spite of . . . the considered judgment of most of his military colleagues.

> The questions such a man of military vision asks are not, or at least not exclusively, "how much [marginal change] is enough?" He asks, "how can I exploit my advantages?" "How can I change the rules of the game?" "How can I make an opponent's investment worthless?" And, if war should ever come, "How can I put the enemy fleet on the bottom?" [8]

I concur with Jim Woolsey; this effort to exploit one's advantages, to change the rules of the game, to make an opponent's investment worthless was the philosophy of Napoleon, the tank genius Guderian, his colleague Rommel, our own Patton, Halsey, and Nimitz, and many other successful military leaders. One probably should add Admiral Gorshkov to that list. And, whether or not one agrees with his policies, one wonders if Admiral Zumwalt would have been a candidate for that list if our system would have permitted him to remain as head of the navy for more than the accepted four years.

What are the advantages we can exploit, how can we change the rules of the game, how can we make an opponent's investment worthless, and how can we put his fleet on the bottom in time of war, especially given the constraints, limitations, inhibited thinking, and attitudes we have today?

With respect to tactical air at sea, first and foremost, the big carrier is successful: World War II, Korea, Vietnam, and a hundred crises have fully demonstrated that. To shouts that they are expensive we must respond, Yes, but so is a soldier, a tank, an airplane, or even a PHM missile hydrofoil. To cries that they are vulnerable, we should quote Churchill: "Anyone can see the risk from air attack which we run. . . . This risk will have to be faced. Warships are meant to go under fire." [9] Rather than vulnerabilities, consider what carriers can accomplish with their speed, mobility, and ability to operate large numbers of aircraft for sustained periods.

---

[8] Under Secretary of the Navy R. James Woolsey, before the Navy League, Arlington, Va., 6 September 1977.

[9] Winston Churchill, Note for First Sea Lord, 15 July 1940.

First, the "next" *Nimitz* should be built, to ensure twelve big-deck carriers are available. This next carrier must take advantage of the savings accrued by adding "one more ship" to the *Nimitz* class (some changes that would not affect basic design could be considered, such as the propulsion concept being put forth by Dr. Reuven Leopold and some others).

Simultaneously, the navy must initiate a V/STOL carrier program; a ship of under 25,000 tons appears reasonable, carrying some twenty-five V/STOL aircraft and helicopters. That ship should be undertaken even at the expense of large cruiser-type ships.[10] Both conventional and V/STOL technology and experience available to the United States today far exceed that available in other nations. This is one of our few areas of leadership.

Thus, as a second recommendation, the navy should proceed at full speed with the V/STOL program. Again, here our advantage over a potential enemy also includes the large number of surface ships that already have helicopter facilities that can be upgraded to VTOL aircraft. The larger ships—thirty modern destroyers and fourteen cruisers—can be fitted to carry and support V/STOL aircraft, as can numerous amphibious ships. Many of our eighty frigates built and building could be fitted to land V/STOLs, which would be supported aboard other ships. The availability of *over 150 potential* V/STOL *platforms in the fleet*—plus the carriers and new-construction V/STOL ships—could be a way to change the "rules of the game" significantly.

Third, antiship cruise missiles, the Harpoon and especially the longer-range Tomahawk, are another way to change the "rules of the game." These cannister-launched missiles can be placed aboard several classes of cruisers, destroyers, and even frigates.

This proliferation of tactical cruise missiles aboard U.S. ships will increase the "high value aim points" beyond our twelve or thirteen carriers, and provide some compensation for our limited offensive capability in areas where a carrier is not available. Over-the-horizon targeting is a problem, but V/STOL, improved C³ (Command, Control, Communications), acoustic sensors, and multiship tactical operations will permit effective use of long-range cruise missiles, again, to change the "rules of the game."

A fourth area that could be exploited is offensive mine warfare; however, that subject is beyond the scope of this paper, except for the

---

10 Arguments for a nuclear cruiser program to provide AEGIS AAW missile platforms can be refused on the basis of modernizing the existing nuclear missile cruisers (including the *Long Beach*) with AEGIS, and constructing the planned AEGIS-configured *Spruance*-class destroyers (DDG-47).

comment that the most effective means available today to plant mine-fields is with aircraft, either land based or carrier based. (Although sub-marines can plant mines, their normal loading with torpedoes only, slow transit times, and other mission requirements make them a less favored minelaying platform at this time.)

All four of these concepts are based on the extensive use of sea-based tactical aviation. Land-based aircraft, except in the instance of offensive mining, simply are not as effective because of the limited num-bers that probably would be available, limiting basing options, delays in reaching objective areas, and other factors.

Rather, as history has shown, as current operations indicate, and as analytical analysis demonstrates, sea-based tactical aviation will be important to American use of the sea for the foreseeable future. And, the United States is today more dependent upon use of the sea for advancing its political, economic, and military well-being than probably ever before in the nation's history.

Land-Based Aircraft Options
for Sea Control

Dov S. Zakheim

Sea control is the navy's primary wartime mission within the nation's overall forward-defense strategy. It encompasses the navy's tasks of protecting sea lines of communication between the United States and her overseas forces and allies and of carrying materiel and manpower to overseas forces. "Sea control," as defined by Admiral James L. Holloway, the present chief of naval operations, is "the engagement and destruction of hostile aircraft, ships and submarines at sea . . . or the deterrence of hostile actions through the threat of destruction." [1] In his view, "maritime threats can be attacked and destroyed on the high seas or in their base areas." [2] For the past thirty-five years, naval aircraft have been the primary naval systems for achieving that destruction. These aircraft have been both land- and sea-based. However, most of the navy's offensive firepower has come from sea-based tactical aviation. The aircraft carrier, capable of transiting long distances, enhanced the range of naval aircraft; together, carrier and aircraft became the navy's dominant offensive system during World War II. They continue to dominate the U.S. fleet.

Recent advances in technology, notably the advent of precision-guided munitions, have, however, resulted in a new threat to U.S. carrier survivability. Whereas carriers previously operated virtually as safe havens, out of the range of enemy land-based aviation, they now must face not only long-range bomber threats in certain locales, but a more widespread threat from cruise missile–equipped nuclear-powered submarines. The decline in fleet size, and particularly in the size of the carrier force, has added to the impact of increased carrier vulnerability

Views represented herein are entirely those of the author. The Congressional Budget Office, where he is employed, bears no responsibility for the contents of this paper or the opinions of the author.

[1] Statement of Admiral James L. Holloway III, USN, before the U.S. Congress, House, Committee on Armed Services, concerning the *FY 1978 Posture and FY 1978 Budget of the United States Navy,* March 7, 1977 (processed).

[2] Statement of Admiral James L. Holloway III, USN, before the U.S. Congress, House Subcommittee on Seapower and Strategic and Critical Materials of the Committee on Armed Services, February 23, 1977 (processed), p. 1.

upon overall naval effectiveness. The loss of one carrier today would be far more damaging to the fleet than its loss would have been twenty years ago; yet the loss of that carrier is far more likely today than it would have been then.

The decline in the size of the carrier force has, of course, stemmed in a large part from the increasing costs of carriers themselves and, indeed, of the forces procured to protect them. Carriers now cost in the region of $2 billion; surface escorts cost anywhere from $300 million to over $1 billion, depending on their propulsion and the systems they carry. Carrier air wings include planes that operate primarily for defense of the carrier, the S-3A being a prime example. The thirty-year life-cycle costs of defending the large deck carrier, even with air wing excluded, would exceed $7 billion. To be sure, escorts will have an offensive capability of their own once they are fitted with the Harpoon surface-to-surface missile. However, as long as they are to operate with the carrier as a task force, and carriers clearly will require escort protection for the foreseeable future, their offensive capabilities will remain secondary to their task of defending the carrier; it is for that latter purpose they they will be procured.

The increasing vulnerability of aircraft carriers, the growing costs of both building and protecting them, and their declining numbers have led analysts to search for alternative means of providing the navy with the air power necessary to assure the success of its sea-control mission. One of these alternatives is that of widening the navy's utilization of land-based aviation. As noted above, it has been an intrinsic part of the navy for well over thirty years, and indeed predates the use of carrier aviation.

This paper will address land-based aviation as a complement, rather than as a full alternative, to carrier aviation. Carriers will remain in the fleet until well into the twenty-first century. Indeed, with the service life extension program (SLEP), nearly the entire programmed twelve-carrier force will be in active duty until the 1990s. Furthermore, unless the United States has access to any land mass it desires, and has developed a fighter plane with a combat radius than can be measured in thousands, rather than hundreds, of miles, there will remain ocean areas that will be inaccessible to U.S. tactical aviation unless it is launched from a carrier. Neither of these conditions is likely to be met during the next quarter century. There will remain a need for some carriers, and carriers will be available to meet that need. However, U.S. maritime requirements may extend beyond present carrier-based air capabilities. These requirements address not only the mission of sea control, to which major importance would be attached in the event of a worldwide war with the Soviet Union, but also power projection in a NATO war, as well as in smaller contingencies that might take place anywhere in the world. The ability to respond quickly to contingency requirements for tactical aviation generates a need for forward carrier deployments. These deployments in turn generate demands for backup carriers. Thus the possible use of land-based tactical aviation for sea control might be viewed not only as complementing the inherent sea-control capabilities of the carrier force, but also as freeing elements of that force for projection of power ashore, a mission for which it is admirably suited, particularly in remote areas. The question this paper will address is one of optimizing our marginal procurement for sea-control air power in light of our overall maritime tactical aviation needs. Put another way, it will ask: Can the mix of aviation procured for the mission of sea control be altered to increase the present proportion of land-based to sea-based aircraft while maintaining and possibly enhancing overall U.S. maritime effectiveness at less cost?

Sea Control and the Evolving Soviet Threat: Outlook for the 1980s

The magnitude of the navy's sea-control task is directly related to the nature of the Soviet maritime threat. As noted above, the nation's forward-defense strategy calls for the navy to protect sea lines of communication between the United States and its overseas forces and allies and to transport materiel and manpower to overseas forces. Over the past two decades, the Soviet Union has organized an impressive maritime force, composed of surface ships, submarines, and aircraft, which are geared to disrupt the U.S. effort. This force continues to diversify and to improve its capabilities. It now seriously threatens not only transoceanic shipping, but all naval units, including the carrier, and forward-based naval and air defense installations as well. The diversity of the Soviet threat is such that it poses complications for allied planning regardless of the assumptions one makes about the nature of the war that might be fought.

Overview of the Soviet Threat. The Soviet submarine fleet is the world's largest. It includes 231 general purpose units divided among four fleets, the Northern, Black, Baltic, and Pacific, with the largest number attached to the Northern fleet. The fleet is as modern as it is large. It includes Charlie-class nuclear-powered submarines that can fire cruise missiles 30 nautical miles (nm) while submerged, as well as Echo-II–class nuclear submarines, which can fire the longer-range (300nm) SS-N-3 missile, and the fast (over 30 knots) torpedo-carrying Victor class. Both

231

the Charlie and the Victor are considered to be second-generation submarines, comparable to the U.S. 594 class, though not as capable. Experts have been anticipating the appearance of a "third-generation" submarine, which would likely be quieter and more difficult to detect than its predecessors, but equally as fast. Some analysts have pointed to the Alpha submarine as a prototype for this new class of submarine.[3] In any event, it appears likely that the first few of these new submarines may appear before the end of the 1980s, thereby enhancing Soviet potential for sea denial while complicating U.S. antisubmarine warfare (ASW) efforts.

Of the four fleets, the Northern fleet poses the greatest threat to America's sea lanes to its allies. It numbers about 125 torpedo and cruise missile submarines, 47 of them nuclear powered. It also has year-round, ice-free access to the open oceans.[4] Recent estimates posit that by 1985 the total Soviet submarine force will rise from its present level of 84 nuclear-powered attack submarines (SSN) to about 165 SSNs. Given present proportions, the Northern fleet would claim about 92 of these, with most if not all of the remainder in the Pacific fleet. This number is about equal to the present total U.S. diesel and nuclear attack submarine force in service or under construction. Nevertheless, these estimates may be conservative. They assume the continuation of current annual production rates, which are significantly below the capacity of Soviet shipyards.[5]

The Pacific fleet poses a threat to U.S. shipping seeking to resupply Japan and other Asian allies that is comparable, though of somewhat lower order, to that of the Northern fleet in the Atlantic. This fleet includes thirty-one nuclear-powered attack submarines (SSNs) as well as thirty-eight conventionally powered torpedo and cruise missile boats. The other fleets are not likely to play a significant part in a conflict on the high seas, since the exits from both the Baltic and Black seas could well be cut off early in the war by allied ASW tactics, notably mining.

Soviet naval aviation provides an important complement to the fleet mission of denying the sea lanes to the Western allies. The naval air arm of the Soviet navy presently numbers about 1,200 aircraft,[6] of

---

[3] See K. J. Moore, Mark Flanigan, and Robert D. Helsel, "Developments in Submarine Systems, 1956-76," in Michael MccGwire and John McDonnell, eds., *Soviet Naval Influence: Domestic and Foreign Dimensions* (New York: Praeger, 1977), pp. 174-76; Michael MccGwire, "Soviet Naval Programs," ibid., p. 340.

[4] Robert P. Berman, "Soviet Naval Strength and Deployment," ibid., p. 324.

[5] MccGwire, "Soviet Naval Programs," ibid., pp. 342, 355.

[6] Norman Polmar, "Soviet Naval Aviation," *Air Force* Magazine, March 1976, p. 69.

which about 645 are combat aircraft.[7] The latter figure includes about 280 medium-range (1,500 to 2,000 nm) Badger bombers, armed with air-to-surface missiles with ranges of over 100 miles. It also includes at least thirty Backfire long-range bombers.[8] The latter are estimated to have a combat radius of anywhere between 1,750 and 3,500 nautical miles, though it probably would be lower if the plane flew continuously at low altitudes or dashed long distances at supersonic speed. The Backfire carries two AS-4 missiles with ranges exceeding 100 miles.[9] It may eventually carry the AS-6 missile, with ranges reported up to 500 nm,[10] though the optimally effective range will probably be considerably lower.[11] More Backfires are expected to enter the Soviet naval air force each year until a level of well over 100 bombers is reached.[12] As the Backfire level increases, that of Badgers is likely to decline. In addition, the total Backfire force level is estimated to reach at least 400, with at least 300 planes expected to enter the Soviet long-range aviation (LRA) force.[13] Sea interdiction is a collateral mission for that force. Thus, while the magnitude of the Backfire threat should not be exaggerated, since the plane has other priority missions in its LRA role, it certainly is possible that more than just the naval air component of Backfire could be used to attack allied shipping.

The naval air force also includes Beagle light bombers, short-range Blinder bombers, and reconnaissance variants of the Badgers and long-range (8,000 miles) Bear aircraft.[14] These aircraft pose a secondary threat to NATO shipping and forces, particularly in areas near the U.S.S.R. A recent addition to the Soviet naval air arm is the force of Forger vertical take-off and landing (VTOL) aircraft, presently deployed only aboard the "antisubmarine" carrier *Kiev*. They are, how-

---

[7] International Institute for Strategic Studies, *The Military Balance: 1976-1977* (London: International Institute for Strategic Studies, 1976), p. 9. The Soviet Union also could employ its long-range aviation in a maritime role.

[8] *The Military Balance: 1976-1977*, p. 9.

[9] William D. O'Neil, "Backfire: Long-Shadow on the Sea-Lanes," *United States Naval Institute Proceedings*, vol. 103 (March 1977), pp. 29-30; Polmar, "Soviet Naval Aviation," p. 70.

[10] Charles M. Gilson and Bill Sweetman, "Military Aircraft of the World," *Flight International*, March 5, 1977, p. 591.

[11] O'Neil, "Backfire," p. 30.

[12] Gilson and Sweetman, "Military Aircraft," p. 591. The initial assignment of half of Backfire production to the navy, as well as the current ratio of about 500 Badgers in long-range aviation and 300 in naval aviation both point to a total SNA Backfire force well in excess of 100 aircraft.

[13] Ibid.; O'Neil, in "Backfire," p. 30, cites CIA sources for this estimate.

[14] Polmar, "Soviet Naval Aviation," p. 71. The Blinder has been rated "unsuccessful" in the strike role (ibid.).

ever, also likely to be deployed aboard the *Kiev*'s newer sister ships as they enter the fleet.[15]

Not generally included in estimates of Soviet air capability in the maritime sphere are other Soviet tactical aircraft, such as the SU-19 Fencer, and the Mig-23 Flogger. The Fencer, a fighter carrying missiles with a range of about 50 nm, has an estimated combat radius of over 400 nm.[16] Newer versions of this plane are predicted to have radii of about 1,000 nm.[17] The Flogger also carries air-to-air missiles, though of somewhat shorter range. Its combat intercept radius is estimated at between 550 and 700 nm.[18] At present, neither of these fighters has the range to enable it to escort Soviet bombers from their present bases to likely points of conflict along the northern air corridors from the Soviet Union to the North Atlantic Ocean. These corridors extend through the Barents Sea north of the Kola peninsula, around North Cape, and down through the Norwegian Sea between Iceland and Britain or through the Denmark Straits between Iceland and Greenland. Both involve transits in excess of 1,400 nm. However, these aircraft, if deployed from East Germany, could provide fighter escort for bombers across the Baltic and North Sea exits to the Norwegian Sea.

The Soviet surface fleet is not considered to be as great a threat to U.S. missions as the submarine or aviation forces.[19] Nevertheless, the capabilities of Soviet surface units are considerable, and rapidly improving. The newest Soviet cruiser classes, the Kara and Kresta II, mount SS-N-14 antisubmarine missles as well as antiaircraft missiles and guns.[20] The Krivak-class destroyer likewise mounts tubes for the SS-N-14 as well as launchers for the SA-N-4 short-range surface-to-air missile, torpedo tubes, mine rails, and four 76-mm guns. Finally, the most significant and recent development in the surface fleet has been the appearance of the first of a new class of antisubmarine aircraft carriers,

---

[15] U.S. Congress, House Committee on Armed Services, *Hearings on Military Posture and H.R. 5068 (H.R. 5970) and H.R. 1755*, part 4, 95th Congress, 1st session, 1977, pp. 40, 51.

[16] Gilson and Sweetman, "Military Aircraft," pp. 577, 590. This assumes the Fencer flies at low altitudes throughout.

[17] Ibid., p. 590.

[18] Low estimate: ibid., p. 577; high estimate, Georg Panyalev, "The MIG-23 Flogger—A Versatile Family of Soviet Combat Aircraft," *International Defense Review*, vol. 10 (February 1977), p. 49.

[19] Testimony of Admiral Holloway, in U.S. Congress, *Hearings before the House Appropriations Committee, Department of Defense Appropriations, Fiscal Year 1977*, part 8, 94th Congress, 2nd session, 1976, pp. 180-81.

[20] The SS-N-14 has often been referred to as the SS-N-10. It has been described by one authoritative source as "a 30-mile missile with a payload similar to the U.S. Asroc for attack against submarines." Letter from Commander John B. Shewmaker, *Detroit News*, September 18, 1976.

the *Kiev*. As noted above, this ship, with its complement of Forger aircraft, in addition to surface-to-surface missiles, complicates Western air defense strategy because it provides the Soviets with their first-ever sea-based offensive tactical air capability.

The Soviet submarine, surface, and air arms all function in a highly coordinated manner. Indeed, it is their capacity for coordinated command and control, as displayed in the 1975 Okean exercises, that lends credence to their overall capabilities and underscores the severity of the Soviet threat to allied operations.

The Soviet Threat in a Long War Scenario. The nature of the Soviet threat and its naval missions, as well as allied operations, will vary with the type of war that is fought and with the type of warning that precedes it. In the case of a *long war* (several months or more), preceded by several weeks' warning, it is the submarine that will pose the longest-term and most-sustained threat to allied operations. The allied effort in a long war in Europe or Asia (or in Europe *and* Asia) could not be supported without a huge convoy operation on the part of the United States. One of the missions of the Soviet navy would be to prevent successful convoy operations. The convoys, and carriers providing "umbrella" protection for them,[21] would be particularly vulnerable to attacks by submarines, whose stealth and, in the case of SSNs, unlimited range would make detection and localization an exceedingly difficult task for allied forces.

A relatively long mobilization period before the outbreak of war could be particularly favorable to the Soviet submarine effort. A large number of submarines could be deployed to the open ocean before the war began (though an equally large number might be retained close to home to protect nuclear-powered ballistic missile submarines). The Soviet merchant fleet might be organized to serve as a source of resupply for the submarine fleet, thereby compounding allied efforts to attack submarines upon their return to home base.

As noted above, the Soviet threat is heightened by the coordinated capabilities of its forces. Aircraft would certainly menace convoy shipping. Under optimum conditions, Backfire flying high-altitude, subsonic profiles could threaten shipping along the mid-Atlantic transit routes and, if deployed in the Kamchatka peninsula, west Pacific routes to Japan. Badger aircraft, though possessing less range than the Backfire, could nevertheless reach the sea lanes in the eastern Mediterranean, as well as the westernmost approaches to Japan. In addition, the Soviet

---

[21] Anticarrier operations are a separate and important Soviet naval mission. These operations are likely to be independent of the Soviets' projected length of the war.

surface fleet could operate in conjunction with the air and subsurface forces in the eastern Mediterranean, where it could launch a preemptive attack that would severely impair the capabilities of U.S. forces deployed there.[22] Surface ships would also pose a problem in the north Norwegian Sea, where the combined air cover of long-range bombers and *Kiev*-based aircraft would allow for coordinated tactics against U.S. and allied forces.

Nevertheless, in general it is the submarine force that the allies would find hardest to neutralize, because submarines will first have to be found. And, in a long war, particularly if preceded by a considerable mobilization period, finding submarines will be a difficult and time-consuming task.

Scenario for a War Preceded by Little Warning. As noted above, convoy shipping is unlikely to play a primary role in the resupply of allied forces during the early weeks of a war. If the war lasted only a few weeks, airlift, rather than sea lift, might well be the key to allied fortunes. However, because the length of a war cannot be predicted, it is difficult to envisage that the Soviets would hold back those forces, notably submarines, that could be utilized for anticonvoy operations. Some convoys might reach Europe, even in a short war, and the submarines could be directed against them. In any event, they would be needed for missions against U.S. and allied carriers and other military units. Nevertheless, the role of submarines could well be secondary in a short war, and would be particularly so in a war preceded by little warning.

It is in the case of a "short warning" conflict that the relative roles of Soviet forces clearly changes, with implications in turn for allied force requirements. The Soviets can control the length of warning far better than they can the length of war. For example, they could withhold their submarines—potentially a sign of Soviet intentions—until after they have launched their attack.[23] Recent pronouncements by Lieutenant General Hollingsworth and Senators Nunn and Bartlett, among others, have pointed to the ability of the Soviets to launch their forces across central Germany with far less warning than has generally been assumed by allied planners. There could well be a maritime

---

[22] It should be noted that the likelihood of such an attack is, of course, highly scenario-dependent. But, given a Soviet attack, damage to the U.S. fleet would be significant.

[23] They might only deploy a few more—leaving allied commanders uncertain as to their intentions and possibly lax in taking responsive measures. For the importance of submarine deployments as a signal of Soviet intentions, see Robert E. Weinland, "The State and Future of the Soviet Navy," in MccGwire and McDonnell, *Soviet Naval Influence*, p. 411, and remarks of Congressman Les Aspin, *Congressional Record*, February 7, 1977, p. H913.

counterpart to this scenario—with Soviet submarines held in port while long-range bomber aircraft seek to neutralize allied bases in northern Norway and Iceland. Soviet airborne units might then seize a small number of key bases in northern Norway. If successful, the Soviets would create an imposing barrier to convoy operations across the Atlantic. Convoys would have to face not only submarine attacks, but also attacks by bombers undeterred by allied air defense forces, and possibly even deployed from some of the bases formerly held by allies. This situation could tempt the West European allies to sue for peace, since their hopes for long-term support would be exceedingly dim.

The short-warning scenario places a premium, for the Soviets, upon their long-range bomber forces; it is these forces that most threaten allied maritime interests, albeit indirectly, since the initial targets would be allied airfields rather than the convoys themselves.

As in the case of a long-warning/long-war scenario, surface forces would not be the primary threat to allied interests. But, if the Soviets successfully knocked out allied airfields in northern Europe, the Soviet ship-based tactical air force would confound allied tactics. It could now venture much further south into the Norwegian Sea with the assurance that the Soviets, not the allies, commanded the air space in that region.

Combatting the Soviet Threat of the Mid-1980s: Geography and the Opportunities for Land-Based Aviation

The Soviets have a significant capability to disrupt allied maritime operations during a war based in Europe and/or Asia. It is enhanced by the present uneven state of allied defenses. While U.S. antisubmarine warfare capabilities appear to be equal to the threat they face,[24] U.S. air defense capabilities, notably in the North Atlantic where the air threat is greatest, leave considerable room for improvement. U.S. early-warning and interceptor forces in Iceland are obsolescent; the proximity of Norwegian air bases to Soviet territory renders them vulnerable to surprise attacks and even seizure; no carrier is deployed to the North Atlantic region on a full-time basis.

Fortunately, the Greenland-Iceland-United Kingdom (G-I-UK) gap provides a natural geographic barrier for the early detection and interdiction of hostile Soviet aircraft, as well as submarines. As such it constitutes the foundation for a potentially significant land-based contribution to the defense of the Atlantic sea lanes against the Soviet

---

[24] See Dave Shilling, "A Perspective on Anti-Submarine Warfare," reprinted in U.S. Congress, Senate Budget Committee, *Hearings on the First Concurrent Resolution on the Budget, Fiscal Year 1978*, 95th Congress, 1st session, 1977, p. 245.

bomber and submarine threats, and therefore to allied defenses regardless of the length of a war, or the warning that precedes it.

Early Warning and Air Defense. Present U.S. early-warning and interceptor capabilities in Iceland consist of twelve obsolescent F-4C Phantom interceptors and three EC-121 early-warning aircraft, as well as one ground-based radar on the southern part of the island. The EC-121s have seen, on the average, over twenty-one years of service life. Their systems are hardly equal to the capabilities that the Soviet naval air force can muster. With considerable warning, the navy could deploy carriers to the G-I-UK gap to provide the needed interceptor and early-warning capabilities. But carrier forces will also be needed elsewhere: to reinforce carriers in the Mediterranean, to defend the Pacific lines, to provide umbrella-type escort for convoys crossing the Atlantic. With only about a week's warning, carriers may not arrive in time to blunt Soviet attacks on the Iceland air base.

The substitution of a more modern early-warning plane—AWACS or the E-2C—for the EC-121, together with a more capable interceptor, such as the F-14, for the F-4, would significantly improve U.S. defenses. AWACS is the more costly of the two early-warning systems. It also is the more capable, having greater range and on-station time. It can vector more planes in an aerial combat, and it possesses greater jamming-resistant capabilities. In terms of cost-effectiveness per orbit, the two planes are virtually equivalent.[25]

Both planes could be used in conjunction with the F-14 fighter. The F-14, with its Phoenix system, can fire long-range air-to-air missiles at six targets simultaneously. If given timely warning from AWACS or E-2C at stations of about 450 nm, the F-14's dash speed should permit it not only to intercept bombers seeking to destroy the air complex at Keflavik but also to intercept bombers crossing the G-I-UK gap at distances of up to 350 nm.[26] Two squadrons of F-14s should provide sufficient air defense capability to render a Soviet attempt at attacking the Iceland base highly unproductive. One of these squadrons could replace the F-4Cs at Keflavik. Another could be stationed in Britain, to be redeployed to Iceland within forty-eight hours. Perhaps a more effective deployment would be to Greenland. This would permit fighters to

---

[25] Dov S. Zakheim, *The U.S. Sea Control Mission: Forces, Capabilities, and Requirements*, U.S. Congress, Congressional Budget Office, Background Paper, June 1977, pp. 22-24, 63-69.

[26] Specific calculations of AWACS/F-14 responsiveness to Backfire crossings of the G-I-UK gap appear in ibid., pp. 63-66. Protection of Iceland is easily subsumed within requirements for early warning/interception capability against the Backfire crossings. Ibid., p. 24, n. 4.

respond to bombers crossing the gap west of Iceland without necessitating a transfer of more planes to Keflavik and possible congestion
at that airfield.[27]

The cost of employing land-based air in the G-I-UK gap is far less
than the equivalent cost of stationing a carrier in that area or, indeed,
of operating a carrier elsewhere with a view to its rapid redeployment
in the gap. Recent analysis has indicated that the differential in terms
of both procurement and operating costs could be as great as $2.5
billion, even if no new carrier is procured. If one were procured for the
air defense mission in the G-I-UK gap, that differential could rise to $6.5
billion (see Table 1).

It is, of course, extremely difficult to compare the capabilities or
effectiveness of the small land-based Iceland force with a large carrier
air wing. The carrier option provides more aircraft than are likely to be
available for operations in the G-I-UK gap if the aircraft are stationed in
Iceland and supplemented by a squadron in Britain or Greenland. The
key aircraft for the air defense mission, interceptors, and early-warning
planes appear in comparable numbers, however, in both the land-based
and the carrier options. Other aircraft carried aboard the carrier, while
useful in other contexts, may be somewhat superfluous to overall defense
requirements in the G-I-UK gap. For example, even a small carrier air
wing would probably include a complement of S-3 and SH-3 antisubmarine aircraft. These planes and helicopters would contribute mar-
ginally to the ASW effort, but hardly in a significant way, since, as will
be shown below, the Iceland-based P-3 ASW patrol force already provides
airborne antisubmarine coverage in the area. Similarly, P-3s armed with
Harpoon could also substitute for A-6 and A-7 carrier-based attack
aircraft for the antishipping mission. Indeed, the P-3, with its known
capability for low-level flight, could avoid appearing on the radar
screens of Soviet surface ships until it released its Harpoon at ranges
beyond those of Soviet shipborne air-to-surface missiles.[28] Even the
Kiev aircraft carrier would be vulnerable to the P-3-launched Harpoon.
The limited range and speed of Forger aircraft would not permit them to
intercept the P-3 even if they were in a full alert mode.[29] The P-3,
though a slow aircraft, would have an advantage of at least 50 nm
(Harpoon's range), which would permit it to get beyond Forger's dash-

---

[27] This discussion assumes that the United Kingdom would provide Nimrods or
other AEW planes to patrol the eastern portions of the G-I-UK gap.

[28] I am indebted to Commander John Shewmaker, USN (ret.) of the Congressional
Budget Office for his observations concerning P-3 tactics.

[29] The *Kiev* does not have ship-based AEW aircraft. It could not economically
maintain its Forgers on combat air patrol: the VTOL aircraft simply does not have
the endurance to sustain a patrol of any significant duration.

Table 1

Costs of Carrier Options and Land-Based Aviation Options

(in millions of fiscal year 1978 dollars)

Option	Procurement/Base Alteration Costs	15-Year Operating Cost	15-Year Total Cost
AWACS/2 F-14 squadrons	1,625	1,292	2,917
E-2C/2 F-14 squadrons	1,877	839	2,717
No new carrier procured	——	4,860	5,188
Procure one carrier/ associated air wing/ 5 associated escorts	5,190	4,086	9,276

Source: Congressional Budget Office Defense Resources Model, in Zakheim, *The U.S. Sea Control Mission*, p. 32.

speed radius before being overtaken.[30] Thus, cost comparisons unequivocally favor the choice of land-based aviation for the G-I-UK air defense, but considerations of effectiveness, though difficult to posit with precision, do not appear to favor the carrier to the point of offsetting its greater cost.

Antisubmarine Warfare: The Land-Based Contribution. Present and programmed aircraft capabilities limit the employment of land-based aviation for air defense to the G-I-UK area. The expanses of the Pacific and Indian oceans simply are too great for present interceptor capabilities to be meaningful. Antisubmarine warfare is, however, a totally different matter. The P-3 and other aircraft have a major role to play in both the Atlantic and the Pacific/Indian Ocean theaters. P-3s have operated in the North Atlantic for some time. Their range, speed, and payload are such that they form a useful complement to submerged sonar systems as well as attack submarines that conduct ASW missions. The P-3's range also permits it to play a significant role in Pacific and Indian Ocean operations. Indeed, the development of Diego Garcia is particularly important to P-3 operations in the Indian Ocean. P-3s, with an

---

[30] Given a P-3 speed of 405 knots, and a Forger maximum speed (at altitude) of Mach 1.05, Forger would only overtake P-3 at 200 nm, which is the limit of its absolute combat radius. Given (1) limitations upon Forger's range and (2) the time required for the plane to take off, the chances of Forger's overtaking P-3 are nil. (Source for flight characteristics: Gilson and Sweetman, "Military Aircraft," pp. 575, 577.)

operational radius of 1,400 miles for a three-hour patrol, can now provide the navy with data extending to the Indian Ocean entrances to the Arabian Sea without reliance upon other foreign bases.

The P-3 is a multipurpose plane, and two of its alternative roles have yet to be fully exploited. The first, antiship operations, was noted above, in the context of the G-I-UK area. The P-3, with Harpoon, poses a threat to every Soviet surface system, not excluding the carrier *Kiev* and its sister ships. The second role, that of mine-laying operations, is extremely important to U.S. ASW activities, particularly with the imminent introduction into the U.S. force of the encapsulated torpedo (CAPTOR). A P-3 can carry six CAPTOR mines. Were the requirement for a CAPTOR minefield in the G-I-UK gap approximately five hundred mines (that being one estimate of CAPTOR needs in that area),[31] a squadron of nine P-3s flying two sorties a day coud lay the entire field within five days.

Of course, the actual number of mines required for the field is a function of many factors, not the least of which is the precise location of the field. Similarly, the tempo of P-3 operations and the availability of P-3s might vary, so that more or fewer planes could be employed to lay the field. In light of these considerations, as well as problems of estimating comparative effectiveness between a field of fixed mines with "one shot" only and a group of highly mobile submarines that can perform many missions, it is extremely risky to posit that one or the other system is the more cost-effective. Nevertheless, employing P-3s with an effective deep-water mine would significantly enhance U.S. antisubmarine capability while perhaps also freeing SSNs for other missions.

P-3s are not the only system that could be employed in mine warfare. B-52s are another likely candidate: the B-52D models are aging but still capable systems. One B-52 carries 18 mines; returning to the 500-mine example, the entire field could be laid in less than three days by only six aircraft. Put in real-world terms, that means that with minimum warning, it might still be possible to mine the G-I-UK gap immediately upon the onset of hostilities.[32]

---

[31] See Richard L. Garwin, "The Interaction of Anti-Submarine Warfare with the Submarine-Based Deterrent," in Kosta Tsipis, Anne H. Cahn, and Bernard T. Feld, eds., *The Future of the Sea-Based Deterrent* (Cambridge, Mass.: MIT Press, 1973), p. 104.

[32] The conditional nature of this statement should not be ignored. Laying the field would depend upon the factors noted above, namely (1) the actual number of mines required and (2) the number of bombers employed and the number of sorties they flew, as well as the time required to clear the target area of all friendly ships.

The G-I-UK gap is but one fruitful area for mine-laying operations. The Pacific offers possibilities as well. For example, mines laid across the entrances to key Soviet Pacific ports certainly would complicate Soviet naval operations. Both the P-3 and the B-52 have the range for operations of this sort. However, whereas fighters based in Japan could escort mine-laying operations in the Sea of Japan, U.S. fighters presently could not accompany B-52s or P-3s if they sought to mine the entrance to Petropavlovsk.[33]

Recapitulation. It appears that geography has afforded the United States with the opportunity to improve upon its sea-control capability well within the next decade, perhaps without having to resort to the construction of expensive ships. Land-based AWACS (or E-2C) early-warning aircraft, and interceptors such as F-14, would radically improve present obsolescent air defenses in the G-I-UK area. P-3s armed with Harpoon could perform the antiship mission there. So, for that matter, could B-52Ds, or F-111s,[34] if they were armed with the new antiship missile. P-3s already make a major contribution to the ASW effort. The advent of CAPTOR affords more scope for their use, or for the utilization of B-52s in the mine-laying role.

The limitations upon land-based aircraft, and the consequent continued need for carriers, are primarily those of endurance. Carriers can go where land-based aircraft cannot. As the interests of the United States continue to encompass the world's oceans during the next ten years, carriers will continue to serve as key rapid-reaction forces by providing air bases in areas where no others are available. Nevertheless, the unique capabilities of carriers should not obscure land-based aircraft's potential contribution to the sea-control effort. That has been the case in the past; it need not be so now, nor indeed, in the future, as the following section will attempt to show.

The 1990s and Beyond: Nature of the Threat and the Prospects for Land-Based Aviation

Prediction is an inherently difficult task: at best it is only educated guesswork. Nevertheless, the maritime arena happens to be one that, relative to other military spheres, perhaps allows for some confident speculation. Ships take five to ten years to build. Unless they are sunk in war, or accidentally damaged, major warships and support ships can

---

[33] B-52s would likely be more effective than P-3s in laying mines near Soviet Pacific ports.

[34] See *Aviation Week*, August 15, 1977.

operate for twenty, thirty, or in the case of very large support ships and aircraft carriers, as much as thirty-five or more years. Thus, U.S. ships authorized in programs of fiscal years 1973–1977 will enter the fleet only in the late 1970s and early 1980s, and will remain in that fleet into the twenty-first century. Indeed, one can state with assurance that well over a fifth of the present U.S. authorized or operating fleet (approximately 130 ships), including at least 5 aircraft carriers, will be operating as late as the year 2000. A broadly similar observation may be made about the Soviet fleet: the larger warships that have just entered service or will soon do so are likely still to be conducting their operations at the close of the century.

Several other factors also may not change. Geography is, of course, one such factor. For the purposes of this paper, the membership of both major alliances and the bases they make available for a major war may be taken as a second constant. To be sure, Eurocommunism threatens both Italy and France, and Iceland has flirted with neutralism as recently as four years ago. The neutrality of any of these states would further constrict our operations and would force us to rely even more upon our own devices and independent sea-based capabilities. Nevertheless, no country has left the Atlantic alliance for over thirty years. All members of the alliance continue to benefit from economic systems that are incompatible with those that Communists foster. Lastly, if many of our allies on the Continent deserted us, the question would not merely be one of possessing an independent capability to protect Europe. Rather it would be one of protecting ourselves in the face of a hostile Europe. That effort would force radical shifts upon our strategy and posture that would go well beyond the question of the availability of one or another base. Such shifts and their force implications are beyond the scope of this paper and will not be addressed.

Uncertainties in Prediction: The Soviet Threat. Uncertainties arise primarily in terms of the systems capabilities of missiles, aircraft (which have shorter service lives than ships), and electronics systems. We therefore must hedge against the possibility that the Soviets could achieve advances in all of these areas. In specific terms, that means that the Soviets might:

- develop interceptor and attack aircraft with combat radii in excess of 1,000 nm and equip them with longer-range air-to-air missiles

- improve upon the range, speed, and weapons load of their v/stol carrier-borne aircraft

- improve the guidance and anti-ecm capabilities of their missiles

243

- improve the noise abatement, sensors, and weapons of their submarines

- improve their ASW capabilities, and their reconnaissance capabilities

- improve their command and control capabilities.

All of these developments are not beyond Soviet capabilities; indeed, they would achieve most of them by matching many of the capabilities of our present systems. To be sure, it is unlikely that the Soviets would produce improved systems in large numbers before the year 2000. The Soviets have tended in most cases to pursue incremental improvements and not to retire old systems in light of new developments. Thus newer systems, such as longer-range aircraft, might be making their first appearance during the 1990s.

The implications of these developments nevertheless are significant for U.S. planners. Longer-range tactical aircraft, with improved air-to-air missiles and ECCM techniques and better command and control would allow for the escort of long-range bombers on missions such as the destruction of G-I-UK bases or of major U.S. fleet or convoy units. Surface ships would have a much larger air umbrella under which to operate, and would benefit as well from the improved capabilities of V/STOL aircraft on board the ships themselves; as well as from improved reconnaissance capabilities. Lastly, quieter submarines would enhance that element of the Soviet naval threat which our naval commanders consider the most awesome.

Planning Ahead against the Soviet Threat. Prospects for improving U.S. maritime capabilities are as bright, if not brighter, than those of the Soviet Union. As one observer has recently noted,

> The United States starts with the world's richest reservoir of scientific resources. Constant feedback between civil and military markets encourages entrepreneurism and technological chain reactions not remotely equalled by our Russian rival. As a result, options still closed to the Soviets are completely open to us.[35]

The same study lists the U.S. as having a clear superiority in aircraft, air-to-air missiles, electronic counter- and counter-countermeasures (ECM and ECCM), look-down shoot-down systems, and survivable submarines.[36] Since the programs undergoing research and development

---

[35] John M. Collins, "American and Soviet Armed Services, Strengths Compared 1970-76," reprinted in *Congressional Record*, August 5, 1977, p. S14068.
[36] Ibid.

244

today are those that will likely be authorized in the next ten years, and will become initially operable in the next fifteen to twenty years, it appears that the United States could, with the requisite effort, maintain its present maritime superiority over the Soviet Union.

One great inhibiting factor for R&D programs, indeed for all programs, is cost. It is the constraints of recent budgets that have limited the growth of the navy, and these constraints may be with us for many years to come. However, as noted above, land-based options might ease the budgetary strain on U.S. maritime capabilities in the immediate future by providing significant sea-control capabilities in selected areas in a less costly manner than carrier task forces. In the same way, land-based aircraft may ease the heavy financial burden that will be imposed upon navy budgets of the 1980s and 1990s if even two-thirds of the present carrier force level is to be maintained well into the twenty-first century.

The essential thrust of post-1990 land-based options is likely to be the same as those of today: air defense capabilities, including early warning; antisubmarine patrol; antiship missions; and mine-laying capabilities. These missions could be combined into one air frame.

Recent discussions regarding a possible follow-on to the P-3 maritime patrol aircraft have focused on the possibilities afforded by the concept for a moderately large, subsonic (about 450 knots) aircraft termed LMNA (land-based, multipurpose naval aircraft). The LMNA could utilize its size, speed, and endurance in carrying out antiship strikes, or it could serve as an interceptor against oncoming bombers or as an ASW patrol aircraft. In the antiship case it might remain at high altitude, possibly utilizing remotely piloted vehicles (RPVs) for better surveillance and employing Harpoon or Tomahawk for long-range attacks. As an interceptor, the LMNA would be most useful in the G-I-UK gap, where it would remain on patrols against bombers that it would detect with long-range radars and attack with long-range missile systems such as an improved Phoenix. Lastly, its additional speed and endurance would ensure that the plane in its ASW role could cover far larger tracts of ocean per hour, for more hours, and at greater distances than could the P-3. Furthermore, the LMNA's speed would enhance its defense. As the originator of the concept has noted, "running away can be a good defense."[37] The LMNA could also be equipped with radars and defensive armament against oncoming missiles that might be fired from enemy aircraft or, indeed, from a submarine.

---

[37] William D. O'Neil III, "Land-Based Multi-Purpose Naval Aircraft (LMNA) Concept," (processed: Office of the Secretary of Defense, September 15, 1976), p. 5. All LMNA characteristics outlined in the text are drawn from this study.

Apart from range and time on station, it is, however, uncertain to what extent LMNA would add to present capabilities in all three sea-control areas. With respect to ASW, it might be difficult to exploit fully LMNA's potential for greater on-station time than that of the P-3, since the duration of its patrol might be limited by the endurance of the crew. Furthermore, were Soviet fighters or bombers capable of carrying air-to-air missiles at ranges that would permit them to attack patrol aircraft, it remains uncertain whether even LMNA could survive such engagements.[38]

While LMNA could perform a useful antishipping role, Harpoon or the longer-range Tomahawk can also be carried by the P-3 and other aircraft. Since, as noted above, Harpoon permits a plane to shoot at enemy warships beyond the range of their shipboard missiles, it is difficult to assess the value of LMNA's augmented defenses to its antishipping role.

LMNA's greater range and endurance clearly would permit it to remain on combat air patrol for longer periods of time and/or greater distances than those fighters such as the F-14 and F-15 presently can attain. It also would carry the early-warning sensors that would be aboard an AWACS or E-2C. Therefore, fewer planes would be required to support these stations if LMNA performed the air defense task in place of tactical fighters and EW aircraft. LMNA could not match their speed and maneuverability, however, and these characteristics are crucial for an interceptor's survivability once it has fired its long-range missiles. The loss of even one LMNA would be a serious blow to the air defense network in the North Atlantic, since the cost of LMNA (estimated at $80 million in fiscal year 1978 dollars) renders it unlikely to be procured in quantities as large as those of present fighter programs.

The notion of an aircraft capable of performing a variety of maritime missions is an attractive one. Given the uncertainties regarding the development costs of LMNA and the degree to which it really adds to the effectiveness of present forces, it would appear, however, that this concept ultimately may not be as productive as the incremental improvement of different types of aircraft for each of our different maritime needs.

Turning first to maritime air defense, it should be recognized that Soviet improvements in both aircraft range and air-to-air missilery are likely to be more than matched by U.S. improvements in these areas. Indeed, the YF-12A, currently a NASA test aircraft, but once part of an interceptor program, has a reported cruising speed of Mach 3 and has achieved average speeds in excess of Mach 2.5 while carrying a 2,000 kg payload over a 625-mile closed circuit. In addition, the YF-12A pro-

---

[38] A Backfire armed with air-to-air missiles is likely to possess the range and endurance to chase and overtake the LMNA.

gram also included development of the AIM-47 air-to-air missile, with a reported speed of Mach 6 and a range of 100 nm.[39] A modified YF-12 and missile exhibiting similar characteristics would be a potent interceptor system against Backfire, which is likely to be the mainstay of the Soviet antiship bomber force in the 1990s. It would also counter such long-range interceptors as might have entered into operation. If equipped with the most modern ECM and ECCM capabilities, as well as an advanced long-range missile guidance package, the YF-12 should be superior to the new fighter models appearing in the Soviet air force. The plane should be capable of coordination with an updated AWACS, which should still be in operation during the 1990s.

The costs of an improved long-range interceptor are sure to be high, but the costs of major capital ships with complex weapons suites are certain to rise in real terms as well. The land-based air defense option should remain less expensive than the carrier task force concept, and competitive with it in terms of effectiveness in geographic sectors, such as the G-I-UK gap.

Airborne antishipping operations, unlike air defense, may require completely new tactics to accompany the systems of the 1990s. A P-3 launching a missile with somewhat greater range than Harpoon may still be vulnerable to V/STOL planes developed in the 1990s, or to conventional aircraft if the Soviets construct a carrier with catapults. P-3s, or other aircraft, could, however, launch Tomahawk or RPVs, which in turn would fire antiship missiles. Updated F-111s could also perform the antiship mission. Their speed should enable them to fire long-range missiles and avoid being overtaken by any enemy aircraft. Nevertheless, by the year 2000 the best antiship capability may reside in the submarine. If the Soviets seriously threaten our carriers with the Charlie-class sub and its thirty-mile missile, how much more threatening would our SSNs, armed with a long-range Tomahawk (or even Harpoon), be to their surface warships?

P-3s still could make a valuable contribution to ASW. The cost of developing a new airframe for ASW is likely to be extremely high. Adding some endurance to the P-3's present capacity would be far less costly, yet, when accompanied by improvement of the ASW sensors that it carries, would be a highly productive exercise. Improved mines should also enhance the value of a maritime patrol aircraft to the navy without forcing a significant change in its present P-3 airframe. As noted above, an improved mine capability might substitute for, or complement, submarine barrier requirements. More SSNs might then be devoted to anti-

---

[39] *Jane's All the World's Aircraft,* 1974-1975, 1976-1977; *Jane's Weapons Systems,* 1974-1975, 1977.

ship and other missions, as required, without forcing a significant, and costly, expansion of the SSN force.

Where do all these developments leave the aircraft carrier? The answer, as was indicated at the outset of this paper, is that carriers will remain very much a key element of the navy for the next twenty-five years. While the navy may hope to retain the overseas bases it now operates, it is unlikely to add to them. Many of the areas of the world that are of great or increasing concern to the United States—the Indian Ocean, the Eastern Mediterranean, the South Atlantic—provide little opportunity for land-based aviation. The stretches of ocean are too vast, the land bases are unavailable. Carriers will remain the most effective way of rapidly bringing U.S. air power to bear in these areas. Even if we move to a system of flexible deployments, there will be a need for a carrier force larger than that which existing assets will support after the year 2000. New carriers may have to be built. However, the extent to which the navy comes to rely upon land-based air power for sea control will determine whether the force level will have to be maintained at twelve high-cost, large deck carriers, necessitating the construction of five or more carriers in the next fifteen to twenty years; [40] whether a larger number of small deck carriers, still at great cost, will be constructed; or lastly, whether somewhat lower levels of either type will suffice, allowing for significant savings. Land-based aviation for sea control is an option available to the navy today; it will remain available and become even more important during the next quarter century.

---

[40] The Department of Defense has announced a service life extension program (SLEP) for the *Forrestal* and later carriers. A two-year overhaul at about the carrier's thirtieth year of operation is expected to extend its service life another fifteen years. DOD projects that Forrestal-class carriers would enter overhaul at two-year intervals. If the program is realized, the carrier force would stand at eleven in the year 2000. However, a similar plan for two Midway-class carriers was cancelled after the first carrier's overhaul: the overhaul had taken fifty-two months, not the planned twenty-four, and had cost well over twice the original $88 million estimate. Even if the present SLEP program succeeds for as many as five ships, the carrier force would stand at seven as early as 1995.

COMMENTARIES

Robert Kirksey

It was thoughtful of Norman Polmar to bring the definitions of the mission and the functions of the navy. We sometimes have a tendency to get hung up on definitions. One definition may well determine force level sizes for the next ten or twenty years. The mission of the navy is sustained combat operations at sea. To me, that is simple to understand, and that is why we have a navy.

We have added words to that, and we have underscored some of them, such as projection and sea control. Then the definition becomes a force-sizing tool that is frequently used to the disadvantage of the navy. It is a fact that the force cannot be built for collateral functions, and projection of power is a collateral function of the U. S. Navy at sea, with tactical aviation. It was pointed out that the carrier is very well suited for projection. Before going any further, we should clarify definitions. It has been the perception of the chief of naval operations and of the operators at sea that definitions should be understood in their proper time sequence. Antisubmarine warfare operations, for example, are not merely a matter of floating across the seas and listening for submarines. In a blue-water confrontation with another navy, we would be projecting power in the same fashion as the missions flown against land-based targets in World War II, Korea, and Vietnam.

We would be facing the same defenses, a very formidable surface-to-air missile threat like the ones that circled Hanoi and Haiphong, only better. The requirements for the navy should always expand to counter new threats.

I was recently asked if I thought the F-14 was a cost-effective aircraft for the navy. To answer that question, we would have to determine what the threat is and then either pay the price to counter that threat or stop playing the game. We can draw an analogy to a fellow who has a 35-caliber weapon at home. If he had to pay $135 for one round of ammunition to stop a burglar, he might consider it cost effective. If he did not want to pay that price, he might get knocked on the head.

Most of the papers under discussion talk about an increasing threat. Refreshing alternatives are offered, and we certainly should be paying attention to them. Some of them use words like "bottom line" and "marginal capability" and the "crunch." There are practical things we have to face up to in life, but we should do so with our eyes completely open. People who make recommendations to the secretary of defense and to the civilian secretaries of our uniformed services should spell out exactly what capability we are up against, and how much of a margin in capabilities we have lost to defend the sea lines of communications.

And from that, I would like to address a few items in Norman Polmar's paper—first, the alternatives to taking an investment as heavy as the $2-billion carrier to sea. One alternative may be through the use of more flexible aircraft that could operate from smaller and more economical platforms.

V/STOL has become the rage of the Pentagon. Two and a half years ago, I came here from eighteen months' duty aboard the U.S.S. *Kittyhawk*. Not one person had ever mentioned "V/STOL" to me, or that it might alter the flight deck of that aircraft carrier, or change the way it operated. But there is a certain fever, if you will, that makes some of us see V/STOL as the panacea to many of our problems.

A certain synergistic effect may be obtained when the V/STOL can be utilized at sea. Norman Polmar touched on the possible sit-down on barrier or shoulder pickets, which would give us a zero-fuel-flow type of a deck-launch intercept ready to go at any moment. If it does, in fact, complement the carrier task force and its operation, we would probably achieve more than a marginal benefit, and probably more than a one-unit effect, from that V/STOL aircraft. We should encourage this development. The research and development on V/STOL, however, carries a very big price tag. We cannot afford that price tag. We cannot at the same time afford an R&D effort on a VPX, or a follow-on P-3, or a super-duper P-3, or an LMNA, because, if $2 billion for one aircraft carrier seems a big price, this one would be mind boggling.

I am looking at a projected VPX model right now, one that would probably do some of the things Mr. Zakheim mentioned, and its cost is estimated at about one-half times the price of an LMNA. It is a $44 million to $50 million aircraft.

Such prices per unit of equipment are very high. The technology and the R & D effort required for V/STOL are penalties we have to pay in dollars. We have to be sure that those dollars we are subtracting from other programs will pay off in benefits against the threats we will face in the twenty-first century.

At the same time, if this technology can lift a mass with a short takeoff roll or none at all, why isn't the same technology applicable to, let's say, the F-14 aircraft? And if it is applicable, do we want the F-14 aircraft to go faster, or do we want to shrink it and have it operate off the same ship, but maybe with a smaller target profile, maybe with lighter-weight advance radars, and with a capability equal or superior to the V/STOL aircraft?

CTOL capability at sea will scarcely stop because of the expense of the technology to develop an engine that will lift a heavier mass straight up into the air.

If this is true, ships the size of the *Nimitz* would provide an amazing flexibility for a CTOL-V/STOL combination. We examined that possibility on the *FDR* in a very, very low-key manner, using an AV8 Bravo or an AV8 Alpha, and we found there was a lot of flexibility. An interceptor could be launched while we were running downwind, or crosswind, or what have you. The aircraft just went up and away. It did not go very far, and it soon had to come back, but that could be worked into normal launch and recovery operations aboard the carrier when it was required to turn into the wind. Turning into the wind, of course, just gives a benefit to V/STOL aircraft.

With a four-and-a-half-acre flight deck, the *Nimitz* could provide all kinds of flexibility for the navy in the twenty-first century, using a mix of CTOL and V/STOL aircraft. The same technology should be used to improve something like the F-14, so that we don't find ourselves waiting for a fifteen-year effort to deliver a product. Carriers are said to be bad because they require seven or eight years from authorization to delivery of the ship. But the air force calls for fifteen years for the development of aircraft, including complete R&D.

I favor the large carrier, rather than smaller ones. In my personal and professional opinion, the CVN-71 should be afloat.

The small carrier is suggested as an alternative to these big expensive items. But, as was pointed out, the newly designed smaller carriers, conventionally powered or nuclear powered, entail a penalty that far exceeds the acquisition price of a follow-on *Nimitz*- or *Vincent*-class ship. Other arguments for the large carrier include the lower cost per ton, the shaft-horsepower-per-ton advantage, and the length profile of the ship, as well as everything else that has been developed empirically for a ship of the U.S. Navy over thirty-plus years to accommodate the growing sophistication of the air wing.

251

The smaller carrier involves some trade-offs, even with V/STOL aircraft operations. Many of our studies show that the 22,500-ton VSS that Norman Polmar mentioned has no side protection. The answer to that is, the ship should be operated in low- and medium-threat areas, or with a very large umbilical cord to a large-deck aircraft carrier that can protect it.

I submit, once again, there is no low-threat area. In ASW operations, unless there is some breakthrough that I cannot even conceive of at this time, a so-called low-threat area could be teeming with the submarines of another nation in forty-eight hours.

So, I don't feel that this is going to exist. And one other item, on a practical point of view, is the smaller carrier alternative.

If CVVs are authorized and constructed, it could take two of them to match the capability of the *Nimitz*. That ship would cost about a billion dollars more than the *Nimitz,* but would it deploy on a two-to-one ratio? The answer to that, in my opinion, is no. Because if I were the type commander in the CINC and I had requirements to SACLANT and SACEUR and I had a 60,000-ton carrier, and they said, "You've got to give me a carrier," I'd send them one 60,000-ton carrier. The day the war starts—and I realize this is a pretty soggy cliché—we will fight it with what we have in place at that time. I have little confidence in a policy of decreasing capabilities in the face of an increasing threat.

In regard to the ARAPAHO concept of taking V/STOL or helicopters to sea, we will find out that we have a problem in trying to get the best of both worlds—that is, taking equipment to sea but not paying the penalty of supporting it. The support of ships at sea—including beans and butter and bullets and everything—takes the same volume that is needed in the large aircraft carriers.

In regard to Mr. Zakheim's paper, when we look at the penalty of providing escort for carriers—whether it consists of an air wing or of other ships—we have to put it in the perspective of a task force built for a synergistic effect. Such a force is not built merely to protect ships at sea, because that would not be cost-effective. Every one of the ships has an offensive strike capability, and every one of the ships exercises its strike capabilities.

I agree that the LMNA "Big Mother" is not the best thing possible. There are people who would say that it is, that it can do anything and can counter every type of scenario. One problem with Mr. Zakheim's paper is that we need carriers to operate as complements to tactical air at sea, unless we operate in a relatively permissive society and forget about stationing time, logistics, and everything else. In my time in the navy, I have seen the southern littoral of the Mediterranean become relatively closed to the United States. My experience in the western Pacific areas has demonstrated that we are not particularly welcome there. Land-based air cannot work as a complement when the land bases have shrunk and the capabilities of affording that land-based air are already stretched.

William S. Lind

On balance, Polmar argues convincingly for the viability of sea-based tactical aviation for the present and the near future, despite some over-statement of his case. In the latter category I must place his statements that "Even against the Soviet Union the modern attack carrier . . . seems to present a viable threat," and that ". . . for the foreseeable future (the twelve-carrier force's) capability for sea control and pro-jection missions will remain high."

One might argue that the attack carrier presents a viable threat to Soviet forces under some conditions in certain locales. But to sug-gest that a carrier task force could operate effectively against the Soviet homeland would be to underrate both Soviet air and naval defenses. The Okean exercises, which Polmar cites, show the very considerable homeland defense capability of the Soviet navy. At least against the submarine component of Soviet naval forces, a carrier task group's defenses appear wholly inadequate to approach within striking range of the Soviet Union itself.

Similarly, to characterize the capabilities of our twelve-carrier force as generally "high" seems an overstatement. The projection capability probably does remain high—although declining—against many Third World states. But the sea control capability of our twelve carriers against the Soviet submarine force—and, increasingly, against the sub-marines of smaller powers—appears inadequate. While some might suggest that the navy has destroyers and frigates for ASW, the ASW effectiveness of surface ships was inferior to that of aircraft even in World War II and the submarine has improved its capabilities relative to the surface ship since that time. Sea-based air will be a most im-portant component of any effective ASW force, and the limited number of S-3s on our twelve existing carriers, along with the LAMPS on the escorts, would not seem adequate to give a "high" sea control capability.

Polmar recognizes the need for sea-based aircraft in most missions, and he draws a logical conclusion from it: that we should trade planned investment in surface ships—he mentions cruisers—for larger numbers of air-capable ships, such as VSS and Air Capable DD-963s. In this he is fully correct. Most of the weapons systems on our cruisers, destroyers, and frigates—five-inch guns, Tarter, ASROC, torpedoes—are of little effectiveness against present and future Soviet systems. The greater part of our escorts' capabilities is in on-board aircraft—LAMPS—and passive detection systems—TACTAS. Clearly, greater total effectiveness is possible by trading typical surface ship weapons systems for more LAMPS or other aircraft—which is to say, building aircraft platforms instead of cruisers, destroyers, or frigates.

The aircraft for these platforms must be V/STOL; CTOL aircraft require overly large and expensive platforms. Polmar notes the navy's lack of enthusiasm for V/STOL. The navy attitude is an unfortunate product of a fundamental misunderstanding of aircraft performance requirements. In the projection mission, high performance aircraft are often required because the opponent's land-based air force includes high performance aircraft. But the Soviet navy has virtually no high performance tactical naval aircraft. A medium performance V/STOL, such as the AV-8B Advanced Harrier, has adequate performance for the sea control role: it can strike Soviet surface ships and intercept incoming "Backfires" well beyond the range of these systems' antiship missiles. As the Guam Interim Sea Control Ship tests demonstrated, the Harrier is useful in ASW. Because of the extraordinary maneuverability provided by the vectored thrust system, the Harrier is a highly capable air defense fighter, even against high performance aircraft. Yet, because the navy thinks of aircraft performance only in terms of "higher-farther-faster," the Harrier has been rejected—and with it, V/STOL in the early 1980s—by the navy.

The most important point in Polmar's paper originates not with him, but with James Woolsey, the under secretary of the navy. If we are to reverse the trend in the naval "correlation of forces," a trend that favors the Soviet Union, we must indeed "shatter the conventional wisdom," and ask, "How can I change the game?" Ultimately, as the question is asked, part of the answer is likely to be "By replacing manned systems, such as sea-based aircraft, with unmanned systems." A fundamental technological trend of our time is for unmanned systems to increase in capability relative to manned systems. For a variety of reasons—the special capabilities of the submarine being a major one—the replacement of manned aircraft by missiles and RPVs probably will not come as quickly at sea as on land. When it does occur, the ships we now build as aircraft platforms will adapt: sea-based aircraft are essentially modules sitting on the flat deck of a module carrier, and the deck cares little what variety of module it supports.

We must not let the current correctness of Polmar's advocacy of sea-based air hinder our acceptance of the replacement of manned with unmanned systems, any more than we should permit the vested interests of the "surface union" within the navy to hinder the substitution of aircraft platforms for traditional cruisers, destroyers, and frigates.

Zakheim's paper is something of a paradox. It is a thoughtful, well-balanced, and objective examination of the potentials and weaknesses of land-based naval aviation, coupled with an unsupported and sweeping generalization at the conclusion—that lower levels of sea-based aviation will suffice, "allowing for significant savings," if greater use is made of land-based aircraft for sea control.

The paper sensibly presents land-based aircraft as a supplement to, rather than a replacement for, sea-based aircraft: It does not offer land-based aircraft as a panacea, as some promoters of the LMNA have done, to the discrediting of their own proposal. Zakheim's specific recommendations—increased use of Iceland for controlling the G-I-UK gap, and utilizing P-3s or other land-based aircraft for minelaying and antiship warfare—should be evaluated in a positive spirit, and most should probably be adopted. Certain objections can be raised to elements of these recommendations: His discussion of using Harpoon-equipped P-3s against the *Kiev*, for example, neglects the fact that the *Kiev* will probably have Bear or other Soviet land-based aircraft providing reconnaissance and early warning support. In general, however, his recommendations appear sound.

The paper would have been strengthened by a more comprehensive discussion of the strengths and weaknesses of land-based aircraft in antisubmarine warfare. His dubious assumption that U.S. antisubmarine warfare capabilities appear to be equal to the threat they face may have led to the relative neglect of this key aspect of the U.S. maritime problem.

It is in ASW that U.S. land-based naval aircraft currently play their greatest role. Arguments can be advanced that they are highly cost-effective in this function, especially in comparison with traditional-design destroyers and frigates. At the same time, certain questions regarding possible degradation of their effectiveness should be addressed. How vulnerable is SOSUS to destruction or disruption, especially if nuclear explosives are used for this purpose (a step that might or might not cross the nuclear threshhold)? How reliable are communications between P-3s and sensors or sensor platforms other than SOSUS? What would be the impact of P-3 cost-effectiveness of the development of a submarine-to-aircraft missile? Will we see the deployment of the "Backfire" as a long-range interceptor, and if this occurs, how will it affect P-3 survivability in ASW (and minelaying and antisurface) missions?

The paper would have been strengthened by a discussion of the potential of lighter-than-air (LTA) as applied to land-based naval aircraft requirements. If the LMNA is to prove viable, it will probably have to be an airship rather than an airplane. Only an airship can have the endurance to raise the ratio of time-on-station to transit time to a truly useful level. Only an airship can provide sufficient crew comfort to permit extended operations. And, thanks to its "free" static lift, only an airship can keep large military payloads aloft for long periods economically: Some recent estimates place the cost of one ton of lift by LTA at a twentieth of the cost of the same ton lifted by a heavier-than-air craft.

Unfortunately, it is difficult to have LTA considered objectively by most defense analysts. While schoolchildren, too many of them were treated to movies of the *Hindenburg* crashing in flames. Few of those movies pointed out that the thirteen passenger fatalities in the *Hindenburg* crash were the only passenger fatalities in the history of the Zeppelin company, which included both the post-World War I operations of the *Graf Zeppelin* and the *Bodensee,* and the pre-war operations of DELAG.

In fact, both the rigid Zeppelin airships and the U.S. Navy nonrigid blimps had a remarkably successful history, particularly in the sea surveillance and ASW tasks for which the LMNA is being considered. During World War II, not one of the 89,000 ships escorted by U.S. Navy blimps was lost to an enemy submarine. Tests in the 1950s with the latest blimps demonstrated the long endurance of these ships and their good capability in bad weather. With full utilization of modern technology for propulsion, framework, and envelope, the airship could potentially solve many of the conceptual problems facing current LMNA proposals.

Land-based naval aircraft could provide a useful supplement to sea-based aircraft in a number of mission areas. Even if all the potentials of land-based air are realized, however, we will probably be unable to defend effectively against the Soviet navy with lower levels of sea-based aircraft. On the contrary, a larger requirement for sea-based aircraft is suggested by the increasing importance of geographically remote areas, by the continuing rise in the naval capabilities of the U.S.S.R. and potentially hostile Third World nations, and, perhaps most importantly, by the mounting evidence that sea-based aircraft on small aircraft platforms are far more effective in many roles than are cruisers, destroyers, and frigates. Strategic and technological realities seem to dictate not the trading off of sea-based for land-based aircraft, but increased investment in *both* at the expense of planned investment in traditional surface ships, in U.S. Air Force tactical aircraft, and in obsolete types of ground forces, such as foot infantry. This is the logical conclusion to Mr. Zakheim's paper, and the paper would have been improved by making it.

George Spangenberg

In view of the great impact of the V/STOL aircraft program on the future of the navy, a detailed review of the program is warranted. From the evidence publicly available, it appears that the decision makers have been victimized by overzealous salesmanship perhaps coupled with some breakdown in communications between the navy's technical community and the program planners.

As now described, the navy is to transform itself toward an all V/STOL fleet of aircraft deployed on both aviation and nonaviation ships. A similar goal, believed achievable by some in ten years, was suggested in the Bureau of Aeronautics in the early 1950s after the success of early developmental tests on "tail sitter" models. The twin problems of capability and cost, which caused abandonment of the plan then, remain, with little hope in the future for a simultaneous solution when compared with more conventional approaches.

First, let us consider the case involving the large carrier and its ultimate replacement. We have the option of continuing to buy carriers with complements of conventional carrier aircraft, which we will call CATOAL, for catapult assisted take-off and arrested landing, or we can buy ships of the same size operating V/STOL aircraft of the same capability but without benefit of catapult and arresting gear. For this case, it can be shown that:

(1) Procurement and operating costs for ships of either type are small compared with the costs of the air group, on the order of one-third.

(2) The differential in ship costs due to inclusion of catapult and arresting equipment is small, probably on the order of 10 percent.

(3) The differential in air group costs between a new V/STOL group and a new CATOAL group is large, probably at least 50 percent with individual design variations costing an additional 20 to 100 percent.

With these facts, V/STOL obviously cannot be justified. In the real world, one must consider also the possibility of procuring not new CATOAL airplanes, but only more of those already in service. The weight differential between a new V/STOL and an old CATOAL would be reduced. The cost differential is less capable of treatment by broad generalizations

257

because of the different production status of each of the service models. It is probable, however, that unless the total force level is increased, the old airplanes will cost even less than their new and lighter replacements. That issue, however, can be deferred for handling on a case-to-case basis, since any new carrier could handle the current aircraft.

For nonaviation ships, the issue is almost as clear-cut despite the confusion caused by discussion of both V/STOL A and V/STOL C for this application. If "C" were the only V/STOL for this application, and it were designed as the LAMPS III replacement, the decision on its development could be deferred since there is no coupling with the carrier issue or the other V/STOL designs. If V/STOL A is assumed capable of use on modifications of the DD-963 and other larger ships, it must be considered against LAMPS III and other helicopters. The low disk loading helicopters are virtually certain to be more successful within their own operating envelope, but have limitations in speed and altitude. At present, it would be difficult to justify the probable cost spread of two or three times between V/STOL A and LAMPS.

In addition to the large unit production and operating cost penalties associated with the V/STOL program, it is burdened with by far the most expensive R&D program ever laid out for naval aviation. That cost, of course, must also be amortized.

The V/STOL program should be drastically revised. With naval aviation already seriously underfunded from its position vis-à-vis the threat for years past, the plan greatly aggravates the situation. The issue of small, medium, or large carriers should be made on the merits of each and not confused with the V/STOL issue. On a positive note, carriers and carrier-based airplanes have done their job well. The world's most capable tactical STOL aircraft are now deployed. The concept is proven, sound, and can do the job in the future.

Norman Polmar

I have nothing to say on the specific points, but I would make a general point. Primarily for political reasons, we cannot keep going the way we have been going. And George Spangenberg is right, I made the comment about eighty *Kennedy*s or fifty *Nimitz*es facetiously, in the Washington political environment. On an analytical basis, I'll sit down with anyone here and make what I consider to be some strong and objective arguments for that. Politically, we cannot continue the way we are going. Congress won't fund that. We can afford it, but not under our current way of thinking about budgets and dollars. Even though some of the arguments put forth by others may be wrong in an absolute sense, on a practical basis we cannot do what is right anymore.

I have had a big fight about using merchant ships for underway replenishment. Navy UNREP is the correct way to go, but we cannot afford it anymore, politically or environmentally.

We have to change, whether it is right or wrong to change. Going the way we have been going will not work anymore. Second, we have to change because our potential enemies—the Soviet Union and the Third World countries—have had a chance to react to the way we are doing things. They have had time to read what we have written, and to watch us in Vietnam, and even to capture our equipment there. A-6s, EA-6s, and other aircraft can be found in a number of laboratories and air centers around the world outside the United States. We have to look for alternatives, whether they are right or wrong. Psychologically, we have to look for alternatives, for other ways of doing things, in order to upset the balance. Right now, too many of the trends are going against us.

Dov S. Zakheim

The problem the navy in particular has is that it is trying to fight the cost crunch, or trying to wish that it would go away, instead of trying to sidestep it. For example, when Mr. Spangenberg said that the problem with carriers is one of cost, he then went on to say that V/STOL is too expensive and that YF-12A is too expensive. Subconsciously, we are all faced with the same problem of cost.

Cost, in itself, is not the only factor. In all cases, we have to look at the cost of a system, at its effectiveness, and at the context in which it will function. And this is something that frequently is ignored.

Some people say that System A is more or less costly than System B, and, therefore, they are for or against it. Other people look at the output, at the number of sorties, at the speed, at the tonnage, without considering the return on that additional dollar spent on the system—the marginal effectiveness relative to the marginal cost. We have sunk a lot of cost, and we have bought a lot of systems; but we are only buying on the margin.

The context is critical. The North Atlantic is not the same as the Indian Ocean. What makes sense in one does not necessarily make sense in the other.

When I said that the land-based option might save money on the carrier force, it was because without that land-based option, we would have to use carriers in place of land-based aircraft in those particular

259

areas. If we were to buy another carrier for the North Atlantic, it would cost that much more. Now, I have not gone into enough detail yet to know how many carriers we might need for missions other than the North Atlantic one, but let's say, for example, that it is a dozen. With additional North Atlantic tasks, it may go up to fourteen. That would be two extra carriers we would be spending money on. The cost would be less with land-based air.

Remember, anybody who looks only at cost is a fool, and anybody who looks only at missions is unrealistic. We have to look at all three—costs, effectiveness, and context missions.

DISCUSSION

JAMES MAYO: I have been around naval aviation long enough to think we may have narrowed our discussion too much. I have had the rare pleasure of landing a pretty good V/STOL aircraft, a TBF, on the *Wolverine,* on a paddlewheel excursion boat used on the Great Lakes. I have also had the 75,000-pound MK-2 Vigilante on the *Enterprise.* Between those, it seems to me, we have a wider choice than either the *Nimitz* or the 22,000-ton CVSS, and than either the helicopter or the Mach 2 or 3 V/STOL. I agree with George Spangenberg, but I also agree with Norman Polmar: we cannot plan on that high-performance V/STOL, because it just costs too much, but we have to change things.

I'd like to ask some of our distinguished panelists whether there aren't cheaper ways to build big carriers, for example. Aren't there cheaper ways to get intermediate performance capabilities on our carriers, rather than having either the helicopter expense on one end or the very high-performance V/STOL on the other?

ADMIRAL KIRKSEY: I had the privilege of spending six to eight months on the CVNX study, culminating in 1976, which was specifically aimed at what we were addressing. That is, how can we develop a nuclear-powered carrier that would be cheaper—with the lead-ship cost and and follow-ship cost being amortized over a period of time—using the technology we have at hand and working under the somewhat artificial constraint of having it authorized in a certain fiscal year?

We studied every aspect of the designs we have today to save R & D dollars. It was the conclusion of the study—and, again, people said, "We knew before you even started"—that the *Nimitz*-class ship was the most cost-effective ship we had. This cost was translated into many things. There were over a thousand iterations done on a carrier conceptual model of such factors as safety factors for pilots. Naturally, as the length and the breadth of the ship are reduced, safety problems develop, as they did on our *Essex*-class carriers. We did not feel it was fair to the U.S. Navy to increase the risk factor of pilots landing aircraft.

We looked at new radars, we looked at new design systems, we looked at every feather-merchant scheme that they had carried forth to us, to see if we could incorporate it into a carrier. We modified the *Nimitz*. We removed the flag bridge, of all things. The admiral had no place to go. We did many things to it, and it took months and months of study. Our conclusion was that, among nuclear-powered ships, the *Nimitz*-class ship was certainly the most cost- and combat-effective.

That review has been thoroughly gone over by the Congress and by the office of the secretary of defense, and no one, to this date, has argued the conclusion is unsound.

I know that there are options in new designs. We have to continue the study of new designs for aircraft and for carriers, even though it is time consuming, and the cost of a new design will be substantial. We would have to build a new design carrier and approximately five follow ships to amortize the cost to that of building a repeat *Nimitz*.

The empirical data that led us to the *Nimitz* from the Detroit and Cleveland *Wolverine* have saved lives and given us a combat-effective platform. A lot of combined intelligence has gone into that decision.

MR. ZAKHEIM: We looked at that study at CBO, and the fundamental conclusion, I think, is correct. I think everybody agrees that in buying one ship on the margin, the *Nimitz* is the most cost-effective. But remember the effectiveness measure that was used in that study was sorties. Sorties, in themselves, are usually associated with what's called "projection."

It does not necessarily take account of all the functions that would be incorporated into sea control. When different sorts of scenarios and contexts are considered, the importance of sorties—particularly, given the scenarios that were set up in that study—may not be as great as were made out.

One other point is that I am not convinced, as the people on the right and left of me are, that V/STOL, as they present it, is our only option, although I am pretty sure that we do have to disperse our air-capable platforms. If, however, we went all the way with V/STOL ships, then we might not stop at five ships. And if we bought more than five, as Admiral Kirksey just said, they would become the more cost-effective.

The argument very much depends on how many ships we want to buy and what exactly we want to do with them. What measure of effectiveness are we talking about?

MR. EDWARDS: On Mr. Lind's comments, while it is true that no ship might have been lost, the water area covered by the blimps was not great, and, in fact, the number of submarines sunk by blimps could be assembled in this room. I would not put the future of ASW on the blimp. Mr. Lind mentioned the lack of high-performance aircraft in the Soviet navy. The Soviets have just got into carrier aviation, and certainly what they have today is not what they will have ten years from now, or twenty-five years from now. So, don't plan a future U.S. Navy on what the Soviet navy is today.

On Mr. Zakheim's point about the vulnerability of the carrier, it's true that we were told the carrier would never last out World War II. And the truth is that no *Essex*-class carrier was sunk during World War II, even though the capability of doing it was there. I submit that, in the present situation, the carrier's vulnerability can be very largely cured in a general war by our method of deploying. Certainly, we would never allow a Soviet missile-capable ship to be 2,000 yards on the starboard quarter in plane guard station. We would keep it well clear. With its own reconnaissance capability, we should be able to ensure that. We would then be dealing, as we dealt all through World War II, with the submarine problem as the principal one.

On Mr. Polmar's point about underway replenishment, that we ought to buy the Merchant Marine and get rid of navy UNREP, I hope we have some capability to bring the crew under the control of the OTC. In World War II, a merchant ship did UNREP us near Espírito Santo, but we had to put a whale boat over and go over to that ship in order to handle the lines, because the crew was at lunch.

MR. LIND: The blimp, of course, per se is quite restricted as a nonrigid ship. Obviously, for long-range capabilities and a heavy payload, a rigid ship is needed. Some people have suggested that if we had the *Akron* and the *Macon* and a few other rigid airships in the Pacific, it might have been a little harder for the Japanese to pull off Pearl Harbor.

On the question of aircraft performance, obviously if shooting down attacking Soviet aircraft is the only consideration, we don't have much of a problem today. The whole point of the seminar, however, has been that aircraft can do much more than that. My argument would be that an aircraft such as the AV-8B has adequate performance capabilities for many, if not most, of those missions today.

MR. POLMAR: Airships do give a fantastic endurance time on station. With respect to putting all of the German submarines sunk by airships into this room, we are now finding out that we can put virtually all of the German submarines sunk by carrier aircraft in World War II—

twenty-some of them—into this room, if we discount those we found because we were reading the German Enigma Code.

As a search platform, an airship is far superior to a carrier-based aircraft—in many scenarios. We are now learning that part of the reason for the fantastic success of the British and the United States against the U-boats in World War II was that we were reading the German codes, and we knew where they were going and at what speed of advance. This is aside, of course, from the ones we actually killed trying to close with convoys, in tactical operations.

JOE WATSON, chief engineman, Naval Enlisted Reserve Association: Admiral Kirksey commented that the V/STOL could be the panacea. Vice Admiral Crowe said the future of sea-based tactical air power depends, to a large extent, on the investment we make now in the V/STOL technology. Norman Polmar's paper says the navy should proceed at full speed ahead with the V/STOL program. Mr. Lind appears to agree.

In the September issue of *Sea Power*, however, L. Edgar Preener says that the decision has already been made by Secretary Brown, in his PDM of August 16, to delay V/STOL development until the mid-1980s. My question is, does the PDM make the V/STOL question academic?

MR. LIND: The latest understanding, unofficially, is that the secretary has reversed himself on the V/STOL R & D for the Type A and Type B V/STOLs. He apparently is still moving, however, to kill the advanced Harrier. In the view of some of us, this would be catastrophic. Although the navy will not now accept the Harrier as a naval aircraft, if we can put a VSS into the budget this next year, the navy would not have much choice. And if we do not have the AV-8B, the advanced Harrier, we will be in real trouble through the 1980s. If V/STOL does not come until the 1990s, that will be too late. The Soviets will be so far ahead, and our own key platforms will be so few and so vulnerable, that, like the Spanish Armada, we will sail in expectation of a miracle.

ADMIRAL KIRKSEY: I think Mr. Lind's interpretation of the secretary's PDM and his intentions is correct. The AV-8, the Bravo, or the Superplus may be in some jeojardy. If the VSS is the option authorized for a 1979 ship, it would be rather embarrassing to have this ship delivered and no air wing to go on it. Even if this program decision were reversed in the favor of V/STOL as Mr. Lind indicated, however, it would be in the late 1980s before a fly-off would exist for the procurement phase for that type of air wing, which would not be deployable until the 1990s.

This does allow us, I believe, certain breathing room in the R & D effort. I think Bob Kirksey's interpretation of Secretary Brown is that there has been a certain stampede. We should back off a notch and look at how the R & D effort will be spread out. Will the return for that effort, in fact, provide the capabilities needed for that time frame? If any decisions are reversed, and VSS is authorized, it will be authorized as a replacement in the 1985 time frame of the so-called twelve deployable carriers.

The navy is attempting to get a carrier to replace a carrier. If it is a VSS, then I feel that the United States has taken a major step backwards in capability.

ADMIRAL MILLER: I will now take advantage of the prerogative of the moderator to summarize, and also to add a couple of points that I had hoped might be addressed and were not.

First, relative to carriers and their escorts, I had hoped that in discussing the future of sea-based aviation, we would have heard about attack submarines as escorts for aircraft carriers, as opposed to surface ships. There are many of us who were on active duty, who had some role in pushing this idea. For the Mediterranean, I wanted fourteen attack submarines for peacetime purposes, to cover the situation. That got me some interesting messages involving the word *chutzpah*. We spent quite some time looking up the definition, but we eventually got it. But the idea of tying ourselves to surface ships as escorts has been accepted by a great many people other than those who operate aircraft carriers. On active duty with a task force, if I find a surface ship on the same side of the horizon as an aircraft carrier, two guys are going to get canned, and one of them will be the guy in charge. The collision between the *Kennedy* and the *Belknap,* as far as I am concerned, stemmed from an improper use of the assets in the hands of the individuals.

Surface ships have great capabilities. I want some of them to serve as scouts and in skirmishes. I want something that has a capability to sense what is under the ocean and in the skies and to alert me, and to act as a sacrificial lamb. I am a product of World War II, and of the suicide destroyer attacks, and I lived in cruisers more than I ever did in aircraft carriers. I wish that submarines had been addressed as possible escorts.

I wish there had been some discussion of devoting one or two of those twelve big carriers, in the event of a war, specifically to the ASW role. I seriously question whether or not we can perform both the missions that are assigned to the current CV from one deck. I regret that I did not fight this decision harder when I was an admiral on active duty. I should have taken my stand on the CV.

In regard to the use of land-based air and allies, I support much of what Dov Zakheim said. In the Mediterranean, I used to discuss this subject constantly. It does not matter whether tactical aircraft are shore-based or land-based. As long as I get tactical air, I don't care where it comes from. After we have three times as much as we need, I will debate the efficiency of shore-based versus land-based air power.

And why isn't Tunisia a member of NATO? It is a friendly Arab country, sitting in a strategic position. I could have used a base there, if the State Department had read the messages and done more than they did about cementing relations.

On the future of naval aviation, I want to report on the discussion that Admiral Moorer and I had with the secretary of the navy.

Some of you may have been aware that the current administration has some ideas to get away from the past and to change things a bit. One of them was that all helicopter pilots from all the armed services will be trained by the army in Fort Rucker, and there have been some people who objected to that. In the course of the congressional hearings, Admiral Moorer and some other retired admirals made a few points. To summarize, with a lot of help and the wisdom of many, many people, the Senate defeated the idea seventy-five to twenty-one.

The spokesman for the administration was a fine individual, the secretary of the navy. So, here we had a group of old retired officers going against the civil authority, to look at it in the worst light.

Admiral Moorer and I were concerned about that, and we went in to see the secretary of the navy. It was not the most satisfactory discussion in the world, but other things that he addressed that afternoon were of considerable significance to this conference.

We got on the subject of the future of the navy, V/STOL, aircraft carriers, and so forth. He talked at great length about the AV-8B, and how much payload it could carry with a 600-foot deck run.

We tried to point out that if a 600-foot deck run is put on an AV-8B, there could not be many aircraft aboard the carrier, but these were incidental points. The most significant point of the whole conversation was his statement to us about the future of sea-based aviation.

He stated—and I give it almost directly—he said, "Gentlemen, do you realize that there are a great many people in this administration who believe that the only sea-based aviation we need is a few long-range shore-based aircraft strictly for the reconnaissance missions."

We have considerable work ahead. We have to do a lot of educating, a lot of informing of a lot of people, on a very, very significant aspect of the defense posture of this country.

266

PART FOUR

BALANCE OF THE FLEET

What will be the balance of the fleet as we enter the twenty-first century? Will we have radical ship designs? Can the fleet of the future be protected? What will the size of the fleet be?

In his paper, Reuven Leopold, one of the navy's top civilian ship designers, tells us that there will undoubtedly be some changes, but not the radical changes that some contemplate or desire. First, as Leopold notes, although there are some interesting ship-hull designs upcoming— such as the small waterplane area, twin hulls, hydrofoils, air-cushion craft, and surface-effect ships—he predicts that the conventional displacement-type hull will remain the dominant ship design, with gas turbines the main form of propulsion. The paper also goes into future weapon systems, from laser beams to eight-inch guns, and projects some highly sophisticated electronics and communications systems. But, as Leopold concludes, which of the innovations will be actually accepted is as much a "sociological as a technological issue."

David Kassing, president of the Center for Naval Analyses, tackles the very difficult question of protection of the fleet. He opens with a reminder that while protection is necessary, its purpose is really only to make sure the navy can do "what it was created for." The question of the fleet's ability to protect itself has come about because of four technological changes—nuclear weapons, nuclear propulsion, antiship missiles, and ocean surveillance—and one other major change: the size and composition of the U.S. Navy. Another factor that Dr. Kassing raises is a "threat that's apparent to anyone who looks at advertisements in the front and back of Jane's," *namely, that anyone who can meet the price can buy himself some very sophisticated military technology. The paper then goes into some of the technologies that will change and others, like antisubmarine warfare, that probably will not change that radically. He concludes with six implications for the future, one of which is the importance of intelligence and satellite surveillance, which may become crucial around the twenty-first century.*

Admiral Trost, director of Navy Systems Analysis Division, concludes the conference by tackling another very difficult question, the size of the fleet. In the introduction of this paper, he points up the difficulty of making predictions by showing a 1957 projection, in which the size of the fleet of the 1970s is given as 927 ships, whereas the actual size is 464—approximately half. The paper also includes some useful tables on the size of the fleet since 1950 and some comparisons between American and Soviet shipbuilding, which is not entirely encouraging. Admiral Trost then describes some of the force-structure issues and trends and comments on the future force size. His conclusion is that the size of the fleet will depend on our national strategy around the twenty-first century.

Surface Warships for the Early Twenty-First Century

Reuven Leopold

To gaze into the future and predict its course is an ancient art. Back when the Greeks ruled the civilized world the oracle of Delphi was asked to predict such events as the outcome of battles between the Greeks and their enemies. While we have no statistical information relative to the success of those predictions, we have seen within the last two decades or so that this art has again become very popular, with practitioners springing up like mushrooms after a heavy rain. In spite of the availability of techniques and the proliferation of practitioners, however, there are at least as many doubters as believers.

One of the believers is Simon Ramo who, in a recent article, defended the need for forecasting in these words:

> If you are going 10 miles an hour in broad daylight on a good straight road, with little traffic, then it is sufficient to look ahead for only a few feet and even to turn your gaze away from the road quite often. Nothing too serious will happen to impede your travel. But ours is a bumpy, poorly lighted street with high-speed or drunk drivers, and surprising intersections and obstacles. We had better look well ahead and learn how to translate what we see into appropriately timed steering wheel, throttle, and brake activities.[1]

Peter Drucker, on the other hand, appears to sprinkle doubt on our ability to predict the future by saying:

> The impacts of technology tend to be threshold phenomena; until they reach a certain level, there is no impact at all. Pollution is, of course, the obvious example. It is a fairly old and rather well-proven theorem that threshold phenomena cannot be predicted. They are noticeable only after the threshold has been passed. From the bottom of the pitcher one cannot predict *when* it will overflow—indeed not even that it *will* overflow.[2]

---

[1] Simon Ramo, "Comment: The Anticipation of Change," *Technology and Culture*, vol. 10 (October 1969), p. 514.

[2] Peter Drucker, "Comment: Is Technology Predictable?" *Technology and Culture*, vol. 10 (October 1969).

However, Dr. Ida R. Hoos may have delivered the most vitriolic critique when she wrote:

> With technology forecasting, the prime stock in trade of these adventurers into the unknown, we might share the further de-professionalizing note offered by an aerospace engineer: "There are two occupations," he said, "for which previous experience is not necessary. One is streetwalking and the other is technology forecasting."[3]

Since I am not a professional technology forecaster but a warship designer, it is understandable that I have embarked upon the writing of this article about warship design for the early twenty-first century with some apprehension. Predicting the characteristics of warships for the twenty-first century entails a great deal of forecasting—forecasting the international political environment that will make it necessary to have one sort of naval capability rather than another; forecasting the economic environment that might, for example, make large aluminum-hull ships more cost effective than steel-hull ships; forecasting what will encompass the myriad technologies behind the numerous mechanical, electrical, electronic, and weapons systems that compose a warship. Though not unaware of the impacts that political and economic factors could have on our twenty-first century navy, I will assume for this discussion that current trends will persist without abrupt or dramatic change and, for the most part, I will concentrate on technological changes that will affect various parts of a warship and will tend to make the warship different in the early twenty-first century.

I will attempt to avoid making judgments relative to the navy's needs for various numbers of different types of ships, since opinions tend to vary widely. Specifically, I mean to avoid such theses as those advocating use of land-based aircraft for the tasks of many surface warships, or those favoring a navy that consists only of large aircraft carriers and submarines, or those favoring a navy that consists only of very fast high-performance ships and submarines. I will also avoid predicting which faction will come out the winner in the current dispute over the size, propulsion machinery type, and aircraft type for aircraft-carrying surface ships of the future.

I will assume that moderation will prevail over those who wish to eliminate versatility in our navy, and that we will keep our options open by continuing to have a navy composed of surface, air, and submarine arms in proper balance. I guess by having made this statement, I have already made my first forecast.

---

[3] Ida R. Hoos, "Criteria for 'Good' Future Research," *Technological Forecasting and Social Change Journal,* vol. 6, no. 2 (1974).

From an operational viewpoint, U.S. Navy ships and craft are broadly classified by their missions: warships, auxiliary ships, and so on. Warships are the backbone of the fleet, representing the offensive and defensive capacity of the United States on the world's seas. The foremost group of warships is, of course, the combatants, consisting of aircraft carriers, battleships (not presently in commission), command ships, cruisers, destroyers, and submarines. A second group consists of frigates, patrol types, mine warfare types, and riverine types. A third group of combatants is the amphibious warfare type, consisting of command, inshore fire support, assault, cargo transport, and landing ships. These three groups constitute the major fighting capability of the U.S. Navy at the present time. To service and supply warships, there is another group—the so-called auxiliaries—consisting of tenders, ammunition ships, oilers, hospital ships, stores ships, general cargo ships, tugs, salvage ships, oceanographic ships, and others.

This impressive list of different types of ships should give an idea of the breadth and diversity of our fleet, and thus a hint as to how long this paper would be if it included all of the issues that drive each particular design. Since I cannot cover all that today, I shall focus on the surface combatants—cruisers, destroyers, and frigates—representing most of our surface warships. It should be apparent, however, that much of what I say also applies, in varying degrees, to many of the other ship types. To start, I will describe the basic principles governing the current state-of-the-art limitations for further advances in ship design and explain what one could expect to find in the fleet by the early part of the twenty-first century.

The primary elements of a warship are: (1) a hull to provide form and structure and to contain and support all other components of the ship; (2) propulsion machinery to give it mobility; and (3) a combat system consisting of weapons and sensors and data handling devices to provide its fighting capability. These three basic elements, or categories, form the framework for my discussion of technological trends in U.S. warship design.

Types of Hull Form

The identification and classification of ship types, as enumerated above, are meaningful to the ship operator; they relate to his military operational demands and his functional requirements. The ship designer, however, needs a different ordering based on engineering considerations. Surface ships versus submarines, conventional versus high-performance types, single-hull versus multihull-types—these are but some of the

271

options that have a major impact on design. If a ship designer were asked to name the qualities of an ideal ship hull form, he would list the following: low resistance to forward motion; good seakeeping behavior; good maneuverability characteristics; good internal arrangement (boxiness); light weight.

As with most engineering systems, a ship form is normally a compromise among these various factors, with each element of desired capability and performance weighted according to its relative value to the decision maker. With conventional displacement-type surface ships, for example, a shape that is efficient for stowage has poor hydrodynamic characteristics—a barge is an extreme example. I should explain that a displacement-type ship is one that is supported by buoyancy as opposed to craft, such as hydrofoil ships or surface effect ships, which are supported by dynamic lift. In a commercial tanker, maximum cargo capacity is desirable and speed is relatively unimportant—a fat, boxy ship is the result. In a navy guided-missile frigate, speed is considered important, and internal arrangement is subjugated to the need for a fine, lean hull that minimizes the ship's resistance to being pushed through the water. The greater the horsepower a ship requires, the greater the fraction of weight-carrying capability that must be devoted to propulsion machinery and fuel and the smaller the fraction of weight-carrying capability that is available for purposes directly related to the ship's mission (guns, missiles, radars, and the like).

Displacement-Type Ships. In the area of hull form design for displacement-type ships, there are three current lines of development that I consider particularly important for our future navy. The first is in the direction of reducing the resistance a ship encounters to its movement through the water. Since that resistance increases as the speed of the ship increases, more horsepower is required to overcome it. The problem is that each increment of speed becomes more and more costly in terms of additional horsepower required. For a typical surface combatant, for example, a 10 percent increase in speed at 20 knots would require roughly a 30 percent increase in horsepower. At 30 knots, a 10 percent increase in speed would require more than a 50 percent increase in horsepower. At 40 knots, a 10 percent increase in speed would require something on the order of a 100 percent increase in horsepower.

Although some improvements in this picture are anticipated through advanced work in ship hydrodynamics, the displacement-type hull is clearly up against barriers inherent in its physical characteristics. Thus, it seems equally clear that future ships requiring speeds in excess of 40 knots or so will not utilize displacement-type hulls. This is actually less of a penalty than it might seem. With the current sophistication, smartness, agility, and increasing range of weapons systems as well as the increasing potential of surveillance and worldwide communication systems, the value of speed has actually decreased for many naval missions. In view of the declining emphasis on speed and the natural advantages of the displacement-type hull for most applications, this ship form will probably be as dominant in our navy of the early twenty-first century as it is today.

The second important line of development for displacement-type hulls is in the direction of reducing the motions induced on the ship by ocean waves—that is, improving its seakeeping capabilities. In the rolling and pitching of a ship in stormy seas, its bow may be raised completely out of the water, as waves crash down on its decks. Such conditions tend not only to impair the operational capabilities of the ship—its speed and maneuverability, the performance of its weapons and sensors, the efficiency of its crew, and so on—but also to damage the ship and its weapons and equipment.

Sheer size is one way to promote good seakeeping ability, but most naval missions do not require ships large enough to be really effective in this respect. By incorporating such devices as antiroll tanks or underwater fins, the designer can reduce the roll component of the ship's motion. The greatest potential for improved seakeeping, however, seems to be the small waterplane area, twin hull (SWATH). The SWATH is a rather unconventional type of displacement ship, basically a development of the twin-hulled catamaran. It consists essentially of a pair of submarine-like hulls below the surface of the water that support a box-like structure above the water by means of long, slender struts. The parts of the ship that provide its buoyancy are below the waves, while the part that contains most of the equipment and personnel and armament is held high above the waves. This design enables the ship to proceed in heavy seas with almost undiminished speed. Compromises must be made, however, and SWATH's seakeeping excellence is obtained at the cost of a somewhat greater investment in steel and propulsion machinery to carry a specified payload. (If the ship's payload is useful only when ship motions are moderate—aircraft, for example—then SWATH may well be the least expensive solution to the design problem.) The speed of the SWATH ship is roughly the same as that of conventional ships (20–40 knots) but, because of its geometry, it can maintain this speed into much higher sea states (that is, higher winds and larger waves). The SWATH ship provides a steady platform and wide deck, lending itself to helicopter or vertical takeoff aircraft operations that do not require ships as large as conventional displacement-types. For

273

example, a 3,000-ton SWATH-type frigate would have seakeeping abilities equal to those of a 6,000-ton or a 7,000-ton conventional frigate.

The third important current line of development for displacement-type hulls has to do with simplified construction, better utilization of existing materials, optimization of structural geometry, and amenability to rapid and economical reconfiguration to keep up with rapid technological advances in the weapons and electronics features of contemporary and future warships. This interesting and significant area of development pertains to how ships are put together rather than to their gross physical and functional characteristics. I will not go into any details at this point but will come back to this subject toward the end of this discussion.

I mentioned that for many naval missions the value of ship speed has diminished in recent years. While this is true, there are still a variety of special missions for which speed seems to have an increased tactical significance. Consequently, we are trying to move on a new front, beyond the displacement-type hull, in our attempts to overcome the natural barriers to speed on the oceans. That search takes place in the realm of what we call high-performance ships.

The displacement-type ship operates in a unique environment; unlike the submarine or the airplane, each of which is designed to operate essentially in a single medium, it travels at the interface between two enormously different media: air and water. The detrimental influences of this interface on speed and seakeeping capability have led to vehicles that diverge away from it in both directions: submarines below the water, high-perfomance ships above it. The sections that follow describe several basic types of high-performance ships: hydrofoils, vertical sustention craft, and hybrid forms.

Hydrofoils. The hydrofoil ship has most of the attributes of a conventional displacement ship, because, at times, it must be capable of operating in the displacement mode. In its own specialized, preferred mode of operation, however, it is supported by underwater wings—hydrofoils—attached to long struts. Hydrofoils work in a manner directly comparable to the airfoils, or wings, that give an airplane its lift, but are smaller since they operate in water—a medium 800 times as dense as air. Raising the hull out of the water removes the greatest source of the ship's resistance to movement through the water; thus, high speeds can be achieved—roughly double those possible with conventional ships. But exploitation of this concept requires high technology and very expensive materials, welding techniques, equipment, and machinery—and lots of fuel per ton-mile. While today's hydrofoil boats (250 tons) have limited endurance—requiring a "mother ship" for extended open-ocean operations—current navy studies include designs for hydrofoils in the 1,400–2,400-ton range, having thirty-day mission duration capability, and foilborne ranges of 2,500 and 3,600 nautical miles, with all onboard maintenance done by the ship's crew. The hydrofoil is less self-sufficient than a conventional ship and requires support bases for extended deployments in distant areas. However, there does not seem to be any particular limitation on the size of future hydrofoils, which can be at least as large as 3,000 tons.

The hydrofoil provides a high-speed capability into very rough seas with very little degradation of either speed or seakeeping ability. Speeds of 50 knots could be considered typical, but current U.S. Navy developments employing variable-geometry foil features indicate that 70 knots can be achieved in a militarized vessel. The seakeeping characteristics of a hydrofoil, a key feature, offer very significant improvements over an equivalent displacement-type ship for a given speed and sea state.

Over the last fifteen years, the navy has designed and constructed, with industry support, a series of engineering-prototype hydrofoil craft. Steady development, starting with pure R&D craft and progressing through operational evaluations of a pair of militarized craft off South Vietnam in 1969, has resulted in the design and construction of the PHM-1 class of missile-armed combatant hydrofoils; the navy will acquire six by 1982. The PHM-1 carries eight Harpoon surface-to-surface missiles and a 76-millimeter gun with integrated fire control systems.

Vertical Sustention Craft. A relatively new and very promising class of naval craft is characterized by its novel technique for vertical support or sustention. Instead of being held up by static buoyancy or by dynamic forces produced by submerged foils, it sits on a cushion of air generated by powerful fans thrusting downward and contained by a flexible skirt surrounding the lower hull. This craft comes in two basic types: the air cushion vehicle (ACV) and surface effect ship (SES). ACVs are typically much smaller than SESS, ranging up to roughly 200 tons, and have the unique ability to cross the shoreline, from water to land and back again. This amphibious capability comes at a price, however—with no part of the craft projecting below the water, the use of water propellers or water for propulsion is ruled out, necessitating the use of less efficient air propellers. The SES, on the other hand, has long catamaran-like hulls forming its sides, with flexible skirts at bow and stern only. Not only are water propellers and water jets feasible propellers for the SES but the craft derives additional vertical support from the buoyancy of the side hulls, enabling it to carry greater payloads and to support itself statically in the water should the lift fans become inoperable for some reason.

ACVS are relatively small and relatively unsuited to open-ocean operations, especially of any lengthy duration. They would be useful either in applications requiring an actual amphibious capability, such as landing craft for assaults over the beach, or in applications requiring a shallow water capability, such as patrolling rivers or marshy areas, near-shore mine countermeasure operations, hydrographic surveying, and search and rescue operations. The navy currently has a program to develop a class of air-cushion landing craft, the first prototype of which is planned for construction beginning in late fiscal 1981, with construction of production craft beginning in 1986. Current ACVS have speeds on the order of 50 knots, but as much as 100 knots or more can be expected in the future.

The SES will play a more traditional deep-ocean naval role. The navy's current SES development program focuses on the design, development, construction, and comprehensive testing of a 3,000-ton ship. The 3KSES, as it is called by Rohr Industries, is 266 feet long with a beam of 108 feet. It has a longitudinally framed aluminum-alloy hull and is powered by six General Electric LM-2500 gas turbines: two turbines driving lift fans to raise the ship on its cushion, the other four driving water-jet pump propulsions for forward movement at speeds of up to 80 knots. The centrifugal-type lift fans are approximately 15 feet (4.58 meters) in diameter. The ship will accommodate 125 officers and crew. After completion (scheduled for 1982), this armed, developmental prototype will undergo approximately two years of testing by the navy, including fleet operations simulating anticipated ship capabilities in a realistic environment. The operational concept of an SES frigate requires it to sprint out well ahead of the convoy at regular intervals, stop, and then, with helicopter assistance, listen for submarines. Operating clear of the convoy, the high-speed SES/helicopter team will be able to detect and destroy submarines long before they have an opportunity to close in on the merchant ships. It has been suggested that a few SESS will provide a far more effective shield than three times as many displacement-type warships.

Future development efforts include the planning and preliminary design studies for such fleet-frigate surface-effect guided-missile (FFSG) ships as well as for much larger ships incorporating antiair warfare, anti–surface-ship warfare, and amphibious assault capabilities. At present, the navy is testing a pair of experimental prototype SESS weighing about 100 tons each. The SES-100A, operating at the navy's test facility in Maryland, is being used to test the new bow and stern seals intended for large surface effect ships; the SES-100B, operating at the navy's Coastal Systems Laboratory in Panama City, Florida, set a record for this type of craft earlier this year when it attained a speed of 89 knots (103 miles per hour, or 165 kilometers per hour) during a crossing of St. Andrew Bay. During another test, an SM-1 medium-range guided missile was successfully launched from the SES-100B traveling at a speed of 60 knots. The missile then flew accurately to its target five miles away.

Hybrids. The advent of high-performance ship concepts has led to categorizing the various hull types according to their means of sustention, such as:

- buoyancy (conventional displacement hulls and SWATHS)
- dynamic lift (hydrofoils)
- powered static lift (ACVs and SESS).

This classification, in turn, generated the idea of combining different sustention mechanisms in a single craft, which led to the idea of developing hybrid craft incorporating some combination of buoyancy, dynamic lift, and powered static ·ft. One major advantage of hybrid craft is that they add variables, enabling the designer to fit his design to specific requirements and constraints. The technology by the twenty-first century should be sufficiently advanced to produce such hybrids without significant problems. Whether or not they actually are built depends on how far their added complexity is offset by economic and/or performance gains and, of even greater importance, on how much value the navy of the twenty-first century attaches to speed.

Propulsion

Having discussed the basic hull types available to the designer of surface warships of the early twenty-first century, let me present some of the considerations involved in the selection of propulsion plants to drive those ships. The power-plant types presently in use as main propulsion prime movers of warships are steam, nuclear, gas turbine, and diesel.

Prime Movers. At the start of World War II, nuclear and gas turbines existed only in theory or as small-scale experimental models. Diesels had been in use for over twenty years in the U.S. Navy, mostly in submarines but also as small, slow-speed escort propulsors. One of the reasons for the limited use of diesels in warships—then and now—is that diesels are relatively large and relatively heavy for a given horsepower. Diesels small enough in size and weight to be considered for warship application today are limited to the 8,000–10,000 horsepower range. A typical warship requires on the order of 40,000–80,000 horsepower, and aircraft carriers, our largest ships, can require as much as 300,000 horsepower. A diesel plant simply eats up too much of the volume and the weight-carrying capability of a warship. Diesels do find application in the noncombatant auxiliary ships, however, since the requirement for speed, and thus horsepower, is considerably less for auxiliaries than for combatants, and also because volume and weight are less critical. Since this paper is directed at the combatants—the warships—I will not discuss diesels in any greater detail.

Steam. The predominant propulsion system in the navy's warship fleet today is the steam plant. Steam is produced in large boilers and then directed into turbines, which drive the ship's propellers through reduction gears. Steam has been a reliable and versatile medium for propulsion over the years, and it has come a long way—from 300 pounds per square inch pressure in the 1930s to 600 pounds per square inch pressure at the end of World War II to 1,200 pounds per square inch pressure today, with comparable increases in steam temperature at each step. Increasing the pressure and temperature of the steam has greatly increased the amount of energy available in given amounts of steam and, correspondingly, reduced the physical size of the propulsion plant per given amount of horsepower. At the same time, it has greatly increased the efficiency with which the fuel is converted into power. But, each increase in pressure and temperature led to increased complexity in the equipment associated with a steam plant and greatly increased the demands on the materials composing it. The navy is still wrestling with some of the problems resulting from the introduction of 1,200-pound steam some thirty years ago. The question is: Where will steam go from here?

It appears unlikely that we will be able to continue the pattern of decreasing the size and increasing the efficiency of steam plants in the foreseeable future. Even if we could, it would most likely be at the cost of greater complexity. Complexity is something else that must be considered carefully—greater complexity means more things can fail; bigger stocks of spare parts; higher crew skill levels; higher costs for construction, maintenance, and repair; greater difficulty in automating plant operation; and so on. The steam plant does have virtues that will make it useful for a variety of applications into the twenty-first century, but its tenure as the workhorse of the fleet seems certain to end within the next ten years. The workhorse of the fleet after that and into the early twenty-first century will be the gas turbine.

Gas turbines. The gas turbine was considered for application in nearly every new U.S. destroyer design from the late 1940s to the late 1960s. It was not until 1971 that the decision was finally made to install gas turbine propulsion plants in a new class of warship, the DD-963 destroyers. Since then, only gas turbine propulsion plants have been selected for new-design surface combatants. From 13 ships today, the number of gas turbine driven warships will climb to over 100 ten years from now. The great virtue of the gas turbine is that it can produce a relatively large amount of power for its size and weight—and in a warship such virtue is most appreciated. In fact, in the case of the high performance-type warships—the hydrofoils and surface effect ships—one can be even more emphatic: their very existence depends on the availability of gas turbine prime movers. There are no trade-offs to make. Without light, compact gas turbines, these ships would not be feasible.

Both General Electric and United Technology are currently developing so-called third generation gas turbine engines that should be available for use in warships within three years.

It is very disappointing to have to dismiss, certainly for the first half of the twenty-first century, nonfossil-fuel but nonnuclear solutions to warship propulsion. Yet, all indications are that alternative sources such as solar energy, photovoltaic generators or other heat collecting/converting devices, ocean thermal energy converters, or the simple wind generator will not be practical for warship propulsion, at least in the early part of the twenty-first century. For example, to collect 50 kilowatts of energy for a warship from the sun, the entire topside would have to be devoted to solar energy collection; yet 50 kilowatts represents only a fraction of 1 percent of the power needed by such a ship.

Because of improved designs, the specific fuel consumption of gas turbines has been decreasing steadily over the last twenty years. Engines that incorporate the latest developments are not yet in service on naval ships but are expected to be in the 1980s. Two primary technological advances responsible for gas turbine design improvements are new materials that can better withstand higher and higher temperatures and new methods of cooling the gas turbine blades in the first and second rows adjacent to the combustion chamber. New blade materials, such as ceramics, offer the potential for even further increased inlet gas temperatures and the attendant improvement in fuel consumption. We are also perfecting techniques that do much more than merely improve individual component performance.

Combined power plants. It appears to me that the combined power-plant approach which the navy has often employed in the past to introduce new, untried sources of power into the fleet—for example, sails with steam, reciprocating steam engine with steam turbine, and steam turbine with gas turbine—will find a somewhat new purpose in the future. Combined plants will be used to improve fuel consumption of a base plant or to better adapt the capabilities of a specific type of propulsion prime mover to a segment of the warship's mission profile.

The most advantageous application of the combined plant is in warships requiring high speed for short intervals of time and long cruising ranges at lower speeds. This requirement is ideally satisfied by a combination of a base-load plant of moderate weight and high efficiency plus a booster plant of very light weight and not necessarily as high an efficiency, since it is used only during an insignificant portion of the life of the ship. Although no warship in the active U.S. fleet today utilizes the combined power-plant concept, I envision the adoption of combined power plants to exploit the higher combined life-cycle efficiency, primarily because fossil fuel prices and availability will probably be prohibitive by the twenty-first century.

One combined power plant, COGAS, has been receiving substantial attention in recent years. The COGAS concept consists of a gas turbine power plant combined thermodynamically with a steam power plant. Simple cycle gas turbines currently in use yield specific fuel consumption in the range of 0.40 pound per horsepower hour. The COGAS cycle appears to offer a specific fuel consumption in the range of 0.33 pound per horsepower hour, using the General Electric LM 2500 gas turbine.

A COGAS plant for the Spruance class destroyer (DD-963) would have an acquisition cost in the neighborhood of $140 per horsepower, while the annual overhaul cost would be about $236,000, as compared with $116 per horsepower acquisition cost and $200,000 overhaul cost for the gas turbine power plants now in use. However, the higher COGAS acquisition and maintenance costs would be substantially offset by the savings in fuel of 0.07 pound per horsepower hour.

I anticipate that gas turbine power plants will dominate the warship propulsion scene in the U.S. Navy of the early twenty-first century. These plants will experience improved thermodynamic efficiencies by incorporation of materials that can withstand higher temperatures as well as by application of the combined-plant concept.

Power Transmission. Having listened to a discussion of potential advances in energy conversion devices for propulsion, one might wonder, how that energy gets from the energy conversion devices to the propellers that deliver the thrust that pushes the ship forward. There has been an extremely interesting development in this respect.

A radical change in power transmission may soon be effected by the introduction of new kinds of electrical machinery (generators and motors) having weight and volume characteristics only one-fourth to one-fifth of that presently available. I am speaking of superconducting machinery.

The interesting aspect of this development is that its impact is not restricted to the propulsion system—it will generate major changes to the entire warship configuration. For example, it will eliminate the need for the reduction gear, for most of the heavy propeller shafting, and for the controllable and reversible pitch propellers, as well as for a significant portion of the air intake and uptake ductwork. The main propulsion gas turbines will no longer have to be in line with the propeller, thus introducing a degree of design flexibility heretofore unattainable for high-powered warships. Flexibility of power distribution from one prime mover to more than one propeller will be introduced, leading to improved part-load gas turbine performance at cruise speeds and to reduced fuel consumption. The total gains from these improvements will permit a significant reduction in ship size for the same payload, speed, and endurance.

Although the basic phenomenon of superconductivity has been known for sixty years, the technology has only recently been developed to the point of practical application. Detail design and construction of a 3,000 horsepower motor for laboratory and shipboard experimental evaluation by the navy is now under way. This prototype is intended to demonstrate the materials, design parameters, fabrication, and assembly approaches required for full size (40,000 horsepower) systems.

For the first time it appears that electrical transmission systems will be more attractive than the currently used mechanical reduction gears or state-of-the-art electrical machinery. A reduction gear for a 40,000 horsepower system would weigh about 280,000 pounds, and the equivalent state-of-the-art electric generator set would weigh about 375,000 pounds. With superconducting technology applied to the generator and motor, the unit would weigh only about 85,000 pounds, thus enabling the kind of ship configuration options alluded to earlier in the paper.

Manning Automation

Another issue of great significance to naval designers—one that is bound to be impacted by the technology of the twenty-first century—is the manning level of a warship. One of the most important factors underlying the increasing size of U.S. Navy warships per given payload and performance is the high standard of ship habitability. Since warships are volume limited, and habitability standards have increased substantially since World War II, every added man costs much more in increased ship size today than he did in World War II. Attempts to reduce the number of required personnel have been successful in recent designs, but the number of cubic feet per man has continued to grow. The need to reduce ship manning levels has also been forced by rising manpower costs, decreasing defense appropriations, and declining availability of qualified personnel. Nearly sixty cents of every defense dollar is now spent for payroll and related personnel expenses.

Thus, the issue is how to get people off warships and how to reduce the impact on ship acquisition cost of those who must remain on board. The instinctive first reaction is to automate. One hears prognostications of unmanned ships controlled by satellites. Some speak of peacetime versus wartime crews or of changes in maintenance philosophy, specifically, "maintenance by replacement," as opposed to repair on board. Unfortunately, there does not appear to be a simple solution.

From a technological viewpoint, remotely controlled, unmanned ships can certainly be built today. Unmanned machinery spaces exist in the U.S. Navy as well as in commercial ships and ships of foreign navies. Automatically fired guns responsive to certain incoming target characteristics are realized today by the Vulcan/Phalanx close-in weapons system; the bridge that can be operated by one man is also a current reality. However, much of this outward appearance of automation is not true automation, nor has it taken man out of the control loop. It provides more adequate information and allows remote and centralized activation, which helps reduce manning but does not eliminate it.

The repair-by-replacement concept reduced the manning level of the recently developed Perry FFG-7 class frigate but at the cost of having to store much larger, more expensive whole units on the ship or on a tender. Also, it places penalties on ship size; for example, more space is required for removal of large units from a ship repair-by-replacement than for removal of smaller parts, as is now done under the repair-in-place concept. The overall impact would be a higher fleet cost. As an example, imagine that every time a car had a major carburetor problem, the garage removed the entire engine and sent it to a special repair shop where the carburetor would be repaired. Moreover, some of the personnel eliminated from the crew because of adoption of the repair-by-replacement concept would not be deleted from the operating force of the fleet. Instead, they would be stationed on tenders or at onshore repair facilities. The navy would still have them on its payroll.

There is a further complication to the problem of warship manning. One reason warships are designed to withstand a certain amount of damage in combat is the presence of so-called damage control parties. Trained in damage control, these men are stationed in key locations throughout the ship during general quarters, ready to limit the impact of wartime damage to the ship's viability by extinguishing fires, stopping progressive flooding, or cross-flooding undamaged spaces to prevent the ship from capsizing—tasks that could not be executed on unmanned ships. Reduced manning would also affect the accomplishment of house-keeping chores on a warship that is on the high seas for extended periods and vulnerable to the degrading effects of salt water, ship motions, and vibrations. These kinds of considerations tend to make the navy rather conservative about adopting automation concepts that proved useful in industrial sectors, notably aerospace.

Under the circumstances just discussed, there is a certain validity to the question, Why invest in automation if it does not get people off the ship? If we want to reduce the cost and size of our warships, we will have to adopt radically new operating concepts, not just simple auto-mation. Without such new concepts, I do not foresee major reductions in manning levels, regardless of how much automation is incorporated.

Combat Systems

Up to this point, I have been talking primarily about a ship's hull and about the propulsion plant that is provided to move that hull from point A to point B at a certain speed. However, a ship is not designed and built for the existential pleasure of seeing it go but to put a particular collection of weapons and weapons-related systems out on the ocean where they may be needed. It is those weapons and their associated systems—what we refer to as the combat system—that make a warship what it is and give it a reason for being.

To accomplish its mission, a warship must be able to detect ships, planes, and weapons—that is, targets—and verify that they are in fact enemy targets; to launch appropriate weapons at those enemy targets; and to direct those weapons accurately to their targets. This part of the discussion focuses on the particular means our warships employ now and are likely to employ in the future in accomplishing these functions.

We classify the various types of engagements our surface warships may enter into as antisubmarine warfare (ASW), antiair warfare (AAW), and surface warfare (SUW), which includes action against other ships or shore targets.

The basic ASW weapons are an acoustic torpedo launched either from shipboard or from a helicopter, and a standoff rocket (ASROC) that can carry either a homing torpedo or a nuclear depth charge within a range of about five miles. In the newest surface warship, the Perry (FFG-7) class frigate, the standoff rocket has been discarded in favor of helicopter delivery, which provides a greater range at the cost of some loss in bad-weather capability.

However, weapons are only the visible part of the ASW system. Much depends on the sensors, which in the U.S. Navy, are predominantly very powerful active sonars. Recently, the navy has begun to experiment with large, towed, passive arrays that will perform even better—especially against noisy Soviet submarines. In addition, the helicopters flown from many ASW ships can sow fields of sonobuoys, which greatly extend the effective range of shipboard ASW sensors.

Silencing is an essential and invisible element of surface-ship ASW design, but it is expensive in terms of other ship characteristics. For example, engines must be acoustically isolated from the surrounding hull structure to ensure that most of the engine-generated noise is not transmitted into the water. This means that greater machinery box volume is needed for a given horsepower or that a ship of a given size will have less power, hence less speed. Our efforts in submarine silencing have received appreciably more publicity than have our efforts in surface ships. Yet silence is an important characteristic of these newest U.S. surface ships.

One other ASW point well worth mentioning concerns reloads. Most U.S. ASW units have substantial reload capacity. For example, the new Spruance class destroyers are supplied with three launcher loads, totaling twenty-four rounds of ASROC as well as fourteen MK-46 torpedoes that are fired from onboard torpedo tubes and another six that are dropped by helicopter.

The Soviets appear to have applied their cruise missile technology to the SSN-14 standoff rocket, whereas the U.S. ASROC (and SUBROC) is a ballistic weapon whose course cannot be updated during flight. Elsewhere in the West, the Australian Ikara and the French Malafon use cruise-missile technology to deliver a homing torpedo. Presumably, Harpoon would offer the United States similar capabilities should a command-control link be developed for the basic antiship missile—a weapon that could be available for U.S. warships of the early twenty-first century.

Antiaircraft weaponry is a matter of great complexity. The U.S. Navy began antiaircraft missile development late in World War II and produced three major series: a large, long-range ramjet, Talos; a long-range, two-stage rocket, Terrier; and a short-to-medium range, single-stage rocket, Tartar. Rocket fuel development has not brought Tartar well beyond the capabilities of the early Terriers, and in fact, the two programs have merged under the designation Standard. Future anti-aircraft-missile ship construction is likely to be based on Standard, the missile component of the new Aegis weapons system.

As an almost last ditch defensive measure, the already-operational basic point defense missile system—essentially a modified air-to-air missile (Sparrow) launched from shipboard—is to be mounted aboard nearly all U.S. warships, so that even non-AAW ship types, such as the ASW frigates, will have some organic air defense.

The brief descriptions given above leave out the important question of the sensors and guidance systems that determine the value of the missile defenses—a concession necessitated by time and space limitations. However, I do wish to consider for a moment the new Aegis system, which is designed to overcome saturation attacks and does not require an enormous ship to carry it. Current missile-carrying ships are limited in the number of targets they can engage simultaneously, because each missile requires the full attention of a guidance radar from launch to explosion. However, the newest generation of missiles, Standard II and the airborne Phoenix, have autopilots, which means that they can be fired into the area of a target and then guided by a dedicated radar.

Systems such as Aegis require tracking radars capable of following many missiles simultaneously, so that the guidance signals can be properly directed at the right moment—and a fast computer is required to choose that moment. These requirements are being met by a light-weight, phased-array radar, Spy-1, and a computer that can readily be fitted into relatively small ships, thanks to recent advances in solid-state electronics. Spy-1 radars are expected to enter service aboard a new class of destroyer (DDG-47) in the early 1980s and can be expected to remain in production through the late 1990s. Thus, they are expected to dominate the surface-warship radar scene in the early twenty-first century.

The Command and Decision Element. Although not readily visible, another feature of a modern navy combat system is the naval tactical data system (NTDS), which enables ships in a task force to exchange information automatically and virtually instantaneously, permitting a task force to operate in a highly integrated fashion against incoming threats. This computer-based system makes possible a layered defense: Sparrow or Phoenix missiles out where the Soviet bombers must operate; then Talos; then Standard in both long-range and short-range forms; and finally, the point defenses. All must be coordinated if incoming threats are to be handled properly. I will discuss some expected advances in this area a little later.

Anti–Surface-Ship Missiles. As far as anti–surface-ship capabilities are concerned, the U.S. Navy has been relatively backward because of a lack of suitable targets. Even its aircraft have received relatively few antiship standoff weapons. This situation is about to change. United States forces are beginning to receive Harpoon, an autonomous antiship weapon launchable from ships, submarines, and aircraft, with a range of about sixty miles. Harpoon was designed for compatibility with existing launching systems, hence its limited dimensions (13.5-inch diameter) and relatively small warhead (500-pound blast type). For the future, the navy is developing the much bigger, longer-ranged Tomahawk (350 miles, 21-inch diameter), which will also be compatible with submarine torpedo tubes.

A strategic version of Towahawk will also be built. It will have a thermonuclear warhead, a range of about 1,700 miles, and a high-precision radar-mapping guidance system. Mounted on surface ships, Tomahawk would force the Soviets to conduct the equivalent of anti-carrier operations against all U.S. surface ships—quite possibly against all NATO surface ships. However, it is not clear what the status of Tomahawk will be under a new strategic arms limitation talks (SALT) agreement, or what, if anything, could be developed to replace this weapon, which is itself still in the development stage.

Missile Launchers. Against aircraft at long distances as well as against large antiship missiles launched from long-range, land-based aircraft, such as the Backfire, missiles have no rival. Their effectiveness naturally assures them a place on the warships of the early twenty-first century.

In addition to the MK-26/MK-13 rail launchers aboard current ships, recent and near-term developments will provide means (not in the current U.S. Navy inventory) of launching the variety of our present and future AAW/SUW/ASW missiles, specifically, individual box launchers mounted on deck and vertical launcher/magazines. The question arises, What launching system will the early twenty-first century surface warships use?

The best launcher mix appears to depend on the ship class. On a PHM hydrofoil boat (250 tons displacement), for example, the box launcher is the only practical solution because of weight and space limitations. When we reach the FFG-7 size of ship (3,600 tons), other alternatives, including a mix of types, become possible. However, in general, double-ender ships with vertical launchers for medium- to long-range missiles and above-deck launchers for short-range self-defense missiles offer an efficient launcher mix that maximizes rate-of-fire, minimizes weight and cost, and provides adequate redundancy.

The most cost-effective solution may not lead to a fierce-looking ship. To accomplish that objective would require that "the fierce look factor" be more heavily weighted than the cost and effectiveness factors. Therefore, a fierce look may not be realized in the future any more than it is today. Consequently, I expect that current criticism of U.S. Navy warships in comparison with Soviet ships will continue; that is, Soviet ships appear to be heavily armed with many weapons of different types and are generally fierce looking, while U.S. ships seem to have only a limited number of weapons, generally creating the impression of a lesser fighting capability.

With future availability of box and vertical launchers (that is, new hardware options), I anticipate a departure from the current practice of having one or two multipurpose rail-arm launchers per ship. Instead, we will see a shift toward a mix of vertical, box, and rail-arm launchers. However, since vertical launchers/magazines are even less fierce looking than the current MK-26/MK-13 arm-rail launchers, the appearance of our early twenty-first century warships will not be any fiercer than today's U.S. warships, even though their potency will be substantially increased.

Guns. A visible and important warship weapon not addressed so far is the gun. Guns are very versatile weapons at sea. The traditional role of the gun is in long-range ship-to-ship as well as ship-to-shore bombardment. After World War I, increasing proportions of gun and gun firecontrol development were directed toward antiaircraft defense. All three of these roles for the gun still exist and are expected to continue into the twenty-first century, but with substantial improvements.

At present, the U.S. inventory of modern naval guns consists of the 5 inch and the 76 millimeter varieties. Two new developments are nearing completion, one larger caliber and one smaller, that is, the 8 inch and the Phalanx 20 millimeter for Close In Weapon System (CIWS).

The smaller caliber Phalanx gun is designed as a last ditch defense in very close ranges of up to one mile. This gun is tied to a sophisticated radar that uses adaptive prediction procedures to keep its lock on the incoming missile or plane. In this role, the gun is expected to be on ships of the twenty-first century, unless high-energy lasers with virtually zero flight time prove to be so much more effective that they replace them. The 8 inch, 5 inch, and 76 millimeter guns have antiair, antiship roles in addition to their shore bombardment role.

The need for first-round accuracy against increasingly lethal and highly maneuverable targets and the desire to reduce ammunition expenditures gave rise to the "smart ordnance" concept. Borrowing from air-dropped guided munitions and missile technologies, the navy adopted terminal guidance for the 8 inch projectile. Because its semiactive laser seeker was adopted from the Paveway bomb, this weapon has become known as the Paveway guided projectile. The projectile program currently under way is expected to increase the effective range of the gun as much as 40 percent over that of contemporary ballistic ammunition, against both air and surface targets.

An even newer program has been started for a further extended-range 8 inch guided projectile to eventually replace the Paveway. This new 8 inch round is expected to exhibit a fivefold increase in accuracy over the Paveway. Since the cost of this sophisticated projectile will be only a fraction of the cost of a missile, and since we can talk about reloads per ship on the order of hundreds (versus tens for missiles), it is expected that large caliber guns of up to 8 inches will still be mounted on surface warships, and perhaps on smaller frigate-size ships, in the early twenty-first century.

Another hard-kill weapon expected to be a standard on warships of the twenty-first century is the high-energy laser (HEL). It appears from current R & D work that this kind of weapon will make an effective close-in weapons system, primarily because of its agile retargeting capability and zero time of flight. Ongoing navy and Department of Defense R & D programs are continuing to provide strong evidence that the HEL technology can be effectively employed as part of warship combat systems. Based on results from these R & D programs, a number of candidates will reach the engineering development stage in the form of an operational weapons configuration for the ship self-defense mission.

Electronic Warfare. So far I have discussed only "hard-kill" weapons. However, within the last decade it has become evident that an essential element of future war at sea will be electronic warfare (EW) systems of the highest sophistication.

In the past, most naval strategists preferred to place their faith in hard-kill weapons systems. EW was looked upon with much skepticism, and its importance was never fully appreciated. In fact, until the 1973 Arab-Israeli war, no navy had really experienced the effectiveness of electronic countermeasures (ECM) in combat. Since ECM is designed to thwart and deceive the enemy, hard evidence of its effectiveness is available only through the simulation of enemy missile attacks or actual experience. As a result, EW was relegated to a back-seat position relative to hard-kill options.

Having recognized the degree of current and future threats, most navies have started procuring EW systems for retrofit into their ships. Much of this EW effort has gone into the development of electronic support measures (ESM) systems, many of which are of a very sophisticated nature. A typical advanced system includes equipment for the reception, analysis, and identification of radar signals as well as for the classification of threats on a priority basis.

Other EW techniques that will definitely be used on U.S. warships of the early twenty-first century are jamming and decoys. Unfortunately, time does not permit me to say more about this subject.

Air Capability. Another very important feature of future surface warships is air capability. Through use of the organic air capability, the ships' sphere of influence will be greatly expanded by an over-the-horizon target detection, classification, and engagement capability that most likely will be used for surface-to-air and antisubmarine roles and even in such versatile activities as ECM, sea-air rescue, medivac, personnel transport, and vertical replenishment.

The current naval air capability, which reached the fleet about six years ago, is the helicopter-based light airborne multipurpose system (LAMPS). The function of LAMPS aircraft is to assist in screening operations and to redetect, classify, and attack submerged submarines whose presence in the tactical area is initially determined by some other means. With the availability of vertical/short take-off and landing (V/STOL) aircraft within the next decade, it is expected that surface warships will devote even more of their space and weight to air capability. With the advent of RPVs it is quite likely that these unmanned aircraft will also find their way onto surface warships. The ability to gain a third dimension for warships, such as that provided by its organic air capability, is not expected to be missed by warship designers of the twenty-first century. This later feature is expected to change even the outward traditional appearance of today's warships.

Anticipation of Future Combat System Changes. An expected change in warships toward the twenty-first century relates to the design and production approach to the ship and its major weapons system components. To keep pace with the changing technology of the payload, warships undergo modernization procedures several times during their life, each taking from 1.5 years to 2.5 years. Since this means that a ship is not available to carry out its mission for a significant percentage of its useful life, the navy has to have more ships just to maintain the required fleet size. It also means tax dollar expenditures of major magnitude for labor and materials invested in the modernization task at the shipyard.

To reduce such expenses, naval ship designs in the twenty-first century are expected to call for decoupling the payload from the platform in order to facilitate changes in either the payload or the platform (ship). The success of this decoupling concept depends not only on technological advances but also on the navy's ability to implement an entirely new approach to the design and procurement of warships. The technical aspects of this concept include:

- Standard size and standard configuration of weapons system stations to allow for rapid exchange of modules.

- Standard size distributive systems (cables, pipes, and ducts) and generation components (pumps, chillers, generators, fans).

- Extensive use of microprocessors to accomplish necessary computations immediately prior to weapon launch (with computers which are a component of each weapons module, as opposed to the current practice of using a centralized computer complex). As a result, reprogramming and the impact on the ship's central computer at the time of changeover from one weapon to another will be greatly reduced.

- Extensive use of multiplexing—a technique for carrying multiple signals on the same cable, using either time or frequency division to separate messages; multiplexing will also enable quick changeover from one weapon to another.

- Incorporation of fiber optics cabling systems; for example, to increase manyfold the number of messages which can be carried on a certain cable size. Fiber optic cable which can carry 2,000 simultaneous phone calls requires a 3-inch diameter cable compared with the many twisted pairs of copper wires in the current state-of-the-art technology.

Even without implementation of the above-mentioned new technologies, the trend toward the standard ship has already started. Several warships have already been redesigned using the same basic platform to enable the installation of revised weapons/sensor suites (for example, DD-963 to DD-993, DD-997, DDG-47).

Conclusion

Of the various hull forms discussed in this paper, displacement-types require fundamentally low technology; they use the least fuel per ton-mile; and they can be constructed for long endurance at relatively modest cost. SWATHS are energy efficient but a step up in cost and in level of technology. Hydrofoils and SESS are at the other end of the scale, requiring high technology and intensive energy; they have low endurance and are expensive. The hybrids offer corresponding advantages and disadvantages. Of the various high-performance craft, some exist only on paper and others have not gone much beyond the prototype stage. None has joined the fleet as an operational unit, and none is likely to prior to the early 1980s (with the exception of the single 250-ton hydrofoil that joined the fleet in 1977). Primarily because of the high acquisition and life cycle cost associated with the high performance hull types and the questionable value of high ship speed for most missions, their future application will be mainly for special missions where high speed is of great importance.

Advances in individual subsystem technologies will influence the characteristics of both high performance and conventional displacement warships, which I believe will still dominate the surface warship scene of the early twenty-first century. However, this apparently conservative prediction does not mean that surface warship design will be stagnant. Compared with the most recently commissioned destroyer, the DD-963 (7,600 tons), and the frigate to be commissioned early next year, the FFG-7 (3,600 tons), even the outward appearance of twenty-first century warships is expected to be different. Moreover, the introduction of significant new technologies may not be evident from a a cursory external observation. Some of the features contributing to this new appearance, as well as internal subsystem changes, will be:

- a greater portion of the ship dedicated to aviation capability;
- placement of the propulsion system much farther aft than at present, and, instead of the usual in-series arrangement with the propellers, propulsion prime movers will be vertically stacked and moved toward the stern;
- elimination of conventional stacks on ships powered by fossil fuel and much shorter intakes and exhaust that will not interfere with topside antenna arrangements;
- replacement of typical missile rail launchers; with more visible, single-purpose and dispersed missile launchers as well as some totally invisible vertical launchers;

- addition of close-in weapons systems such as the laser gun and the Vulcan-Phalanx gun/radar system;
- replacement of some typical rotating antennas with 3-D stationary face radars;
- transfer of Combat Information Center (CIC) and other key combatant functions down into the hull (versus the present more vulnerable superstructure location);
- changes in the character, size, and manning of the bridge to achieve a more functional space;
- standardization of basic ship configurations to gain mission flexibility and simplify combat system changeover;
- allocation of more space to electronic warfare systems; and
- inclusion of large caliber guns like the 8 inch on smaller warships than was possible heretofore.

In this rather long discussion of the advances expected to be incorporated into our surface warships of the twenty-first century, I certainly did not cover every function for which systems and equipment presently exist. However, I believe that those functions for which future developments will result in the most major visible impact on the warships as a whole have been covered.

Let me add a last word of caution. The mere existence of a certain technology is by no means assurance that it will be incorporated into new warships. The problem of adopting innovations by large bureaucracies like the navy is a very complex one. Which of the innovations discussed (as well as others that have not been mentioned) will be adopted into surface ships of the twenty-first century is as much a sociological as a technological issue. Therefore, the actual characteristics of our future surface warships will be a function of threat perception, the outcome of bureaucratic battles over which innovation to adopt, and the availability of technological advances.

Protecting the Fleet

David Kassing

The 1970s have seen a continuing debate about the size and structure of the U.S. Navy's general purpose forces. Some of the issues stem from changes in how the need is perceived. Other issues arise from the sharp increases in costs. But many of the issues arise out of concern about the basic ability of the fleet to perform its functions in the face of ever more capable opposition.

This paper considers some of the problems involved in allocating resources to protection of the fleet. It concentrates on the contribution of surveillance, antisubmarine, antiair, and antisurface ship systems to protection of the navy's main fleets.[1] The paper begins with a discussion of some of the concepts involved in thinking about protection of the fleet. Then it examines some of the major changes in technology and in forces that have made protection more difficult. The threats to the fleets are described briefly. The discussion then shifts to the problems of protecting the fleet in two kinds of conflict with the Soviet forces—tactical nuclear war and nonnuclear war. Finally, there is a brief assessment of the problems of protecting the fleet from attack by third-country forces.

Basic Considerations

To carry out its main wartime functions—gaining sea control and projecting power ashore—the fleet must be able to withstand enemy attack. There is a need for protective systems to help the fleet survive. But survival of the fleet is not, of course, the purpose of a naval force. Protection is only one of several capabilities essential to the main wartime mission.

The author is president of the Center for Naval Analyses. The views expressed in this paper are his, not those of the Center, the Department of the Navy, or the Department of Defense.

[1] That is, it focuses on issues involved in protecting the U.S. Navy's general purpose forces, not its sea-based strategic missiles, Poseidon and Trident. Also, although tactical air strikes at enemy ports and bases help protect the general purpose forces, these tactics are not examined in this paper. Nor does it consider the sometimes important contribution of mines and mine countermeasure forces.

The need to protect naval forces from attack creates a problem for naval planners at every level. Resources devoted to protection compete directly with resources devoted to the main naval functions. The ship designer—constrained by size or cost—realizes that self-defense systems, such as armor, detract from striking power. The fleet commander—constrained by size of available forces—realizes that deploying his force for better protection may detract from their ability to carry out their main functions. And the naval force planner—constrained by budgets—knows that resources directed to defensive systems will not be available for buying offensive capability.

The analyst can prescribe the correct principle for resolution of these problems. Resources should be devoted to protection up to the point where additional investment in protection adds as much to offense as would additional investment in offense. In short, an additional dollar should buy the same amount of added offensive punch for the fleet, whether spent on offense or on protection.[2]

The principle implies that protection will not be perfect as long as resources are limited. Technical questions aside, to provide a perfect defense against even a modest threat would result in a misallocation of limited resources. And, of course, resources are always limited.

Therefore, protection—and its complement, survivability—must be considered in probabilistic terms. Navy ships, as the saying goes, are designed to sail "in harm's way"; some will inevitably be harmed. All forces—whether attacking or defending—are vulnerable to some degree. Vulnerability per se, therefore, should not be the main issue in the sizing and structuring of naval forces. Rather, the question is this: Allowing for relative vulnerabilities, can naval forces meet a specific need at lower cost than any alternative means—and, if so, what types of naval forces should be selected?

Although it is easy to state the analytical principle for balancing between protective and offensive capabilities, putting it into practice is quite difficult.

First, there are problems of definition. An individual weapon system cannot always be categorized as either offensive or protective. For example, some defensive antiair missiles also have an antiship capa-

---

[2] This can be suggested by a simple example. Suppose that a defensive system with a life cycle cost of $25 million enables a carrier task group to fly an additional attack sortie a day. Suppose that the attack aircraft for offensive operations have a $50 million life cycle cost and add one sortie a day. Buying one less aircraft costs one sortie, but permits acquisition of two defensive systems, which, in turn, result in two sorties. If the threat is taken as fixed, the incremental returns to defense systems will fall, and this daily sortie capability of aircraft will increase. When the incremental sortie rates are equal—at, say, 1.6 per day—the proper balance between offensive and defensive systems has been achieved.

bility that can be used offensively; an antiship missile, on the other hand, may be used offensively or defensively, depending on the tactical situation. Another example is naval mines, which may be employed for either purpose.

Second, the key questions are obviously quantitative, and the numbers are hard to estimate. Just how much will specific offensive and protective systems add to the fleet's total firepower? The quantitative answers depend on a host of uncertain and uncontrollable factors: the time and place of the conflict, the amount of warning and the level of readiness, the skill and experience of the commanders, the contributions of allied forces, and so on.

Third, the reaction of the enemy to the introduction of new weapons is fundamental to any assessment of their effectiveness; this is very hard to determine. Clearly, the relative ability of the enemy to counter our new systems—such as Harpoon, Tomahawk, Aegis, shipboard intermediate range combat system (SIRCS), and lasers—affects the desired balance among these systems. Since we cannot know the potential enemy's intentions and resource limitations, we cannot be sure about his specific reactions, but we can be certain that the measures we take to protect the fleet will draw countermeasures.

These countermeasures can take any form—from adjusting a simple design to restructuring an entire fleet. Designers of individual systems must consider the characteristics of opposing systems, present and future. In the long run, moreover, the force structure of a navy adapts to counter the capabilities of the opposing force. The present balance between the U.S. and Soviet navies reflects the slow evolution of measure and countermeasure.

The U.S. Navy has long—and for good reason—relied on the carrier as the main element of its striking power: for strategic delivery in the 1950s, for conventional tactical air power and antisubmarine warfare in the 1960s and 1970s. Thus the Soviet navy has had a relatively "steady target" for a long period and could design its forces aimed at this relatively fixed threat. The Soviets have now evolved a substantial anticarrier force. Their task has become easier as a result of the reduction in U.S. forces from twenty-four carriers to thirteen in the past ten years. Viewed in this long long-term context, U.S. countermeasures to Soviet anticarrier capabilities are just beginning.

Changes since World War II

The ability of the fleet to protect itself has come into question largely because of five major changes since World War II. Four are technological developments—nuclear weapons, nuclear propulsion, antiship missiles, and ocean surveillance systems. The fifth has to do with changes in the composition of the U.S. Navy.

(1) Nuclear weapons. By the end of World War II, the U.S. Navy had developed reasonably effective defenses against air and submarine attacks. Major combatants built during the war were larger, more heavily armored, and more heavily armed than prewar designs. Antisubmarine warfare (ASW) techniques, employing surveillance, land- and sea-based air and ASW escorts, were well developed. In the Atlantic, the German submarine force was rapidly being defeated. In the Pacific, the fleet was able to withstand attacks by several thousand kamikazes.

But the 1946 tests at Bikini Atoll demonstrated the awesome effects of nuclear bursts on ships. Ships were sunk or severely damaged by bursts thousands of feet away. Radar and radio antennas were stripped away at even longer ranges. To achieve comparable destruction with conventional weapons would have required one or more direct hits. Clearly, this major increase in the lethality of antiship weapons reduced the need for large numbers of weapons and great accuracy of delivery. Indeed many, in both East and West, argued that the day of the large surface ship had passed.

(2) Nuclear propulsion. By the mid-1950s, both the U.S. and Soviet navies had learned to use nuclear power for submarine propulsion. The submarine thus acquired a tremendous increase in capabilities relative to those of antisubmarine forces. The submarine's main advantage is the stealth that comes from remaining submerged. A diesel submarine must come close to the surface to charge its batteries and can, at best, remain fully submerged for only a few days at a time. But nuclear power permits the submarine to remain submerged for two or three months at a time, making it much harder to detect and counter. In addition, nuclear power provides higher sustained speeds for reaching station and maneuvering in combat.

Nuclear power in submarines has reversed the situation that obtained at the end of World War II. The antisubmarine forces no longer hold the upper hand. As a result, the seas have become an attractive hiding place for strategic missiles. Moreover, our ability to protect our sea lanes from submarine attack has been sharply reduced.

(3) Antiship missiles. Although mines sank or damaged many ships,[3] the main antiship weapons of World War II were guns, torpedoes,

---

[3] Mines accounted for 7 to 8 percent of sinkings of naval forces and about one out of eight of the more than 12,500 merchant ships sunk.

and bombs. These weapons required the attacker's ships, aircraft, and submarines to come quite close to their targets, where they could then be engaged by defensive forces. Moreover, the chance that a single weapon could hit its target was small, and multiple attacks were generally needed to ensure a kill.

The antiship missile met both problems. Cruise missile technology permits the attacker's ships and aircraft to launch their attacks from outside the range of most defensive systems. In addition, cruise missiles have been designed to fly at supersonic speeds and along trajectories that make it hard for the defense to detect and engage them. The guidance and control systems incorporated into antiship missiles permit them to home in on the targets and hit with high reliability.

The consequences for the protection of surface ships are clear. The attacker's weapons can more easily penetrate the fleet's defensive systems, and the effect of each penetrating weapon is increased.

(4) Ocean surveillance systems. The ability to hide in the vastness of the oceans has always been one component of the fleet's ability to survive and carry out its missions. During World War II, the main surveillance systems were high-frequency direction-finding networks, which detected enemy radio transmissions, and aircraft, which searched visually and electronically. These systems added somewhat to our knowledge of the enemy's operations and our ability to find and attack his forces, but often intelligence—codebreaking, in particular—added much more. By and large, U.S. ships were free to range the oceans safely, if they took routine safety precautions—zigzagging, running dark, and so on.

Today, such measures are not enough to ensure ships at sea against being located. The technologies of World War II have been retained and improved. New technologies have been added. Long-range radars, mounted on satellites, can detect ships. Electronic signal monitoring equipment, out in space, can detect emissions from ships. There are infrared detectors and acoustic arrays.

As a consequence, large surface ships can be located with some precision almost anywhere on the oceans. There remain, however, difficulties in identification and tracking under some circumstances.

These technologies illustrate the difficulty in classifying naval capabilities as either offensive or defensive. Although these advances in technology make protection of the fleet more difficult, they can also help protect it, as will shortly be shown.

(5) Changes in the U.S. Navy. In addition to technical developments, changes in the size and composition of the U.S. Navy have added

to the difficulties of protecting the fleet. Over the past thirty years, the main striking power of the U.S. Navy has been concentrated in fewer and fewer units. In the 1950s, the last battleship was retired;[4] in the 1960s, a decline in carrier force levels began. This year, the navy will operate thirteen carriers and deploy four carrier task groups overseas.

Part of the reason for this concentration is economic: large ships generally provide more offensive capability per dollar invested, particularly if they are not opposed, as has been the case with U.S. carriers since 1945. Part of the reason is fiscal: older, smaller carriers were retired in the early 1970s when defense budgets were particularly tight. And part of the reason is the technical change just discussed. These changes have induced the navy to invest more in costly, sophisticated defense technologies; as a consequence, fewer units can be procured and operated.

Whatever the reasons, the consequences of this concentration are clear. It is easier for potential enemies to concentrate against the fleet, easier to achieve tactical surprise, and easier to knock out a substantial fraction of the forces.

Threats to the U.S. Fleet

The need to protect the fleet so that it can survive and carry out its main functions does not derive from technological developments per se. The fact is that all these technologies have been incorporated in the forces of our main potential opponent—the Soviet Union—and some have been incorporated in the navies of other potentially hostile nations. In the future, more and more navies will be acquiring the technologies that are now called "modern."

Soviet Navy. It is not necessary to detail here the growth in the Soviet naval forces and their capabilities. These have been described and examined by many observers.[5] Suffice it to say that the Soviet navy has

---

[4] The battleship *New Jersey* was returned to service for action off Vietnam and was again decommissioned in 1969.

[5] For example, Arnold Moore discusses the changes in the Soviet navy since the mid-1960s in a chapter on "General Purpose Forces: Navy and Marine Corps," in *Arms, Men, and Military Budgets: Issues for Fiscal Year 1977,* ed. W. Schneider, Jr., and F. P. Hoeber (New York: Crane, Russak, 1976), pp. 57-69. An earlier but more comprehensive analysis of the evolution of Soviet naval forces was done by Barry M. Blechman, *The Changing Soviet Navy* (Washington, D.C.: Brookings Institution, 1973). For a detailed description of Soviet naval forces

enough forces, widely deployed, to pose a real threat to the U.S. fleet in the event of war.

The Soviets cannot, however, allocate all their naval forces to attacks on U.S. surface forces. Although defense against carrier task groups has a high priority in their navy, the priority of strategic missions is even higher. Some portion of the Soviets' submarine and antisubmarine forces would probably be assigned to protection of their strategic missile-launching submarines—in enclaves or redoubts—and others would be directed against U.S. strategic missile submarines.

The main Soviet forces for attack on the U.S. surface fleet are cruise missile submarines and antiship bombers. Beyond question, the cruise missile submarines are designed and deployed against U.S. carrier forces. Today, the Soviets have sixty of these submarines, forty-four nuclear-powered and sixteen diesel-powered. Considering the requirements for overhaul and maintenance and the long distances they must sail to reach U.S. carrier operating areas, the numbers that can be deployed continuously are much smaller. In time of crisis or rising tension, the Soviets might be able to get as many as forty submarines into position to attack U.S. forces.

The Soviet navy also has a force of more than 300 bombers that are obviously designed and armed for antiship warfare. As many as 80 to 90 percent of them could be brought to bear against U.S. carrier forces. In addition, the Soviets might assign some of their long-range aircraft (LRA) to naval tasks.

Some Soviet surface ships are equipped with long-range (250-nm) antiship missile systems: the Kiev-class carriers, four Kresta I cruisers, and four Kynda cruisers. The Soviets are also equipping Kashin and Kildin class destroyers with a modernized version of the SSN-2, a thirty-mile missile. This program may eventually extend to all twenty-three ships of the Kashin and Kildin classes. Finally, the Soviets have seventeen Nanuchka class corvettes (850 ton) each armed with six 150-nm SSN-9 antiship missiles.[6] Some of these ships have occasionally deployed to the Mediterranean.

---

and their characteristics, see John E. Moore, *The Soviet Navy Today* (New York: Stein and Day, 1975).

Michael MccGwire has organized several conferences on the Soviet navy. Papers from these conferences have been published as Michael MccGwire, ed., *Soviet Naval Developments, Capability and Context* (New York: Praeger, 1973); Michael MccGwire, Ken Booth, and John McDonnell, eds., *Soviet Naval Policy Objectives and Constraints* (New York: Praeger, 1975); Michael MccGwire and John McDonnell, eds., *Soviet Naval Influence: Domestic and Foreign Dimensions* (New York: Praeger, 1977).

[6] John E. Moore, ed., *Jane's Fighting Ships 1977-78* (New York: Franklin Watts, 1977), p. 706.

To help these forces find their targets, the Soviets have significant capability for surveillance of the ocean's surface. They have been scanning the ocean's surface with radar satellites since 1967. During Okean-75, two radar satellites reported on a simulated convoy in the Bay of Biscay. According to *Aerospace Daily,* "The radar spacecraft are able to sweep large areas with a signal strong enough to provide data that can be analyzed by commanders on land or sea."[7] A radar satellite could detect large surface ships but might have difficulty in distinguishing warships from large, fast merchant ships.

The Soviets deployed a second type of ocean surveillance satellite in December 1974. Satellites of this type do not use radar and are therefore assumed to be electronic listening or television devices. Either type of sensor could help identify ships. An electronic listening satellite, of course, requires a "cooperative target," one that is operating its radars or radios.

Once the U.S. forces had been located, the Soviets could attack them with torpedoes and antiship missiles.[8] Of Soviet torpedoes, little can be said here. There are at least two types, and they may be armed with conventional or nuclear weapons.[9] But their range, speed, and guidance mechanisms are kept secret.

More can be said about Soviet antiship missiles. For a long time, the Soviets have led the world in the development and deployment of antiship missiles. At least ten different antiship missiles are now deployed in their fleet. Four can be launched from ships on the surface (including surfaced submarines), one can be launched at ships from submerged submarines, and five can be launched at surface targets from aircraft. The main characteristics of these missiles are listed in Table 1.

Table 1 shows a variety of stand-off ranges, missile speeds, and warhead types. The missiles employ radar and infrared homing mechanisms in the terminal stages of attack. About half the Soviet navy's antiship missile launchers are aboard submarines, 40 percent more are on aircraft, and the remainder are on surface ships.

Soviet naval writings and exercises tell us something about their plans for employing these weapons. Admiral Gorshkov has set down his views quite clearly. He expects future combat to be quick and decisive:

---

[7] From "Soviets Seen Operating Two Types of Ocean Surveillance Satellites," *Aerospace Daily,* June 2, 1976.

[8] The Soviets also have a substantial inventory of antiship mines, but most would probably be employed defensively in waters close to the Soviet Union.

[9] Kosta Tsipis, *Tactical and Strategic Antisubmarine Warfare* (Cambridge, Mass.: MIT Press, 1974), p. 93.

Table 1

Soviet Naval Missiles for Attacking Surface Ships

	Range (nm)	Speed (mach)	Warhead Type	Initially Operational
Surface-launched				
SSN-2 (Styx)	23	0.9	HE	1960
SSN-3 (Shaddock)	150–250	1.5	HE or Nuclear	1961–1962
SSN-9	150	1.0+	HE or Nuclear	1968–1969
SSN-12	250?	?	?	
Submerged-launched				
SSN-7	30	1.5	?	1969–1970
Air-launched				
AS-2 (Kipper)	115	1.0+	?	1960
AS-3 (Kangaroo)	400	1.5+	?	1961
AS-4 (Kitchen)	185?	2.0+	?	1965
AS-5 (Kelt)	120	0.9	?	1968
AS-6	150	3.0	?	1970–1971

Note: HE = high explosive

NATO code names are given in parentheses

Source: John E. Moore, ed., *Jane's Fighting Ships 1977-78* (New York: Franklin Watts, 1977), pp. 781–782.

The combat activity of the navy in the future will be a complex combination of simultaneous and successive combat operations, swift and brief, ending with the attainment of decisive goals . . .

In many cases the grouping of enemy naval forces will have to be destroyed within a very short, specified time, before they can fully employ their own weapons.[10]

This suggests concentration of air, surface, and submarine forces against the opposing fleet and the employment of surprise, coordinated attacks. This interpretation of the Soviet approach is confirmed by a review of the Soviet navy's major exercises. In both 1970 and 1975, major Soviet naval exercises showed that they could conduct coordinated antiship attacks in ocean areas near the Soviet Union where the U.S. fleet might well be deployed. In 1975, special emphasis was apparently placed on attacks on surface ships, mainly by aircraft equipped with

[10] Sergei G. Gorshkov, *Morskaya moshch' gosudarstva* (Moscow: Military Publishing House, 1976), pp. 370-371. I am indebted to James M. McConnell for the translation.

antiship missiles. In this exercise, the Soviet navy demonstrated that its surveillance, command and control and attack systems could organize and conduct attacks on an opposing fleet.[11]

Other Navies. Much of the new naval technology, both U.S. and Soviet, has already appeared in other navies; more is likely to find its way there in the next ten to twenty years. How far this trend goes depends on the costs of the systems and the budgets available for naval procurement.

Satellite surveillance systems are probably beyond the means of all but the superpowers, and the costs of nuclear submarines will preclude development and acquisition by all but a few states. This is also true of most modern ASW systems.

But there are now a variety of naval missile systems, as well as small-ship sonars, radars, and combat information systems, on the market. Some of this technology is now in the hands of smaller navies— for example, the Gabriel, the Seacat, the Otomat, the SS-12—and more will undoubtedly be acquired. Table 2 lists the main missile systems now available for antiship warfare. Note that most of these are relatively short-range weapons.

The diffusion of this technology is well under way. Antiship missiles are now employed by the navies of such diverse states as India, Malaysia, Senegal, South Africa, and Venezuela, as well as China, Cuba, North Korea, and Vietnam. In the future, therefore, even small nations may pose some threat to at least the surface forces of other nations.

These developments in the Soviet and other navies have been under way for many years and are well understood. They have given rise to considerable concern about the utility of large surface warships in future combat. When asked to give his assessment of attrition to U.S. forces in conflict in the mid-1970s, Admiral Holloway stated his views very clearly:

> I think I can answer it in one brief paragraph. In a conflict with the Soviets, I would expect very heavy losses to our carrier forces if nuclear weapons were used. If nuclear weapons were not used, I would predict about a 30 to 40 percent attrition of our carriers. We have no figures, statistically, because we have no view into the future with the infinite set of scenarios in which we could go to war. That is my judgment.

---

[11] For a more complete description of the 1975 major Soviet naval exercise see B. W. Watson and M. A. Walton, "Okean-75," *U.S. Naval Institute Proceedings,* vol. 102/7/881 (July 1976), pp. 93-97.

Table 2
Selected Antiship Missiles

Type	Developer		Range (nm)	Speed (mach)
Surface- to- surface	France	Exocet	20	1.0+
	France	SS.11	1.6	?
	France	SS.12	4.4	Subsonic
	Intl.	Otomat	32	0.9
	Israeli	Gabriel	14	0.7
	Italy	Seakiller I	6	1.9
	Italy	Seakiller II	13	1.9
	Italy	Seakiller III	24	1.9
	Norway	Penguin	14.5	0.7
	Sweden	Rb08A	100?	0.85
	UK	Sea Dart	40	?
Air-to- surface	France	Martel	30	?
	France	AS 20	4	?
	France	AS 30	6	1.5
	Italy	Airtos	6	1.5
	UK	Sea Skua	5?	?

Sources: *Jane's Fighting Ships 1977–78*, pp. 780–781 and General Dynamics Corporation, *The World's Missile Systems*, 3rd ed., November 1976.

If we go to war with a client of the Soviet Union, as we have historically since World War II, I think that carrier attrition would measure less than 10 percent.[12]

Protecting the Fleet in Tactical Nuclear Warfare

The task of protecting the fleet is most difficult if nuclear weapons are used to attack it. Tactical nuclear warfare is often equated to combat with low-yield nuclear weapons. In naval warfare, however, this is not necessarily true. Designers of naval nuclear weapons have not been constrained by any need to limit collateral damage or to permit early entry of their own troops.

Instead, designers of nuclear systems for naval use have incentives that could lead them to larger warheads. High yields can compensate for some of the common limitations of naval warfare, such as the diffi-

[12]U.S. Congress, Senate, Committee on Armed Services, testimony of Admiral James L. Holloway, chief of naval operations, *Hearings on Fiscal Year 1976 Authorization,* 94th Congress, 1st session, part 2, February 11, 1975, p. 742.

culty of differentiating the primary target from other enemy ships in the vicinity. They make the utility of "dead man" fuzing higher, and this reduces the effectiveness of ship-based protective systems. High yields offset the difficulties of locating a target precisely, and they reduce the need for terminal homing mechanisms that are vulnerable to decoying or jamming. Finally, they economize on scarce shipboard magazine space: Higher yields make for surer kills, and fewer weapons are needed per target.

From the viewpoint of protection, the defenses against nuclear weapons must be highly effective. Penetration of the protective screen by one or two weapons can spell disaster or, as Admiral Holloway put it, "very heavy losses."

Nevertheless, the debate over the size and structure of the U.S. fleet has barely touched on tactical nuclear war. Most broad assessments of naval capabilities—posture statements, net assessments, campaign analyses, general reviews—focus almost entirely on war with conventional weapons. This does not mean that there has been no work on naval warfare with nuclear weapons. Of course, there have been many point papers and memoranda, design studies, analyses of individual weapons systems, and even an occasional CNO statement of policy. But the basic rationale for the navy's tactical nuclear posture has, in fact, received little attention. The literature on naval warfare with nuclear weapons is negligible. Even the critics of the U.S. Navy seem to have ignored the issue.

There are several reasonable explanations for the omission. One is the great, steady emphasis that has been placed on planning forces for only the conventional defense of Europe. A second explanation is that the U.S. and Soviet navies are apparently the only ones with major tactical, independent nuclear programs. A third explanation is the most likely of all: During the 1960s, when studies were made of tactical nuclear warfare at sea, the results were both clear and distasteful. According to one assessment that was made at the time:

> It is apparent from official comment . . . that . . . a preponderance of opinion is emerging that, even on purely tactical considerations, the resort to nuclear weapons would not favor the West with its large investment in both military and civilian surface fleets.[13]

The recent assessment by Admiral Holloway also points out that tactical nuclear weapons would make a substantial difference in the survivability of surface ships. But just such considerations could well

---

[13] L. W. Martin, *The Sea in Modern Strategy* (New York: Praeger, 1967), p. 89.

have led the Soviets to emphasize the use of nuclear weapons against surface ships.

As we have seen, the Soviets do seem to be planning for the kind of short, sharp naval combat that is consistent with tactical nuclear weaponry. And their ships are faster but have less endurance; they have more immediate firepower, but many lack reloads for their missile launchers. Moreover, Gorshkov's writings do not distinguish between nuclear and conventional weapons.

There has been, then, a difference between the U.S. and Soviet navies in their basic attitude toward use of nuclear weapons at sea. This difference has followed from the differences in missions. Nuclear weapons are highly effective against both surface ships and submarines—in fact, all kinds of targets. For a long time, the Soviet navy had the mission of defending Soviet territory from carrier-launched strikes. A carrier is large and easy to find, but hard to sink with conventional weapons unless it is hit many times. A single nuclear weapon, however, can put it out of action.

The Western navies have felt most threatened by the Soviet submarine force. The hardest task for an antisubmarine force is detecting and localizing the submarine, not attacking it once found. Once a submarine has been localized, nuclear weapons can destroy it most effectively, but the kill radii are not large enough to compensate for normal uncertainties about the position of the submarine.

The general assessment, therefore, has been that nuclear weapons would be of little help to the antisubmarine forces of the Western alliance, but would greatly reduce the survival ability of carrier forces, amphibious assault groups, and convoys. One consequence is that thinking about tactical nuclear war at sea has been minimal in the West.

The U.S. Navy has retained nuclear weapons for several systems (see Table 3). The presence of nuclear weapons aboard U.S. ships may have a deterrent effect on Soviet use of nuclear weapons against them, as does the prospect that tactical nuclear war could quickly escalate to general nuclear war. Carrier forces or military convoys represent sizable military capabilities; destruction of them with nuclear weapons might easily evoke a nuclear response at a higher level. On the other hand, the Soviets may reason, as others do, that if use of nuclear weapons is limited to the oceans, escalation is much less likely because damage is limited to the military forces.[14]

Many factors that weigh in the tactical nuclear balance have changed since the 1960s. But, regardless of changing conditions, the

---

[14] See Edward Wegener, *The Soviet Naval Offensive,* trans. H. Wegner (Annapolis: U.S. Naval Institute, 1975), p. 11 for an example of this argument.

Table 3
Present and Potential Tactical Nuclear Weapons
of the U.S. Navy

	Present	Under Study
Antisubmarine	SUBROC ASROC Mk 45 torpedo B-57 bomb	Mk 46 torpedo
Antiair	Talos Terrier	Standard missile
Antiship		Harpoon Tomahawk

Source: F. P. Hoeber and W. Schneider, Jr., eds., *Arms, Men, and Military Budgets: Issues for Fiscal Year 1978* (New York: Crane, Russak, 1977), p. 127.

basic vulnerability of surface ships to nuclear weapons remains unmistakable. Dispersed carrier formations and convoys only increase the number of weapons needed to kill a given number of ships; they do not reduce the inherent vulnerability of ships to the nuclear blasts. Since the enemy has nuclear weapons and may be a net gainer from using them, U.S. forces must be designed for nuclear—as well as conventional—combat.

To do so may require major redesign of U.S. forces. Investing more in submarines and proliferating the numbers of small but potent surface ships are possible responses. High-speed surface effect or hydrofoil craft can be employed to enhance the survival ability of surface warships.

But such options do little to enhance the ability of carriers and convoys to survive nuclear attack. The cost of building a high-speed carrier of any size would be colossal, and merchant cargoes are likely to continue being transported in economical, relatively slow surface ships. The vexing problem of defending these high-value surface units against nuclear attack, therefore, will probably continue.

To defend such forces will require great improvements in protection, protection best achieved through destruction of the enemy's weapons before they can be launched. The prospect of tactical nuclear war should therefore shift emphasis even more toward destroying enemy aircraft and ships; here, land-based aircraft can make an important contribution. Better surveillance is needed to alert the defending forces in time to intercept the attackers before they can reach launch position.

Protection against nuclear-armed antiship missiles also requires air-defense missile systems of longer range. Such systems—designed to hit missiles with missiles—are likely to be complex and costly. Last-ditch point-defense missile systems are of only limited value; the ranges are too short.[15]

Before the navy decides on major changes in its force structure to reflect the possibility of sea war with nuclear weapons, it is important to examine the change that has taken place since the 1960s. Beyond the improvements in surveillance and the deployment of antiship missiles that have already been discussed, these evolutions include:

- changes in U.S. and Soviet forces
- improvements in acoustic detection
- changes in antisubmarine strategy and tactics, and
- new technology for tactical nuclear weapons.

It is hard to gauge the net effect of all these changes. But it is apparent that there is no simple solution to the problem of protecting surface ships from nuclear attack. War at sea with nuclear weapons would probably result in a quick double knockout of many Soviet and U.S. surface ships. The use of nuclear weapons would also accelerate the pace of antisubmarine warfare, the advantage going to the side with the best detection and localization systems. Here, the U.S. submarine force would likely prevail.

As long as U.S. forces are planned for conventional conflict, the ability to protect the fleet in nuclear war will derive mainly from developments for nonnuclear war. This is the subject of the next section.

Protecting the Fleet in Nonnuclear War

U.S. naval forces—like other general purpose forces—have been sized and evaluated for worldwide nonnuclear war with the Soviet Union. In such a conflict, the fleet would be most likely to engage Soviet forces in the Mediterranean, in the North Atlantic close to Europe, and in the Western Pacific. Under some circumstances, the U.S. and Soviet fleets might fight in the Indian Ocean as well. In any of these areas, the U.S. forces involved could include aircraft carriers, amphibious forces, and logistic support groups. The chief of naval operations has made this assessment of the threat these forces will face:

---

[15] The U.S. Navy is doing research on faster ships, better protective systems, and so on. The most important of these programs are discussed in the next section of this paper.

> We rate the Soviet maritime threat in this order. The most severe threat is their submarine force, the second most severe threat is the air force, and the third in ranking is their surface navy.
>
> The reasons for this are complex. They have a great many submarines and their submarines are hard to detect. On the other hand, they have a great many aircraft with air-to-surface missile systems, and the important thing about their air forces is that they can shift them rapidly from one theater to another and deploy them quickly against our forces. Their surface navy is formidable, that is true, but it is substantially less of a threat than the first two, because it takes longer to deploy, and can be kept under continuous surveillance.[16]

To attack a fleet, an enemy must take several steps. First, he must find out where it is and acquire enough information to predict its general movements. He must also find out enough to distinguish his main targets from other ships in the vicinity. Then he must prepare his forces for attack, arming them with the proper weapons and countermeasures. His forces must then get into position to launch their attack; to do this they may have to overcome several layers of defense. To coordinate an attack with several kinds of forces, moreover, requires extensive communication. The weapon must withstand additional defenses, select its intended target, and hit it with enough strength to put it out of action.

Accomplishment of these tasks depends on having detailed information about U.S. and allied forces, their system designs, and their tactics and countermeasures—information acquired in peacetime through intelligence and surveillance.

The likelihood of success in such an attack depends on a variety of circumstances. Planning a preemptive or surprise attack in peacetime is the least difficult of all.[17] Information about the positions and movements of the U.S. fleet can be supplied continuously by ships acting as "tattletales." Preparation for the attack can be leisurely and the attack timed carefully. Since shooting has not started, the attacking forces can move into position without opposition. Finally, if they achieve surprise, the defenders are likely to be less ready. Such an attack by the Soviets might focus on four or five U.S. task forces.

---

[16] U.S. Congress, House, Subcommittee on the Department of Defense, testimony of Admiral James L. Holloway, *Hearings on the Department of Defense Appropriation for 1978,* 74th Congress, 1st session, part 2, p. 523.

[17] Planning and conducting an attack in a peacetime exercise against one's own forces is, of course, even easier. Safety and resource constraints remove some of the problems that would complicate plans for a real attack. Because of these artificialities, one can discount somewhat the performance achieved in such major fleet exercises as Okean-75.

But, even a few days into a major war, circumstances are different, and mounting an attack on a U.S. carrier group is much harder. The attacker has less information—and poorer information—to go on, and his attacking forces face stronger, readier defenses.

Some of the protective measures that the fleet can take are implied by the attacker's problems. As with the attacks, effective protection requires a great deal of information about the enemy's forces, his weapon systems and operations, his state of readiness, and his tactics. Protective measures can be characterized in several ways, depending on when they take place, where they take place, what they protect, and how they protect.

Some of the most important protective measures must be taken in peacetime. Gathering intelligence about the enemy is crucial. But proper training and readiness are also vital to effective protection. How the fleet is operated in peacetime can help complicate the enemy's problem in formulating his attack strategy. If the defenders' deployments are varied, the enemy finds it harder to prepare his attack. Finally, the way the fleet is structured can either help or hinder the defense. As noted earlier, concentrating the fleet's main striking power in fewer and fewer units aggravates the problems of the defenders. But if the defenders disperse their striking power more widely—through reliance on larger numbers of smaller ships and proliferation of long-range cruise missiles on many ships—they can acquire a measure of protection that is not otherwise possible.

Other protective measures, such as jamming the enemy's communications, destroying his surveillance systems, and attacking his forces, are available in wartime.

Another way to characterize protective measures is by their location:

Forward protection—including forward surveillance and intercept systems—is far from the defender's naval forces.
Area defenses protect all the ships in the vicinity.
Local defense protects the area immediately around that fleet.
Point defense protects only the ships they are mounted on.

Protective systems can also be defined by the way they operate to nullify the enemy's attack. "Hard-kill" systems destroy his ships, aircraft, or weapons. "Soft-kill" systems neutralize the effects of the weapons by diverting them from their targets.

Just as Soviet forces may combine multiple elements to attack the fleet, the U.S. Navy employs multiple units to protect it. The kinds of protective measures just discussed are used in a great variety of combinations, a concept often called "defense in depth." Individual components of the defenses are designed to take advantage of various weaknesses in the opponent's position, weapons, or tactics. Generally, a defense in depth is well hedged—an enemy breakthrough in one technology or tactic will not defeat the entire defense. Rather, the defense will degrade gradually as specific elements in it are neutralized or destroyed.

The remainder of this section discusses protection of U.S. naval forces against submarine attack and air attack by Soviet forces. In each case, we will state the problem briefly, discuss the near-future (1980s) prospects for protecting the fleet—based on the U.S. Navy's development and procurement programs—and then look at more distant possibilities (1990s) on the basis of present trends in research.

Antisubmarine Warfare (ASW) Protection. The CNO places the Soviet submarine threat at the top of his list because the Soviets have many submarines and they are hard to find.

Locating the enemy submarines and sinking them before they can get into position to attack is the classic ASW problem. In World Wars I and II, the submarine's presence was often not revealed until it had made its attack. A torpedo hit on a ship then served as a "flaming datum," attesting to the presence of at least one submarine. Modern nuclear-powered submarines are even harder to detect than the conventional diesel-powered submarines of earlier times.

The addition of antiship missiles to the submarines' armament adds a further complication. These weapons travel much farther than torpedoes. Against the submarines that fire these cruise missiles, ASW forces must therefore provide protection at much greater ranges.

The best known technique for detecting a submarine is to listen for the noises generated by its machinery and hull. But the transmission of sound through the water varies greatly with acoustic frequency and such water conditions as temperature and salinity. Detection of submarines must therefore be viewed in probabilistic terms. Indeed, no single ASW action to detect or attack a submarine has a high probability of success. Consequently, ASW is a matter of probabilities. ASW relies on the cumulative effect of several different kinds of measures to defeat the submarine. The navy has procurement and development programs under way on a variety of measures to enhance ASW capabilities in the 1980s.

ASW in the 1980s. The best guess about antisubmarine technology in the 1980s is that it will move along currently recognized paths. For many years, some research managers held out hope for a breakthrough in ASW that would make it easy to see through the water and find submarines. So far, there has been no such breakthrough. Rather, improvement in ASW has resulted from a steady accretion of small advances in sensors and weapons. Much of the improvement stems from the application of modern computers and sophisticated methods to the processing of acoustic information. Still, the detection of submarines is likely to be the central ASW problem of the 1980s. Success in ASW will depend on coordinated action by diverse forces, organized to create ASW defense in depth.

The U.S. Navy monitors submarine activity in areas where enemy submarines might go to make their attacks. Information about any submarines detected can be passed to force commanders for use in directing their antisubmarine searches. The information provided by surveillance makes the search force far more effective than it would be if it had to depend entirely on random search of broad ocean areas. A force commander can also use this type of surveillance information to protect his forces by directing them away from suspected concentrations of enemy submarines.

The navy's surveillance systems are now being improved for the 1980s in several respects. Processing and communications techniques are being sharpened to increase the numbers of detections and to extract more useful information from those detections.

A mobile surveillance sensor system is being developed to provide fleet commands with a deployable capability in the 1980s. This system will augment the other surveillance coverage and will enhance surveillance in important areas—for example, where a carrier is operating.

Because most Soviet submarines must sail through relatively narrow choke points before getting into position to attack the U.S. fleet, a strategy of setting up protective barriers in these areas offers sizable advantages. The main elements of the Soviets' submarine force are in their Northern and Pacific fleets. Submarines based in northwestern Russia must sail through the Barents Sea and the gap between Iceland and either the United Kingdom or Greenland to reach the Atlantic. In the Pacific, some Soviet submarines are based in the Sea of Japan and must pass through one or another of the narrow passages between it and the open ocean. ASW forces in these passages can intercept Soviet submarines.

Which types of forces to employ depends on the distance of the barrier from the Soviets' defensive forces. Close to the Soviet Union, submarines are most suitable, being better able to survive. In more distant areas, remote from Soviet defenses, the barrier operations can be conducted by aircraft and surface ships. ASW mines can also contribute substantially to the effectiveness of barriers.

The U.S. Navy is improving every component of its ASW force for the 1980s. As many as forty nuclear attack submarines of a new class— the SSN-688s—will enter service in the 1980s. They should be even more effective than earlier generations of U.S. Navy attack submarines in barrier operations because their improved sensors will extend their detection range.

The navy's land-based patrol aircraft are being updated through the next generation of ASW patrol aircraft and will probably not appear in significant numbers until late in the 1980s. New sonobuoys and processors will improve the ability of the P-3Cs to detect, identify, and attack submarines.

In the 1980s, many ASW surface ships will be equipped with tactical towed array sonars. These will lengthen the range at which surface ships can detect a submarine, thus making them far more effective in a barrier role. To prosecute submarine contacts, ASW surface forces will employ the LAMPS helicopter. With sonobuoys, radar, electronic warfare equipment, magnetic anomaly detectors, and torpedoes, LAMPS will find and attack enemy submarines. Use of these helicopters greatly extends the range of ASW operations by surface ships.

Finally, the Captor ASW mine, long under development, should enter service in the 1980s. It will be particularly effective in antisubmarine barriers.

Most of the system will then be able to operate in ASW barriers and help provide U.S. carrier and amphibious forces with local protection. Land-based patrol aircraft, nuclear attack submarines, and ASW surface ships will all help screen task groups from enemy submarines. The improvements represented by SSN-688s, improved P-3Cs, and the tactical towed array/LAMPS team will also add to the fleet's ability to protect itself against submarines that penetrate outer layers of protection. In particular, the employment of nuclear submarines in support of carrier operations represents a fairly recent application of a highly effective ASW tactic. As we move into the 1980s, the fleet's tactics for operating SSNs in carrier groups should become significantly more effective.

The carriers themselves, of course, contribute to ASW capabilities. The S-3A, a modern carrier-based ASW aircraft, will be in the fleet throughout the 1980s. In addition, the carrier force itself may begin to change during the 1980s. If new, smaller carriers are acquired, the fleet's capacity for ASW in distant areas will be increased. Perhaps an even smaller V/STOL carrier or VSS (V/STOL Support Ship) will be built

312

by the end of the 1980s. Such a ship will rely largely on such helicopters as LAMPS for its ASW capability.

Unless the Soviets unveil a surprise in the form of a wholly new and greatly improved submarine force, the steady relative improvement that was observed in the 1970s in the U.S. Navy's ASW capabilities should continue in the 1980s.

ASW in the 1990s. Projections of ASW posture and capability to the end of the century are necessarily speculative. The best approach is to identify the research activities and concepts that may lead to successful applications, rather than predict the approaches that will be preferred when technical limitations, operational performance, and costs are better understood.

The types of improvements in acoustic ASW techniques sought in the 1970s will undoubtedly continue to be goals of research. For example, the Defense Advanced Research Projects Agency (DARPA) has a program in the technology of large acoustic arrays, studying hydrophone technology, telemetry of acoustic data, and deployment techniques for large arrays. Another DARPA ASW program is studying the oceans to determine the limits of performance by acoustic arrays.[18] Improvements in the power of computers for ASW will surely continue. Faster computing is important in ASW information processing, and computing is one field in which the United States holds a substantial technological lead over the Soviet Union.

Scientists have also been investigating a variety of nonacoustic techniques. Although more than one ASW technology has failed to fulfill its early promise, it would be unwise to write off nonacoustic techniques. Advanced research programs are looking at all the ways in which submarines disturb the natural environment, searching for alternative means of detecting submarines. The main signatures being studied are electromagnetic, hydrodynamic, and material.[19]

High-speed ASW surface ships also offer advantages for some ASW applications. Hydrofoils, surface effect ships, and wing-in-ground-effect (WIG) vehicles are much faster than conventional surface ships with displacement hulls. Although high speed is not essential to some ASW tasks—such as convoy escort—it permits a sprint-and-drift tactic that may yield higher search rates than is available to destroyers and frigates. Moreover, there are situations in which a force of modest size, prosecuting a moderately distant contact, may have to respond quickly. A

---

[18] Statement by the director, Defense Advanced Research Projects Agency of U.S. Department of Defense, *Fiscal Year 1978 Program for Research and Development,* February 1977, p. I-12.

[19] Ibid., p. II-30.

high-speed surface ship with a small complement of helicopters would be highly useful in such circumstances.

Submarines will continue to be effective ASW vehicles in the 1990s. Some research, now under way, may open the way to the development of small, militarily effective submarines. If research into low-drag technology is successful, deployment of a force of small submarines may become possible.[20] These submarines could both strengthen barriers and enable the barriers to degrade more gradually under attack.

The Navy Department is also studying the use of large land-based aircraft for ASW. Large aircraft offer several possible improvements in ASW. One is that they can carry more sensors or larger sensors and thus cover more ocean area. Another advantage is the possibility of carrying more on-board processing equipment, to improve the chances of detection. A third advantage is the capacity for more ASW weapons, enhancing the chances of hitting any submarine taken under attack. Larger aircraft could also have higher speeds, valuable in prosecuting distant contacts. In addition, they could stay longer on station.

Finally, there is V/STOL aviation, which may well find an application in ASW in the 1990s. The navy has embarked on an ambitious V/STOL program, one of whose early objectives is to develop an ASW V/STOL aircraft. Such aircraft, operating on many small V/STOL carriers or air-capable ships, could sweep large areas free of submarines and make those waters safe for convoys or carriers.

Antiair Warfare. The chief of naval operations described Soviet aircraft as the second most serious threat to the fleet because of their numbers and speed. If Soviet aircraft were to launch concentrated attacks on individual carrier groups, they could saturate the defenses, although saturation attacks could not, of course, be mounted against all U.S. carriers at the same time. To prevent saturation attacks, the navy must be able to exact so heavy a price from the enemy that such attacks will appear unprofitable.

As in the case of ASW, protection of the fleet from air attack relies on a defense in depth. Because events in air warfare move so swiftly, however, defense must succeed the first time; the probability of detection, intercept, and kill must therefore be high. It is true that a large warship is armored and compartmented so that it can take some hits from nonnuclear weapons, but each hit increases the chance that the ship or its weapons will be put out of action.

In addition to defense against aircraft, the fleet must be defended against antiship missiles launched from submarines and surface ships.

---

[20] Ibid., p. II-18.

In discussing protection against coordinated air-, surface-, and sub-marine-launched antiship missiles, it is useful to divide the process into two steps: destroying the weapon launcher before it can fire, and de-troying the missile after it has been launched.

Detecting aircraft is much easier than detecting submarines. Yet the speed of aircraft is so high and the standoff range of their air-launched weapons so great, that the battle for air superiority at sea is greatly compressed in time. There is therefore a premium on readiness and the ability to engage several enemy aircraft or missiles at once.

The problems of detecting and destroying submarines before they can launch their missiles have already been discussed. Defense against the SSN-7 submerged-launch antiship missile is severely limited; its short range (30 nm) and high speed (M 1.5) leave little time for the defense to react. Here again, therefore, there is a premium on readiness and quick response by the defense.

The problems posed by antiship missiles launched from surface ships are different. If the opposing surface forces are intermixed, the one that strikes first gains an advantage; it is sure to launch most of its antiship missiles. If the attack is a surprise, the advantage is even greater; retaliation may be delayed—or even avoided entirely. The vulnerability of surface ships to antiship missiles, therefore, makes for an unstable situation when two surface forces are in the same area at a time of high tension.

If the opposing forces are separated, however, surveillance systems may be so important that each side may find it necessary to destroy the satellites of the other. If they are, in fact, destroyed, the pace of naval warfare will turn out to be far slower than is now envisioned. The result can be likened to a night baseball game with many of the lights turned out and others dimmed. Pitchers would have trouble reading signals from the catchers. Batters would not get signals from the third base coach. There would be many errors and passed balls, and innings would last a long time.

Regardless of the fate of surveillance satellites, protection of the U.S. fleet from attack by large surface ships is not likely to be a serious problem. The Kievs, Krestas , and Karas would be the first of the Soviets' major forces to sustain heavy losses.

Defense against air attack in the 1980s. In the 1980s, the U.S. carrier forces will still be able to destroy the Soviet surface fleet. This capability will be strengthened by the wide deployment of Harpoon antiship missiles and the longer-ranged Tomahawk missiles. Problems in long-range targeting will be largely overcome by a variety of on-board and off-board surveillance and targeting systems. The Soviet surface fleet can be expected to launch many of its missiles at U.S. forces on D-day. Protection against these missiles will require improved antimissile systems and soft-kill systems. After D-day, the Soviet surface forces will add little to the threat to the U.S. fleet.

The main elements of the U.S. fleet's protection against Soviet aircraft in the 1980s—land-based early warning systems, land-based interceptors, the large-deck carrier, and the F-14/Phoenix system—are already in place. NATO surveillance and early warning systems will be in position to detect Soviet aircraft long before they can reach the operating areas of the U.S. fleet. Although Soviet air attacks may be flown by circuitous routes or at low altitudes, either option will reduce their attack radius. In many areas, land-based interceptors will be able to engage Soviet attackers long before they can arrive at their launch points. In these engagements, some of the attackers will be killed and, fully as important, the coordination of the Soviet attack will be broken up.

Soviet bombers that survive this combat with land-based interceptors and reach the fleet operating areas will be engaged by carrier-based forces. The E-2C aircraft will provide early warning and aerial combat coordination. The F-14A, now widely deployed, has a substantial capability for intercepting the Soviet navy's strike aircraft. Cumulative attrition by land-based interceptors and carrier-based F-14s will greatly reduce the number of antiship missiles actually launched at U.S. surface ships.

In the late 1980s, the ability of the fleet to detect, intercept, and either destroy or evade antiship missiles should have been greatly enhanced by newly introduced systems. The most prominent of these is Aegis. This system will have a fixed, phased-array radar resistant to enemy countermeasures. The system will be managed or directed by modern computers. Aegis will incorporate a rapid-fire launching system for the new SM-2 missile. Introduction of the Aegis system will substantially increase the fleet's ability to defeat enemy missiles. The net effect will be to make saturation of the fleet's air defenses far more difficult. In the 1980s, deployment of this large, expensive system will be limited to the few large surface combatants that operate with carrier task groups.

A new point defense or close-in weapons system, Phalanx, is being developed for last-ditch defense against antiship missiles. This is a 20 mm Gatling gun that has its own search and track radars and fire control system. The system is small enough to be mounted on a wide variety of U.S. Navy ships.

316

Electronic warfare (EW) systems will also be important in protection of the fleet in the 1980s. Their purpose will be to provide electromagnetic warning and surveillance. EW systems will, in addition, incorporate active countermeasures to deny targeting information and to decoy enemy weapons away from their targets. As with "hard-kill" defenses, EW will make extensive use of computers to correlate detections, identify threats, and pick the right responses.

Defense against air attack in the 1990s. Improvements in fleet protection against air and missile attacks will continue through the 1990s. U.S. antiship missiles should be more sophisticated and better able to locate Soviet ships and penetrate their defenses. Improvements in surveillance systems will make employment easier. Consequently, the threat from Soviet surface ships should remain the least serious part of the problem of protecting the fleet.

Incorporation of the Aegis systems into the fleet is likely to continue into the 1990s. Undoubtedly, parts of the system will be modified and improved to keep pace with developments in Soviet missile and EW technology.

A new system—shipboard intermediate range combat system (SIRCS)—is planned to arrive in the late 1980s; it will be available in sizable numbers in the 1990s. SIRCS is intended to provide intermediate-range surface-to-surface and self-defense capabilities to naval surface combatants not equipped with Aegis. In its present concept, the system is designed for fast reaction, sizable area coverage, and potent firepower. When deployed, SIRCS will greatly enhance the self-protection of naval combatants.

Scientists are also studying the use of high-energy lasers in naval warfare.[21] This work involves research into phenomenology and development of individual components of a laser system, such as a pointer/tracker and automatic aimpoint selection. Although this program is directed at use of high-energy lasers for protection against missiles, it is far too soon to tell what roles high-energy lasers may play in the fleet of the 1990s.

The high speed of aircraft means that there is a premium on early detection of their launch and tracking of their progress. The air force reportedly has at least two programs under way for detecting and tracking aircraft from space. One, called Teal Ruby, would employ infrared detectors for spotting aircraft. The second, called HALO, would employ

---

[21] See, for example, D. M. Cordroy et al., *Meteorological Sensitivity Study on High Energy Laser Propagation,* Naval Research Laboratory Report 8077, January 1975.

optical means. Either system might provide early warning of air attacks directed toward the fleet from Soviet naval airfields.[22]

Aircraft will continue to play an important role in defense against aircraft in the 1990s. Investigations of roles for large land-based aircraft in naval warfare include consideration of ways in which these aircraft can strengthen the fleet's air defenses. One possible role is airborne early warning; the possibility of arming the plane with air-to-air missiles must also be considered.

The V/STOL program is a more likely candidate for enhancing the role of aircraft in protecting the fleet in the 1990s. The navy's program for V/STOL includes development of a V/STOL fighter by the mid-1990s. Such a capability would raise a number of possibilities for combating attacks on the fleet in the 1990s.

Future Developments

There is no evidence to suggest either that the day of the surface fleet has passed or that the problems of protecting the fleet will be easily solved. The problems of defending the fleet require consideration of these important possibilities:

1. The fleet can be so disposed as to minimize the risk and damage of surprise attack. Dispersing the fleet's striking power and concealing its operations—as much as possible—are types of actions that can improve the readiness of forces by operational and tactical changes that are relatively inexpensive.
2. The navy can maintain its superiority in submarine design by investing the resources and employing submarines in a variety of antisubmarine roles.
3. Naval warfare will rely more than ever before on intelligence. The navy's planning can provide for denying the enemy vital information about the fleet and its weapons, sensors, and operations.
4. Protection of the fleet will require coordinated action by land- and sea-based systems, including some outside the navy's control. To maintain coordination in the face of enemy countermeasures will require responsive systems of command and control.
5. Surveillance systems may prove to be so important that each side will try to destroy those of its opponent. If these systems

---

[22] See Barry Miller, "Aircraft Detection System Advances," *Aviation Week and Space Technology,* June 20, 1977, pp. 22-23.

are, in fact, destroyed, the pace of naval warfare will turn out to be far slower than is now envisioned. The navy should plan for this possibility.

6. To enhance the effectiveness of the navy's own ASW and to provide it with information about possible countermeasures, the navy can conduct more research in nonacoustic techniques for detecting submarines.

Protecting the Fleet against Smaller Navies

General purpose forces of the navy and marine corps have served as instruments of national policy in a wide variety of situations. According to a Brookings Institution report, naval units participated in more than 80 percent of 215 incidents in which the U.S. leadership used armed forces between 1945 and 1975.[23] In some of these cases, armed opposition was possible; in a few instances, it took place.

In the future, military opposition may be much more effective, as a consequence of the diffusion of modern naval technology. In addition, increases in national claims to the sea and its resources add to the possibility of naval warfare.

The consequences of the new technologies for naval warfare have received little discussion, although some of these "new" technologies have been in naval use since 1958. Since Soviet-made Styx missiles sank the *Eilat* in 1967, perhaps 100 to 150 antiship missiles have been fired in anger, sinking another destroyer, ten to fifteen smaller naval craft, and about five neutral merchant ships.

There is a growing belief that new types of weapon systems will make smaller navies much more capable, for example, of causing temporary embarrassment to superpower navies. The new technologies mentioned most often are: precision-guided weapons, remotely piloted vehicles, V/STOL aircraft, surveillance and targeting systems, and electronic measures and countermeasures. One main theme is that the new technology favors defense forces. Large, visible attacking units, such as carriers and cruisers, are thought to be more easily detectable by the new sensors and more vulnerable to attack with the new weapons. For smaller navies, however, such potentialities lie largely in the future.

At present, the navies of most small nations have only local defense functions and largely outdated equipment for performing them. Some of these countries are modernizing their forces, more with an eye on each other than with any plan to counter the forces of larger naval powers,

[23] Barry M. Blechman and Stephen Kaplan, "Armed Forces as a Political Instrument," *Survival*, vol. 19, no. 4 (July-August 1977), p. 170.

such as the United States, the Soviet Union, the United Kingdom, or France. Modern weapon systems in the hands of a small navy may help deter attack by neighbors, and some could undoubtedly win local naval conflicts. None, however, is equipped to deny local seas to a superpower or to project naval power at a distance.

Could a smaller navy—with frigates and patrol craft mounting antiship missiles, with new diesel submarines, with land-based air, with precision-guided munitions, and so on—stop the navy of a superpower from projecting forces into an area? Probably not.

There are two main reasons. One is relative economic strength. A small navy with new technology might inflict an initial shock if it struck first at the U.S. fleet. We would be less likely to engage in gunboat diplomacy against any nation with such a navy. But a U.S. Navy that is sized to fight the Soviet fleet could, obviously, soon muster the forces to obliterate even the best of the smaller navies.

More importantly: The U.S. and Soviet navies have great incentives for staying ahead in the technology of naval warfare; they will probably stay well ahead of other arms producers. Moreover, neither navy is likely to release its best and latest technologies to any but its firmest allies—and perhaps not even to them. In conflicts with smaller navies, therefore, the U.S. fleet is likely to encounter older or less capable systems and in relatively small numbers.

Predicting the possible evolution of specific small navies is difficult. The future of these forces depends on domestic stability, regional problems, economic development, international alliances, and so on. But it is possible to see what $100–150 million a year spent on naval forces might buy for a typical or nominal smaller navy.

Such a force would contain 150 antiship missile launchers at most and would lack adequate capabilities for distant surveillance and targeting.[24] Experience suggests that smaller nations have even more problems, including maintenance, training, and reliability. Even this nominal modern navy, therefore, would probably be unable to muster more than half its forces for an attack. In all likelihood, such a navy would lack the real-time command and control capability to launch a well-coordinated air, surface, and submarine attack. The U.S. fleet, accordingly, would face no more than a poorly coordinated attack by small numbers of older missiles.

Under such circumstances, such a force might still take on a U.S. carrier task group. In the 1990s, the U.S. group would probably include a single large-deck carrier or several smaller carriers with v/STOL air-

---

[24] Information about the movements of the U.S. fleet could, of course, be furnished by the Soviets.

Table 4
Nominal "Small" Navy of the Future
(millions of 1977 dollars)

	Number	Procure- ment Cost	Annual Operations	Twenty-Year Systems Cost
Diesel submarines	3	$37.0	$3.5	$321
Missile frigates	2	84.5	5.0	469
Frigates	2	70.0	4.0	300
Corvettes	5	40.0	3.0	500
Fast patrol boats	10	12.0	0.7	260
P-3 aircraft	10	18.0	0.8	340
ASW helicopters	10	3.0	0.3	90
Subtotal: Force investment and operational costs				$2,280
Command, training, and administration				
(⅓ of operating costs)				115
Total cost				$2,395
Average annual cost				$ 115

craft. In either case, it would have 75 to 100 tactical aircraft, all of them at least as capable as today's F-14s, S-3s, A-6s, and E-2Cs. There would probably be two Aegis/SM-2 ships in the force and about six other surface combatants. All would have the Phalanx CIWS and up-to-date electronic warfare systems. Submarines would accompany them. The force would also have substantial numbers of Harpoon or Tomahawk launchers. Finally, the commander on the scene would be supported by remote systems for ocean surveillance and computerized systems for command and control.

Unless the small navy achieved complete tactical surprise, its strongest attack could probably inflict only slight damage on the U.S. force. The U.S. force's surveillance, coastal aircraft, and Tomahawk missiles would enable it to stand off and attack the enemy's small surface force from a distance. Its airborne early warning aircraft and fighter aircraft should be able to blunt the enemy's air attack and turn it. And the Aegis systems could easily handle any enemy missiles that survived to be launched at the task group.

Admiral Holloway estimated that the U.S. fleet might lose 10 percent of its carriers in combat with a Soviet client, that is, one to two carriers. The analysis just presented suggests that this is an overestimate. At worst, combat with the nominal small navy might result in one or two hits on a U.S. carrier.

The Size of the Fleet

C. A. H. Trost

with the assistance of

L. Wayne Arny III

The question of the size of the fleet as we approach the twenty-first century is extremely complex. The answer is rooted in the quality and size of the current fleet, the quality and size of the perceived future threats, the cost of desired future capabilities, and other fiscal *and conceptual* constraints under which we will be forced to operate. As Congressman Aspin has recently pointed out, since 1973 the U.S. Navy has been unable to predict with any accuracy what the size of the fleet will be in each succeeding year.[1] The projected size often varies from month to month as various forces act and react upon the system. To attempt to predict the exact size in 1999 would be pure folly, but certain desired directions and concepts can be delineated, and some of the major issues outlined.

In the spring of 1977 the U.S. Navy was asked to declassify a confidential paper, "The Navy of the 1970 Era," issued in 1958 during Admiral Arleigh Burke's tenure as chief of naval operations. This document was prepared twenty years ago, nearly as far in the past as the twenty-first century is in the future. A comparison between the forces described in that paper and the actual forces in existence today (Table 1) provides an interesting example of the problems inherent in discussing the future size of the fleet and illustrates dramatically the potential gap between prediction and reality.

Background

Since the late 1960s the number of navy ships has significantly declined (see Table 2). Although the fleet is smaller today than it was before World War II, it is certainly more capable now than in the prewar years. But there has been a substantial loss in capabilities relative to the Soviet Union, which has emerged as a major naval power.

The reason for this decline in the U.S. fleet has been the failure to construct sufficient new ships to replace those becoming obsolete

---

[1] Press release from Congressman Les Aspin, August 29, 1977.

Table 1

Comparison of 1957 Projections with Actual Naval Forces in 1977

Naval Force	1957 Projection of Forces in 1970s	Actual 1977 Forces
Missile-launching submarines, all nuclear	*50*	*41*
With Polaris or greater	42	41
With short-range missiles	8	0
Surface striking force	*87*	*41*
Modern aircraft carriers (with nuclear prop)	12(6)	13(2)
Large training carriers	3	1
Guided missile cruisers (with nuclear prop)	18(12)	27(7)
Guided missile frigates (with nuclear prop)	54(18)	— a
Antisubmarine warfare (ASW) forces	*398*	*205*
ASW aircraft carriers	9	0
Submarines (with nuclear prop)	75(65)	77(67)
Destroyers	72	64 b
Ocean picket ships	60	0
Ocean escorts	182	64 c
Amphibious forces	*90*	*62*
Helicopter assault	18	8
Assault transports and landing ships	58	47
Command and support ships	14	7
Mine warfare and small patrol	*110*	*10*
Auxiliaries	*190*	*105*
Fast underway replenishment	50	39
Other	140	66
Total	*927*	*464*

a DLGS—a designation no longer used.
b Includes 39 guided missile destroyers (DDGs).
c Includes 6 guided missile frigates (FFGs).
Source: Department of the Navy, "The Navy of the 1970 Era" (1958), p. 7; Department of the Navy, Ships Management Information System, *Active Fleet Historical Force Levels,* September 7, 1977.

(after about twenty-seven years of service, on average). Although individual ships may be retained for a few years beyond their expected service life, the long-term size of the U.S. Navy is largely determined by its building program.

Table 2
Size of The U.S. Active Fleet

Type of Ship	1940	1945a	1950b	1955c	1968d	1976	1977	Change 1968–1977
Carriers								
First line	6	25	11	16	15	13	13	−2
Support	0	73	4	8	8	0	0	−8
Surface combatants								
Cruisers e	52	95	14	20	34	26	27	−7
Destroyers	239	372	137	249	220	69	64	−156
Frigates	0	365	10	64	50	64	64	+14
Submarines								
Strategic	NA	NA	NA	NA	41	41	41	0
Nuclear-attack	NA	NA	NA	1	33	64	67	+34
Nonnuclear	101	237	72	108	72	10	10	−62
Amphibious								
Helo-carriers	NA	NA	NA	NA	8	8	8	0
Other	0	1,256	91	175	151	54	54	−97
Support ships	208	3,295	279	389	344	127	116	−228
Total	606	5,718	618	1,030	976	476	464	−512 (−52%)
Average age (years)			5.4	9.9	17.5	14.0	14.2	

NA: Not applicable.
a World War II high.
b Post–World War II low.
c Korean War.
d Vietnam War high.
e Includes battleships, fiscal years 1940–1968.
Source: Director of Naval History, *Active and Reserve Fleet Force Levels (1908–1973),* letter serial 1748PO93H, April 20, 1973; Ships Management Information System, *Active Fleet Historical Force Levels.*

Three conditions contributed to the current situation in which an insufficient number of ships are being built to maintain the size of the fleet: (1) an overriding requirement to finance the Vietnam War; (2) the rising cost of construction because of inflation and the need to build in greater capabilities to match the increasing threat; and (3) decommissioning in the early 1970s of older, less capable ships to finance a higher rate of new construction and modernization. The increase in decommissionings reflected a judgment that some risk was necessary during the 1970s in order to construct greater numbers of more capable ships for the future. When the national strategy is balanced against the projected threat, it becomes apparent that the overall size of today's fleet cannot be reduced any further. It is also apparent that an overall increase in the size of the U.S. Navy can come about only through an increase in funds for new construction.

Role of the Navy

The size of the U.S. Navy is a function of the national strategy, the potential threat, and judgments as to the acceptable level of risk in carrying out that strategy. The national strategy of the United States is based on considerations of the geopolitics of the two superpowers, the United States and the Soviet Union. The U.S.S.R. is located entirely within the Eurasian land mass. Because its principal allies, the Warsaw Pact nations, are contiguous to its western border, the U.S.S.R. has no need to cross oceans to support them. Similarly, conventional attacks on Russian soil would most likely come from continental adversaries—NATO and the People's Republic of China.

The United States, on the other hand, has no potential enemies on its borders. One U.S. state, several U.S. territories, and forty-one of the forty-three nations with which we have defense treaties and agreements, all lie overseas. It is clear that support of U.S. allies as well as attacks against the United States must be overseas operations. Thus, the oceans serve both as barriers for our defense and as avenues to extend our influence abroad. Although technology has revolutionized our communications and transportation systems, most cargo necessary for both peacetime commerce and wartime military operations is still transported by ships. These fundamental facts mold the development of our foreign policy and related military posture.

Within this strategy, the U.S. Navy has two primary responsibilities: (1) to provide components of our forward deployed forces; and (2) to ensure the security of the sea lines of communication between the United States and its overseas forces and allies. Forces maintained in the highest attainable state of combat readiness and organized into numbered fleets are currently deployed to those areas of the world of critical importance to our security. This posture provides visible reassurance to allies, permits rapid response to local crises, and deters aggression. Should deterrence fail, the initial combat elements necessary for the protection of our essential sea lines of communication are already in place and can immediately initiate combat operations against an aggressor. At the same time, such a posture facilitates rapid reinforcement of both land combat and sea control forces.

This military posture supports two key elements of our foreign policy: deterrence and mutual support with allies. To deter aggression, we seek to maintain a military capability which, without being provocative, confronts an adversary with a credible threat that, should he contemplate an armed initiative, he faces a substantial risk of failure. For mutual support, we seek both to sustain our allies' belief that we will come to their aid if attacked—because our interests are interwined with theirs—and to reduce the overall costs of defense by integrating forces and fully using all available allied capabilities. Successful execution of this strategy thus depends upon a military posture adequate in both overall size *and* capability.

Threat Trends

The Soviet Union clearly poses the principal maritime threat to the United States. It alone has the strength to threaten our ability to execute our strategy. Other coastal states with modern weapons can temporarily threaten U.S. forces or impede their mobility, but these nations lack the numerical strength to sustain that threat in the face of determined U.S. opposition. In contrast, Soviet capabilities have been growing in terms of both the sophistication of their weapons systems and their demonstrated operational capabilities. Table 3 summarizes some of these trends.

Since 1970 Soviet missile-equipped surface combatants have increased by 25 percent, affording the Soviets a greater ability to strike at opposing surface forces while defending themselves against air attack. Soviet nuclear submarines have increased by well over 60 percent, while older, less capable diesel boats have been retired.

These shipbuilding trends have two important practical consequences. First, the Soviet navy has significantly increased its qualitative war-fighting capabilities, even though its total force levels have remained relatively unchanged. Second, the Soviet Union now has the capability to extend its naval operations significantly beyond its home waters. In the international naval exercises, Okean 70 and 75, the Soviet navy showed worldwide command and control of anticarrier and antisubmarine operations and of combined ship, submarine, and aircraft operations against convoys, thereby demonstrating its transformation into a true open-ocean navy.

In the course of modernizing its navy, the Soviet Union has demonstrated its ability to build large numbers and types of ships. As shown in Table 4, the Soviet rate of new construction has outpaced that of the United States by more than five to one.

327

Table 3
Soviet Naval Trends

Type of Ship	November 1970	July 1974	August 1975	July 1976	July 1977	Change 1970–1977
Carriers	0	0	0	1	1	+1
Surface combatants						
Missile equipped	48	64	66	57[a]	60	+12
Other	166	158	151	172	167	+1
Submarines						
Nuclear	85	120	130	140	144	+59
Nonnuclear	265	200	195	195	194	−71
Amphibious	100	100	85	80	84	−16
Patrol craft						
Missile	160	135	135	135	138	−22
Other	520	550	540	560	355[b]	−165
Mine warfare	315	260	255	295	382	+67
Auxiliaries	700+	750	760	765	777	NA
Total	2,359+	2,337	2,317	2,400	2,302	

Out-of-area Operations

	1966	1968	1970	1972	1974	1976
Thousands of ship days	7.8	22.0	18.7	20.0	50.7	44.5

NA: Not applicable.

[a] Defense Intelligence Agency (DIA) redesignated missile destroyers as those with surface-to-air missiles (SAMs) greater than a range of ten nautical miles. Previous years include destroyers (DDs) with short-range SAMs and surface-to-surface missiles (SSMs).

[b] DIA deleted some types of small patrol boats from the order of battle (OOB).

Source: Defense Intelligence Agency, *Unclassified Soviet/Communist Bloc Navy Order of Battle;* U.S. Congress, House Armed Services Committee, *U.S. vs. Soviet Out-of-Area Ship Days,* February 4, 1977.

Table 4
U.S. and Soviet Shipbuilding Deliveries, 1961–1975

Type of Ship	U.S.S.R.	U.S.
Ballistic missile submarines	54	38
Attack submarines	177	57
Major surface combatants (3,000 tons and more)	57	117
Major surface combatants (1,000–3,000 tons)	83	2
Minor surface combatants (incl. amphibious)	1,175	71
Underway replenishment ships	4	25
Other support ships	199	17
Total	1,749	327

Source: Joint Chiefs of Staff, *Soviet Shipbuilding Deliveries, 1961–1975,* May 20, 1976.

Basic Navy Functions

In a recent statement, the U.S. chief of naval operations, Admiral James L. Holloway III, stated that "The true measure of the Navy's value to the nation is its ability to carry out its mission regardless of time, place, or circumstances now and in the future."[2] The mission of the U.S. Navy is to conduct combat operations at sea. Within that mission the two basic functions are sea control and power projection. Sea control is the more fundamental and is a prerequisite for tactical power projection. Power projection includes tactical as well as strategic projections and is a subset of sea control. These are interdependent functions rather than separate options requiring different forces and philosophies.

The U.S. Navy must be able to exercise sea control against a threat which is now and will continue to be three-dimensional. An attack at sea, as has been demonstrated, can come from the air, the surface, or the subsurface, or from any combination of these sources. Against such a threat no single platform is totally effective. Accordingly, the fleet must consist of balanced and coordinated forces.

U.S. forward deployed forces—of which the U.S. navy is a major portion—extend the defense perimeter, provide a measure of conventional and strategic deterrence, are available to the national command authority for crisis management, and represent the pre-positioned initial war-fighting capability in the event of an all-out global conflict. To be creditable as a deployed force, the U.S. Navy must be capable of conducting effective sea control and power projection operations, must be logistically independent, and must be fully mobile.

These national requirements for the U.S. Navy are only one facet of the issue of force size. The U.S. Navy must also be capable of responding to the threat which it may face. One view of that threat has already been presented, but the closed nature of Russian society and the paucity of necessary intelligence gives rise to disagreement over the magnitude and nature of the threat. Indeed, the debate has ranged from whether any threat exists to which year in the near future the threat could become hopelessly overwhelming.

Determining Force Size

These and other factors clearly influence the optimal size of the U.S. Navy. While its value and role are generally understood, the size and structure of the fleet are the subject of continuing debate.

---

[2] James L. Holloway III, "The Transition to V/STOL," *U.S. Naval Institute Proceedings,* September 1977, p. 19.

This question of size is basically one of "how much is enough?" What size fleet is really required to meet national commitments and security needs? Complicating the issue are stringent fiscal constraints imposed in an era of rising costs during which attempts are being made to build up a service that is inherently capital intensive. In addition, each ship funded involves a thirty-five to fifty-year commitment from its inception to its retirement. Consequently, policy makers are increasingly asking such questions as: "Does the Navy need to project power? Does it need a Marine Corps? Isn't it enough simply to control the seas? How much of the sea do we need to control? Why build expensive, vulnerable aircraft carriers? Can't submarines and land-based aircraft do the job? Can we afford nuclear-powered surface ships?"

In considering the future size of the fleet it seems prudent to plan a force clearly capable of defeating the worst possible threat. Although this has often been the stated goal, fiscal realities have dictated otherwise. The present or projected fleet is not of the size required to defeat the worst possible threat. Fortunately, the "worst-case threat" (that is, general war with the Soviet Union) would appear to be the least likely of potential conflict scenarios.

Crisis Management

In a recent study, Blechman and Kaplan stated that "The Navy has been the foremost instrument for the United States' political uses of armed forces: at all times, in all places, and regardless of the specifics of the situation."[3] Of the 215 international incidents they studied, covering the period from 1945 to 1975, the U.S. Navy participated in 177,100 of which involved naval units only. Carriers were used in 106, almost half of the total incidents studied. The amphibious forces participated in 71 incidents; in 56, or about one-fourth, they were employed with carrier task groups providing sea-based air cover.[4]

There are three primary reasons for the predominant use of naval forces in responding to a crisis. First, ships are easier and cheaper to move than ground- or land-based units. They can be deployed more rapidly and are more self-supporting in terms of logistics and communications. Second, upon arrival in the crisis area, they are more flexible, less disruptive psychologically, and less offensive diplomatically

---

[3] Barry M. Blechman and Stephen S. Kaplan, *The Use of Armed Forces as a Political Instrument* (Washington, D.C.: Advanced Research Project Agency, 1976), p. IV-3.

[4] Ibid., pp. IV-3 to IV-7.

than an equivalent land-based force. Finally, since World War II, a significant portion of our active fleet has been forward deployed in areas of the world where crises were most likely to develop. The availability and capability of ships were undoubtedly factors in their frequent use. Thus, the U.S. Navy's value in responding to a crisis stems in part from its policy of forward deployment which places it much closer to the scene than other combat arms. In addition, the U.S. Navy has independent mobility and can operate with little or no external support, and it has developed and maintains a great degree of flexibility with its complete navy/marine team.

In the opinion of many people, the size and configuration of the U.S. Navy should be determined on the basis of scenarios for the most likely intervention or crisis management rather than the worst-case threat of general war. However, a fleet which is designed to meet only the most probable threat may be incapable of surviving the worst, thereby placing our entire national security strategy in jeopardy. The worst-case enemy may well be encouraged to become adventuresome if the chances of being successfully deterred or countered are minimal.

The unique wartime requirements over and above that of traditional crisis management include the protection of vital sea lines of communication with our allies and overseas forces; the conduct of operations against an opponent in more than one theater; the ability to combine the effects of anti-submarine, anti-air, anti-surface, and mine warfare to deal with a three-dimensional threat; and, finally, the ability to conduct amphibious assault-and-strike warfare after sea control is achieved.

Current Force Structure

The U.S. Navy seeks to structure its forces to provide maximum flexibility and balance within fiscal constraints. Several techniques are used to realize this objective, including the "Hi-Lo Mix" concept, maximum use of existing assets, balanced procurement, and procurement of ships with a multipurpose or multimission capability.

The Hi-Lo Mix concept envisions platforms of different sizes and capabilities to meet varying threats. The "Hi" portion consists of the more complex and expensive platforms and weapons, generally in larger sizes and smaller numbers to meet the more advanced threat. The "Lo" portion consists of the less expensive and complex platforms, perhaps with a capability in only one warfare area. In small groups, these ships could counter a lesser threat, while in combination with the Hi forces they could meet more advanced opposition. Generally it is expected that the Lo forces can be procured in greater numbers. The actual mix which occurs in any given force is dependent on the size of that force. As the size of the force decreases, the percentage of Hi ships will increase dramatically, since with fewer ships available each must be more capable of responding successfully to a given threat.

In order to maintain the maximum capability within the constraints of the budget, plans have been made to extend the life of some of the existing forces. Forrestal-class aircraft carriers and the Adams-class guided missile destroyers will undergo a Service Life Extension Program (SLEP), which will extend their useful service lives by fifteen years. A Conversion in Lieu of Procurement (CILOP) program to extend the active service lives of the F-4, A-6, A-7, and AV-8 aircraft by eight to ten years is also planned. Where considerations of military effectiveness permit, the U.S. Navy is manning certain of its support ships with civilian crews in order to reduce personnel costs.

Above all, the U.S. Navy is seeking a proper balance among its air, surface, and subsurface arms. Within this balance, reliance will continue to be placed on versatile, multipurpose ships. Aircraft carriers, for example, are no longer specialized but are capable of performing both attack and antisubmarine operations. Submarines are being designed and built for independent and barrier operations as well as for operations in direct support of surface and air units. New cruisers will be capable of use in antisubmarine, anti-air, and antisurface warfare. The destroyer force will continue to be competent in at least two warfare areas. Finally, the support force will include more tankers and oilers capable of carrying more than one type of supplies.

Issues of Force Structure

The discussion of threats, goals, and desirable capabilities seems simple and straightforward. However, as with all programs subject to the budgetary process, there is controversy or disagreement concerning proper solutions. In the case of the U.S. Navy, the main issues today center on the rationale for aircraft carriers, the proposed transition to V/STOL (vertical/short take-off and landing) aircraft, and the direction of the land-based air program.

Carrier Force Levels. The U.S. Navy's aircraft carrier program has been a source of continuing controversy. A major study is underway in response to congressional direction to assess the costs, capabilities, and effectiveness of all current and potential air-capable platforms. Based on the proven capabilities of the large, modern aircraft carrier (either the CV, which is conventionally powered, or the CVN, which has nuclear power), and on its demonstrated value in support of national strategy, the U.S. Navy has maintained that the CV is the most capable and cost-effective platform for today's CTOL (conventional take-off and landing) aircraft. The U.S. Navy remains concerned about declining carrier force levels and the impact on future naval force capability. However, the costs of large replacement platforms are receiving much attention.

The modern aircraft carrier has tremendous capabilities in all aspects of naval warfare. It acts as a focus of the modern battle group and exploits its synergistic effects. The carrier remains one of the most survivable ships ever built. With its ability to project power ashore and to conduct effective sea control, it has been, and should continue to be, the major force in crisis management as well as a major contributor in a general war situation.

But because the expense of the carrier is of concern to many, the U.S. Navy has developed and plans on improving the Hi-Lo Mix concept with a force of four CVNs, eight CVs, and an increasing number of new CVVs that cost less to construct. As the central component of nuclear battle groups, the CVNs are capable of covering large distances in minimal time, arriving in the high-threat areas ready to fight. The CVs will have essentially the same war-fighting capability but will remain less versatile because of their increased need for refueling and rearming. The CVVs are envisioned as a replacement for the last Midway-class carriers and will be smaller, with about two-thirds of the CV's aircraft capacity. Consequently, the CVVs will be less costly and should be affordable in greater numbers. As the major thrust in the Lo portion of the Hi-Lo Mix, the CVVs will be able to cover more trouble spots, but with a lesser capability than the CV when operating singly. They will, of course, be the equivalent of a CV if concentrated in appropriate numbers. The CVV should offer reduced vulnerability through dispersion of assets, but with decreased individual survivability under high-threat conditions.

The decline in carrier force levels due to aging and to continuing fiscal constraints is of great concern. To help alleviate this decline the SLEP program has been initiated. The fifteen-year life extension this program will permit is currently expected to cost about $450 million per carrier. Each of the eight Forrestal-class carriers will be out of commission for two to three years while the SLEP modernization is performed. The navy will retain a thirteenth carrier in service to provide a total of twelve deployable carriers until the SLEPs are complete.

The U.S.S. *Midway* is aging and will not be modernized. The U.S. Navy would prefer to have one more CVN to replace her. The alternative would be to procure CVVs at greater than one-for-one replacement to compensate for reduced capability. The CVVs will be fully capable of operating with conventional aircraft, but will also serve as the "transition" platforms as V/STOL aircraft are introduced into the fleet. The pure V/STOL support ship (VSS) is the next logical step. While still in the conceptual stage, it is envisioned as a smaller platform to support sea-based aircraft should V/STOL prove feasible.

V/STOL. The carrier discussion leads directly to the second major issue in naval forces today—the V/STOL program. V/STOL aircraft are a potential *major* innovation for the conduct of naval warfare and could, in time, revolutionize not only sea-based air power but also our entire concept of combat at sea. If V/STOL are proven feasible, the U.S. Navy may eventually effect a complete transition of its air arm to these new air craft. By the twenty-first century that transition would be well under way, and with it would come numerous advantages. V/STOL would allow a great increase in operational flexibility. Sea-based air platforms would be relieved of the need to carry the catapult and arresting equipment which require large amounts of energy and manpower. Furthermore, these platforms would no longer need to spend long periods steaming into the wind or moving equipment back and forth to accommodate flight operations. V/STOL should permit smaller, less expensive, and thus more numerous air platforms which would provide great versatility and dispersion. There is every indication that V/STOL's capabilities could be extended not only to conventional aircraft carriers as we know them today, but also to other conventional hull forms on which a flat deck can be placed (merchant vessels, cruisers, and destroyers). Certain unconventional hull forms, such as the SWATH (small waterplane-area twin-hull) and the SES (surface effects ship), appear to be potential air-capable platforms as well.

Where does the V/STOL program stand now? Clearly, a program as potentially revolutionary as this entails high technical risk and expense. To ensure that the service and the public get as much for their money as possible, the U.S. Navy will involve not only its own analysts, but those of industry as well, in the study of the cost-benefit trade-offs of a move from CTOL to V/STOL. The development program is being carefully structured to offer alternatives at each step and to provide decision points for a fallback to CTOL should the program falter. In addition, the Marine Corps' AV-8A Harrier V/STOL aircraft is operational and can be used to test some of the program's assumptions and the recommendations of the studies that have already been completed.

334

The U.S. Navy hopes to reduce cost by extensive use of a common airframe. A modern aircraft carrier currently carries as many as nine different types of airplanes. The V/STOL program would replace these with a subsonic Type A aircraft, a supersonic Type B aircraft, and possibly a quasi-helicopter Type C. The Type A would have a common airframe which would be able to hold modular tactical packages and would be used for antisubmarine warfare (ASW), early warning, and cargo handling. The supersonic Type B would fill the fighter and attack roles with only minor avionic changes. The Type C is envisioned as possibly using the "X"-wing concept to replace current LAMPS (light airborne multipurpose system) and other ASW helicopters. The "X" or rotor of the craft is driven or stopped in flight by air forced from slots along the leading and trailing edges of each blade and is used as a conventional rotor for helicopter-like flight or as an unconventional, cruciform fixed wing for airplane-like flight. Whatever V/STOL types are chosen, each must clearly demonstrate that its cost effectiveness equals or is superior to that of its CTOL predecessors.

Land-Based Naval Aircraft. The last issue to be discussed involves the role of future land-based naval aircraft. How much of the sea control mission can be assumed by advanced land-based airplanes? Opponents of sea-based air argue that all the war-fighting roles of our current fleet can be accommodated by a new generation of land-based aircraft. One specific proposal has been the LMNA (land-based multipurpose naval aircraft). This is a large, high-endurance flying machine capable of air-to-air warfare for its own defense and the protection of other forces while doing its primary job of finding and destroying submarines and attacking enemy surface combatants.

The U.S. Navy does not consider the land-based air controversy as an either-or question. Land-based aircraft have been and will continue to be fundamental contributors to a balanced naval force. The U.S. Navy will continue to improve their design to meet whatever threat may be present or to take advantage of emerging technology or any newly discovered enemy weakness. Studies conducted by the navy staff and the Center for Naval Analyses are currently examining the entire issue.

There are, however, major concerns which affect the LMNA proposal and which these studies may help to answer. As currently envisioned, the LMNA concept competes directly with funding for the V/STOL and other aircraft programs. As a land-based aircraft, its flexibility could be restricted by its dependence on land facilities. If its endurance is such that it can operate exclusively from the continental United States, its time en route might be excessive. If it must operate from overseas bases, it will be subject to the interests of host nations which would increase its vulnerability. Finally, while airplanes such as the LMNA might be promising as future war-fighting machines, there remains considerable doubt that they could provide the visibility, versatility, and staying power necessary for deterrence or crisis management. These factors are important characteristics of a balanced naval force.

Trends in Force Structure

The land-based aircraft, V/STOL, and the role of the carrier are some of the major issues facing the U.S. Navy in the last quarter of this century. Other less visible issues include the size of the force itself, its balance, the role of nuclear power, the form and function of the strategic forces, the form and function of the amphibious forces and of the Marine Corps—the list is endless. What will the force look like for the next quarter century? What will be some of the major trends?

The organization of the fleet in the future will remain much as it is today, with the exception of changes in titles as new missions, concepts, or platforms evolve. There will be four basic tactical units, all of which emphasize flexibility and mobility. The main battle fleet will still center on the carrier task group, both nuclear and conventional, capable of any wartime or peacetime mission. Carrier task groups will be supported by new, more versatile replenishment groups, which will permit the U.S. Navy to remain mobile, flexible, and free of undue reliance on overseas base facilities. Amphibious ready groups will provide the ability to project armed power ashore for both wartime needs and crisis management. Finally, escort forces will protect logistics shipping should an enemy threaten our sea lines of communication. Within the limits of fiscal constraints, all these tactical units will be designed to combat a multidimensional threat of any intensity.

The war-fighting capabilities of the battle fleet will still concentrate on the three main categories of AAW (anti-air warfare), ASW (antisubmarine warfare), and ASUW (anti–surface ship warfare/strike). In anti-air warfare, the F-14 and the E2C will provide the long-range protection until the advent of Types A and B V/STOL and long-range, surface-launched AAW missiles. Mid-range protection will be provided by the new Aegis system and the SM-1 and SM-2 missiles, while point defense will be provided by the NATO Seasparrow Missile System, Close-in Weapon System (CIWS), and updated Electronic Warfare (EW) systems.

In antisubmarine warfare, choke points will be protected by more sophisticated mine fields, especially those using the new CAPTOR (capsule torpedo) mobile mine. Distant protection of fleet units will be supplied by sonobuoy fields monitored by P-3s and S-3s and eventually by the Type A V/STOLs. At moderate distances, the U.S. Navy's increasing experience with nuclear attack submarines in direct support of surface units will be telling, as will be the increasing proliferation of towed array sonars. These will be streamed from surface as well as subsurface platforms. New active and passive systems and new LAMPS helicopters with more powerful sensors will protect main body units at shorter ranges.

Anti–surface ship warfare/strike remains the means by which the fleet will project its power against shore targets as well as enemy fleets. Long-range strikes will still be led largely by manned tactical aircraft— the A-7 Corsair and A-6 Intruder at present, with the F/A-18 Hornet joining the fleet in the 1980s. The Type B V/STOL aircraft will provide striking power in the 1990s. These aircraft will be assisted by the Tomahawk cruise missile for nuclear land attack and conventional long-range attack against enemy surface vessels and eventually by more powerful long-range missiles targeted by V/STOLs, or by other over-the-horizon targeting networks. Mid-range attack will be pressed using the Harpoon anti-ship cruise missile launched from a variety of air, surface, and subsurface naval platforms. Finally, the close-in attack capability will be provided by the MK-48 torpedo and the major caliber light-weight gun using guided projectiles.

Future Issues of Force Size

While the foregoing does not specifically answer the question of fleet size, it does give an impression of the capabilities that can be expected. Ultimate size will depend upon system costs and fiscal constraints, but a modest upturn to a force level of 500 to 600 ships is expected in the next two decades. There are, however, some other issues and trends which should be addressed briefly since they will affect the entire issue of force size and many platform and equipment decisions up to and beyond the year 2000.

Hull Forms. First, there is the matter of new hull forms. In an effort to break the confines of the conventional displacement hull, several new surface platforms have been proposed, including the SES, the hydrofoil, the WIG (wing in ground effect), and the SWATH. Prototypes of each are currently being operated by various nations. The SES and hydrofoil offer the advantages of high speed and a degree of invulnerability to torpedoes.

The WIG provides a combination of boat-like endurance and aircraft-like speed and range. The SWATH, perhaps the most interesting of all, provides a very large deck area for its displacement, exceptional stability, and submarine-like sonar compatibility in a surface vessel. It is still uncertain which type or combination of types will be most successful. There is little doubt, however, that future surface platforms could have hulls that are dramatically different, both in form and capability, from those of today.

Propulsion Systems. New propulsion systems could be the key to making one or more of the above hulls economically competitive with existing displacement hull forms. Existing systems, such as steam, nuclear power, and gas propulsion will continue to be improved. At the same time, the development of newer light weight propulsion plants and supercooled conductors could reduce system costs or provide power-to-weight ratios far greater than those to which we are restricted today.

Precision Guided Munitions (PGM). New developments in weapons systems and munitions are also likely to change the face of naval warfare. Precision guided munitions (missiles, bombs, gun projectiles) are achieving unprecedented accuracies. Because PGMs are increasingly compatible with lighter weight launch platforms, this field of munitions could nicely complement the development of V/STOL aircraft as well as the newer, more revolutionary hull forms.

Fuel-Air Explosives (FAE). Related to PGM are fuel-air explosives, which use aerosol mixtures of fuel and air ignited by charges contained in the weapon. Although still in their infancy, models of these types of weapons are operational with both U.S. and Soviet forces and were used by the United States in Vietnam. FAEs offer blast effects many times greater than comparable weights of TNT, and it is predicted that in the future they will produce effects approaching small tactical nuclear weapons. They have been used to clear mine fields and landing zones in dense jungles, and they appear well suited in naval warfare to inflict blast overpressure damage that will be especially effective against topside antenna systems of modern combatant ships. The continued development and deployment of FAE munitions may dramatically influence warship design and tactical employment patterns.

C3 and ECM. Longer-range and greater speed capabilities in new weapons are already straining the present targeting ability of fleet units. In the past, the naval officer's world was limited by the horizon. Each new system—radio, radar, sonar, airplane—has tended to expand those limits. Now a host of new weapons systems require the use of over-the-horizon targeting and surveillance systems, such as satellites, remotely piloted vehicles (RPVs), high altitude super pressurized aerosats (HASPA), and V/STOL aircraft, to exploit fully their range capability. As a result of this burgeoning scope of surveillance, all types of passive and active electronic countermeasures, as well as new methods of concealment and deception, are likely to receive increased emphasis in future warfare.

The Shore Establishment. The role of the U.S. Navy's shore establishment is often forgotten in discussions of naval warfare. As always it continues to be designed to serve and support the fleet, but newer platforms, more complex weapons, and worldwide communication, surveillance, and targeting systems can only increase its importance. In the Lo Mix maintenance concept, many maintenance functions are removed from smaller ships and placed ashore or on board tenders. The concept uses modular components and equipment with greater reliability to reduce crew maintenance tasks on smaller combatants, but it increases the fleet's reliance on support facilities. Complex weapons and sensor systems, both air and seaborne, are more frequently designed to be delivered to the user in a fully operational condition with only the simplest of shipboard go/no-go checks to be performed. When the equipment malfunctions, it is removed to an external repair facility. Despite increased reliability on the U.S. Navy's systems, its ships and aircraft will still rely on external sources for parts and other supplies.

As the complexity of weapons, hull forms, and propulsion systems increases, so will the need for highly trained personnel. Although the U.S. Navy has consistently attempted to keep pace with improved training techniques, demand has been increasing for personnel in fields that require longer time in classroom training than in the past, and this demand is likely to continue to grow. In addition, the shore establishment must continue to provide necessary personnel support to active duty and retired personnel and their dependents. None of these trends indicates a lessening reliance upon or a decline in the size and importance of the shore establishment.

Civilian Manning/Merchant Marine. The U.S. Navy currently has eight oilers, one stores ship, and four fleet tugs which are fully manned by civilian Civil Service personnel. Studies and fleet experience have shown that certain types of service and support ships can be operated by fewer civilian mariners than navy personnel, and at reduced cost. The U.S. Navy is currently analyzing comparative costs of manning various types of fleet support ships in order to determine whether additional ships could be converted to civilian manning when considerations such as availability, flexibility, and required military capability permit.

Conclusion: the Role of the Navy in National Strategy

The foregoing discussion has provided an overview of the many factors which influence the size and composition of U.S. naval forces. As we approach the twenty-first century, the major consideration for defense and naval planners must be the future role of U.S. sea power in support of our national strategy. An analysis of long-term U.S. political and economic interests and goals, and the strategy which logically supports these goals, highlights the increasing economic interdependence of nations in a world in which political turmoil and instability can be expected to increase. National leaders seek détente, but it appears unlikely that the East-West conflict will be abolished. Nationalism and social awareness are increasing throughout the Third World. New power centers are evolving and threats to worldwide U.S. interests show no decline. Furthermore, the buildup of Soviet military power continues despite public disavowals of any intent to use those forces for purposes other than "self-defense." We must constantly be alert to the threat posed by the capabilities of possible opponents and not be lulled by comforting assessments of their intent.

It is unlikely that the role and responsibilities of the United States as a free-world leader will diminish, nor is there any apparent basis for a change in our traditional forward strategy, which is dependent on a strong maritime posture. Under these conditions, history indicates that our sea services must play an increasing part in support of national strategy. The degree to which this requirement will be fulfilled will depend in large measure on national awareness and on the willingness of our leaders to take requisite action to meet the challenge, both physically and fiscally.

COMMENTARIES

Elmo R. Zumwalt

With regard to the energy situation, it is important to be aware that currently the energy usage of the Department of Defense is just 4.5 percent of what the nation uses. Of that, only one-third, or 1.5 percent, is used by the navy; and of that, only one-half is used by ships, the other half by aviation.

So the fleet uses a very modest fraction of the nation's energy requirement. This is a consideration within which the overall discussion of nuclear power and other kinds of power has to be judged. Obviously, the country will use the energy that it has to use for its ships in a crisis, and we will put on sweaters and do whatever else we have to do. But this does not speak to the long-term situation. We will see the hydrogenation of coal, and, in the long term, other forms of energy will take over.

No discussion of energy should fail to deal with the long-term consequences of running out of oil with regard to the strategic places on the globe. The Middle East, specifically the Persian Gulf, is of critical importance today. By 2015, it will probably be relatively unimportant. There will be a period when what has been the crisis center of the globe will suddenly cease to be that. Nations that today are in a position practically to dictate will survive on the infrastructure they have built for themselves. And they will again rely somewhat on the industrial world.

With regard to the long-term sources of energy, highly industrialized nations will turn to the hydrogenation of coal, to nuclear fusion, and to other exotic forms of fuel, instead of depending on overseas areas. Increasingly these nations will be their own sources of energy.

Certainly, the United States, Canada, and Australia, today have the overwhelming majority of food surplus and the overwhelming fraction of the free world's coal. These nations have a combination that when put together represents a very important element of power.

341

The existence of that energy supply at our end of the supply line will change the nature of our overall weapons and weapons systems.

Similarly, we need to pay attention to those areas of the world that are likely to join the industrial part of the globe by 2000 or later. Nations such as Brazil, which are clearly in this category, will have an impact on the overall strategies within which we consider our problems.

There is another area that we have to examine. Over the last 500 years, mankind has been moving from the European continent across the surface of the seas to the Western Hemisphere and to the African continent. Now we see, at an ever accelerating exponential rate, these civilizations moving together again under the sea. We are just at the leading edge of this movement in offshore exploration. We are beginning to move from the hunting of fish and food in the sea to the farming of fish and food in the sea.

Deep-sea drilling projects on the ocean bed, in ever deeper water, are obviously the way of the future. The problems of navies and how they will deal with the policing and the defense of such projects will have to be considered when examining the generation of ships that will survive until 2015.

The whole question of nuclear proliferation and how that changes the defense situation of the world, as smaller nations acquire the capability to build nuclear weapons, should concern us all in making weapons system decisions.

Perhaps of overriding consequence is the question of which of the two rival views for organization of the globe will prevail. Will the ruthless, tyrannical, power-seeking Soviet view prevail? Or will the strength of man's true free spirit prevail? How will that struggle be played out in future eras when we have not yet learned as a nation to focus on what our enemy tells us he intends to do?

When one examines naval systems, it is very important constantly to keep in mind whether we are looking at a peacekeeping situation or at a war situation. The problem that we have in bringing power to bear in peace time is completely different from the problem of winning a war with the Soviet Union at sea, once that war breaks out.

All that we have done in the past needs constantly to be reexamined in that regard. Nuclear energy is the first subject that comes to mind. No one disagrees that nuclear power is more effective than conventional power. No one disagrees that nuclear power is more costly than conventional power in ships. The issue has always been whether the additional cost is warranted by the additional effectiveness. Clearly, the overriding conclusion is that the cost is justified for submarines and for some nuclear carriers and escorts. Beyond these few, the number of ships that must be given up outweighs the gains in the effectiveness of a unit. The trade-off has constantly to be examined.

The increasing capability of both sides for global command and control and surveillance and reconnaissance is changing the nature of weapons systems. The increasing lethality of even conventional explosives has changed the nature of sea warfare. Therefore, when the job of sea control is projected into the years ahead, we are driven inevitably toward larger numbers of smaller and more cost-effective platforms.

The CNO's decision to head into the CVV is a good one. It hedges the uncertainty as to whether V/STOL will come along rapidly enough. I believe in the more distant future we will see still smaller platforms and true V/STOL operations.

In the later years of this century and in the early years of the next century, we will see V/STOL aircraft increasingly in the role of surveillance, reconnaissance, and command and control. Cruise missiles and remotely piloted vehicles will take over as the lethal end of the system.

We have to take a lesson from our potential enemy, the Soviet Union. We have to be aware of the much more effective job they are doing of tying together all of the platforms available to them, with their total and rather brutal control of the entire Soviet economy, including, for example, their ability to send the merchant marine off in the directions that Admiral Gorshkov desires and to use merchant ships as auxiliaries.

We have a vast and untapped field of opportunity with regard to our ability to group the total force of this country—the army, the navy, the air force, the Coast Guard, the marines, and the merchant marine. The enemy, with regard to accomplishing this, has always been the bureaucracy, which defeats any such effort. Until there is someone who has the authority to bridge the interagency bureaucratic problem, we will not begin to organize to use our total power. It is unconscionable to me that merchant ships which have the capability, with just a few structural changes, to be antisubmarine platforms, to be V/STOL platforms or helicopter platforms, to carry towed and passive arrays, to carry the antisubmarine or antiship rockets, are not being so prepared.

We need increasing numbers of ships at sea because of our increasing dependence on overseas resources. We should be exploiting our merchant ships at the margin, to develop the capability to control the sea, or—more accurately—to defend those platforms by means of the most cost-effective platforms of all, themselves.

Beyond the bureaucratic interface, we have two significant problems. First, there is the reluctance of our leadership, in general, accurately to inform the American public about the Soviet Union—what it says it is up to, and what its actions demonstrate it is up to. And the second problem is that we cannot allow the Soviet Union to outspend us by 60 percent in the strategic field and 50 percent in the conventional field, no matter how optimal we become. We will simply have to begin to match that nation, which, with 60 percent of our gross national product, continues to outspend us. And, within that matching, we must seek, through our greater efficiency, to regain the deterrence capability we have given up in these last five or six years.

Alva M. Bowen, Jr.

In his paper, Admiral Trost indicated an average life expectancy of about twenty-seven years for ships of the U.S. fleet. Applying that figure, almost every ship in the U.S. Navy today, even the newest ones, will either be dropped from the active list or on its last legs by the year 2004. Therefore, we are talking about an entirely new navy when we address the question of sea power in the twenty-first century; new in the sense that there will be few of today's 464 U.S. Navy ships around, and whatever replaces the capability they represent will have joined the fleet in the interim. Whether the U.S. Navy will be "new" in the sense that it is significantly "different" in its deployment and operational concepts, and therefore "different" in kinds of ships and the tasks they are designed to perform, has been the subject of this book.

Looking ahead twenty-five to thirty years is the correct way to consider what changes might be desirable in the navy of the future. Most of us, in our day-to-day work, are constrained by a large inventory of ships whose life expectancies still have a long way to run. Conversion of ships in the inventory to take advantage of emerging technology is expensive and time consuming and, because of these two factors, often judged not cost-effective.

On the other hand, there is a five-to-seven-year building period for new ships and usually seven or more years R & D time for the weapon systems and other key components before that. Ships authorized and funded in 1977 have technology in them that started development in 1970 or earlier. When these ships are delivered in 1984, that technology will be fourteen or more years old. These facts of life make conversion programs imperative and place a high premium on finding ways to improve on the time and expense factors in weapons system development, ship design, shipbuilding industrial performance, and the decision processes that determine all these things. They are also a constraint on innovation. It takes a long time to equip the fleet with new technology.

In addition, ship replacement in peacetime is, or should be, a continuous process to avoid the unsettling effects of peaks and valleys in shipbuilding budgets on both the service and industry. We should not, as a matter of policy, wait around hoping that some promising technological development will miraculously appear to solve our most difficult operational problems: how many ASW capable ships would we have by now if we had waited for the perfect solution to the undersea detection problem? Instead, decision makers must proceed with what is available at the time, which means ship designs are very much determined by what was started in the development pipeline seven to ten years before.

So the conclusion by the authors of the preceding papers that the fleet of the twenty-first century may have many of the same characteristics as today's fleet reflects their knowledge of what is in the R & D pipeline. While there are some things in development that could have a revolutionary effect on the fleet if they prove successful, there are more programs that are only incremental improvements over what we have now, and the authors predict that more of the latter kind of development will make it into production than the former.

The key question is how to provide the future navy with the capabilities now available in sea-based air power. The difficulty of penetrating sophisticated air defense is forcing changes in weapon delivery techniques and technology—standoff weapons and penetration aids are examples. Also, the nuclear warhead, antiship missiles, and vastly more effective ocean surveillance systems have increased the vulnerability of our surface ships, including aircraft carriers. There is a trend toward shifting from manned to unmanned air vehicles and also toward shifting from sea-based to land-based solutions to operational problems requiring manned aircraft. Other studies have developed the pro/con arguments as to whether these trends are helpful or dangerous. This book provides valuable insights into both the stimulus for these trends and the likely rate of change.

The Size of the Fleet. Admiral Trost presented a rationale for the navy's projected fleet size and composition in his paper. The U.S. Navy of the early twenty-first century will be structured and sized for a forward strategy, as it is today, because the considerations that called forth the forward strategy—our national interests overseas and the desirability of retaining the oceans as defensive barriers—will not have changed by then. The navy's mission to conduct prompt and sustained warfare at sea will still obtain, and the functions of sea control and its subset, projection of power overseas, will continue to be navy requirements. Sea control is depicted by Trost as three dimensional, requiring air, surface, and subsurface platforms to prosecute. Informed readers will have little difficulty in agreeing with these conclusions. As Trost states, the issue is the size and structure of the fleet that should be acquired to support these functions.

Trost postulates as the proper criterion for sizing and structuring the fleet the ability to defeat the worst case threat, which he identifies to be the Soviet navy. Capabilities necessary to meet the worst case contingency are to be able to control the sea lanes and to conduct amphibious and strike warfare in more than one theater, after theater control of the sea is achieved. In his view, fiscal constraints have prevented meeting this criterion in today's fleet, and they will be a problem in meeting it in the years ahead. Trost acknowledges that this worst case threat is also the least likely contingency to which the U.S. Navy may have to respond. However, he rejects the alternative, sometimes proposed, to size the fleet for the most probable contingency—crisis management in conditions on the edge of war. In his view that would be likely to lead to adventurism on the part of our adversaries and could lead to defeat in event the worst case contingency arises.

In Trost's view, the carrier will still be the key ship of the main battle force throughout the remainder of this century and into the twenty-first century. To that end, the navy should maintain a force of four CVNs, eight CVs, and some unspecified number of CVVs. Trost notes that life extension overhauls of carriers in the fleet today are planned to prolong their availability through the end of the century. No proposal for their eventual replacement is given, probably because of uncertainty over the success of the navy's V/STOL development program described next.

According to Trost, the V/STOL may replace the conventional take-off and landing aircraft as the navy's principal sea-based aircraft. The V/STOL development program is structured to provide alternative paths at key decision points in the development process that would allow a return to CTOL should this prove necessary. As described by Trost, the navy's planning will permit a serious investigation of V/STOL while retaining the CTOL capability—with the option of renewing and extending CTOL should V/STOL development prove inadequate or should dangerous strategic conditions arise that make the transition to V/STOL temporarily unsafe.

According to Trost, the navy does not view the land-based air option as an either/or choice, but intends to pursue both sea- and land-based solutions to operational problems. Trost notes, however, that land-based options compete for funds with V/STOL development. Why this is so, except in the general sense that all proposed expenditures compete in some measure with all other expenditures, is not explained by Trost. It should be, as other trade-offs come easily to mind.

According to Trost, the U.S. Navy of the twenty-first century is projected to consist of between 500 to 600 ships in four basic functional groupings: a main battle fleet centered on the carrier force, replenishment groups, amphibious ready groups, and escort forces for logistics shipping. Whether this force is adequate to meet the worst case criterion is not addressed in his paper, perhaps because the detailed composition of the basic tactical units and their resulting capabilities are not known with enough precision to say.

Surface Warships for the Early Twenty-First Century. Reuven Leopold has provided a useful technology survey that sheds some light on what is possible in ship design during the remainder of the century, and he has made some predictions about the probable choices that will be made as to hull forms, propulsor, and weapons system technology.

Since displacement hulls are speed limited for all practical purposes to under forty knots, higher speeds can be achieved only by shifting to some nondisplacement hull form that exacts a penalty in cost and complexity for the greater speeds that may then be attained. A trade-off must be made between the operational value of the increased speed and these extra costs. Leopold believes these trade-offs will usually favor displacement hulls. In his view, ship speed is relatively less important for the majority of naval tasks than other characteristics adversely affected by a nondisplacement hull choice such as endurance, payload, and simplicity. However, since there are some tasks where very high ship speed counts, the navy is pursuing hydrofoil, air cushion, and surface-effect technology in search of the most efficient way of providing higher speed where it can be justified. The developments described by Leopold indicate the navy may envision application of these technologies only to small ships. The implication of such a restriction would be to forgo the advantages of greater endurance and payload achievable in large ships, so an explanation would be helpful if these technologies are to be confined to small ships.

A significant innovation possibly affecting the future of sea-based air is the SWATH ship, an unconventional displacement ship whose principal advantage is much improved sea-keeping over ordinary displacement hulls. This advantage, and the boxlike shape of its above-water structure, makes the SWATH concept attractive for aviation application if the design proves seaworthy. Relatively small SWATH ships could operate aircraft in sea states that would reduce the effectiveness of all but the largest displacement hulled ships.

The review of propulsor technology led Leopold to conclude that gas turbines will be the workhorse of the fleet in the twenty-first century, replacing steam. The primary advantage of gas turbines cited by Leopold is their relatively large power output for a given size and weight. For nondisplacement hulls, gas turbines represent the only choice, according to Leopold, by which finding he implicitly rules out a lightweight nuclear power plant, which he does not discuss.

The revolutionary development in propulsion technology will probably be superconducting machinery, which will permit radical re-arrangement of propulsion components. Substituting electrical power transmission for the current mechanical reduction gears and shafting, clutching systems, and controllable pitch propellers will also revolu-tionize space utilization in ships and enable savings in space, weight, and complexity. The result will be significant reduction in ship size for the same payload, speed, and endurance.

The most significant innovation in weapons system technology forecast by Leopold is the plan to modularize the weapons system and thus decouple the "payload" from the ships to enable changes in both payload and platform. The ability to reconfigure a ship in a few weeks from one set of mission equipment to another, or from an older to a more modern weapons suite, or to shift weapons systems from ship to ship is truly revolutionary as the technological age of either the ship or the weapons system, or both, could be adjusted as required, freeing the navy from the severest limitation on conversions discussed at the be-ginning of this paper. This new approach depends not only on technology but also on the navy's ability, as an institution, to implement it.

Leopold is pessimistic about prospects for further significant man-power reductions through automation. He believes that major reduc-tions will come only with the adoption of radically new operating con-cepts. Some of those cited in his paper seem unacceptable. This finding is disappointing, for there remains an urgent need to effect additional manpower savings; commercial ship operators have had more success in reducing seagoing manpower than has the navy.

Protecting the Fleet. In his paper on protecting the fleet, David Kassing analyzes the increased hazards facing surface ships caused by tech-nological innovations since World War II and the special vulnerability of U.S. sea power inherent in our having concentrated almost all our offensive force into a declining number of large carriers. He points out the advantages that have accrued to our adversaries bacause we have relied on a single weapons delivery system, the carrier and its air wing, for so many years, enabling potential enemies to optimize their forces against it. This applies not only to the Soviet Union, but also to lesser navies of Third World countries. But small navies do not have the staying power to do more than deter "gunboat diplomacy" by raising its price.

Kassing makes an important contribution by presenting one of the few analyses of tactical nuclear war at sea available in open source literature. He concludes that the U.S. Navy is at a disadvantage in that form of warfare, and he indicates the kinds of changes in fleet composition and configuration that would be necessary to improve the situation. A shift in emphasis to destruction of hostile weapons carriers before they reach their launch points will be necessary to protect carriers and convoys. Investing more in submarines; proliferating the numbers of small, but potent, surface ships (including high-speed surface effect ships and hydrofoils) for missions that do not absolutely require large carriers; and significantly improving and extending the effective range of ocean surveillance systems are other examples.

Discussing defense against nonnuclear threats, Kassing distinguishes between the peacetime, edge of war, situation, when rules of engagement would allow the intermingling of U.S. and Soviet ships and when surprise of U.S. forces is achievable, and the situation that obtains after a war starts, when the rules change and surprise is less likely. As in the case of tactical nuclear war, one effective corrective measure to improve fleet defensive posture for the D-day "shoot-out" would be to disperse the striking power of the U.S. fleet more widely through reliance on larger numbers of smaller units and proliferation of long-range cruise missiles on many ships.

The importance of orbiting satellites to both sides in the years ahead is highlighted by Kassing, and attention is drawn to the conditions that would exist if the satellites, on which both will come to depend, are rendered ineffective. The importance of integral sea-based aerial surveillance will not be eliminated by satellites, although its role and form can be expected to change.

Summary. Although each of these papers makes an important contribution in its own right, their combined impact is greater than the sum of the parts, particularly as regards the key question of providing the future navy with the capabilities now available in sea-based air power. Admiral Trost demonstrates the continuance of the navy's current missions and key functions. Leopold promises cruisers, destroyers, and other surface combatants that can be reconfigured for different missions almost as easily as carriers. David Kassing details many of the pressures for changing current operating concepts. All three papers describe current navy programs and how they are intended to enable a transition to a more dispersed offensive capability while preserving current offensive air power and the option to renew and extend it.

Although the need to disperse offensive power more widely is generally accepted, and the trend toward transfer of some tasks from naval air power to other kinds of sea power (exemplified by the transfer of the strategic task to SSBNs) is recognized, there is an issue over whether the navy's proposed V/STOL program is the proper "next step" to take. Opponents of V/STOL note that there will always be a capability differential in favor of CTOL over V/STOL in the range-payload-speed characteristics of these two different weapons platforms. V/STOL development is projected to cost vastly more than any new CTOL development now contemplated; and the CVV, which is proposed as a transition ship will be a far less capable ship in its conventional carrier role than is needed and possible. The ship will spend much of its life in this conventional role awaiting the arrival of V/STOL, which may never come. A larger carrier would be an even better V/STOL platform.

Advocates of the navy's plan point out that V/STOL, if successful, would be operable from a variety of platforms, thus helping disperse navy offensive capability more widely in the fleet, which CTOL aircraft cannot do. The capability differential in range-payload-speed can be offset by developing a weapons system sufficiently capable that these platform characteristics are less significant. The F-14 is a step in that direction; the B-1 bomber decision is another example. V/STOL would carry on that trend. The CVV is a replacement for a similar sized carrier, the *Midway*, and will be more capable in the conventional role than the ship it will replace.

An alternative not frequently addressed, but implied by those opposed to the V/STOL proposal, would be to bypass V/STOL and proceed directly to unmanned aircraft solutions.

The questions raised by this debate over the future of sea-based air power primarily have to do with the state of the art and the pace of technological development. The situation is reminiscent of a similar debate in the 1920s and 1930s over the future of battleships.

In 1922, congressional hearings on the structure of the U.S. fleet addressed aircraft carrier–battleship trade-offs. The navy's general board at that time rendered an opinion that battleships were still the capital ship of the fleet and were likely to remain so for the years of interest to the debate. Although their opinion was not tested in combat, it was probably justified for that time because aeronautical technology was not yet sufficiently developed. Battleships continued as the backbone of the fleet, but the *Lexington* and the *Saratoga* were completed as aircraft carriers so the development of the airplane as a weapons system could proceed.

In the mid-1930s, after passage of the Vinson-Trammel Act stimulated a naval shipbuilding program, the trade-offs between carriers and battleships were again assessed. The decision was made to emphasize battleships in the building program that provided the ships for World War II. Events proved that more carriers and fewer battleships would have been a better decision.

The question before us is whether, as in 1922, the state of technological development of alternative capabilities requires that we continue with CTOL-manned aircraft as the backbone of our sea-based air power beyond the beginning of the twenty-first century, or whether we should embark now on programs designed to move toward a more dispersed offensive capability before the end of the century.

The navy's program, as presented in the three papers I reviewed, is a thoughtfully prepared recommendation to proceed now, but with appropriate checkpoints and options provided to accommodate changing perceptions as the program progresses. It has controversial aspects; however, I believe it is an excellent vehicle for stimulating the kind of professional debate that a subject of such significance to the future of the navy and the nation deserves.

Charles E. Bennett

My main quest in life is to have peace in the world, to defend our country, and to keep it secure and strong. I think the best way to do that is to have the strongest possible national defense. I say this because the remarks that follow may otherwise seem out of context. Admiral Trost observed that it is difficult to have a prognosis from the navy, or from the government, as to how many ships we will have. He pointed out that Admiral Arleigh Burke said 927 was about the number of ships we should have today. And we actually have about 460. My staff prepared some statistics for me which show that for every year from 1971 to date the navy has asked for 209 ships. The number they got was 101. That is just about half. If that total of 460 were doubled, the navy would have what it wanted. So Admiral Burke was quite accurate in his prognosis of what he thought the navy should have.

David Kassing quoted Admiral Holloway with regard to the nuclear content of the Soviet navy. If nuclear weapons were not used, Admiral Holloway predicted a 30 to 40 percent attrition of our carriers. Holloway also said he would expect very heavy losses to our carrier forces, if nuclear weapons were used. Kassing pointed out many related changes that have occurred since World War II: the presence of nuclear weapons and their entry into the fleet and into the arsenals of many countries; the advent of nuclear propulsion, antiship missiles, and ocean surveillance; and the reduction in size of the U.S. Navy. Kassing then discussed the impact of these changes on decisions to be made.

Dr. Reuven Leopold discussed the various factors in the difference of numbers, and he mentioned bureaucratic inputs and technological inputs. As a professional lifetime politician who sat on the knee of Woodrow Wilson when I was only seven, I would like to add that there are political inputs. There is political input from Congress and political input among mankind.

I never call anybody my enemy. When I run for office, I never look upon my opponents as opponents, really. They are people running for the same job. I had years of front-line, hand-to-hand combat. I have looked into the eyes of a man that I killed. I do not want that killing to persist. Twenty years ago, I drafted a bill called Arms Control and Disarmament Agency Legislation. Two young senators joined me in introducing this bill on the Senate side—Senator Hubert H. Humphrey and Senator John F. Kennedy. That bill finally became law during the Kennedy administration.

I remember the remarks made by Khrushchev—a very candid and, I thought, a very open-minded man—when he was in our country. He said he would bury us. But I noted the context in which he said that. He had confidence in the socialist system. Many people heard the shaking and rattling of guns in the remark, but I did not take it as that. I do not see how a system that takes away the freedom of the average man can survive, or how it can be expanded without arms. History shows that it cannot. But I took it that he felt his system was so much better than ours that it could compete with and destroy ours.

When I consider what Admiral Holloway and others have said in this context, two other things enter my mind. Even as chairman of the Seapower Subcommittee, I had not realized the degree to which the Soviet navy has centered on the first strike with nuclear weapons and the degree to which we have responded with our own nuclear weapons.

I would say the average member of Congress does not understand this today. I would say the average member of Congress does not know we have nuclear tactical weapons all over Europe, ready to fight a nonnuclear war. And, of course, the theory is that nuclear weapons will be used against ships in a nonnuclear war.

As a man who believes in trying for peace without giving up, I would try hard, if I were on the Arms Control Agency, to avoid that new plateau of tactical nuclear weapons, both in Europe and at sea.

In Europe it will be difficult to stop the Russians without tactical nuclear weapons. Admiral Holloway said that on the sea if the Soviets did not use tactical weapons we might lose 40 percent of our carriers. Now, 40 percent sounds quite large to me. Think how much worse it would be in a nuclear confrontation. I would like to see war end, to see peace on earth, to see an opportunity to develop individually, as we can, our own systems—competitively, not by killing each other.

It is a horrible anachronism that in 1977 we are still blowing people's brains out. All of the Japanese that I killed were probably pretty good guys. The ones I captured, I found, were pretty good guys.

I believe that these papers have been important in helping us see the challenges ahead. One fact that should be brought to the attention of the country as a whole, is that both the Soviet Union and the United States are now looking at the possibility of something short of a nuclear war—something called tactical nuclear war—both in Europe and at sea.

In a situation where both parties might gain from some sort of agreement, it seems to me that an agreement can be policed. I am not a man who believes in merely signing papers. To be effective, agreements must be mutually helpful.

I would like to see nuclear wars of all kinds, tactical and otherwise, ended. If a man is called an enemy, he will be an enemy. I believe all men should love each other. I believe we should have peace. I believe that the greatest quest of man is to find peace—permanent peace. But it should be with the liberty of people, and their freedom should be protected.

The national defense of our country is the greatest bulwark of international peace today. But we should not overlook the possibility that there are human hearts abroad as well.

PART FIVE

GUEST SPEAKERS

The Future of the American Merchant Marine

Daniel K. Inouye

During the course of this conference on sea power, we will hear many learned discussions on the future roles and missions of naval forces. I would not presume to add to what will be said on that subject by the many distinguished experts listed on the program. However, as chairman of the Merchant Marine Subcommittee in the U.S. Senate, I would like to share my views with you on the role and mission of an indispensable adjunct to any naval force. I am, of course, referring to a merchant fleet—and to the U.S. merchant fleet in particular.

I believe that a strong American merchant marine is essential to national security. It serves not only as a major supply line for U.S. defense forces throughout the world but also as a means of minimizing political pressures by foreign maritime powers on whom we might depend for shipping services. After all, the United States has no guarantee that it will be able to purchase all the shipping it needs. The seas are very political. In a crisis, some nations or national blocs may believe that hindering U.S. trade is in their best interests.

During the 1973 Middle East war, for example, Liberia—a nation that had pledged not to interfere with its Liberian flag–American owned ships—successfully prohibited such vessels from supplying Israel. Many other nations are building fleets with the dual purpose of capturing foreign exchange and securing political advantage. In February 1976, the chairman of the Kuwait Tanker Company declared that legislation giving preference to Arab tankers for transport of Middle East oil was inevitable, and that 40 percent to 50 percent of his company's oil would be carried in Arab-flag vessels. Saudi Arabia, Algeria, and other petroleum-producing nations are moving in the same direction. What will this mean in the event of another boycott?

At the close of World War II, the U.S. government enacted the Merchant Ship Sales Act of 1946 in order to dispose of its huge wartime merchant fleet. Underlying the act was a postwar national shipping policy that, among other things, affirmed the necessity of maintaining "an efficient and adequate American-owned merchant marine for the national

357

security and development and maintenance of the domestic and the export and import foreign commerce of the United States." In effect, the 1946 legislation was reaffirming the objectives of the Merchant Marine Act of 1936.

The purpose of the 1936 act was to establish and maintain a strong U.S. merchant fleet, owned by American citizens, operated by American crews, and fully capable of serving U.S. international commitments—economic, military, and political—under all foreseeable circumstances. It recognized that even in times of peace, economic and political tensions and other contingencies may seriously disrupt or distort traditional patterns of commerce over international trade routes. As such, it reflected the realization that an international power such as the United States cannot depend on ships owing allegiance to alien flags without threatening its own national security.

By passing the Merchant Marine Act of 1970, Congress further emphasized the basic principles underlying the 1936 and 1946 acts. Thus, our national shipping policy is clear and unequivocal. Moreover, I believe its objectives are eminently reasonable, sound, and most important, essential to national survival.

In case anyone thinks I am being an alarmist on the issue of national security, let me offer the following facts for consideration. The United States is self-sufficient in only three of seventy-one strategic materials essential to national defense. We import 87 percent of our bauxite, 89 percent of our chromium, 98 percent of our maganese, and 45 percent of our oil. Furthermore, our reliance on imported raw materials for all purposes is increasing. In the last decade, seaborne foreign trade has quintupled in magnitude and doubled as a percentage of our total gross national product. In terms of national growth and security—and by this I mean national survival—these figures clearly illustrate our dependence on a strong merchant fleet. In my judgment, it would be fair to say that our national shipping policy recognizes this dependency and our vulnerability because of it.

Our national shipping policy is a sound one—as valid today as it was in 1936, 1946, and 1970. What is at issue is the extent to which it is, in fact, being implemented, and what (if any) obstacles deter its implementation.

The following passage from the International Economic Report of the President, transmitted to Congress in January 1977, offers a good idea about the success of our national shipping policy:

> Despite innovations introduced by the U.S. maritime industry in recent years and the financial assistance provided to it by the federal government, the U.S.-flag merchant fleet ranks 10th

in size among the national fleets of the world and accounts for only a small fraction of the world fleet. [pp. 115-116]

The report goes on to say that in 1976 U.S. vessels carried approximately 17 percent less trade tonnage than in 1970, and that the share of overseas cargo carried on American ships operating under the U.S. flag was a mere 4.4 percent in 1976 in contrast to 42.3 percent in 1950.

In the following testimony before my Merchant Marine Subcommittee, the president of the Transportation Institute, Herbert Brand, described the state of the American-flag fleet as "appalling":

> Our nation's foreign trade—almost all of it—is carried on foreign-flag vessels. Today, less than 5 percent of our export-import commerce is transported on ships that fly the American flag, and only 2 percent of our dry bulk trade and less than 4 percent of our vital oil import trade are carried on American vessels.
>
> Yet, no other major world power permits the carriage of its trade to be so totally controlled by the merchant fleets of foreign nations. The Soviet fleet today carries about 50 percent of Russia's foreign trade. Nearly 40 percent of Japan's foreign trade is carried on its national flag vessels. The Greek-flag fleet carries about 45 percent of its international commerce. For Norway and Spain, the figure is 37 percent. For Great Britain, 34 percent. West Germany and France each carry 30 percent of their foreign trade on vessels flying their national ensigns.
>
> Today . . . nations have come to understand that their economic security is vitally linked to their maritime independence.
>
> In fact, the emergence of national maritime independence among the major world powers makes it more necessary than before that the United States achieve a measure of self-sufficiency in its oceanborne transport capability. As we look at the state of our merchant marine today, we see that we are woefully inadequate to assure American shipping capability ready and able to respond to national and international requirements.

As chairman of the Merchant Marine Subcommittee, I cannot ignore these assessments of our merchant fleet nor their implications for our national security. I also have a special responsibility to determine the reasons for the present situation, and, insofar as I am able, recommend solutions. Let me briefly outline what I perceive as problems, and the process by which my subcommittee arrives at its recommendations.

I consider the rebating situation in the U.S. foreign trade the most serious problem the American-flag carrier faces today. In March 1977, my subcommittee held preliminary hearings to emphasize that rebating is widespread in our liner trades and to seek recommendations for congressional action to correct the situation. As a consequence of those hearings, I introduced legislation (S. 2008) that would provide for a three-year period in which to reach a permanent solution of the rebating practices in the U.S. foreign trade.

Also of high priority is the question of a third-flag bill. The biggest incursions into our shipping are occurring in the vital liner segment, where the Russians and other communist bloc nations are entering pell-mell as cross traders. The Soviets have the fastest growing merchant fleets in the world. While our merchant fleet tonnage was dropping from first to tenth place, they were advancing from twenty-third to sixth place. What's more, they were doing it with new, modern, technologically sophisticated ships—almost all copied from American designs. An interesting point is that the expansion of the Soviet merchant fleet has no relation to the country's trading needs. The Russians are simply interested in deploying their merchant ships into every lucrative trade available.

Of no less importance than a third-flag bill is the enactment of pending legislation to assure U.S.-flag tankers a fair share of our petroleum imports, which—as stated earlier in this paper—is so vital to our national security and survival.

Finally, my subcommittee intends to review the administration of our current cargo preference laws to assure that they do not operate to the detriment of U.S.-flag carriers, given the realities that prevail among other trading nations throughout the world.

Let me thank you for the opportunity of addressing this conference. I did not intend this paper to be an indictment of federal agencies responsible for implementing our national shipping policy nor to use this rostrum for discussion of whatever malaise affects the shipping industry. I did want to give you my assessment of the dangers facing our merchant fleet and to suggest what I believe must be done to restore the status quo—which, in this instance, is a strong merchant fleet owned by American citizens, operated by American crews, and fully capable of serving our international economic, military, and political commitments under all foreseeable circumstances.

Sea Power and the Energy Crisis

John Moore

We have listened to a great deal at this conference—some of it at times confusing because of the phraseology—which lends itself to broad interpretation. I think that one of the dangers we face today is the tendency to wrap everything up and fit it into a package, and then assuming that because the package has "Big Mac" stamped on the outside, everybody will know what is inside. Frequently, the contents of the package are very different from those envisioned. Everyone has his own "Big Mac" recipe and tends to see the contents of a "Big Mac" in terms of his own ingredients and method of preparation.

One thing that has worried me very much while I've been here is reading the newspapers on your President's energy program. Let me assure you that I have no intention of being latched into a domestic argument as I nearly was at a press conference the other day. I will step back very smartly if anybody suggests I am. The point I want to make is that this energy business is an absolutely integral part of sea power. What seems to be missing from the various arguments we have heard about reactors, nuclear power, and related issues is some thought about how we are going to keep the factories running, to keep the people warm, to keep providing all the other energy-dependent products and processes. Nobody has yet told us how this world is going to function if we don't have any ships to carry the raw materials from their sources to their production points. Nobody has said how sea power, in its broadest sense, will be exercised when the petroleum products of this world run out. In fact, nobody has told us *when* they will run out.

On some people's calendars, 2015 is a fairly popular date for the exhaustion of our oil supply. It may be later; it may be earlier. The fact of North Sea oil has managed to keep the British government in the seat of office, but that supply is going to run out before very long. The wells are going to run dry in all sorts of places.

In the debate about energy alternatives one hears about nuclear power of various kinds at one extreme, and solar, geothermal, and hydro-electric power at the other. Nobody talks about ships. Nobody has suggested how all the ships we are talking about at the moment—and brilliantly designing in the room next door—are going to be propelled around the oceans. For those who have not been intimately involved in the design and production of ships, let me suggest that from the moment Admiral Zumwalt envisioned a ship in his bath this morning, saying, "We must have that," to the time that ship is launched, lies an interval of seven to eight years. The hull life of that ship is of the order of twenty-five years. Could we just focus on the kind of time we are talking about? Admiral Zumwalt had an idea for a ship in his bath this morning: seven to eight years elapse between concept and launching—1985; twenty-five years of hull life—2010, that leaves only five years before the oil presumably runs out.

The newest ship designs call for gas-turbine propulsion. Some of the more antique varieties are propelled by steam from an oil-fired boiler; others by diesels. Very few are powered by nuclear power. I know Commandment X says, Thou shalt have nuclear power, but that is a jolly expensive way of pushing ships around the oceans.

What are we going to do? Are we just going to sit back and say we hope some geologist finds another enormous reservoir of oil lurking under the Sahara? Or are we going to turn around and admit that we spend our time arguing about sea power, projection power, and sea control, but none of these things will mean a blind bit of anything if we can't get ships on the ocean. And if we do not have ships circulating, there is no way we are going to be able to run any kind of outfit. This applies particularly to the United States, with its increasing dependence on overseas trade, as so clearly pointed out by Senator Inouye.

I am suggesting that it is time to begin studying the various energy alternatives, because we are not going to have petroleum very much longer—not for much beyond the lifetime of an old fellow like me. The oil will certainly run out within the time scale of my son's life, and will be gone throughout much of my grandson's life.

Although we can foresee many problems for ocean transport by the next century, I have found not a shred of evidence that anybody is really driving ahead with any kind of program to provide us with the merchant ships we need today and will continue to need well into the future. With 99 percent of the world's trade, by weight, transported by sea, I don't see our need for merchant fleets changing very much, unless there is an astonishing breakthrough in air transport, which seems likely.

What then are the possibilities? We hear various assumptions about how long the coal will last—anywhere from 200 years to 500 years. The countries that are coal-rich—such as the United States, the U.S.S.R., Great Britain, the Federal Republic of Germany, and Spain, among others—might liquefy their coal. When the U.S. Navy tried it a few years ago, the process turned out to be extremely expensive. It is conceivable, however, that wider use of liquefied coal would lead to lower costs. So, that's one possibility.

Some people ask, Why can't we have a totally reflective ship that runs on solar energy? My reply is, Well, there wouldn't be a place for the lookouts. I do not think this is the starting point. Somebody else asks, Why can't we have a ship with thousands of vanes rotating up top, providing electrical power in their little generators? I do not consider this a starter, either. The fuel cell seems to have possibilities, but developments are not yet sufficiently advanced to know for certain.

We could go back to the nineteenth century, propelling ships by wind: I doubt if anybody is going to rob us of that commodity. We have some very sophisticated designs for sailing ships that can easily be controlled from the bridge. They use hydraulic power, which implies they need some kind of fuel to run the auxiliary engines that power the hydraulic system.

And then there is nuclear power. From the calculations I have seen, the idea of a nuclear-powered merchant fleet is insupportable. Given the 65,000 ships comprising the free world's merchant fleet today —that is, excluding those of the Soviet bloc—and allowing for a 10 percent increase in merchant ship tonnage each year in Lloyd's list (as reflected over the last ten years) I can see little hope of propelling that lot by nuclear power.

Thus, fifty years from now we will probably have no means of transporting raw materials to points of production or from the points of production to global markets. Moreover, we will have no means of defending merchant ships unless we start doing something about it now, since it is eminently probable that the ship designed in 1980 will, toward the end of its life, have to be running on something other than hydrocarbon oils.

To me, this represents an enormously important undertaking. It will require research and development into all forms of things. At this conference we have been hearing about the dollars being poured into the development of airplanes of various types and of the enormous cost of building a smaller aircraft carrier. It is just possible that the NATO countries have been investing a considerable amount of the money that, at least in my own country, Great Britain, has been wasted in areas (such as sea lines of communication) that may not exist in the first quarter of the next century.

I think that toward the middle of the twenty-first century—and this is merely Moore's dubious projection—we may be confronting some very large nuclear-propelled merchant ships, supported by a very large number of wind-propelled merchant ships, protected by navies whose ships are fueled mainly by liquefied coal, except for those the country concerned can afford to equip with nuclear propulsion. This is a very different picture from that portrayed here today. I do believe it imperative that those considering sea power in its broadest sense should be thinking more about future means of propulsion.